AF248792

Grammatical Theory and Bilingual Codeswitching

Grammatical Theory and Bilingual Codeswitching

Edited by
Jeff MacSwan

MIT Press
Cambridge, Massachusetts
London, England

MIT Press books may be purchased at special quantity discounts for business or sales promotional use. For information, please email special_sales@mitpress.mit.edu.

This book was set in Times LT Std by Toppan Best-set Premedia Limited, Hong Kong. Printed and bound in the United States of America.

Library of Congress Cataloging-in-Publication Data

Grammatical theory and bilingual codeswitching / Edited by Jeff MacSwan.
        pages cm.
    Includes bibliographical references and index.
    ISBN 978-0-262-02789-2 (hardcover: alk. paper)   1. Code switching
(Linguistics)   2. Education, Bilingual.   3. Grammatically
(Linguistics)   I. MacSwan, Jeff, 1961– editor of compilation.
    P115.3.G73 2014
    306.44'6—dc23
                                            2014007218

10 9 8 7 6 5 4 3 2 1

Table of Contents

Acknowledgments

Many people generously invested time and energy into the production of this book.

First and foremost, I'm grateful to the authors for their willingness to participate and give some of their best work for inclusion, and for their patience as we worked through delays. Thanks are due to Shoba Bandi-Rao, Rakesh M. Bhatt, Sonia Colina, Marcel den Dikken, Anna Maria Di Sciullo, Daniel L. Finer, Kay Gonzalez-Vilbazo, Silvia Milian Hita, Monica Moro Quintanilla, Pieter Muysken, Erin O'Rourke, Ana Teresa Pérez-Leroux, Edward P. Stabler, Gretchen Sunderman, and Almeida Jacqueline Toribio. Many of the authors also generously served as reviewers for the project, providing detailed feedback on other chapters in the volume. In addition, I am grateful to Mariana Bahtchevanova, Brian Chan, Hector Campos, Elly van Gelderen, Javier Gutierrez-Rexach, Helene Halmari, Janice Jake, Li Ping, Thomas Roeper, Suzanne Schlyter, and Teresa Satterfield for providing additional reviews of contributions. Michael Clyne, who also served as a manuscript reviewer, passed away in October 2010, and will be greatly missed by all. We are additionally indebted to two anonymous reviewers who provided extensive feedback on the entire manuscript.

Wayne Wright, Peter Sayer, and Gerda Lobo provided skillful assistance in the early stages, as did Kara McAlister, who assisted and collaborated on a number of language contact-related projects. Marie Lufkin Lee, Marc Lowenthal, and Marcy Ross at MIT Press facilitated a very smooth production process, and David Hill provided additional assistance with indexing. Kellie Rolstad generously assisted with proof corrections.

I am also grateful to the many graduate students whose interest and enthusiasm for codeswitching research stimulated thought, research, and sometimes collaborations over the course of this project, especially Kara McAlister, Katja Francesca Cantone, Jane Grabowski, Chatwara Suwannamai, and Ahmed Zeeshan Gul. Ahmed, a young father and doctoral student, tragically suffered an untimely passing in May 2010, and is fondly remembered by friends, family, and colleagues.

I have had the pleasure of presenting work related to this project at a number of venues as an invited guest, and very much appreciated the stimulating conversation at these events. Many thanks to Jürgen Meisel for several opportunities to visit his team at the Centre for the Study of Multilingualism at Universität Hamburg, and to Natascha Müller for invitations to work with her research group at Bergische Universität Wuppertal and to participate in an organized conference there in April 2013. Thanks to Ludmila Isurin, Donald Winford, and Kees de Bot for including me in a Workshop on Codeswitching at the Ohio State University, and for promptly turning the presentations there into an accessible and excellent edited volume. I am grateful to Margaret Deuchar, who invited me to visit her research team at the Centre for the Study of Multilingualism, University of Bangor, Wales, and for stimulating conversation around the work they are doing there on Welsh-English codeswitching. Special thanks to Maria Carmen Parafita Couto for her participation and hospitality at Bangor. Thanks to Max Bane, Juan Bueno Holle, Thomas Grano, April Grotberg, and Yaron McNabb, who graciously included me as a speaker in the special parasession on codeswitching at the 44th Annual Meeting of the Chicago Linguistics Society. Tej Bhatia and Bill Ritchie kindly included me in the Mellon Foundation Symposium on the Bilingual Mind that they organized at Syracuse in 2009, which provided an additional forum for thoughtful discussion on language mixing. For invitations to participate in department colloquia, many thanks to Massimo Piattelli-Palmarini (University of Arizona), Teresa Satterfield (University of Michigan), Katja Cantone (University of Bremen), Matt Gordon and Sandra Thompson (University of California, Santa Barbara), and Kay Gonzáles-Vilbazo and Luis López (University of Illinois at Chicago).

Finally, on a personal note, I wish to thank the people closest to me, whose companionship has sustained me and has served as a continual reminder of the most important things in life. Kellie Rolstad is my wife, friend, and life partner, who makes every day a joy to live. I'm grateful to her and to my delightful, intellectually provocative, and really fun kids—Xander, Katalina, and Skye—for their love and camaraderie. Ila and Al Rolstead, Kellie's folks, have been a warm and loving addition to our family and household in Maryland. Thank you!

On June 15, 2013, I lost my mother, Marian MacSwan, who had lived a long and happy life. She was an inspiration to me, and taught me at an early age the things that have helped me most in life: To love unconditionally, to reject authority, and to be a careful and critical consumer of information and convention. Thanks, Mom!

1 Programs and Proposals in Codeswitching Research: Unconstraining Theories of Bilingual Language Mixing

Jeff MacSwan

Codeswitching (CS) is the alternate use of two or more languages among bilingual interlocutors. The present book focuses on grammatical properties of languages mixed in this way, narrowing in on cases of *intrasentential* CS— that is, language mixing below sentential boundaries, as illustrated in (1).

(1) *Mi hermano* bought some ice cream.
     'My brother bought some ice cream.'

CS is traditionally differentiated from *borrowing*, which involves the phonological and morphological integration of a word from one language (say, English *type*) into another (Spanish *typiar*). CS involves the mixing of phonologically distinctive elements into a single utterance, as illustrated in (1), where the Spanish lexical DP *mi hermano* is mixed into an otherwise English sentence. While considerable attention has been devoted to English-Spanish CS in the literature, examples of the phenomenon could involve any two languages.

The central problem for scholars interested in the linguistic properties of CS is the explanation of the contrast in grammaticality between cases such as (1) and (2).

(2) **El* bought some ice cream.
     'He bought some ice cream.'

Why would a bilingual's grammar permit switching between a lexical DP and verb but not between a pronoun and verb? What principles of grammar might account for the contrast, and what might these analyses tell us about the nature of bilingualism itself? The answers must account for CS between the particular languages in the data on hand as well as for switching between any other pair of languages.

This introductory chapter is organized as follows. I first set the stage by outlining principal disadvantages of proposing constraints in CS research, and then describe two different research programs for CS—the *constraint-based approach* and the *constraint-free approach*. Next I show that the history of CS research largely involves an unfulfilled quest for a constraint-free solution, with technological limitations keeping genuine solutions out of reach – limitations now largely overcome by the Minimalist Program. The minimalist approach to CS is outlined with some illustrative analyses. Finally, a brief overview of subsequent chapters in the book is presented.

1.1 Two Research Programs for Codeswitching

1.1.1 Constraints on Syntax, Constraints on Codeswitching

In 1962 at the Thirteenth Annual Round Table Meeting on Linguistics and Languages at Georgetown University, Einar Haugen staked a claim to the original use of the term *codeswitching*, although the word had first appeared in print in H. Vogt's (1954) review of Uriel Weinreich's (1953) *Languages in Contact* and two years before that in Haugen's *Bilingualism in the Americas*, a bibliography published by the American Dialect Association in 1956. Although much earlier work by Aurelio M. Espinosa (1911) had noted the phenomenon, an actual CS research literature did not emerge until the late 1960s and early 1970s, when work focusing on both social and grammatical aspects of language mixing began steadily appearing with scholarly engagement of previously published research. (See Benson 2001 for further discussion of the early history of the field.)

Among the earliest to observe that there are grammatical restrictions on language mixing were Gumperz and his colleagues (Gumperz 1967, 1970; Gumperz and Hernández-Chávez 1970), Hasselmo (1972), Timm (1975), and Wentz (1977). For instance, Timm's list of restrictions noted that Spanish-English switching between a subject pronoun and a main verb is ill formed but not so when the subject pronoun is replaced with a lexical subject, as the contrast between (1) and (2) shows.

While construction-specific constraints were typical of this early work, a literature soon emerged in which the grammatical mechanisms underlying these descriptive facts were explored. It is well known and uncontroversial that CS is constrained in the descriptive sense, meaning, simply, that CS behavior is itself rule governed. Consider, for example, the contrast in (3) (Belazi, Rubin, and Toribio 1994).

(3a)   The students *habían visto la película italiana.*
        'The students had seen the Italian movie.'

(3b)   *The student *had visto la película italiana.*
        'The student had seen the Italian movie.'

Although the basic word-order requirements are the same here for both English and Spanish, (3b) is judged to be ill formed. Regardless of what account we might construct for the contrast, (3) is sufficient to show that CS behavior, like other linguistic behavior, is constrained or rule governed.

However, research on CS conducted in the *Aspects* era (Chomsky 1965) of generative grammar soon turned to the notion that CS—a broad, horizontal linguistic phenomenon—could be explained by positing the kind of theoretical constraints developed in the contemporaneous syntactic literature to impose vertical limits on transformations and phrase structure. As early as 1955, Chomsky had noted that the transformational component in a hybrid generative-transformational system had the disadvantage of vastly increasing the expressive power of the grammar, permitting the formulation of grammatical processes that did not seem to occur in any language. In response to the problem, Chomsky (1964, 1965) and other researchers such as John Ross (1967) posited constraints on transformational rules. Ross noticed, for instance, that an NP could not be extracted out of a conjoined phrase, as in (4a), accounting for the ill-formedness in (4b) but not in the semantically equivalent (but syntactically divergent) example in (4c).

(4a)   John was having milk and cookies.

(4b)   *What$_i$ was John having milk *and t$_i$*?

(4c)   What$_i$ was John having milk with t$_i$?

Here, constraints were viewed as psychologically real restrictions on the application of transformations to phrase markers and were therefore understood to be part of the grammar itself. Here *constraint* refers not just to a description of intuitions about a set of constructions, but to an actual mechanism of grammar in the mind/brain of a language user—that is, the term is being used in a theoretical sense.

1.1.2   So What's Wrong with Constraints on Codeswitching?

The idea of a constraint in this syntactic/grammatical sense appealed to a number of researchers in CS and was used to articulate the grammatical restrictions observed in CS data. However, there are good reasons for avoiding such mechanisms altogether. For concreteness, consider Joshi's (1985b) Constraint on Closed-Class Items.

(5)   *Constraint on closed-class items*
      Closed-class items (e.g., determiners, quantifiers, prepositions, possessives, Aux, Tense, helping verbs) cannot be switched.

Joshi's constraint, like many similar mechanisms, makes explicit reference to (code)switching; *codeswitching*, of course, denotes a change from one language to another, say, from Hindi to English, or Spanish to Nahuatl. However, all such entities—languages—are classes of expressions defined by the grammar. So a grammar G defines a class of expressions L. We cannot insert L as part of any function of G, because L is itself defined by G. Hence, explicit constraints on CS are not theoretically well defined because they reference language switching, and grammars are formally blind to the languages they generate.

Furthermore, constraints so formulated may serve to provide good linguistic description (to the extent they are empirically correct), but they do not serve to explain or enlighten. Constraints on CS, in the theoretical sense, restate the descriptive facts by telling us which grammatical constructions or properties are evident in CS. While *linguistic description* is an important first step, it does not constitute a *linguistic theory*. Hence, the more serious problem with CS-specific mechanisms is that they threaten to trivialize the enterprise. Rather than explaining descriptive restrictions observed in CS data, CS-specific mechanisms simply note these restrictions within the grammar itself so that no explanation is needed, and one is left still wondering what general principles of grammar might underlie the observations and descriptions.

We might define a CS-specific constraint, then, as a proposed grammatical mechanism that makes explicit reference to (code)switching or language(s), and that is understood to be part of the actual linguistic competence of a bilingual.

1.1.3 The Constraint-Based Research Program

Historically, CS researchers have consistently offered up CS-specific constraints, despite a clear and persistent intuition that a better theory of CS would do without them. Pfaff (1979, 314) appears to have been among the first to consider the question of whether some mechanism external to either grammar is needed in our account of the facts of CS, concluding that no such device should be needed: "It is unnecessary to posit a third grammar to account for the utterances in which the languages are mixed." About the same time Poplack and Sankoff (1981, 12) wrote: "What is more consistent with the data is simply to allow the possibility that in the uttering of a sentence, the rules used to construct its constituents may be drawn at times from one monolingual grammar and at times from another." Echoing Pfaff, Woolford (1983, 522) similarly wrote that "there is no need to propose any sort of third, separate code-switching grammar." Commenting on Spanish-English CS in particular, but on theoretical approaches to CS more generally, Lipski (1985, 83–84) observed that

strict application of Occam's Razor requires that gratuitous meta-structures be avoided whenever possible, and that bilingual language behavior be described as much as possible in terms of already existing monolingual grammars. As a result, preference must initially be given to modifications of existing grammars of Spanish and English, rather than to the formulation of a special bilingual generative mechanism, unless experimental evidence inexorably militates in favor of the latter alternative.

Similar strong preference for a constraint-free approach continued into the 1980s and 1990s, as Di Sciullo, Muysken, and Singh's (1986, 7) influential work on the Government Constraint supposed that CS "can be seen as a rather ordinary case of language use, requiring no specific stipulation." Clyne ([1987] 2000, 279]), working from a different perspective, similarly conjectured that CS is "governed by the kinds of structural constraints applying to monolingual performance." Belazi, Rubin and Toribio (1994) proposed their Functional Head Constraint within the context of a view of CS as "constrained solely by Universal Grammar." Mahootian (1993), also echoing Pfaff (1979) and Woolford (1983), argued against the "third-grammar" approach, claiming in Santorini and Mahootian (1995, 4) that "codeswitching sequences are governed by exactly the same principles of phrase structure as monolingual sequences."

Hence, there has long been an intuition among CS researchers that language mixing is not constrained by actual mechanisms of grammar (a "third grammar" mediating between the two), but technological limitations available at the time made a genuine constraint-free approach difficult or impossible to implement. While a few examples of explicit endorsements of CS-specific mechanisms may be unearthed (e.g., Joshi 1985b; Sankoff 1998), the overwhelming perspective in the field has been that such mechanisms ought to be viewed with some measure of disdain.

Despite the call for constraint-free solutions, however, genuine implementation remained out of reach. Researchers tended to take one of three courses in light of this predicament: (1) explicitly confront the limitations of the formal mechanism and reluctantly but explicitly introduce CS-specific devices (e.g., Sankoff and Poplack 1981); (2) leave the analytic framework inexplicit or inadequately developed so that the issue did not arise (e.g., Woolford 1983; Mahootian 1993; Santorini and Mahootian 1995); or (3) propose explicit CS-specific mechanisms and argue that they are vacuously available to monolinguals too (e.g., Di Sciullo, Muysken, and Singh, 1986; Belazi, Rubin, and Toribio 1994; Myers-Scotton 1993). Let us take up each of these in turn.

1.1.4 Explicitly Confronting the Formal Limitations

One of the most important early contributions to CS was Sankoff and Poplack's (1981) effort to implement the Equivalence Constraint formally. Several
researchers had converged simultaneously on the notion that language switching is controlled by some kind of syntactic equivalence requirement (Lipski
1978; Pfaff 1979; Poplack 1978, 1981). Poplack (1981) proposed two comple-
mentary constraints that are among the best known in the CS literature, shown
in (6) and (7).

(6) *The Equivalence Constraint*
Codes will tend to be switched at points where the surface structures
of the languages map onto each other.

(7) *The Free Morpheme Constraint*
A switch may occur at any point in the discourse at which it is
possible to make a surface constituent cut and still retain a free
morpheme.

As a variationist (see Labov 1963), Poplack believed that linguistic rules correlate with social structure and should be stated in terms of statistical frequen-
cies, hence (6) is expressed as a tendency. The general idea is nonetheless
clear: CS is allowed within constituents so long as the word-order requirements of both languages are met at surface structure. Surface structures derive
from the (cyclic) application of transformations to phrase markers, which
originate as the output of a phrase structure grammar. The constraint in (7)
defines a restriction on morphology in CS contexts, also noted in Wentz and
McClure 1977 and Pfaff 1979. To illustrate, (6) correctly predicts that the
switch in (8) is disallowed, because the surface word order of English and
Spanish differ with respect to object pronoun (clitic) placement; (7) correctly
disallows (9), where an English stem is used with a Spanish bound morpheme
without the phonological integration of the stem.

(8) *told le,* le *told,* him *dije,* dije *him*
told *to-him,* to-him *I-told,* him *I-told,* I-told *him*
'(I) told him.'
(Poplack 1981, 176)

(9) *estoy*   eat-*iendo*
I-am   eat-ing
(Poplack 1980, 586)

Research since Poplack's initial proposals has found persuasive documenta-
tion that her Equivalence Constraint does not hold up to empirical tests
(Stenson 1990; Lee 1991; Myers-Scotton 1993; Mahootian 1993; MacSwan

1999; Chan 1999; Muysken 2000). Note, for example, the contrast in (3), repeated here.

(3a)   The students *habían visto la película italiana.*
        'The students had seen the Italian movie.'

(3b)   *The student had *visto la película italiana.*
        'The student had seen the Italian movie.'

The basic word-order requirements of Spanish and English are alike with regard to the construction in (3), yet a switch between the auxiliary and the verb renders the sentence ill formed, but not so in the case of a switch between the subject and the verb. However, (6) predicts that both examples should be well formed.

Also consider the examples in (10) (MacSwan 1999), where CS occurs between a subject pronoun and a verb, both in their correct position for both Spanish and Nahuatl, yet one example is ill formed and the other well formed.

(10a) *Tú   *tikoas*   *tlakemetl.*
       tú   ti-k-koa-s   tlake-me-tl
       you/SING   2S-3Os-buy-FUT   garment-PL-NSF
       'You will buy clothes.'

(10b) Él   *kikoas*   *tlakemetl.*
       él   0-ki-koa-s   tlak-eme-tl
       he   3S-3Os-buy-FUT   garment-PL-NSF
       'He will buy clothes.'

The descriptive adequacy of Poplack's Free Morpheme Constraint, on the other hand, remains controversial. While it is attested in numerous corpora (Bentahila and Davis 1983; Berk-Seligson 1986; Clyne 1987; MacSwan 1999), others claim to have identified some counterexamples (Eliasson 1989; Bokamba 1989; Myers-Scotton 1993; Nartey 1982; Halmari 1997; Chan 1999; Hlavac 2003). See Bandi-Rao and den Dikken (chapter 7, this volume) and MacSwan and Colina (chapter 8, this volume) for two theoretical perspectives on the ban on word-internal CS.

Although Sankoff and Poplack (1981) expressed a strong preference for avoiding CS-specific mechanisms to mediate between the two languages in contact, they nonetheless concluded that such a mechanism is necessary on empirical grounds. Otherwise, the authors argued, the free union of Spanish and English phrase structure grammars would yield ill-formed results. For instance, whereas English requires prenominal adjectives (NP → Det Adj N), Spanish requires postnominal adjective placement (NP → Det N Adj). A speaker is free to select the Spanish rule and lexically insert an English determiner, Spanish noun, and English adjective (*the CASA white*) or even insert English lexical items for all categories (*the house white*). Therefore, to constrain the grammars so that they do not generate violations of (4), Sankoff and Poplack introduced a superscripting mechanism (sometimes called *bilingual tagging* or *language tagging*) that restricted lexical insertion rules so that the grammar contributing the phrase structure rule would also be the grammar from which lexical insertion rules were drawn. Hence, under conditions of CS, the Spanish phrase structure rule would be annotated as in (11a), generating (11b). The superscripting conventions followed from *heritability conditions*, according to the authors, which essentially allowed phrase structure rules to look ahead and restrict the application of lexical insertion rules.

(11a) NP $\rightarrow$ Det $N^{sp:n}$ $Adj^{sp:adj}$

(11b) the *casa blanca*

Sankoff and Poplack do not make explicit the mechanisms for superscript insertion. Rather, they indicate that phrase structure rules are so superscripted when they are selected in the generation of a CS utterance and are subsequently used to trigger language-specific lexical insertion rules ($N \rightarrow$ casa, e.g. in the case of $N^{sp:n}$). No account is presented as to how the superscript insertion mechanism is able to annotate the appropriate categories correctly—for instance, N and Adj in (11a), but not Det, where either language may be inserted without negative consequences. Despite these limitations, Sankoff and Poplack's work made important contributions to our understanding of the formal properties of CS.

1.1.5 Leaving the Analysis Insufficiently Explicit

Explicitness is an important tool in linguistic theory; as Chomsky (1957, 5) explained,

The search for rigorous formulation in linguistics has a much more serious motivation than mere concern for logical niceties or the desire to purify well-established methods of linguistic analysis. Precisely constructed models for linguistic structure can play an important role, both negative and positive, in the process of discovery itself. By pushing a precise but inadequate formulation to an unacceptable conclusion, we can often expose the exact source of this inadequacy and, consequently, gain a deeper understanding of the linguistic data.

Similarly in CS research, the use of explicit formulation of our theories and analyses will help expose weaknesses and shortcomings.

Like Sankoff and Poplack (1981), Woolford (1983) sought to derive the Equivalence Constraint within the theoretical assumptions of *Aspects*. The best account of CS, Woolford emphasized, would avoid reference to any kind of CS-specific grammar. Woolford recognized, like Sankoff and Poplack, that the rules of lexical insertion must be trained on their language-specific phrase structure rules:

Phrase structure rules are drawn freely from both grammars during the construction of constituent structure trees, but the lexicon of each grammar is limited to filling only those terminal nodes created by phrase structure rules drawn from the same language. Nevertheless, in the event that there are phrase structure rules common to both languages, such rules belong simultaneously to both languages. Lexical items can be freely drawn from either language to fill terminal nodes created by phrase structure rules common to both languages. (p. 535)

Woolford believed that lexical insertion was unconstrained in the case of phrase structure rules common to both languages, but in the case of phrase structure rules that were not shared, lexical insertion was limited to the terminal nodes associated with the phrase structure rule of the grammar to which it belonged. Woolford's system does not seem to achieve its intended goals, because it predicts that Spanish-English CS would require that a language-unique phrase structure rule (for instance, NP → Det N Adj for Spanish) could only be lexically filled by Spanish items (predicting *the casa blanca* to be ill formed, contrary to the facts). In addition, while Woolford's work is an excellent example of the articulation of the goals of CS research, Woolford does not herself present the formal mechanism that might be responsible for achieving the results expected within her framework. No explanation as to how the unique phrase structure rules get linked to language-specific rules of lexical insertion is offered.

Woolford accounts for Poplack's Free Morpheme Constraint by postulating that "the lexicons and word formation components of the two grammars remain separate" (p. 526). While this approach seems preferable to Poplack's, where the prohibition against word-internal switching is simply stated in descriptive terms, no rationale for the separation of the lexicons in terms of principles independent of CS itself is offered, leaving the basis for asserting that the model is free of any CS-specific mechanisms once again inexplicit.

As in Sankoff and Poplack's model, Woolford suggests, somewhat more directly, that a bilingual has two separate lexicons that must be referenced or indexed in some way for the purposes of lexical insertion. However, this stipulation alone does not add to our understanding of CS and bilingualism if it does not include an explicit rationale, making explicit the specific attributes of the language faculty responsible for the separation. The crucial question that remains unaddressed here is the following: What *basic properties of the language faculty* are plausibly responsible for identifying specific subsets of lexical items in a bilingual's repertoire that we might reasonably call language-specific lexicons?

More recently, Mahootian (1993) proposed the Null Theory of CS, formulated within the framework of Tree Adjoining Grammars (TAGs) originally introduced by Joshi (1985a) for applications in computational linguistics and natural language processing. TAG differs from mainstream generative grammar in that the lexical items encode partial tree structures, and use operations of substitution and adjunction to assemble larger trees composed of multiple lexical items. For example, the verb *build* is represented in the lexicon along with its projection, and therefore the branching direction of its complement is lexically specified. A substitution operation allows the DP *a house* to integrate with *build* by substituting the DP (along with its category label) with the object category label of *build*, generating *build a house* along with its projecting tree structure.

Mahootian focused on the complement relation in phrase structure (see also Pandit 1990 and Nishimura 1997), and claimed that (12) was adequate to account for the facts of CS.

(12) The language of a head determines the phrase structure position of its complements in codeswitching just as in monolingual contexts.

Mahootian (1993) used a corpus of Farsi-English CS data that she collected in naturalistic observations. In Farsi, objects occur before the verb, contrasting with basic word order in English. She observed that in CS contexts the language of the verb determines the placement of the object, as (13) illustrates. These facts are consistent with (12).

(13) You'll   buy   *xune-ye*   *jaedid.*
      you'll   buy   house-POSS   new
      'You'll buy a new house.'

Mahootian noticed that the TAG formalism provides an advantage for the analysis of CS data; because structures are encoded in the lexicon, no intervening control mechanism is needed to pair up lexical insertion rules with terminal nodes in a phrase marker, as seen in previous proposals. However, Mahootian's analysis was restricted to head-complement configurations. Not only was (12) too narrow in this regard, failing to comment on CS in other dimensions of syntax, but it also proved insufficiently restrictive with respect to head-complement configurations. Note, for instance, the examples in (1) and (2), repeated here; although all complements are in the correct positions assigned by heads, (1) is ill formed but (2) well formed.

(1)   *El* bought some ice cream.

(2)   *Mi hermano* bought some ice cream.

Furthermore, note that in (3), *visto*, the complement of *habían/had,* is in the position assigned by its head, and therefore adheres to (12), yet (3a) is well formed and (3b) is not. In (14) (MacSwan 1999), Spanish and Nahuatl word order is respected with regard to the placement of the verbal complement of negation, yet (14a) is ill formed but (14b) is not.

(3a)   The students *habían visto la película italiana.*
       'The students had seen the Italian movie.'

(3b)   *The student had *visto la película italiana.*
       'The student had seen the Italian movie.'

(14a) *No NITEKITITOC.
       no ni-tekiti-toc
       not 1S-work-DUR
       'I'm not working.'

(14b) Amo   *estoy trabajando.*
       amo   estoy   trabaja-ndo
       not   be/3Ss   work-DUR
       'I'm not working.'

These examples indicate that restrictions on CS are far more pervasive than the head-complement relation alone, and appear to move well beyond issues of phrase structure alone. While Mahootian's (1993) model significantly took note of the importance of the lexicon in theories of CS, the apparatus provided was far too narrowly focused to account for an appreciably wide range of CS data.

1.1.6 Bilingual Constraints Vacuously Available to Monolinguals

Working within the framework of Government-Binding Theory, Di Sciullo, Muysken, and Singh (1986) proposed the Government Constraint, which posited that there is an antigovernment condition on CS. Using a standard definition of government, in (15), these authors posed (16) as a condition on lexical insertion (where q indexes a category to a language-particular lexicon).

(15)   X governs Y if the first node dominating X also dominates Y, where X
       is a major category N, V, A, P and no maximal boundary intervenes
       between X and Y.

(16)   If X governs Y, ... X_q ... Y_q ...

Di Sciullo, Muysken, and Singh's intuition was that (16) is a narrower and empirically more accurate version of (17), which they viewed as a common assumption in syntactic theory that is never made explicit.

(17) All elements inserted into the phrase structure tree of a sentence must be drawn from the same lexicon.

With these assumptions in mind, the authors maintained that CS "can be seen as a rather ordinary case of language use, requiring no specific stipulation" (p. 7). To permit the head carrying the language index q to percolate up to its maximal projection, Di Sciullo, Muysken, and Singh formalized a condition on CS in the form of the Government Constraint, given in (18).

(18) *Government Constraint*
      (a) If an L_q carrier has index q, then Y^{max}_q.
      (b) In a maximal projection Y^{max}, the L_q carrier is the lexical element that asymmetrically c-commands the other lexical elements or terminal phrase nodes dominated by Y^{max}.

This formalism allows the language of a head to determine the syntax of its maximal projection and imposes the condition that two categories must be in the same language if the government relation holds between them.

Much like Sankoff and Poplack's (1981) formalism, (18) is formulated in an attempt to trigger language-specific lexical insertion by identifying nodes within a phrase marker with a specific language label (termed a *language index* in the present context). Although the authors maintain that the mechanism underlying the language index is vacuously available to monolinguals as well, it nonetheless appears to add few advantages over Sankoff and Poplack's version. Similarly, as in Sankoff and Poplack 1981 and Woolford 1983, we are not told how the grammatical system identifies the subset of lexical items associated with each "language."

Perhaps no less importantly, there are well-known counterexamples to (18), some of which were noted by the authors themselves. For instance, because government holds between a verb and its object and between a preposition and its object, (18) predicts that a verb or preposition must be in the language of its complement. This is shown to be incorrect by examples in (19) (MacSwan 2004, 2013), where switches occur in case-marked (hence governed) positions.

(19a) This morning *mi hermano y yo fuimos a comprar* some milk.
       'This morning *my brother and I went to buy* some milk.'

(19b) *French-Arabic*
       J'ai   joué   avec   *il-ku:ra.*
       I.have   played   with   the-ball
       'I have played with the ball.'

(19c) *Spanish-Nahuatl*
     Mi hermana *kitlasojtla*   *in*   *Juan.*
     mi hermana 0-ki-tlasojtla   in   Juan
     my sister 3S-3Os-love IN Juan
     'My sister loves Juan.'

See Halmari 1997 for further discussion of the Government Constraint in the context of Finnish-English CS.

Belazi, Rubin, and Toribio (1994) proposed the Functional Head Constraint (FHC), which took advantage of recent developments in syntactic theory that had distinguished between lexical and functional categories (Abney 1987). According to Abney (1987), functional heads were responsible for selecting complements with specific feature matrices. For example, *for* is a C^0 and has a feature specifying that its complement must have the feature [−Tense]. Belazi, Rubin, and Toribio argued that the patterns of CS could be correctly described in terms of the generalization in (20).

(20) A codeswitch may not occur between a functional head and its
      complement.

The authors developed the FHC, given in (21), intended as a refinement of Abney's (1987) theory, and saw it as a special case of Abney's system, vacuously available to monolinguals as well as bilinguals.

(21) *The Functional Head Constraint*
     The language feature of the complement f-selected by a functional
     head, like all other relevant features, must match the corresponding
     feature of that functional head.

By *language feature*, the authors had in mind a label identifying the language from which an item was contributed, such as [+Spanish] or [+English]. If the features do not agree (a Spanish functional head with an English complement, for example), then the codeswitch is blocked. Since (21) applies only to f-selected configurations (a complement selected by a functional head), switches between lexical heads and their complements are not constrained.

Mahootian (1993) and Muysken (2000) argued that the FHC was a further elaboration of the Government Constraint, in that it identifies an independently motivated principle of grammar but incorporates language-specific identifiers (for the Government Constraint, a language index; for the FHC, a language feature). Belazi, Rubin, and Toribio, like Di Sciullo, Muysken, and Singh (1986) with respect to the Government Constraint, maintained that the FHC does not constitute a CS-specific constraint. However, because the FHC, like related proposals before it, posited that an *identifier* of the particular languages (a *language feature*) involved in CS plays a role in the grammatical system, and posited the identifier to be part of the basic and psychologically real architecture of the grammar, the FHC must be seen as a CS-specific proposal. As in other cases, we should view as theoretically spurious any mechanism proposed as part of the actual mental architecture of the grammatical system that specifically labels a language (Spanish, English, what have you) on the grounds that such labels represent classes of expressions defined by the grammatical system, and therefore cannot be used as part of the definition itself. Such systems are tautological and can do little more than relabel the descriptive facts of CS.

There are also empirical counterexamples to Belazi, Rubin, and Toribio's FHC. In (22a), for instance, Mahootian (1993) documents a Farsi complementizer, a functional head, before its sentential complement. In (22b), Di Sciullo, Muysken, and Singh (1986) present a switch at the same boundary in French-Italian CS.

(22a) Anyway, I figured *ke* if I worked hard enough, I'd finish in the
       summer.
       'Anyway, I figured that if I worked hard enough, I'd finish in the
       summer.'

(22b) No,   *parce que*   hanno   *donné*   *des cours*
       no,   because   have   given   of the lectures
       'No, because they have given the lectures.'

Similarly, (22) reveals a switch between a determiner, a functional head, and its complement for Spanish-Nahuatl CS (MacSwan 1999).

(23a) Se   *hombre*   kikoas   se   kalli.
       se   hombre   0-ki-koa-s   se   kalli
       a   man   3S-3Os-buy-FUT   a   house
       'A man will buy a house.'

(23b) Arrancó   *in*   vestido   *non*   *de*   *Maria.*
       arranc-ó   in   vestido   non   de   Maria
       pull-PAST/3Ss   IN   dress   which   of   Maria
       'She pulled on Maria's dress.'

See Mahootian 1993, MacSwan 2013, and Muysken 2000 for additional discussion.

Finally, we turn to a class of proposals built around Levelt's (1989) *Speaking* model. Although similar proposals surfaced independently (De Bot, 1992; Azuma 1991, 1993), Myers-Scotton's (1993) Matrix Language Frame (MLF) Model has had a very strong influence on the field of CS. The MLF Model differentiates the languages involved in CS, as other models (e.g., Joshi 1985b) have also done; one language is known as the *matrix language* (ML), the other as the *embedded language* (EL). According to this approach, the matrix language defines the surface structure positions for content words and functional elements.

The MLF Model includes two basic components—the Morpheme Order Principle, which requires that morphemes within a bilingual constituent follow the order prescribed by the ML, and the System Morpheme Principle, which states that all "system morphemes"—defined as morphemes that have grammatical relations with other constituents outside their maximal projections— come from the ML in any CS utterance.

From a theoretical point of view, we see that we immediately encounter the same difficulties as in some other approaches: the grammatical principles responsible for defining the distribution of CS explicitly refer to the separate languages involved in CS without specifying a formal definition of the languages in interaction. Moreover, the general mechanisms are defined in very vague terms, making it difficult to identify the specific empirical predictions of the MLF Model.

Concern over the vagueness of the definition of the ML, in particular, has been voiced by Muysken and De Rooij (1995), Bentahila (1995), MacSwan (1999, 2000, 2005), and Muysken (2000). Jake, Myers-Scotton, and Gross (2002) resolved some of the ambiguities associated with Myers-Scotton's (1993, 69) original definition of the ML as the language contributing the majority of the morphemes in an utterance, which "may change across time, and even within a conversation." In contrast, the Uniform Structure Principle of Jake, Myers-Scotton, and Gross (2002, 73) offered a more structurally oriented definition of the ML: "The ML may change within successive CPs, even within a multi-clausal sentence, but we stress that the ML does not change within a single bilingual CP." In other words, within a single CP, the MLF Model predicts that all grammatical morphemes will be from one language only (System Morpheme Principle), and that the language contributing the grammatical morphemes will also define the surface order of the utterance (Morpheme Order Principle). Jake, Myers-Scotton, and Gross furthermore stress that the ML/EL distinction is universal, existing "in monolingual language as well as bilingual language" (p. 88), though the relevant associated mechanisms can only be detected in bilingual data.

Myers-Scotton and colleagues further stipulate that an "EL island" may occur below the CP: "As well-formed maximal constituents in the EL, [EL islands] are not inflected with ML system morphemes, although they occur in positions projected by the ML, following the Morpheme Order Principle"

(Jake, Myers-Scotton, and Gross 2002, 77). That is, EL islands are essentially lawful violations of the System Morpheme Principle because they contain grammatical morphemes that are not in the ML, but an EL island must be a maximal projection and must remain true to the Morpheme Order Principle (i.e., its position within the utterance must be dictated by the ML). Let us briefly consider some empirical evidence bearing on these predictions, focusing on the System Morpheme Principle. The French-Italian data in (24) are reported in Di Sciullo, Muysken, and Singh 1986.

(24a) No,   *parce que*   hanno   *donné*   *des*   *cours.*
       no,   because   have   given   of the   lectures
       'No, because they have given the lectures.'

(24b) Oui, alors j'ai   dit   quie   *si*   *potev*   aller   comme   ça.
       yes   so   I have said that   REF   could   walk   like   that
       'Yes, so I said that we could go like that.'

Note that in both cases we observe a switch between an auxiliary or modal and its complement. Because these forms have grammatical relations with other lexical heads within the structure, they meet the MLF Model's definition of a system morpheme. Yet, contrary to the requirements of the System Morpheme Principle, each utterance involves system morphemes from different languages below the CP.

To rescue the MLF Model, one might argue that *donné des cours* in (24a) is an EL island, projected as a VP complement of the auxiliary verb, and that (24b) similarly involves an EL island (*aller comme ça*), an IP complement of the modal. However, note that the examples in (24) contrast with Spanish-English data in (3), repeated here, where a switch between an auxiliary and a participle is ill formed. The construction in (3b) is eligible for the same structural analysis as (24a), in which an EL island is hypothesized, yet it is ill formed, contrary to the predictions of the MLF Model.

(3a)   The students *habían visto la película italiana.*
        'The students had seen the Italian movie.'

(3b)   *The student had *visto la película italiana.*
        'The student had seen the Italian movie.'

As an additional example, consider the Spanish-Nahuatl examples in (14), repeated again here. Notice that Spanish negation (*no*) does not tolerate a Nahuatl complement, while Nahuatl negation (*amo*) permits a Spanish complement. Both the agreement morphology on the verbs and negation count as system morphemes since they enter into grammatical relations with other morphemes (in the less obvious case, Negation c-commands a negative polarity item and may form a syntactic clitic with its verb). Hence, according to the System Morpheme Principle, both (14a) and (14b) should be ill formed because system morphemes are mixed below the CP, yet this is not so. Remarkably, the constructions contrast in acceptability, even though they appear to have identical underlying structures.

(14a) *No *nitekititoc.*
     no   ni-tekiti-toc
     not 1S-work-DUR
     'I'm not working.'

(14b) Amo *estoy* *trabajando.*
     amo   estoy   trabaja-ndo
     not   be/3Ss   work-DUR
     'I'm not working.'

Myers-Scotton and colleagues might argue that NegP is an EL island in (14a) but not in (14b), but with no independent evidence of the status of island entities these claims appear to be mere rationalizations. Myers-Scotton (1993) and Jake, Myers-Scotton, and Gross (2002) furthermore allow "internal EL islands," defined as "a constituent in the EL made up of EL morphemes following EL morpheme order, but smaller than a maximal projection" (Jake, Myers-Scotton, and Gross 2002, 76). In other words, not only can maximal projections be "islands," but structural units smaller than EL islands can too, sanctioning essentially any and all CS examples. One must recall that the constraint mechanism proposed as part of a model of CS cannot be selectively applied—that is, we cannot reasonably claim that negation is an island, immune to the System Morpheme Principle in (14b) but not in (14a) where the result is ill formed. Rather, once created, these mechanisms must operate in all cases, and as such they create a universe of expectations where essentially all CS is well formed.

Of course, all CS is not well formed, as is abundantly clear. But there is a historical tendency for CS researchers to rely primarily on naturalistic data alone—evidence of what does occur in CS—making it impossible to discover when a model overidentifies well-formed constructions. In the absence of negative evidence, generally available through grammaticality judgment tasks, one will not be in a position to construct a generative theory of CS with the capability of generating all and only the well-formed cases. (For further discussion in the specific context of the MLF Model, see Bhatia and Ritchie 1999; Ritchie and Bhatia 1999, 2001; MacSwan 2005, 2013.)

1.1.7 The Constraint-Free Research Program

The history of CS reveals a common intuition among researchers that theories about CS should be free of grammatical mechanisms and constraints specific to it. Poplack and Sankoff (1981) noted complications associated with the free (unconstrained) union of two phrase structure grammars, then reluctantly introduced a CS-specific tagging mechanism in response to the empirical demands of the data. Others did not address the issue and formal problems directly, while some proposed CS-specific constraints but argued that the mechanisms applied to monolinguals as well as bilinguals.

However, a true constraint-free approach to CS will permit no such mechanism and will not tolerate any grammatical device that makes explicit reference to *(code)switching* or *language(s)*. The guiding principle for such a program of research might be stated as in (25) (MacSwan 1999).

(25) Nothing constrains CS apart from the requirements of the mixed
      grammars.

In the next section, I offer a minimalist implementation of (25) along with a set of specific analyses intended to serve as proof of concept for it. I will argue that the MP has important advantages for the analysis of CS data, but note that (25) could in principle be implemented in any number of alternative syntactic frameworks (GPSG, OT, or others).

1.2 Implementing a Constraint-Free Approach

In important respects, the theoretical contexts in which many influential theories had been formulated within the constraint-based research program did not provide the tools needed to permit the implementation of a true constraint-free research program. An approach to syntax that built structure from the top down, as in the *Aspects* and later GB models, postponed lexical insertion until well after the word order had been laid out. The approach posed a significant challenge to CS researchers: the structure could not be sensitive to which language contributed a specific lexical item until the end, when lexical insertion occurred, but the language contributing the lexical item appeared to have significant consequences for the syntactic structure at the outset.

The Minimalist Program (MP) provides an opportunity for implementing a rich, constraint-free approach. Within the MP, structures are built from a stock of lexical items, with lexical insertion (formalized as Select) taking place at the outset. This important development permits CS researchers to probe the structural consequences of particular lexical items from specific languages, with no need to keep track of which languages may contribute which specific lexical elements during a final stage of lexical insertion.

1.2.1 The Minimalist Program

According to Chametzky (2003), the "lexical-entry driven" approach to syntax was part of the general effort underlying X′ reduction, with significant contributions from Stowell (1981) and Speas (1990), among others. X′ Theory, which had been introduced in Chomsky 1970, effectively eliminated phrase structure grammar in favor of the view that structures are projected from lexical items; however, remnants remained, with reference to lexical insertion rules reasonably common among GB-era syntacticians (Chomsky 1981; Stowell 1981; Lasnik and Uriagereka 1988). With a return to its derivational roots, minimalist syntax reduced generation to the simplest possible form—free Merge (Chomsky 1995), building structures from the ground (the lexical string) up (the hierarchical phrase structure) based on the specification of lexically encoded features. Independently, Borer (1984) had suggested an account of language variation in which parameters were also associated with the lexicon, rather than with the system of syntactic rules. Hence, the system of rules could be seen as invariant, with all variation associated with the lexicon, the traditional repository of arbitrariness.

In the MP there are two components of grammar: C_{HL}, a computational system for human language, believed to be invariant across languages, and a lexicon, to which the idiosyncratic differences observed across languages are attributed. An operation called Select picks lexical items from the lexicon and introduces them into a Lexical Array (LA), a finite subset of the lexicon used to construct a derivation. Merge takes items from the LA and forms new, hierarchically arranged syntactic objects. Movement operations (Internal Merge) apply to syntactic objects formed by Merge to rearrange elements within a tree (Chomsky 1995, 2000). Phrase structure trees are thus built derivationally by the application of the operations Select and Merge, constrained by checking relationships established among lexically encoded features in the course of a derivation.

Movements are driven by feature valuation and may be of two types. A head may undergo head movement and adjoin to another head, or a maximal projection may move to the specifier position of a head. In either case, the element moves for the purpose of valuing morphological features of case and ϕ (number, person, and gender). More recently, Chomsky (2001) has proposed that agreement involves a relation between a probe and a goal. A probe searches for a goal in its local domain to assign a value to unvalued ϕ-features on the goal. Furthermore, clause structure is built up in phases; at the end of each phase, the relevant substructure is transferred to phonological and semantic components of the grammar, with the result that each successive phase becomes inaccessible for further computation. The phonological component maps the structure to Phonetic Form (PF) and the semantic component generates its Logical Form (LF).

The leading aim of the MP is the elimination of all mechanisms that are not essential on conceptual grounds alone; thus, only the minimal theoretical assumptions may be made to account for linguistic data, privileging more simplistic and elegant accounts over complex and cumbersome ones. These assumptions would naturally favor accounts of CS that make use of independently motivated principles of grammar over those that posit rules, principles, or other constructs specific to it. Hence, implementing (25), which posits that all the facts of CS may be explained just in terms of principles and requirements of the specific grammars in interaction, the formal claim is that, for G_x a grammar of Lx and Gy a grammar of Ly, CS falls out of the union of the two grammars ($\{Gx \cup Gy\}$) and nothing more (MacSwan 1999). Thus, while free union of phrase structure grammars led to the complications noted by Sankoff and Poplack (1981) for reasons associated with late lexical insertion, free union of lexically encoded grammars does not. Mahootian noticed that the TAG formalism she used provided an advantage for the analysis of CS data; because structures were encoded in the lexicon, no intervening control mechanism was needed to pair up lexical insertion rules with terminal nodes in a phrase marker, as seen in previous proposals. However, the version of TAG Mahootian was using (Joshi 1985a) did not include sufficiently rich feature specification in lexical entries to be very useful beyond the limited analysis of head-complement configurations she undertook, as discussed earlier.

Let us consider some sample analyses pursued within the minimalist approach to CS.

1.2.2 Asymmetrical Switches in DPs

Moro (chapter 10, this volume) developed an account of asymmetrical switches in Spanish-English DPs in which a Spanish determiner may precede an English N (e.g., *los teachers* 'the teachers') but an English determiner may not precede a Spanish N (e.g., **the casa* 'the house'). Moro notes that the composition of the set of φ-features differs for English and Spanish. In Spanish, gender and number are morphologically marked on determiners and nouns, but in English only person and number are marked while gender is absent. In monolingual contexts, the feature matrices of Ds and Ns are identical ({person, number} for English, {person, number, gender} for Spanish). However, with respect to the bilingual constructions, the DPs are well formed only if the φ-set of N is included in the φ-set of D.

Moro takes advantage of Chomsky's (2000, 2001) proposal that uninterpretable features (such as the φ-features of D, but not of N) enter the derivation without values specified. The operation Agree values and deletes these features from the narrow syntax "in one fell swoop" (2000, 124), all or none. Thus, in Moro's analysis, expressions like *the casa* crash because the N's φ-features person, number, and gender attempt to value and delete the D's features person, number, and gender "in one fell swoop"; however, the gender feature cannot succeed, because there is no corresponding feature in the English determiner. As a result, the derivation fails to converge, since the uninterpretable features of D are not deleted. In the well-formed case, on the other hand, the φ-features of N (person, number), being included in D's φ-set, successfully value and delete D's uninterpretable features "in one fell swoop," as in the monolingual cases.

1.2.3 Basic Subject/Verb Word Order

MacSwan (2000, 2005) argued that the properties of morphophonology force bilinguals to separately encapsulate distinct lexicons. Phonology is sensitive to inflectional content, and the rules of word formation are presumed to be internal to the lexicon in minimalist syntax, with words entering the derivation with their morphological content fully specified. We therefore face two alternatives: Either (a) there is a single lexicon, and each lexical item is marked for a specific set of phonological and morphological rules that yield the appearance of one language or another, or (b) the lexical items in a bilingual's repertoire are mentally compartmentalized in some way, with a specific set of phonological and morphological operations associated with each subset of lexical items. The second alternative appears more economical, since the morphophonology is associated with sets of elements rather than with individual members, and may be applied to novel items by monolinguals and bilinguals alike. We therefore will assume the latter to be correct, and refer to each subset of lexical items within a bilingual's linguistic repertoire as a distinct *lexicon*. Furthermore, the ban on mixing morphophonological systems has consequences for the syntax of CS, as it extends to head movement contexts, barring language switching in word-like units generally, including complex heads. The relevant condition is known as the PF Interface Condition (PFIC) (MacSwan, 2009, 2013; MacSwan and Colina, chapter 8, this volume).

As a case in point, consider the derivation of basic subject/verb word order in CS. Following standard minimalist assumptions, we take the universal base structure for both SV and VS languages to be underlyingly SVO with a VP-internal subject. V adjoins to T via head movement to value ϕ-features. SV word order results if T further probes the subject DP, causing it to raise to [Spec, T] to value its EPP feature; otherwise, the subject DP remains in situ and VS word order results. Because V raises to T to check ϕ-features, both elements must be drawn from the same lexicon in mixed-language expressions, otherwise the mixed-language complex head would cause the derivation to crash by the PFIC. As a result, the language of the verb will determine the language of T, and T in turn will probe or not probe the subject DP according to the dictates of its feature specifications. In this way the system developed here predicts that the language of the verb will determine the position of the subject—if the verb is from an SV language, the subject should occur preverbally, whether it is from an SV language or not; if the verb is from a VS language, the subject should occur postverbally, regardless of the requirements of the language of the subject. These facts are attested in a wide range of corpora, as shown in (26) and discussed in MacSwan 2004.

(26a) *VS verb (Irish), SV subject (English) (Stenson 1990)*
   Beidh *jet lag* an tógáil a pháirt ann.
   be-FUT   taking its part   in-it
   'Jet lag will be playing its part in it.'

(26b) *VS verb (Irish), SV subject (English) (Stenson 1990)*
   Fuair sé *thousand pounds.*
   get-PA he
   'He got a thousand pounds.'

(26c) *VS verb (Breton), SV subject (French) (Pensel 1979)*
   Oa   ket   *des*   *armes.*
   be-3S IMP NEG of-the arms
   'There were no arms.'

(26d) *VS verb (Breton), SV subject (French) (Troadec 1983)*
   Setu oa   *l'état-major* du-se   barzh ti Lanserot.
   There be-imp the military-staff down-there in   house Lanserot
   'There was the military staff down there in Lanserot's house.'

(26e) *VS verb (SLQ Zapotec), SV subject (Spanish) (MacSwan 2004)*
   S-to'oh *mi esposa el coche.*
   DEF-sell my wife the car
   'My wife will definitely sell the car.'

1.2.4 DP-Internal Word Order

It has similarly been observed that the language of the adjective determines word order in CS contexts (Cantone and MacSwan 2009). Consider, for instance, the following examples of German-Italian CS.

(27a) Una *glückliche Frau*
'A happy woman'

(27b) *Die französische* cucina
'The French cousin'

(27c) Una   *Gegend*   fredda
A   region   cold
'A cold region'

Cinque (2005) posits that DP-internal word order is underlyingly D Adj N in both Romance and Germanic. In the case of Romance, the NP raises to check features in the specifier position of Agr, deriving D Adj N word order. To derive D N Adj word order, as in German, the NP remains in situ. We further note that adjectives raise to value features with Agr by head movement, just as V raised to T in our account of the VS/SV facts just considered.

We may now account for the facts in (27) in a straightforward manner. We are assured that Agr is in the language of the adjective because the adjective adjoins to Agr by head movement, and mixed constructions in head-movement contexts are disallowed by the PFIC. Italian Agr has an EPP feature, forcing the NP to raise overtly to its specifier position. German Agr, by contrast, does not probe the NP's EPP feature, causing it to remains in situ. Hence, Italian Agr forces the NP to raise overtly, while German Agr does not, accounting for the descriptive generalization noted, namely, that the language of the adjective determines the position of the NP relative to the adjective. (See Di Sciullo, chapter 3, this volume, for further discussion of properties of adjectives in CS contexts.)

1.2.5 Pronominal and Lexical Subjects

As a final example, consider the well-known ban on CS in pronominal subjects illustrated in (2) in contrast to (1), repeated here.

(1)   *Mi hermano* bought some ice cream.
'My brother bought some ice cream.'

(2)   **El* bought some ice cream.
'He bought some ice cream.'

Van Gelderen and MacSwan (2008), following a line of work treating pronouns as heads rather than phrases (Abney 1987; Longobardi 1994;

Cardinaletti 1994; Cardinaletti and Starke 1996; Carnie 2000), propose that subject extraction from a VP-internal shell proceeds according to a principle of economy proposed in Chomsky 1995, 262: "F carries along just enough material for convergence," where F is the target of movement. (Compare Takahashi 2000.) As such, van Gelderen and MacSwan (2008) argue that Ds may check features with T via head movement, while lexical DPs must move as phrases, pied-piping their phonetically filled complements. Since D-to-T movement would result in a mixed-language complex head, ruled out by the PFIC, the pronominal subject case (as in (2)) crashes at PF. However, in (1), the lexical DP moves as a phrase to the specifier of T with no ill-formedness resulting. Corroborating evidence involving coordination of pronouns with lexical DPs in CS contexts further supports the analysis.

I have offered some specific examples of analyses of CS conducted within a constraint-free research program to support the claim that such analyses are both possible and fruitful. The analyses give rise to new families of questions about other language pairs with related and distinct properties, and about general properties of linguistic theory. Other illustrations may be reviewed in the chapters that follow, or in previously published research (for instance, van Dulm, 2007, 2009; González-Vilbazo and López, 2011; Lotfabbadi, 2002; Cantone and Müller, 2005; Cantone, 2007; Radford, Kupisch, Köppe, and Azzaro, 2009; and MacSwan, 1999, 2013).

1.3 Evaluating Theories and Programs

It is important to note that a research program is not itself a theory, but rather constitutes an analytic framework that in turn spawns theories and proposals, as Boeckx (2006) has noted in the context of a more general discussion of linguistic research programs. Lakatos (1970), a philosopher of mathematics and science best known for his defining work on scientific research programs, noted that the "typical descriptive unit" of scientific achievement was not a particular theory or proposal, but indeed a research program. As Boeckx (2006, 89) elaborates, a research program is made up of a core with a "logico-empirical character": "Whatever the constitutive elements of a program's core may be, that core is rightly characterized by Lakatos as 'irrefutable,' and 'stubbornly defended.' Wittgenstein would have called it 'unassailable and definitive.' The core is tenaciously protected from refutation by a vast protective belt of auxiliary hypotheses."

Research programs, according to Lakatos, are not to be distinguished as right or wrong but rather as progressive or degenerating—that is, as fertile or sterile. A progressive research program is one that gives rise to new families of questions and leads to the discovery of new facts. A program is degenerating or sterile, on the other hand, if the theories it spawns are conceived only to account for known facts. Boeckx further notes: "As Lakatos points out, one must treat budding programs leniently: programs may take decades before they take off and become empirically progressive. As Lakatos observes, 'criticism is not a Popperian quick kill, by refutation. Important criticism is always constructive: there is no refutation without a better theory'" (p. 91). Note that (25), the agenda for a genuine constraint-free approach to CS, is similarly not a particular theory about CS but a program for CS research. It gives rise to particular theories or proposals, each formulated with a commitment to tolerate no CS-specific device. Because (25) is not itself a theory, it is not subject to falsification; rather, it should be abandoned as an agenda for CS research only if it proves sterile or unsuccessful.

We might reasonably argue that CS research conducted in the constraint-free program constitutes a dramatic departure from theories articulated within the constraint-based program. A review of the constraint-based literature shows that CS constraints were proposed fundamentally to account for known facts, with each successive proposal offering criticisms of previous ones with no significant or new insights provided. The effort to identify overarching constraints on CS has been exhausted, and the program appears sterile (or regressive, in Lakatos's terms).

Furthermore, it is not meaningful or informative to make empirical comparisons between theories formulated within a constraint-free approach and those formulated within a constraint-based approach, as has been done (for instance, Herring and colleagues, 2010). If relevant counterevidence is presented regarding a proposed constraint on CS, constraint-oriented researchers either attempt to disprove the counterevidence or augment the system of constraints in some way. One sees this notably among proponents of the MLF Model, whose system of constraints has admitted increasingly numerous add-on mechanisms, principles, and hypotheses that are successively intended to inoculate the model from falsification.

Conversely, if a particular theory proposed within the constraint-free program is shown to be false, it does not lead researchers within the program to turn to CS-specific constraints but rather to adjust the analysis to newly discovered data. Suppose, for instance, that evidence from additional language pairs suggested that Moro's (chapter 10, this volume) theory of DP-internal checking, or van Gelderen and MacSwan's (2008) theory about subject licensing in CS contexts, was incorrect. Researchers within the constraint-free program would be expected to discard the previous analyses in favor of improved alternatives covering a greater range of empirical ground. But such data would not be interpreted as evidence that the very "logicoempirical character" of the program should be rejected. That conclusion would follow only if continued research appeared fruitless in light of insurmountable barriers, and the project grew sterile—a result that is not likely to obtain soon, given the enormous promise of ongoing research.

1.4   Contributions to the Present Book

The book is divided into four parts. Part 1 includes five chapters with detailed grammatical analyses of CS. In chapter 2, Dan Finer examines movement triggers and reflexives in Korean-English CS, concluding that the grammatical characteristics follow from the nature of the lexical and functional items selected into the numeration or lexical array. Finer concludes his discussion with attention to new questions raised by his analysis, and notes that the data of CS is relevant to general linguistic theory as data from traditional sources, and ought to be used to shape theory about the monolingual grammar, too. In chapter 3, Anna Maria Di Sciullo explores the data of CS in relation to the Asymmetry Hypothesis proposed in her previous work in the context of monolingual grammar. She discusses three striking facts evident in Italian-English-French CS, suggesting that the complement/noncomplement asymmetry in the grammars of (monolingual) languages is also manifested in CS. In chapter 4, Almeida Jacqueline Toribio and Kay E. González-Vilbazo observe patterns of word order in *wh*-questions, negative fronting, and relative clauses in English, Spanish, German, English-Spanish, and German-Spanish CS, and propose that the patterns may be explained by checking theory. Like Finer, the authors argue that the data and analysis show the utility of CS as a source of valuable information for general linguistic theory. In chapter 5, Pieter Muysken asks how categorial mismatches in the syntax and lexicon might be resolved in language contact, with a focus on the Amerindian languages, Popoloca in particular. Finally, in chapter 6, Rakesh M. Bhatt pursues an Optimality approach to CS, with attention to Kashmiri-English, Hindi-English, Spanish-English, and Swahili-English CS.

Part 2 is devoted to phonological and morphological issues in CS that revolve around the question of whether CS is permitted word-internally. In chapter 7, Shoba Bandi-Rao and Marcel den Dikken examine word-formation properties in Telugu-English CS, proposing a Distributed Morphology (DM) solution. The authors present some criticisms of MacSwan's PF Disjunction Theorem, which is revised as the PF Interface Condition in chapter 8, where Jeff MacSwan and Sonia Colina present experimental evidence regarding the phonological nature of word-boundary CS.

Part 3 includes two contributions on the semantics of CS. In chapter 9, Monica Moro Quintanilla analyzes the semantics and syntax of DPs in English-Spanish CS, addressing intriguing asymmetries in the distribution of determiners in mixed-language utterances. In chapter 10, Silvia Milian Hita, also focusing on the semantics of English-Spanish CS, analyzes the aspectual requirements of the participating verbs in Spanish-English CS in three communities. Hita's work illustrates that bilingual speakers know what features are uninterpreted in each of the participating languages.

Part 4 focuses on CS and language processing. In chapter 11, Edward P. Stabler and Jeff MacSwan implement a computational parser for CS, showing that a computer system can parse bilingual utterances using a fully lexicalized grammar with no CS-specific mechanisms, with a focus on the computation of morphophonology. Finally, Ana Teresa Pérez-Leroux, Erin O'Rourke and Gretchen Sunderman conclude the volume with a psycholinguistic study of language dominance and CS. The authors ask whether there is a processing cost associated with CS, and conclude that CS is an effortless and natural language phenomena, and is not affected by language dominance.The agenda for a constraint-free research program might be implemented in any formal theoretical framework, with different degrees of success, as illustrated in the historical discussion earlier in this chapter. While most contributors to the present book are engaged in MP-style analyses, Bhatt's work is conducted within an OT framework, and Bandi-Rao and den Dikken explore the possibility of a Distributed Morphology approach. In addition, the approaches to minimalism used in the book span nearly the full range of implementations, though all with the same basic commitment to lexicalism noted earlier. One sees similar theoretical variation in other recent work, including Lotfabbadi 2002; van Gelderen and MacSwan 2008, Van Dulm 2007, 2009; González-Vilbazo and López 2011; and MacSwan 2013.

The linguistic study of CS is still very much in its infancy, but it is an exciting and intriguing field. I hope that continued research will lead to refinements and new insights in the fields of bilingualism and grammatical theory, and I invite other scholars to join the work – perhaps inspired, at least in part, by the exciting chapters that follow.

References

Abney, S. P. 1987. The English noun phrase in its sentential aspect. Doctoral dissertation, MIT.

Azuma, S. 1991. Processing and intrasentential code-switching. Doctoral dissertation, University of Texas, Austin.

Azuma, S. 1993. The frame-content hypothesis in speech production: Evidence from intrasentential code switching. *Linguistics* 31:1071–1093.

Bandi-Rao, S., and M. den Dikken. 2014. Light switches: On v as a pivot in codeswitching, and the nature of the ban on word-internal switches. In J. MacSwan, ed., *Grammatical Theory and Bilingual Codeswitching*. Cambridge, MA: MIT Press.

Belazi, H. M., E. J. Rubin, and A. J. Toribio. 1994. Code switching and X-Bar Theory: The Functional Head Constraint. *Linguistic Inquiry* 25 (2): 221–237.

Benson, E. J. 2001. The neglected early history of codeswitching research in the United States. *Language & Communication* 21 (1): 23–36.

Bentahila, A. 1995. Review of *Duelling Languages: Grammatical Structure in Codeswitching*. *Language* 71 (1): 135–140.

Bentahila, A., and E. E. Davis. 1983. The syntax of Arabic-French code-switching. *Lingua* 59:301–330.

Berk-Seligson, S. 1986. Linguistic constraints on intrasentential code-switching: A study of Spanish-Hebrew bilingualism. *Language in Society* 15:313–348.

Bhatia, Tej K., and William C. Ritchie. 1999. The bilingual child: Issues and perspectives. In William C. Ritchie, Tej Krishan Bhatia (eds.) *Handbook of Child Language Acquisition*, 569–643. San Diego, CA: Academic Press.

Bhatia, Tej K., and William C. Ritchie. 2001. Language mixing, typology, and second language acquisition. In Rajendra Singh (ed.), *The Yearbook of South Asian Languages and Linguistics 2001 Tokyo Symposium on South Asian Languages: Contact, Convergence and Typology*, 37–62. London: Sage.

Bhatt, R. M. 2014. Argument licensing in optimal switches. In J. MacSwan, ed., *Grammatical Theory and Bilingual Codeswitching*. Cambridge, MA: MIT Press.

Boeckx, C. 2006. *Linguistic Minimalism: Origins, Concepts, Methods, and Aims*. Oxford: Oxford University Press.

Bokamba, E. G. 1989. Are there syntactic constraints on code-mixing? *World Englishes* 8:277–292.

Borer, H. 1984. *Parametric syntax: Case studies in Semitic and Romance languages*. Dordrecht: Foris

Cantone, K. 2007. *Code-Switching in Bilingual Children*. Dordrecht: Springer.

Cantone, K., and J. MacSwan. 2009. The syntax of DP-internal codeswitching. In L. Isurin, D. Winford, and K. de Bot, eds., *Multidisciplinary Approaches to Codeswitching*, 243–278. Amsterdam: John Benjamins.

Cantone, K., and N. Müller. 2005. Codeswitching at the interface of language-specific lexicons and the computational system. *International Journal of Bilingualism* 9 (2): 205–225.

Cardinaletti, A. 1994. On the internal structure of pronominal DPs. *Linguistic Review* 11 (3–4): 195–219.

Cardinaletti, A., and M. Starke. 1996. Deficient pronouns: A view from Germanic: A study in the unified description of Germanic and Romance. In Hoskuldur Thrainsson, Samuel David Epstein, and Steve Peter, eds., *Studies in Comparative Germanic Syntax*, vol. 2, 21–65. Dordrecht: Kluwer.

Carnie, A. 2000. On the definition of X^0 and XP. *Syntax* 3 (2): 59–106.

Cinque, G. 2005. Deriving Greenberg's Universal 20 and its exceptions. *Linguistic Inquiry*, 36 (3), 315–332.

Chametzky, R. A. 2003. Phrase structure. In R. Hendrick, ed., *Minimalist Syntax*, 192–225. Oxford: Blackwell.

Chan, B. H.-S. 1999. Aspects of the syntax, production and pragmatics of code-switching with special reference to Cantonese-English. Doctoral dissertation, University College London.

Chomsky, N. 1957. *Syntactic Structures*. The Hague: Mouton.

Chomsky, N. 1964. *Current Issues in Linguistic Theory*. The Hague: Mouton.

Chomsky, N. 1965. *Aspects of the Theory of Syntax*. Cambridge, MA: MIT Press.

Chomsky, N. 1981. *Lectures on Government and Binding*. New York: Mouton de Gruyter.

Chomsky, N. 1995. *The Minimalist Program*. Cambridge, MA: MIT Press.

Chomsky, N. 1998. Some observations on economy in generative grammar. In P. Barbosa, D. Fox, P. Hagstrom, M. McGinnis, and D. Pesetsky, eds., *Is the Best Good Enough? Optimality and Competition in Syntax*. Cambridge, MA: MIT Press.

Chomsky, N. 2000. Minimalist inquiries: The framework. In R. Martin, D. Michaels, and J. Uriagereka, eds., *Step by Step: Essays on Minimalist Syntax in Honor of Howard Lasnik*, 89–155. Cambridge, MA: MIT Press.

Chomsky, N. 2001. Derivation by phase. In M. Kenstowics, ed., *Ken Hale: A Life in Language*, 1–51. Cambridge, MA: MIT Press.

Clyne, M. 1987. Constraints on code switching: How universal are they? *Linguistics* 25, 739–764. Reprinted in *Bilingual Reader,* pp. 257–280. Ed. Li Wei. New York: Routledge, 2000.

De Bot, K. 1992. A bilingual production model: Levelt's "speaking" model adapted. *Applied Linguistics* 13 (1): 1–24.

Di Sciullo, A. M. 2014. On the asymmetric nature of the operations of grammar: Evidence from codeswitching. In J. MacSwan, ed., *Grammatical Theory and Bilingual Codeswitching*. Cambridge, MA: MIT Press.

Di Sciullo, A. M., P. Muysken, and R. Singh. 1986. Government and code-switching. *Journal of Linguistics* 22:1–24.

Eliasson, S. 1989. English-Maori language contact: Code-switching and the free-morpheme constraint. *Report from Uppsala University.* Uppsala, Sweden: Department of Linguistics, Uppsala University.

Espinosa, A. M. 1911. Studies in New Mexican Spanish, Part II: Morphology. *Revue de Dialectologie Romane* 3:251–268.

Finer, Daniel L. 2014. Movement triggers and reflexivization in Korean-English codeswitching. In J. MacSwan, ed., *Grammatical Theory and Bilingual Codeswitching*. Cambridge, MA: MIT Press.

González-Vilbazo, Kay, & Luis López. 2011. Some properties of light verbs in code-switching. *Lingua* 121, p. 832–850.

Gumperz, J. 1967. On the linguistic markers of bilingual communication. *Journal of Social Issues* 28 (2): 48–57.

Gumperz, J. 1970. Verbal strategies and multilingual communication. In J. E. Alatis, ed., *Georgetown Round Table on Language and Linguistics*, pp. 129–147. Washington, DC: Georgetown University Press.

Gumperz, J., and E. Hernández-Chávez. 1970. Cognitive aspects of bilingual communication, pp. 115–125. In W. H. Whitely, ed., *Language and Social Change*. Oxford: Oxford University Press.

Halmari, H. 1997. *Government and Code Switching: Explaining American Finnish.* New York: John Benjamins.

Hasselmo, N. 1972. Code-switching as ordered selection. In E. S. Firchow, ed., *Studies for Einar Haugen,* 261–280. The Hague: Mouton.

Herring, J, Deuchar, M, Parafita Couto, M. C. and Moro Quintanilla, M. 2010. "I saw the madre": evaluating predictions about codeswitched determiner-noun sequences using Spanish-English and Welsh-English data. *International Journal of Bilingual Education and Bilingualism*, 13(5), 553–573.

Hlavac, J. 2003. *Second-Generation Speech: Lexicon, Code-Switching, and Morpho-Syntax of Croatian-English Bilinguals.* Berlin: Peter Lang.

Haugen, E. 1956. *Bilingualism in the Americas: A Bibliography and Research Guide.* Jacksonville, IL: American Dialect Society.

Jake, J., C. Myers-Scotton, and S. Gross. 2002. Making a minimalist approach to codeswitching work: Adding the Matrix Language. *Bilingualism: Language and Cognition* 5 (1): 69–91.

Joshi, A. K. 1985a. How much context-sensitivity is necessary for assigning structural descriptions? Tree adjoining grammars, pp. 206–250. In D. R. Dowty, L. Karttunen, and A. M. Zwicky, eds., *Natural Language Parsing: Psychological, Computational and Theoretical Perspectives.* Cambridge: Cambridge University Press.

Joshi, A. 1985b. Processing of sentences with intrasentential code switching. In D. R. Dowty, L. Karttunen, and A. M. Zwicky, eds., *Natural Language Parsing: Psychological, Computational and Theoretical Perspectives*, 190–205. Cambridge: Cambridge University Press.

Labov, W. 1963. The social motivation of a sound change. *Word* 19:273–309.

Lakatos, I. 1970. Falsification and the methodology of scientific research programs. In I. Lakatos and A. Musgrave, eds., *Criticism and the Growth of Knowledge*, 91–195. Cambridge: Cambridge University Press.

Lasnik, H., and J. Uriagereka. 1988. *A Course in GB Syntax: Lectures on Binding and Empty Categories.* Cambridge, MA: MIT Press.

Lee, M.-H. 1991. A parametric approach to code-switching. Doctoral dissertation, State University of New York at Stonybrook.

Levelt, W. J. M. 1989. *Speaking: From Intention to Articulation.* Cambridge, MA: MIT Press.

Lipski, J. 1978. Code-switching and the problem of bilingual competence, 250–264. In J. Paradis, ed., *Aspects of Bilingualism.* Columbia, SC: Hornbeam Press.

Lipski, J. 1985. *Linguistic Aspects of Spanish-English Language Switching*. Tempe, Arizona: Center for Latin American Studies, Arizona State University.

Longobardi, G. 1994. Reference and proper names: A theory of N-movement in syntax and logical form. *Linguistic Inquiry* 25 (4): 609–665.

Lotfabbadi, L. N. 2002. *Disagreement in agreement: A study of grammatical aspects of codeswitching in Swedish/Persian bilingual speech*. Doctoral dissertation, Department of Linguistics, Stockholm University.

MacSwan, J. 1999. *A Minimalist Approach to Intrasentential Code Switching*. New York: Garland Press.

MacSwan, J. 2000. The architecture of the bilingual language faculty: Evidence from codeswitching. *Bilingualism: Language and Cognition* 3 (1): 37–54.

MacSwan, J. 2004. Code switching and linguistic theory, pp. 415–462. In T. K. Bhatia and W. Ritchie, eds., *Handbook of Bilingualism*. Oxford: Blackwell.

MacSwan, J. 2005. Codeswitching and generative grammar: A critique of the MLF Model and some remarks on "modified minimalism." *Bilingualism: Language and Cognition* 8 (1): 1–22.

MacSwan, J. 2013. Code switching and linguistic theory. In T. K. Bhatia and W. Ritchie, eds., *Handbook of Bilingualism and Multilingualism*, 2nd ed., 223–350. Oxford: Blackwell.

MacSwan, J. 2009. Generative approaches to codeswitching, pp. 309–335. In A. J. Toribio & B. E. Bullock (eds.), *Cambridge Handbook of Linguistic Codeswitching*. Cambridge University Press.

MacSwan, J., and S. Colina. 2014. Some consequences of language design: Codeswitching and the PF Interface. In J. MacSwan, ed., *Grammatical Theory and Bilingual Codeswitching*. Cambridge, MA: MIT Press.

Mahootian, S. 1993. A null theory of code switching. Doctoral dissertation, Northwestern University.

Milian Hita, S. 2014. Codeswitching and the semantics/syntax interface: The role of aspectual features in constraining intrasentential codeswitching. In J. MacSwan, ed., *Grammatical Theory and Bilingual Codeswitching*. Cambridge, MA: MIT Press.

Moro Quintanilla, M. 2014. The semantic interpretation and syntactic distribution of determiner phrases in Spanish-English codeswitching. In J. MacSwan, ed., *Grammatical Theory and Bilingual Codeswitching*. Cambridge, MA: MIT Press.

Müller, N., and K. Cantone. 2009. Language mixing in bilingual children: Code switching? In B. E. Bullock and A. J. Toribio, eds., *Cambridge Handbook of Linguistic Codeswitching*, 199–220. Cambridge: Cambridge University Press.

Muysken, P. 2000. *Bilingual Speech: A Typology of Code-Mixing*. Cambridge: Cambridge University Press.

Muysken, P. 2014. Categorial mismatches in the syntax and the lexicon: Evidence from language contact research. In J. MacSwan, ed., *Grammatical Theory and Bilingual Codeswitching*. Cambridge, MA: MIT Press.

Muysken, P., and V. de Rooij. 1995. Review of *Social Motivations for Code-Switching: Evidence from Africa* and *Duelling Languages: Grammatical Structure in Codeswitching. Linguistics* 33:1043–1066.

Myers-Scotton, C. 1993. *Duelling Languages: Grammatical Structure in CodeSwitching.* Oxford: Clarendon Press.

Nartey, J. S. 1982. Code-switching, interference or faddism? Language use among educated Ghanaians. *Anthropological Linguistics* 24:183–192.

Nishimura, M. 1997. *Japanese/English code-switching: Syntax and pragmatics.* New York: Peter Lang.

Pandit, I. 1990. Grammaticality in code switching, pp. 33–69. In R. Jacobson, ed., *Codeswitching as a Worldwide Phenomenon.* New York: Peter Lang.

Pensel, I. 1979. Testeni. *Hor Yezh* 126:47–73.

Pfaff, C. 1979. Constraints on language mixing: Intrasentential code-switching and borrowing in Spanish/English. *Language* 55:291–318.

Poplack, S. 1978. Quantitative analysis of constraints on code-switching. In *Centro Working Papers.* New York: Centro de Estudios Puertorriqueños, City University of New York.

Poplack, S. 1980. "Sometimes I'll start a sentence in Spanish y termino en Español": Toward a typology of code-switching. *Linguistics* 18:581–618.

Poplack, S. 1981. The syntactic structure and social function of code-switching, pp. 169–184. In R. Durán, ed., *Latino Language and Communicative Behavior.* Norwood, NJ: Ablex.

Radford, A., T. Kupisch, R. Köppe, and G. Azzaro. 2007. Concord, convergence, and accommodation in bilingual children. *Bilingualism: Language and Cognition* 10 (3): 239–256.

Ritchie, William, and Tej Bhatia. 1999. Codeswitching, grammar, and sentence production: The problem of light verbs. In Elaine C. Klein and Gita Martohardjono , eds., *The Development of Second Language Grammars*, 273–291. Amsterdam: John Benjamins.

Ross, J. 1967. Constraints on variables in syntax. Doctoral dissertation, MIT.

Sankoff, D., and S. Poplack. 1980. A formal grammar for code-switching. *CUNY Working Papers*, 8. New York: Centro de Estudios Puertorriqueños, City University of New York.

Sankoff, D., and S. Poplack. 1981. A formal grammar for code-switching. *Papers in Linguistics* 14:3–45.

Sankoff, D. 1998. A formal production-based explanation of the facts of code-switching. *Bilingualism: Language and Cognition* 1 (1): 39–50.

Santorini, B., and S. Mahootian. 1995. Codeswitching and the syntactic status of adnominal adjectives. *Lingua* 96:1–27.

Speas, M. 1990. *Phrase Structure in Natural Language.* Dordrecht: Kluwer.

Stabler, E. P., Jr., and J. MacSwan. 2009. A minimalist parsing model for codeswitching. In J. MacSwan, ed., *Grammatical Theory and Bilingual Codeswitching.* Cambridge, MA: MIT Press.

Stenson, N. 1990. Phrase structure congruence, government, and Irish-English code switching. *Syntax and Semantics* 23, 167–197.

Stowell, T. 1981. Origins of phrase structure. Doctoral dissertation, MIT.

Takahashi, D. 2000. Move F and raising of lexical and empty DPs, pp. 297–317. In Martin, R., Michaels, D., Uriagereka, J. (Eds.), *Step by Step: Essays on Minimalist Syntax in Honor of Howard Lasnik*. MIT Press, Cambridge.

Timm, L. A. 1975. Spanish-English code-switching: El porqué and how-not-to. *Romance Philology* 28:473–482.

Toribio, A. J., and K. E. González-Vilbazo. 2014. Operator movement in English-Spanish and German-Spanish codeswitching. In J. MacSwan, ed., *Grammatical Theory and Bilingual Codeswitching*. Cambridge, MA: MIT Press.

Troadec, B. 1983. Tri fennad-kaoz gant an Itron Bernadette Troadec. *Hor Yezh* 71–127.

Van Dulm, O. 2007. *The grammar of English-Afrikaans code switching: A feature checking account.* Utrecht: Netherlands Graduate School of Linguistics (LOT).

Van Dulm, O. 2009. English-Afrikaans intrasentential code switching: Testing a feature checking account. *Bilingualism: Language and Cognition*, 12(2), 193–212.

Van Gelderen, E., and J. MacSwan. 2008. Interface conditions and codeswitching: An F-movement analysis of pronouns and lexical DPs. *Lingua* 118 (6): 765–776.

Vogt, H. 1954. Review of *Languages in Contact*. *Word* 10:79–82.

Weinreich, U. 1953. *Languages in Contact*. The Hague: Mouton.

Wentz, J. 1977. Some considerations in the development of a syntactic description of code-switching. Doctoral dissertation, University of Illinois, Urbana-Champaign.

Wentz, J., and E. McClure. 1977. Aspects of the syntax of the code-switched discourse of bilingual children, pp. 351–370. In F. J. Ingemann, ed., *1975 Mid-American Linguistics Conference Papers*. Lawrence: University of Kansas.

Woolford, E. 1983. Bilingual code-switching and syntactic theory. *Linguistic Inquiry* 14 (5): 520–536.

Grammatical Analysis

2 Movement Triggers and Reflexivization in Korean-English Codeswitching

Daniel L. Finer

The explosion of research on issues of comparative grammar initiated by Chomsky 1981 continues, with the focus on aspects of the lexicon rather than on grammars themselves. That is, instead of hypothesizing that the lines along which languages differ are the effects of parameters defined globally across grammars (such as the mid-1980s branching direction or subjacency parameters), researchers in the Minimalist Program (cf. Chomsky 1995, 2001, 2008) have suggested instead that differences in, for example, word order among languages are the results of movement triggered by properties of the lexical items in the syntactic structure.[1] This chapter attempts to explicate the phenomenon of codeswitching among Korean-English bilinguals by means of the minimalist approach to syntactic variation among the world's languages. Central to the discussion will be the claim that the majority of the codeswitching patterns derive from the different properties of the items in the Korean and English lexicons and the way they interact with each other in the syntactic structure. I begin with a brief discussion of some general properties of the theory, and then move on to material more directly related to codeswitching.

A minimalist derivation begins with the selection of a set of lexical items (the numeration), and then the syntax constructs sentences in a bottom-up fashion, assembling the elements of the numeration into phrases by the Merge operation (Chomsky 2001, 2008). Items move out of their initial position in order to create local configurations with other categories in the structure, and these configurations are typically linked to aspects of inflectional morphology such as Case or verbal inflection. The relation between lexical and functional categories carries a good deal of the burden in the accounts of syntactic variation, and differing properties of the functional categories that populate an enriched view of phrase structure are responsible for whether various kinds of overt movement are observed or not. Among the functional categories are determiners, complementizers, and auxiliary verbs, as well as other categories that do not necessarily have word-sized manifestations, such as v, tense or agreement features. According to the theory sketched in Chomsky 2001, 2004,, functional categories bear features that need to be matched up with (checked against) counterpart features on other categories such as nouns, verbs, or their phrasal projections. Checking can be accomplished via the Probe-Goal relation, where Agree obtains between the relevant categories. In earlier versions of the theory (Chomsky 1995), checking environments could be created under two types of syntactic movement, when a head raises and adjoins to another head, or when a phrasal category moves to the specifier position of the projection headed by the relevant head. In the Probe-Goal system, however, movement is separated from checking, and it is accomplished via a separate feature (EPP[2]) on the Probe. The earlier distinction between strong and weak features, realized in terms of overt versus covert movement (where strong features are checked via overt (visible) movement, and weak features via covert movement), can be expressed via the presence or absence of an EPP feature. An EPP feature on a head requires that the corresponding specifier be filled, and movement is one way to accomplish this. Since EPP features (as well as the earlier strong and weak features) may constitute part of the lexical entries themselves, it follows that the overt syntax is a function of the properties of these lexical entries, and so, to put it into a slogan, parameters are in the lexicon, in particular in the features of the functional categories.

An analysis of the contrasts found among languages with respect to verb placement, for example, appeals to a distinction in features between the functional categories that enter into a checking relation with the verb. Such a contrast between French and English on the one hand or Danish and Icelandic on the other is illustrated below (examples (1a) and (2) are from Vikner 2001; see also Emonds 1978 and Pollock 1989), where the relative order of the verb and adverb is seen to vary (the verb is underlined and the adverb is italicized). Similar facts are also observed with negation.

(1) a. *French*

Je	crois	que	l'acteur	<u>voit</u>	*vraiment*	le	film.
I	think	that	the actor	sees	really	the	film

b. *English*

I think that the actor *really* <u>sees</u> the film.

(2) a. *Danish*

Jeg	tror	at	skuespilleren	*virkelig*	<u>ser</u>	filmen.
I	think	that	the actor	really	sees	the film.

b. *Icelandic*

Ég	tel	að	leikarinn	<u>sjái</u>	*áreiðanlega*	myndina.
I	think	that	the actor	saw	really	the film

Under the natural assumptions that (i) the main verb of each clause enters the derivation as the head of the VP, and (ii) the placement of negation and certain adverbials in phrase-structure is uniform across languages, the analytic task then becomes one of accounting for the differences that the different languages show with respect to verb placement (abstracting for now away from effects of Germanic verb-second). The differences in these examples can be accounted for by hypothesizing that adverbs and negation enter the derivation once the v/VP is constructed and that verbs in French and Icelandic move from their position internal to the vP to a position defined by a functional category outside the vP, while the verbs in English and Danish remain in place. Under the assumption that the relevant functional heads in English and Danish do not attract V+v while those of French and Icelandic do, V+v will raise overtly to adjoin to the functional head in the latter, but not the former.[3]

The structure in (3) illustrates the uniformity of syntactic structure I will be assuming throughout this chapter, and (4) summarizes the effects achieved by the parameterization of feature strength on T. The light verb structure (vP) is adopted, and the subject DP originates in the specifier position of that category, where it receives the θ-role appropriate to its status as the external argument[4] and is shown to have raised to Spec of TP. Adverbs are adjoined to vP, and V is shown as having raised to v.[5] Copies of moved items in strike-through typeface do not receive a phonetic interpretation.

(3)

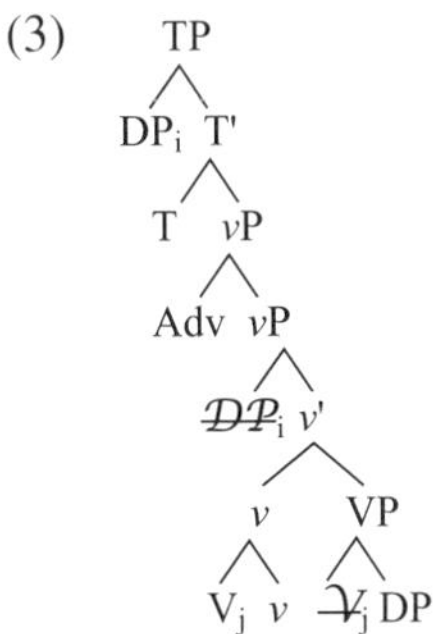

(4) a. T attracts V + v.

  b. T does not attract V + v.

This distinction generalizes to other cases of movement, and is thus in principle able to account for a wide class of word-order variation among different languages. If a head implicated in valuing a Case has an EPP feature, the DP bearing the correspond Case feature will raise to the Spec position projected by that head. If there is no EPP feature on the head, the DP remains in situ. In Finer 1997, for example, it is suggested that the VOS order of Selayarese, an Austronesian language, results from features attracting V and the direct object out of vP. The subject remains inside vP; the head that values its Case feature does not attract DP. The word` order of English, in contrast, can be accounted for by hypothesizing opposite values, which induce raising of the subject DP while the direct object and the V+v remain internal to vP.[6]

(5)   a. [$_T$ la-jañjang-i [$_{v\text{P}}$ tedoŋ-ñjo [$_{v\text{P}}$ i Baso? [$_{v'}$ ~~V~~ [$_{VP}$ ~~V~~ ~~DP~~]]]

      3ERG-see-3ABS   buffalo-DEF   CL

      'Baso saw the buffalo.'

   b. [$_{TP}$ John   T [$_{Pv}$ ~~DP~~ [$_{v'}$ saw [$_{VP}$ ~~V~~ the cow]]]]

2.1   The Hypothesis

With this brief introduction to the feature-checking mechanism as a partial account of the syntactic variation among languages, imagine two languages, L_A and L_B, that differ with respect to the feature composition of one or another functional category.[7] Now imagine that both languages are controlled by the same speaker. Part of the speaker's dual competence, under this view, consists in maintaining separate lexicons that differ in the categories that may be specified for EPP, among many other things. Now imagine a syntactic system that draws from both lexicons when a sentence is constructed. According to what was sketched above, under the plausible assumption that the set of features that are relevant to movement are drawn from a universal set, we expect that, in principle, a functional category from the lexicon of L_A with an EPP feature on a given head should be able to attract a phrase, regardless of whether that phrase comes from L_A or L_B. On the other hand, if the head carries no EPP feature (or, following earlier terminology, if the feature is weak), there will be no such attraction, and no movement. We would also expect an arbitrary lexical element from L_A to select its complements according to syntactic category (determined in part perhaps by the particular θ-role borne by the complement), but not necessarily according whether the complement also comes from L_A. This, I suggest, is a reasonable first hypothesis with which to approach the phenomenon of codeswitching; if nothing extra beyond the separate grammars needs to be specified, bilingual codeswitching emerges as a natural consequence of the syntactic system interacting with a set of categories whose elements are drawn from two lexicons.[8] This is the central thesis of much recent work in the field (see especially MacSwan 1999, 2010, Mahootian 1993, van Gelderen and MacSwan 2008, among others). According to this logic, there need be no higher-order grammar of codeswitching that controls the elements in, or the structure of, the switch.

I consider in this chapter a small corpus of Korean/English codeswitched sentences (drawn from Lee 1991) from this perspective. I conclude that the account of these sentences adds little beyond a specification of the separate grammars. If a particular category enters the derivation from the lexicon of one language, it brings along its specifications for EPP and/or selection, and it and the other elements in the structure react accordingly. The syntax of codeswitching according to this view, then, is simply no more than syntax.

2.2   The Generalizations

Four major syntactic generalizations emerge in the examples from Lee's (1991) study. They are given in (6)–(9).

(6) a. If the main verb of the sentence is Korean, the complements will occur preverbally.
     b. If the main verb of the sentence is English, the complements will occur postverbally.

(7) a. If the main verb of the sentence is Korean, the complements will bear Korean Case particles.
     b. If the main verb of the sentence is English, the complements will not bear Case particles.

(8) a. English *wh*-phrases are displaced from their argument positions.
     b. Korean *wh*-phrases occur in situ.

(9) a. Korean long-distance reflexives can have long-distance antecedents.
     b. English reflexives do not have long-distance antecedents.

These patterns, from one point of view, should not be surprising, since within the separate grammars of Korean and English, this is precisely what is found (e.g., there are no case particles on English DPs, English *wh*-phrases move, Korean is SOV, etc.).

What is interesting from the codeswitched perspective, however, is that if the main verb is Korean, the complements appear preverbally, whether or not they themselves are Korean, and the Case particles occur on complements of the Korean verb, regardless of the language from which the complement comes. That is, in both switched sentences and monolingual sentences, English DPs and Korean DPs bear Korean Case particles if they are complements of Korean verbs. Similarly, a Korean complement of an English verb in a switched sentence is postverbal and does not carry the Korean Case marker.

Lee adopts the Government and Binding (cf. Chomsky 1981) framework in her discussion, and she argues that the morphosyntax of the VP of the switched sentence is largely determined by the head of the VP. According to her analysis, the verb assigns Case and thematic roles in a certain direction with a particular morphosyntactic effect in both Korean sentences and switched sentences with a Korean verb. A switched sentence containing an English verb, on the other hand, has a VP that depends on an alternate set of specifications for the head. The direction of assignment of Case and thematic roles differs, as does the morphosyntax of the VP. According to Lee, in both the separate languages and the switched language, the head of the phrase controls the Case marking and position of its complements. The behavior of the *wh*-phrases found in sentences from the separate languages is mirrored in switched sentences. An English *wh*-phrase moves across Korean material, while a Korean *wh*-phrase remains in situ, even though it can be found in a [+wh] clause selected by an English verb. This suggests once more that lexical parameterization is at work. The separate lexical items and phrases enter the derivation, and the interaction of their particular properties determines the outcome. There is no particular parameter defined globally over the switched grammatical system. If there were, we would expect the *wh*-phrase to either move or remain in situ in the switched language, perhaps according to a general markedness calculation. The fact that each *wh*-phrase behaves as if it were in a sentence in its own language indicates that there is no general always-move/don't-move/move-optionally parameter defined across the switched syntactic system.

Pursuing this a bit further, we can conclude that it is due to the lexical parameterization hypothesis that only the English *wh*-phrases, not the Korean *wh*-phrases, move in the switched system. The elements that interact to produce movement are specific values for specific features that are properties of lexical items. In more current terms, to say that English has overt *wh*-movement is simply to say that the lexicon of English contains categories with such and such features that induce overt movement.

A similar conclusion can be drawn from the behavior of the reflexive pronouns. There is no language-wide parameter that sets a large or small binding domain, but rather the domain is set according to the particular anaphoric lexical item (a point made in Wexler and Manzini 1987 and Manzini and Wexler 1987). Under this picture, the Korean-English switched system is not that different from Chinese, Japanese, or Korean itself, languages that also contain reflexives that have different binding domains.

The goal of the current discussion is to see if a coherent view of the data can emerge from a syntactic framework guided by minimalist assumptions. The major hypothesis to begin with is that the functional categories in the separate lexicons maintain their EPP settings, and that this is responsible for the major effects seen in the switched sentences. Once an Agree relation is established between the Probe and the Goal, an EPP feature associated with a Probe from either language should attract a Goal from either language. Putting aside the two qualifiers "from either language" in the previous sentence, we are left with nothing more than basic tenets of the theory: that feature checking involves the Probe-Goal relation between categories, and movement involves the EPP feature. This is the larger claim that I believe the data to be discussed point toward: there is nothing special about codeswitched systems that goes beyond ordinary monolingual syntax. If we follow the idea that variation is localized in the lexicon, once we draw the elements of the numeration from more than one lexicon, the switched syntax should proceed as if nothing special is taking place.

2.3 Some Syntax

To begin the discussion, I will need to make certain assumptions about the syntax of English and Korean, as well as about the general theory of syntax. To start, I will assume that the basic structure of the category containing the arguments of a transitive verb is as shown below (vP). Following general minimalist tendencies, I assume that the direct object is selected as a sister of the verb, and the subject of the clause is introduced as the specifier of the "light" verb v, which takes VP as its complement. In addition, I will assume the general outlines of Kayne's (1994) antisymmetry framework, which yields the right-branching structure shown in (10) (SB = subject, OB = object), but I will allow multiple specifiers, in the sense of Chomsky 1995 and later work.

(10)

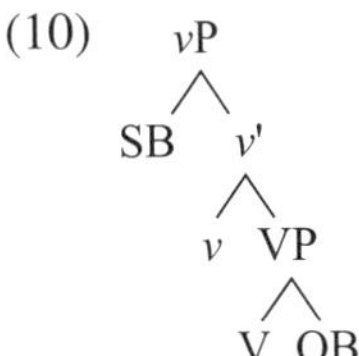

As mentioned, a DP in a Probe-Goal relation with an EPP-marked functional head will move to the specifier of that head. In the above structure, v values the Case feature of OB, and if EPP is present on v, it will induce overt raising. In the absence of EPP, OB remains in place. Once T is introduced into the structure as a sister of vP, its features will either attract the V complex or not, Further, the nature of T will determine whether the subject DP raises overtly. If T bears an EPP feature, DP raises. This is restated below, where the two checking environments that overt movement creates are shown.

(11) a. *Head adjunction*

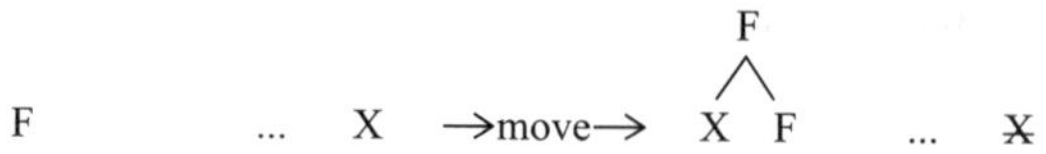

$$\text{F} \qquad \dots \quad \text{X} \quad \rightarrow\text{move}\rightarrow \quad \text{[X F]}_{\text{F}} \quad \dots \quad \text{X}$$

b. *Movement to Spec*

$$[\text{F}_{[\text{EPP]}} \dots \text{XP}]_{\text{FP}} \rightarrow\text{move}\rightarrow [\text{XP} [\text{F}_{[\text{EPP]}} \dots]_{\text{F'}}]_{\text{FP}} \dots \text{XP}$$

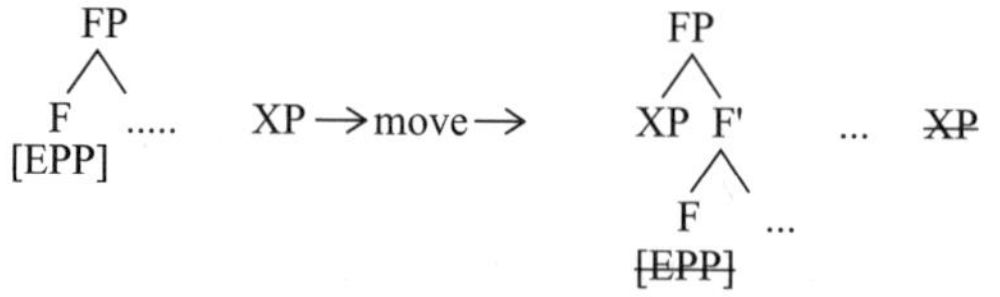

This characterization of movement relies on the notion "attract"; the EPP feature on the F-head attracts the counterpart X-feature on the selected category, and the category moves to the specifier.[9]

2.3.1 Some Korean Syntax: Word Order

The first property of Korean that I discuss is word order. Korean is an SOV language; the object occurs before the verb, and one can entertain at least two hypotheses concerning the derivation of this order. One is that SOV order is derived from an SVO *v*P of the sort shown above, and the other is that SOV word order is generated directly. For the purposes of the present discussion, either approach is possible, but for simplicity of discussion and uniformity, I will assume that the derivation initially constructs an SVO *v*P. The SVO structure is argued by Kayne (1994) to be a feature of all languages, and if this is so, then this simplifies the question of what the *v*P looks like in codeswitched systems.

The following examples (taken from Hagstrom 1996) suggest, given the earlier assumptions about *v*P and the placement of negation, that objects raise overtly (MacSwan 1999 also suggests that Korean objects raise from an SVO *v*P but does not discuss the occurrence of Case particles in codeswitched sentences).

(12) John-i   ppang-ul   an-mek-ess-ta.
     John-NOM   bread-ACC   NEG-eat-PAST-DECL
     'John did not eat the bread.'

Given our assumption that Negation enters the derivation after the basic *v*P has been assembled, the derivation of the above example involves movement of both the subject and object out of *v*P.[10]

Another piece of data that can be used to reinforce the idea that objects raise overtly is shown below (adapted from Lee 1991) where an adverb intervenes between the direct object and the verb.

(13) Na-nun   ceonyek-ul   pali   meokeotta.
     I-SM   dinner-OM   quickly   ate
     'I ate dinner quickly.'

This word order is also consistent with an analysis in which the object raises out of vP across a vP-adjoined adverbial.

Cho (2000) argues that the double Case marking found in certain possession constructions in Korean is also a function of object raising, followed by further extraction and adjunction of the possessor (see Cho 1998, 2000, for details). The data below show the effects of the interactions of this movement with the Merge operation that adjoins the adverbial to vP.

(14) a. Mary-ka   John-ul   tali-lul   seykey   cha-ess-ta.
       Mary-SM   John-OM   leg-OM   hard   kick-PST-DECL
       'Mary kicked John's leg hard.'
     b. Mary-ka John-ul seykey tali-lul cha-ess-ta.
     c. Mary-ka seykey John-lul tali-lul cha-ess-ta.

Both (13) and (14a) suggest that the object raises across an adverbial that was merged with vP prior to object raising. (14b), on the other hand, can be derived by first raising the object, then merging the adverb with vP, and then raising out the possessor. (14c) shows the effects of object raising followed by possessor extraction, followed by the merger of Adv and vP.

If the object raises, we also must assume that, given the SOV order, the subject raises as well. Here, Korean and English are similar. I will assume that the subject raises due to an EPP feature on T in each languages.

The word-order difference between English and Korean is illustrated in (15) (the Korean analysis will be modified slightly below). The object raises in Korean, and adverbials adjoin to vP in either language, but Korean, because of the availability of object raising, offers two such adjunction sites as the derivation progresses.[11]

(15) a. *Korean*   b. *English*

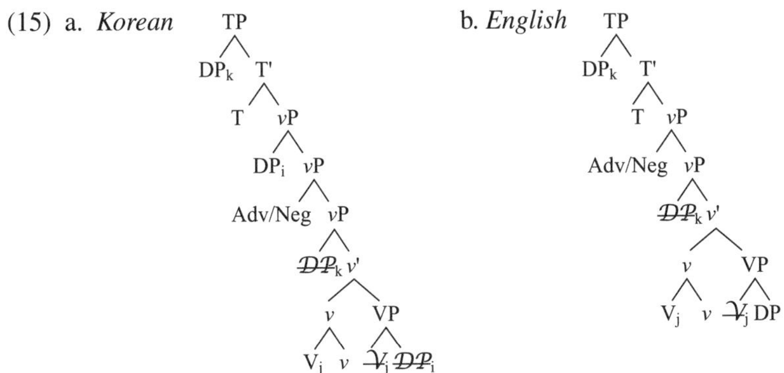

We have so far said little about the trigger for object raising;[12] I will assume that the operation is involved at least with checking accusative Case, and there may be other factors as well. An Agree relation is established between v and the direct object, and an EPP feature of v attracts the DP to the outer specifier position of vP. In English, however, v does not bear an EPP feature, so the object remains within VP once Agree values its Case feature.

2.3.2 Overt Case Particles

Overt Case marking is another feature that distinguishes the two languages. DPs that are arguments of the Korean verb, for example, bear distinctive particles. It does not seem to be the case, however, that the particles can uniformly be mapped onto Case markers. Whitman (1999) argues that the particles that have been associated with Japanese and Korean nominative Case are actually inflectional clausal heads that cliticize to the subject in the phonological component. In the syntax, they are functional heads, as sketched in (16), where SM is the particle in question (see also Saito 1985 for arguments against the claim that the Japanese subject marker is a structurally assigned nominative Case).

(16)   TP
        /\
   SUBJ T'
        /\
    T vP
   SM △

The marker on direct objects, however, does appear to be a reflex of structural Case—for example, its distribution in passive and active sentences parallels what one would expect were it a marker of structural case (Saito 1985 makes the parallel argument for the Japanese -o). There are thus alternations in Korean in single-clause passive as well as in Exceptional Case Marking/ Raising-to-Object contexts such as the following (Cho 2000 and personal communication):

(17) a. Mary-ka   maykcwu-lul masi-ess-ta.
       Mary-SM   beer-OM drink-PST-DECL
       'Mary drank beer.'
    b. Maykcwu-ka   masie-ci-ess-ta.
       beer -SM   drink-PSV-PST-DECL
       'Beer was drunk.'

(18) a. John-i　　　Mary-ka　　　chencay-lako　　　mit-ess-ta.
　　　　John-SM　　Mary-SM　　genius-COMP　　believe-PST-DECL
　　　　'John believed that Mary was a genius.'
　　b. John-i　　　Mary-ka　　　yeppu-tako　　　sayngakha-n-ta.
　　　　John-SM　　Mary-SM　　pretty-COMP　　think-PRES-DECL
　　　　'John thinks that Mary is pretty.'

(19) a. John-i　　　Mary-lul　　　chencay-lako　　　mit-ess-ta.
　　　　John-SM　　Mary-OM　　genius-COMP　　believe-PAST-DECL
　　　　'John believed Mary to be a genius.'
　　b. John-i　　　Mary-lul　　　yeppu-tako　　　sayngakha-n-ta.
　　　　John-SM　　Mary-OM　　pretty-COMP　　think-PRES-DECL
　　　　'John thinks that Mary is pretty.'

The analysis that I will suggest for the Case particles rests on a particular set of assumptions concerning the existence of the category KP (similar to the KP of Bittner and Hale 1996, though distinct from the KP of Cho 1998, 2000). I will assume that in general, the existence of KP in a grammar correlates with the overt manifestation of Case as a phrasal particle rather than, for example, as an affix on a head. Languages in which Case morphology is realized on the head of the NP or DP, for instance, would not necessarily have KP, these alternations in Case morphology being a matter of inflectional morphology.

A verb in a language with Case particles, then, will be assumed to select KP rather than DP, and the occurrence of particular exemplars of K will correlate with the particular categories that check structural or inherent Case, in much the same way that DPs with particular morphology are checked against functional heads. For present purposes, I will assume that the Korean object marker particle enters the derivation as the head of KP. The DP within KP raises to the specifier of KP, V raises to v, and then KP raises to the outer Spec of v.

The situation with respect to the subject is somewhat more complicated, but I will follow Bittner and Hale and assume that the argument bearing nominative Case is a DP. It is in an Agree relation with T, and it raises overtly to Spec TP, and following Whitman 1999, I assume that T is realized as the SM clitic. The final result then resembles a structure such as the following, where SM symbolizes the nominative/finite clitic in T and OM represents the object marker. As above, the struckthrough copies of moved items are phonologically null.

(20)

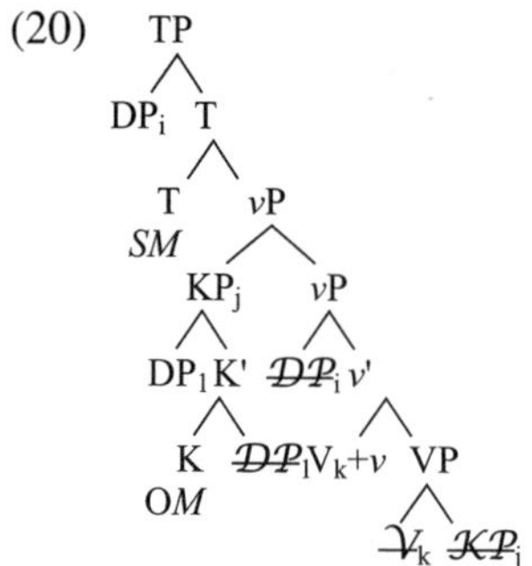

In summary, the analysis is the following: Korean accusative DPs are encased in KPs; v bears an EPP feature, and it values Case on KP. V raises to v, and KP raises to the outer Spec of vP. The DP subject raises to Spec TP, attracted by EPP. The V need raise no higher than v in the overt syntax.

Let us now turn to English. The analysis of the English counterparts of the above Korean sentences proceeds similarly, except that V selects DP throughout rather than KP, and v does not bear an EPP feature. This latter specification ensures that DP remains within VP. T, as in Korean, has an EPP feature that attracts the subject, although T is not overtly realized in the same way as in Korean (but see Pesetsky and Torrego 2001 for discussion of the relation between nominative Case and T). Item (15b) above illustrates English structure.

2.4   The Switched System

2.4.1   Word Order and Case

In a minimalist derivation, the elements that occur in the sentence are first drawn from the lexicon to form the numeration, and then the elements of the numeration are assembled into a sentential structure. At a certain stage in the derivation, the structure is "spelled out." A Spell-Out sequence containing unvalued or uninterpretable features is ruled out at Spell-Out. In the best case, therefore, all features will be valued or deleted prior to Spell-Out, and since the EPP features trigger syntactic movement, this means that all the syntactic movement should have taken place.

The codeswitched sentences in (21) (from Lee 1991) would have the numerations shown in (22) (for ease of exposition I omit functional categories here).[13]

(21) a. Na-nun   *dinner*-lul   pali   meokeotta.
         I-SM   dinner-OM   quickly   ate
         'I ate dinner quickly.'
     b. I   ate   *ceonyek*   *pali*.
         I   ate   dinner   quickly
         'I ate dinner quickly.'

(22) a. N = {na, nun, dinner, lul, pali, meokeotta}
     b. N = {I, ate, ceonyek, pali}

Note that a convergent derivation of (21b) will contain a step in which the Case feature of the Korean direct object *ceonyek* is valued by the English v. This indicates that the Korean DP must be endowed with unvalued accusative features. The overt realization of accusative in the two languages certainly differs; one is essentially null and the other involves the Case particle (K). For the moment, I will assume that the accusative features valued by v in each instance are identical, but that the Spell-Out form that v induces is where the difference lies. The v's in the separate languages thus differ according to EPP and Spell-Out consequences, but I will assume that the uninterpretable features checked in each case are identical. An English v, then, can check accusative Case borne by a Korean DP, as in (21b).[14]

The numeration in (22a) contains a Korean verb, and so it will select a KP. Further, a factor that partially determines the word order of the switched sentence is controlled by the EPP feature borne by the Korean v. Once it enters the derivation, the complement of V will ultimately raise to vP, the EPP feature will be checked against KP, and the occurrence of a particular Case particle (K) is legitimized by v. The derivation of sentence (21a) thus contains the following crucial steps:

(23) a. Merge {[$_{DP}$ dinner], [$_K$ lul]} =
     a'. DP raises to Spec, KP

     b. Merge {KP, [$_v$meokeotta]} =

     c. Merge {v, VP}, adjoin V to v, =
        Merge {vP, [$_{DP}$ na]}

     d. Adjoin KP$_j$ to vP =

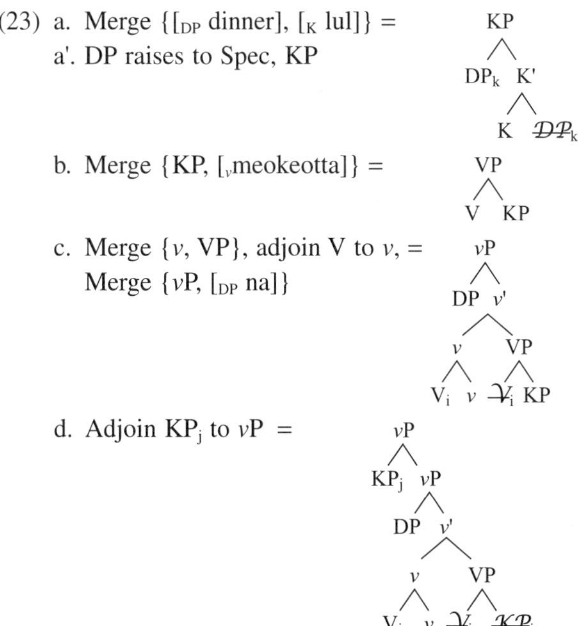

The structure in (23d) is merged with [$_T$ nun], and then the subject [$_{DP}$ na] raises to Spec, TP.

Since there is no EPP feature on the English *v*, DP will not raise in (21b). The English V selects DP rather than KP, and so no Case particle will occur (the adverb is omitted from the representation). A schematic representation is shown in (24).

(24)

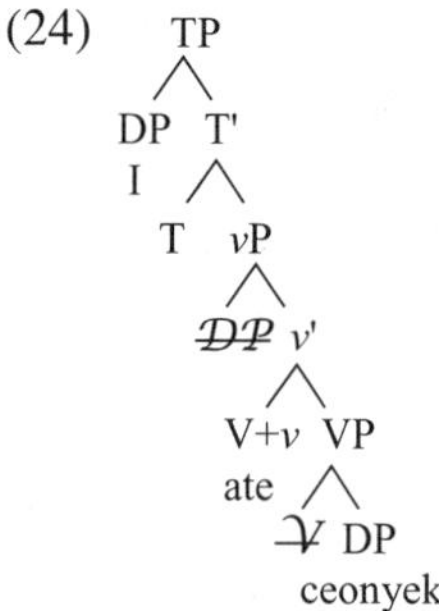

The fact that the accusative particle occurs only with Korean verbs in Lee's corpus is accounted for straightforwardly by selection in the above analysis, but the distribution of the nominative particle needs further clarification. If it is indeed a clausal head, as argued by Whitman, then it is a manifestation of Korean T, and it presumably attracts DPs, as suggested by Bittner and Hale. A DP with a Korean subject marker, however, is incompatible with an English verb in a switched sentence, and so more needs to be said. I suggest that this fact follows from an analysis in which English V+*v*s and the subject DP are probed by T. Korean shows no subject-verb agreement; this suggests that Korean T does not have agreement features. Therefore, if Korean T is the head of TP, it will be unable to value the agreement features of V+*v*, and so the features remain unvalued, causing the derivation to crash. Korean and English are thus distinguished in part by the nature of T; English T bears agreement features, Korean T does not. From the standpoint of Universal Grammar, a system in which there is no distinction between the functional categories from different languages might be preferable on one level of analysis. However, if the variation in the grammars of different languages resides in the functional categories to a large degree, there would be little linguistic variation to account for if functional categories behaved identically across languages.

Other examples showing the above effects are given in (25) (from Lee 1991). Lee emphasizes in her discussion that, among Korean-English bilinguals, the verb *put* counts as either English or Korean. A mother is speaking to her daughters, Hana and Meena. Hana understands both English and Korean, while Meena's dominant language is still Korean.

(25) a. Hana, put   *cangnakam* in the basket quickly and go home.
              toys
     'Hana, put the toys in the basket quickly and go home.'
  b. Meena, *basket*-aneta *all the toys*-lul   pali   put-ha-ko cipe kaca.
                  in   OM   quickly put-do-and home go
     'Meena, put all the toys in the basket quickly, and go home.'

Other naturally occurring examples are given in (26), and here, in addition to the Case markers and postpositions that we see in construction with English DPs in (26a), we also see a Korean direct object having raised across an English adverb in (26b).

(26) a. Cinanpeone *motor vehicle department*-eseo   nae *driver's*
        license-lul *mistake*-lo   kaengsinhaecuci   anhaetseoyo.
        last-time   -in   my
             OM   -by   renew   did-not
     'Last time, by mistake, they did not renew my driver's license at the DMV.'
  b. Kutul-i   il-ul   *often*   kuleoke   haeyo
     they-SM thing-OM   like-that   do
     'They often do a thing like that.'

2.4.2 Remarks on Heads and V + *v*

In Lee's corpus, it is the head of the category that determines the grammar of the phrase. Thus, a Korean verb takes a preverbal direct object with a Case particle, and an English verb takes a postverbal direct object without a Case particle. It is logically possible, of course, that the nature of the phrase could be determined by the complement instead of the head. The generalizations here instead would be: a Korean direct object requires a Case particle, and a Korean direct object must precede the verb. It is therefore a question of some interest as to why a sentence such as (27) is ill formed according to Lee's informants.

(27) *I   ceonyek(-lul)   ate.
      I   dinner(-OM)   ate
     'I ate dinner.'

The reason the head appears to control the overall word order follows, I believe, from the nature of the feature-checking mechanism. That is, consider a grammar in which feature checking was instead implemented via the a feature on the Goal. Under this Greed-based approach, we could analyze SOV word order as arising through a particular feature of the head of KP rather than the EPP feature on the attracting head. The rationale behind object raising in this case would be that this feature of the direct object requires overt checking against the relevant head. Given this organization of the grammar, one would fully expect that a Korean direct object would raise, regardless of the language from which the *v* comes. Under the EPP/attract theory adopted here, however, it is the features on the probing head that trigger the movement, not the features of the moving item themselves; we thus do not expect that an English *v* will attract a Korean KP or DP.

A word or two needs to be said about the relation between V and *v*, however. While V in the above discussion has determined the form of the direct object in each language (DP vs. KP), *v* has been responsible for the placement of the direct object (preverbal or postverbal). The most straightforward analysis of the above examples in the present framework would be to claim that both *v* and V are drawn from the same lexicon. But while it is certainly reasonable to expect that *v* and V should come from the same lexicon in codeswitching contexts, it is hard to see why this should be necessary.

In fact it appears as though it is not necessary. The following examples are from Choi 1991 (brought to my attention by Brian Chan). Given the current assumptions, they suggest that an English *v* and a Korean V can co-occur. Further, it appears as though the Korean V need not always select KP; a DP is sufficient.

(28) a. *Appa* was about to   *pēlyē*   my *ippal*.
         Daddy   throw away   tooth
         'Dad was about to throw away my tooth (that was pulled out).'
     b. I have to   *ttakē* my hand.
                           wash
         'I have to wash my hand.'

Since there is no KP in these examples, and since the direct object is postverbal, these examples can be analyzed as involving an English *v* that checks Case on the DP object without movement. Given that the English *v* does not have an EPP feature, the DP does not raise, and SVO word order results. Further, the ability of the Korean verb to select either a KP or DP, it turns out, is not restricted to codeswitching environments. Direct objects need not be marked with the OM, especially in colloquial Korean.

The example in (27) now becomes problematic. If we consider Lee's and Choi's data as a combined corpus, an asymmetry is apparent. While an English *v* and a Korean V are compatible, a Korean *v* and an English V are not.[15] Although I cannot give a satisfactory account of the asymmetry at this point, I will suggest that perhaps it follows from a difference in status between *v* in

English and *v* in Korean. In particular, the Korean *v* is undoubtedly implicated in light verb constructions in that language, and this points toward a more complex feature composition for it than would be plausible for its English counterpart.[16] In brief, V-to-*v* raising results in feature checking, and if English *v* carries a subset of the uninterpretable features carried by the Korean *v*, then an English verb adjoining to a Korean *v* should result in fewer features of *v* being checked than if a Korean verb adjoins to a Korean *v*, and this result should create a crash. Conversely, if the English *v* has only a subset of the features of the Korean *v*, then they should be able to be checked by either an English or Korean V under adjunction.[17]

2.4.3 Reflexive Binding

Lee (1991) conducted a questionnaire-based study involving twenty-one Long Island Korean-English bilinguals in order to determine the binding properties of reflexives in codeswitched sentences. In the monolingual grammars, the English reflexive requires a local antecedent, while the Korean reflexive *caki* shows a preference for a long-distance antecedent. Her results for switched sentences show that the Korean reflexive is able to take a long-distance antecedent, and that the antecedent for the reflexive can come from either language. Further, the material intervening between the antecedent and the reflexive can come from either language. English *self*-anaphors, on the other hand, take a local antecedent regardless of syntactic context.

There were four example types that Lee investigated, illustrated in (29).

(29) a. Tom-i   sengkakhakilul *Bill likes himself.*   (type A)
          Tom-SM   thinks
          'Tom thinks Bill likes himself.'

   b. Tom thinks that   *Bill-i*   *caki-lul*   *cohahanta.*   (type B)
          Bill-SM   self-OM   likes
          'Tom thinks that Bill likes himself.'

   c. Tom-un Bill-i *himself*-lul   cohahantako sengkakhanta. (type C)
          Tom-un Bill-SM   -OM   likes   thinks
          'Tom thinks that Bill likes himself.'

   d. Tom believes that Bill likes *caki.*   (type D)
                                                          self
          'Tom believes that Bill likes himself.'

For all types, 187 out of 210 responses to sentences with the English reflexive chose the local antecedent, regardless of which language was used in the rest of the sentences. Out of 210 responses to sentences with the Korean reflexive, 167 chose the nonlocal antecedent, again regardless of which language was used in the rest of the sentence. The breakdown by types is as follows:

(30) a. Type A: 90% local
      b. Type B: 88% nonlocal
      c. Type C: 88% local
      d. Type D: 71% nonlocal

There is clearly a pattern here; the choice of antecedent for the reflexive depends not on the language of the rest of the sentence, but on the reflexive itself. If it is English, a local antecedent is preferred, and if it is Korean, a nonlocal antecedent is preferred. This is strong support for the hypothesis that parameters are associated with lexical items.[18]

Nearly any recent theory of binding is applicable here, as long the local/ nonlocal distinction can be expressed as a property of the anaphor itself. There may be further correlations with the nature of the projection of the anaphor (XP vs. X^0) (as in, e.g., Pica 1987; Cole, Hermon, and Sung 1990; Cole and Sung 1994) or variation in the size of the binding domain, but in order to account for Lee's data under any of these analyses, we simply need to assume that the reflexives retain their native properties in the switched language, and the facts then follow directly.

2.4.4 *Wh*-Movement

The discussion so far has argued that the proper characterization of Korean-English codeswitching involves nothing beyond the syntax of the separate languages, except for access to both lexicons. The numeration drawn from the lexicons can thus contain items from either language, and they enter the derivation carrying their own features. Further, the Probe-Goal mechanism insures that the properties of the Probe, not the Goal, will determine the nature of the system to a large degree. The set of data that involves *wh*-constructions in the switched language is not large, but it is very suggestive, and it follows the trend that we have seen whereby the behavior of the *wh*-phrase in the switched language acts as it would in its own language.

Korean *wh*-constructions do not show overt movement of phonetically interpreted material, although there are alternations in clause-final particles that can indicate the scope of the operator. In the examples below, *nunci* and *ni* are such particles, whereas *tako* and *ta* convey declarative force.

(31) a. John-i   eoce   muet-ul   sat-ni.
          John-SM   yesterday   what-OM   buy-Q
          'What did John buy yesterday?'

    b. John-un [Mary-ka   muet-ul   sat   nunci]   kungkumhaehata.
       John-SM [Mary-SM what-OM buy   Q]   wonder-DECL
       'John wonders what Mary bought yesterday.'

    c. John-un   [nuku-ga   chek-ul   sat   tako]   mit-ni.
       John-SM   [who-SM   book-OM   buy   DECL]   believe-Q
       'Who does John believe bought books?'

The Korean verbs corresponding to *wonder* and *believe* are similar to their English counterparts in their selectional properties. *Kungkumhae* 'wonder' takes a [+WH] clause, while *mit* 'believe' takes a [-WH] clause. Observe now the following codeswitched sentences containing *wh*-phrases (Lee 1991):

(32) a. I wonder [*John-i*   *eoce*   *muet-ul*   *sat*   *nunci*].
            John-SM   yesterday   what-OM   buy   Q
       'I wonder what John bought yesterday.'

    b. *Na-nun*   *kungkumhae* [what he bought yesterday].
       I-SM   wonder
       'I wonder what he bought yesterday.'

    c. *Na-nun   kungkumhae *he bought what yesterday*.
       I-SM   wonder
       'I wonder what he bought yesterday.'

Putting aside the question of the placement of the complement CP in (32b–c), we see that the Korean *wh* remains in situ while the English *wh*-phrase moves; note the ungrammaticality of (32c). Also, the [+WH] properties of the subordinate CPs of either language can be accessed by the selecting verbs of either language. Lee notes that sentences such as (32b) are quite common, even among children.

(33) Eomma,   aleo   *what Daddy bought for me*?
     mommy,   know
     'Mommy, do you know what Daddy bought for me?'

The following contrasts are observed in other cases of switching:

(34) a. I wonder he bought   *muet* yesterday.
                       what
     'I wonder what he bought yesterday.'

    b. *I wonder *muet* he bought yesterday.

The Korean *wh*-phrase remains resolutely in place, not moving to the Spec CP position, and apparently not able to scramble to a sentence-initial position in the English context either.

When an English *wh*-phrase is surrounded by Korean lexical material, movement, whether scrambling or *wh*-movement, is possible.[19]

(35) Na-nun mucheok kungkumhae[*who*-lul ku-ka   eoce   mannat nunci].
     I-SM   very much wonder   -OM he-SM yesterday met   Q
     'I very much wonder who he met yesterday.'

If *wh*-movement is triggered by the attract relation via the presence of an EPP feature on C, the contrast shown in (32–35) is somewhat surprising, since it appears as if it is the *wh* phrase itself (the Goal) that is determining whether movement takes place or not.

However plausible a Greed-based theory of movement initially looks in this case (an English *wh*–phrase moves to check features while a Korean *wh*-phrase has features that can be checked in situ), I will suggest that it is in fact possible to reconcile the *wh* constructions with the Probe-Goal approach.

The tack I will take here is to deny that there is no movement in these examples, and argue, following Watanabe's (1992) analysis of Japanese *wh*-constructions, that there is movement of an empty operator in the overt syntax. At this point, I do not know whether Watanabe's arguments will fully extend to Korean-English codemixing,[20] but the empty operator analysis is most compatible with both the facts and the assumptions under which we have been working. The zero-operator analysis would make available the representations given below, where the [+WH] C has an EPP feature in both cases. The representation of the codeswitched example in (34a) would be as shown in (36c).

(36) a. John-un [Op$_i$ C [Mary-ka [e$_i$ [muet-ul]] sat nunci]] kungkumhaehata.
        John-SM   [Mary-SM   what-OM buyQ]   wonder-DECL
        'John wonders what Mary bought yesterday.'
     b. I wonder [what$_i$ C [he bought e$_i$ yesterday]]
     c. I wonder [Op$_i$ C [he bought [e$_i$ [*muet*]] yesterday]]

This approach distinguishes the two languages not by the feature content of C (it bears an EPP feature in both cases), but by the nature of the moving items. One is phonologically interpreted, the other phonologically null. In each case, though, the EPP feature on C attracts a *wh*-element to Spec CP, and depending on the language-particular properties of *wh*-phrases, full pied-piping takes place or not.

2.5 Conclusion

I have attempted in this chapter to provide a minimalist-style analysis of a set of codeswitched Korean-English sentences, and the theme of the discussion has been that there is nothing special about the codeswitched sentences beyond the independently necessary separate grammars, as argued at length by other researchers for different corpora. The properties of the sentences simply follow from the nature of the lexical and functional items that were drawn into the numerations from the separate lexicons. It is, of course, an open question whether the hypothesis can be supported for Korean beyond the fragment discussed here, and if so, whether it generalizes to other cases of codeswitching. It should be recognized, however, that data from switched languages bear on issues of linguistic theory and Universal Grammar just as do data from traditional sources, and evidence from the behavior of the bilingual is relevant to theorizing about the shape of the monolingual grammar. Certain kinds of evidence and argumentation (cf. the discussion of Greed vs. Attract) may only be available in a codeswitched system; when grammars collide, perhaps they break apart at the joints.

Notes

I am deeply indebted to Mee-Hwa Lee and her 1991 Stony Brook dissertation, which provided the data and inspiration for this contribution. Thanks also to Christine Sungeun Cho, Yoonjung Kang, Pieter Muysken, and John Whitman for helpful discussion, and thanks to Jeff MacSwan for rekindling my interest in codeswitching (originally sparked by Sridhar and Sridhar 1980 and Woolford 1983). I am grateful to Brian Chan, Anna Maria Di Sciullo, and Jeff MacSwan for comments on an earlier draft. Some of this material was presented at the third International Symposium on Bilingualism University of the West of England, Bristol and I am grateful to my fellow participants for comments and discussion.

1. See Borer 1984, Lebeaux 1988, Wexler and Manzini 1987, Borer and Wexler 1987, as well as Manzini and Wexler 1987 for earlier statements of lexical parameterization. Other proposals in the direction of lexical parameterization from Koopman 1984 and Travis 1984 concern possible directionality in Case and θ-role assignments.

2. The EPP feature derives from Chomsky's (1981) Extended Projection Principle, which ensures that the subject position of a clause is occupied. It has generalized to apply to specifier positions in general.

3. This discussion assumes that head movement is available in the overt syntax, an assumption that has been challenged for various reasons. See Roberts 2011 for discussion. In subsequent discussion of head movement, I will use the fairly neutral term "attract" to do the work done by strong features in earlier versions of the theory. See Alexiadou and Agnastopoulou 1998 for a proposal that head movement can be driven by an EPP feature.

4. I assume that θ-role assignment for the subject as well as Case checking for a raised complement take place via a conspiracy between V and v. The particular choice of θ-role and the particular choice of Case are determined largely by the V, while the assignment/checking relation is activated by v.

5. Cinque (1999) proposes that adverbs are introduced as specifiers of separate functional categories; adoption of this proposal would require another step in the movement of V from v to T in languages exemplifying (4b).

6. The original 1997 analysis employed the strong/weak distinction as well as Agr projections. The discussion in the text has been recast. Abbreviations in the morpheme-by-morpheme glosses are as follows: ERG = ergative, ABS = absolutive, DEF = definite, CL = noun classifier, SM = subject marker, OM = object marker, PST = past, PSV = passive, DECL = declarative.

7. The inventory of functional heads includes at least C, T, D, and v. In Chomsky 1995, strength of the uninterpretable features associated with the functional heads varies according to parameterization, and in later work, it is the EPP feature that drives movement, a view that will be adopted here.

8. See also Finer 1990 and Lee 1991 for sketches of an association between codeswitching and lexical parameterization.

9. Another way of understanding movement is by reversing the relation; the moving item moves because of the nature of its own features. In strong/weak terminology, if one of its features is strong, the category moves to a place where the feature can be checked. This is characterized as "Greed" (Chomsky 1995). See below for further discussion of Attract versus Greed.

10. Hagstrom adopts a variant of the "split VP" hypothesis, wherein the object remains within vP, having moved across a vP-internal negation. The following example exemplifies the "short form" of Korean negation, in which the object precedes negation. There is another construction, the "long form," in which both the object and verb precede negation; Hagstrom suggests that the V + NP constituent raises in this case.

11. The availability of the second vP projection created by object raising opens up the possibility that the long form of Korean negation can be derived by merging negation with vP after object raising has taken place, in the same way that the alternative orders of adverb and direct object were handled in the text.

12. With different assumptions about the structure of, or the order within, vP, as well as the role of scrambling in Korean, other conclusions about the existence of, and the reasons for, object movement may (or may not) follow. Also, an analysis of an SOV language with this SVO vP will require several other auxiliary hypotheses to account for other movements unrelated to Case checking that appear necessary.

13. Since I will not discuss the morphology of the verb, I have not decomposed it further into a string of heads, if that is its proper analysis. The adverb *pali* in (21b) is either right adjoined to VP or is a low complement inside the VP shell (cf. Larson 1988, 2003). It would be hard to argue that both the English verb and the Korean object raise out of vP in this example.

14. Muysken (2000) cites Turkish/Dutch codeswitching examples from Backus that show a Dutch complement of a Dutch verb bearing the Turkish Spell-Out of accusative Case. This could presumably be analyzed as the use of a Dutch V with a Turkish v. See below for Korean/English cases of V/v mixing.

15. I continue to assume that 'put' counts as a Korean verb for Lee's bilingual consultants. If it were considered English, then the asymmetry noted in the text would disappear, but we would be faced with a violation of MacSwan's (1999) PF Disjunction Theorem, which prohibits codeswitching below the X^0 level. Also see MacSwan and Colina, chapter 8, this volume.

16. The relation between *v* and light verb constructions is fairly murky, and I cannot offer clarification here. See Baker 1988, Grimshaw and Mester 1988, Miyagawa 1989, Ahn 1991, Hale and Keyser 1993, and Kratzer 1996, Folli and Harley 2007, Butt 2010 for discussion of some of the issues. See also Gonzalez-Vilbazo and Lopez 2012 for a discussion of *v* in Esplugish, a German/Spanish codeswitching variety. Its role is very similar to that of the Korean and English versions illustrated here.

17. If this line of analysis is correct, the features remaining on the Korean main verbs that would otherwise check the features of the Korean *v* cannot be uninterpretable, otherwise the derivation would crash when the Korean verb and an English *v* interact. Other cases where functional categories from one language and lexical categories from another interact are discussed in Finer 2001. The cases range from examples that have single-word switches to cases where there is wholesale substitution of lexical categories from one language into the functional matrix of the other, such as Media Lengua (Muysken 2000) or Makassarese Malay (Steinhauer 1988).

18. Lee also investigated the subject-orientation properties of the anaphors in switched sentences, and the results converge again with the notion that the anaphor, rather than the language context, determines antecedent choice. *Caki*'s subject orientation was preserved, as was the availability of an object antecedent for the English reflexive.

19. Lee's corpus does not contain codeswitched examples in which an English *wh* is in a subordinate non-[+WH] clause and takes higher scope. The status of such examples would help in distinguishing *wh*-movement from scrambling. Kayne (1994) suggests the reason that head-final languages seldom display *wh*-movement is that the IP preposes into Spec-CP, and this prevents *wh*-extraction. If this is the case, then (35) should perhaps be analyzed as IP-internal scrambling rather than *wh*-movement.

20. Since Huang's (1982) proposal that Chinese *wh* in situ involves LF movement, there have been several proposals for *wh* in situ that involve mixtures of LF and movement to varying degrees. See, for example, Watanabe 1992, Aoun and Li 1993, Tsai 1994, and Cole and Hermon 1998. According to Yoon 1999. Korean, like Japanese, observes *wh* islands but not Complex NP islands. This is essentially the same pattern that Watanabe notes for Japanese, and so I will tentatively adopt his analysis for Koan, leaving open the question of island effects in bilingual codemixing.

References

Ahn, H.-D. 1991. Light verbs, VP-movement, negation, and clausal architecture in Korean and English. Doctoral dissertation, University of Wisconsin, Madison.

Alexiadou, A, and E. Agnastopoulou. 1998. Parameterizing Agr: word order, V-movement, and EPP-Checking. *Natural Language and Linguistic Theory*. 16.3:491–539.

Aoun, J., and A. Y-H Li 1993. *Wh* elements in situ: syntax or LF? *Linguistic Inquiry* 24.2:199–238.

Baker, M. 1988. *Incorporation: A Theory of Grammatical Function Changing*. Chicago: University of Chicago Press.

Bittner, M., and K. Hale. 1996. The structural determination of case and agreement. *Linguistic Inquiry* 27:1–68.

Borer, H. 1984. *Parametric Syntax*. Dordrecht: Foris.

Borer, H., and K. Wexler. 1987. The maturation of syntax. In T. Roeper and E. Williams, eds., *Parameter Setting*, 123–172. Dordrecht: Reidel.

Butt, M. 2010. The light verb jungle: Still hacking away .In M. Amberber, B. Baker, and M. Harvey, eds. *Complex Predicates: Cross-Linguistic Perspectives on Event Structure,* 48–78. Cambridge: Cambridge University Press.

Cho, S. 1998. A new analysis of Korean inalienable possession. *Proceedings of the Northeastern Linguistics Society* 28:79–93.

Cho, S. 2000. Three forms of case agreement in Korean. Doctoral dissertation, SUNY at Stony Brook.

Choi, J. 1991. Korean-English code-switching: Switch-alpha and linguistic constraints. *Linguistics* 29:877–902.

Chomsky, N. 1981. *Lectures on Government and Binding*. Dordrecht: Foris.

Chomsky, N. 1995. *The Minimalist Program.* Cambridge, MA: MIT Press.

Chomsky, N. 2000. Minimalist inquiries: The framework. In R. Martin, D. Michaels, and J. Uriagereka, eds., *Step by Step: Essays on Minimalist Syntax in Honor of Howard Lasnik,* 89–156. Cambridge, MA: MIT Press.

Chomsky, N. 2001. Derivation by phase. In M. Kenstowicz , ed. *Ken Hale: A Life in Language.* 1–52, Cambridge, MA: MIT Press

Chomsky, N. 2004. Beyond explanatory adequacy. In A. Belletti (ed.) *Structures and Beyond: The Cartography of Syntactic Structures, Volume 3,* 104–131 Oxford: Oxford University Press.

Chomsky, N. 2008 On Phases. In R. Freidin, C. P. Otero and M.-L. Zubizarreta (eds) *Foundational Issues in Linguistic Theory, Essays in Honor of Jean-Roger Vergnaud.* Cambridge, MA: MIT Press.

Cinque, G. 1999. *Adverbs and Functional Heads.* Oxford: Oxford University Press.

Cole, P, and G. Hermon 1998. The typology of *wh*-movement: *WH*-questions in Malay. *Syntax* 1:3–221–258.

Cole, P., G. Hermon, and L. Sung. 1990. Principles and Parameters of long-distance reflexives. *Linguistic Inquiry* 21:1–22.

Cole, P., and L.-M. Sung. 1994. Head movement and long distance reflexives. *Linguistic Inquiry* 25:355–406.

Emonds, J. E. 1978. The verbal complex V-V' in French. *Linguistic Inquiry* 9:151–175.

Finer, D. L. 1990. Modularity and lexical parameterization in the adult grammar. *Linguistics* 28:905–927.

Finer, D. L. 1997. Contrasting A' dependencies in Selayarese. *Natural Language and Linguistic Theory* 15:677–728.

Finer, D. L. 2001. Codeswitching as lexical merger. Paper presented at the third International Symposium on Bilingualism, University of the West of England, Bristol.

Folli, R. and H. Harley 2007 Causation, obligation and argument structure: On the nature of little v. *Linguistic Inquiry* 38.2:197–238.

Gonzalez-Vilbazo, K and Luis Lopez. 2012. Little *v* and parametric variation. *Natural Language and Lingistic Theory* 30.1:33–77.

Grimshaw, J., and A. Mester. 1988. Light verbs and θ-marking. *Linguistic Inquiry* 19:205–232.

Hagstrom, Paul. 1996. Object shift in Korean negation. Paper presented at the 1996 LSA meeting, San Diego.

Hale, K., and S. J. Keyser. 1993. On argument structure and the lexical expression of syntactic relations. In K. Hale and S. J. Keyser, eds., *The View from Building 20*, 53–110. Cambridge, MA: MIT Press.

Huang, J. 1982. Move wh in a language without wh movement. *The Linguistic Review* 1.4:369–416.

Kayne, R. S. 1994. *The Antisymmetry of Syntax*. Cambridge, MA: MIT Press

Koopman, H. 1984. *The Syntax of Verbs: From Verb Movement Rules in the Kru Languages to Universal Grammar*. Dordrecht: Foris.

Kratzer, Angelika. 1996 Severing the external argument from its verb. In J. Rooryck and L. Zaring, eds. 109–137. *Phrase structure and the lexicon*. Dordrecht: Kluwer Academic Publishers.

Larson, R. K. 1988. On the double object construction. *Linguistic Inquiry* 19:335–391.

Larson, R. K. 2004. Sentence-final adverbs and "scope". In M. Wolf and K. Moulton, eds. 23–43 *Proceedings of NELS 34*. Amherst, MA: GLSA.

Lebeaux, D. 1988. Language acquisition and the form of the grammar. Doctoral dissertation, University of Massachusetts at Amherst.

Lee, M.-H. 1991. A parametric approach to code-mixing. Doctoral dissertation, SUNY at Stony Brook.

MacSwan, J. 1999. *A Minimalist Approach to Intrasentential Code Switching: Spanish-Nahuatl Bilingualism in Central Mexico*. New York: Garland.

MacSwan, J. 2010. Unconstraining codeswitching theories. In *Proceedings of the 44th Annual Meeting of the Chicago Linguistics Society*, 151–168. Chicago: University of Chicago Press.

Mahootian, S. 1993. A null theory of code-switching. Doctoral dissertation, Northwestern University.

Manzini, R., and K. Wexler. 1987. Parameters, binding theory and learnability. *Linguistic Inquiry* 18:413–444.

Miyagawa, S. 1989. Light verbs and the ergative hypothesis. *Linguistic Inquiry* 20:659–688.

Muysken, P. 2000. *Bilingual Speech: A Typology of Code-Mixing*. Cambridge: Cambridge University Press.

Pesetsky, D., and E. Torrego. 2001. T-to-C movement: Causes and consequences. In Michael Kenstowicz, ed., 355–426. *Ken Hale: A Life in Language*, Cambridge, MA: MIT Press.

Pica, P. 1987. On the nature of the reflexivization cycle. In Joyce McDonough and Bernardette Plunkett, eds., *NELS 17*, 483–499. Amherst: GLSA, University of Massachusetts.

Pollock, J.-Y. 1989. Verb movement, UG and the structure of IP. *Linguistic Inquiry* 20:365–424.

Roberts, I. 2011. Head movement and the minimalist program.195–219. In Cedric Boeckxx, ed., *The Oxford Handbook of Linguistic Minimalism* Oxford: Oxford Press.

Saito, M. 1985. Some asymmetries in Japanese and their theoretical implications. Doctoral dissertation, MIT.

Sridhar, S. N., and K. K. Sridhar. 1980. The syntax and psycholinguistics of bilingual code mixing. *Canadian Journal of Psychology* 34.407–416.

Steinhauer, Hein. 1988. Malay in East Indonesia: The case of Macassarese Malay. In Mohd. Thani Ahmad and Zaini Mohamed Zain, eds., *Rekonstruksi dan Cabang-Cabang Bahasa Melayu induk*, 108–151. Kuala Lumpur: Dewan Bahasa dan Pustaka, Kementerian Pendidikan Malaysia.

Travis, Lisa. 1984. Parameters and effects of word order variation. Doctoral dissertation, MIT.

Tsai, W.–T. D. 1994 On economizing the theory of A-bar dependencies. PhD dissertation, MIT.

van Gelderen, E. and J. MacSwan 2008. Interface conditions and code-switching: Pronouns, lexical DPs, and checking theory. *Lingua* 118.6:765–776.

Vikner, Sten. 2001. V°-to-I° movement and do-insertion in Optimality Theory. In Géraldine Legendre, Jane Grimshaw, and Sten Vikner, eds., Optimality-Theoretic Syntax, 427–464. Cambridge, MA: MIT Press.

Watanabe, A. 1992. Subjacency and S-structure movement of Wh-in-situ. *Journal of East Asian Linguistics* 1:255–291.

Wexler, K., and R. Manzini. 1987. Parameters and learnability in binding theory. In T. Roeper and E. Williams, eds., *Parameter Setting*, 41–76. Dordrecht: Reidel.

Whitman, J. 1999. Kayne 1994: p. 143, fn. 3. In G. Alexandrova, ed., *The Minimalist Parameter*, 77–100. Amsterdam: John Benjamins.

Woolford, Ellen. 1983. Bilingual code-switching and syntactic theory. *Linguistic Inquiry* 14:520–536.

Yoon, Jeong-Me 1999. Decomposing WH-questions: WH-marking and WH-scoping movement *Studies in Generative Grammar* 9.2:153–199.

3 On the Asymmetric Nature of the Operations of Grammar: Evidence from Codeswitching

Anna Maria Di Sciullo

3.1 The Asymmetry Hypothesis

This chapter supports the Asymmetry Hypothesis, according to which asymmetric relations are core relations of the language faculty. This hypothesis is central to Asymmetry Theory (Di Sciullo, 2005). It has consequences for the properties of morphological structures (Di Sciullo 1996, 1999, 2000, 2004, 2014),[1] as well as for the relations between features in morphological derivations (Di Sciullo 1997, 1998, 2009; Di Sciullo and Tenny 1997; Di Sciullo and Slabakova 2005; Di Sciullo and D'Alessandro 2008; Di Sciullo and Landman 2009).[2] Furthermore, it provides a rationale for the presence of complement/noncomplement asymmetries in a variety of languages (Di Sciullo, Paul, and Somesfalean 2003; Jakab 2003; Di Sciullo 2006; Di Sciullo and Isac 2008b, a.o.). Moreover, it provides a novel approach to language development (Di Sciullo 2011, Di Sciullo and Nicolis 2011, Di Sciullo and Somesfalean, 2013).[3]

I consider here the consequences of the Asymmetry Hypothesis for intrasentential codeswitching and show that it predicts possible and impossible switch sites. If intrasentential codeswitching is governed by the properties of the language faculty (hereafter LF) and the core relations derived by the operations of LF are asymmetrical, then asymmetry is central in intrasentential codeswitching.

The theoretical framework that I assume is the Minimalist Program (Chomsky 1995, 1998, 2001, 2005, 2008, 2013). The empirical evidence that I bring forward is based on corpus data,[4] and elicited judgments. The data suggest that the complement/noncomplement asymmetry with respect to the merger and the extraction of syntactic constituents also manifests itself in codeswitching.

The complement/noncomplement asymmetry underlies an array of apparently unrelated constraints. Such constraints include X-bar theory (Chomsky

1970, 1981), the Internal Subject Hypothesis, (Koopman and Sportiche 1991) for asymmetries of projection; the Empty Category Principle (Chomsky 1981), the Condition on Extraction Domains (Huang 1982), Relativized Minimality (Rizzi 1990), and the Minimal Link Condition (Chomsky 1998) for asymmetries of extraction. If the complement/noncomplement asymmetry follows from the operations of LF and not from specific constraints, it is possible to envision a unified explanation for typical properties of the grammars of natural languages whether they are the manifestation of a unique set of parameters (monolingual grammars) or more than one set of parameters (multilingual grammars) giving rise to codeswitching.

The organization of this chapter is as follows. I start by identifying the main aspects of the Minimalist framework and codeswitching relevant to my purpose. I then consider the consequences of the Asymmetry Hypothesis for codeswitching and discuss three striking facts that emerge from the corpus. Lastly, I address the issue of crosslinguistic variation with respect to switch sites, and propose a way to account for the diversity.

3.2 Minimalism and Codeswitching

According to the Minimalist framework, LF provides (a) a set of features, valued or unvalued,[5] (b) a set of principles for assembling features into lexical items,[6] and (c) a set of operations, namely Internal and External Merge, which lead to feature valuation.[7] The features include formal features, (including category, φ-features, Case, and EPP), semantic features and phonetic features. I refer to the full set of features of a grammar as the G-features. The G-features of a given grammar are carried through the derivations and feature valuation must take place before Spell-Out.[8] Full Interpretation requires that no unvalued features reach the interfaces.

Given Merge and feature valuation, parametric variation is reduced to a minimal difference between lexical items. Parametric features are unvalued features associated to functional items, such as the unvalued feature D, attracting N to D, or the unvalued feature T, attracting V to T, or the unvalued feature EPP, attracting a constituent, say a subject, to the specifier of TP.

I take codeswitching grammars not to be different from noncodeswitching grammars in that they both rely on the computational procedure of LF;[9] however, codeswitching grammars range over more than one set of G-features. I posit the following, which makes codeswitching a particular case of linguistic variation, namely the case where a change in G-features occurs in the course of the derivation of a linguistic expression.

(1) *Derivational codeswitching*

  Given $\{G_1, G_2, \ldots, G_n\}$, there are points in the derivation of a linguistic expression where G_2 can be substituted for G_1.

I propose that this substitution may occur at the critical points in the derivation, where parametric features are valued. The mechanism responsible for this change is the very mechanism that makes grammars learnable and that allows linguistic variation.

Under the proposed view, codeswitching is basically a derivational substitution of G-features in a feature valuation site. Given that there is only one Grammar (LF), the asymmetric properties of LF are expected to be part of codeswitching grammars as well, and in particular, the complement/non-complement asymmetry should manifest itself in these grammars. All things being equal, codeswitching is expected to be possible in configurations where unvalued functional features are valued and impossible otherwise. Given the properties of feature valuation, codeswitching is more likely to take place in the functional field. In contrast, codeswitching is not likely to occur in sites where there is no functional head attracting a category for feature valuation, as is the case in the head-complement relations generated in the lexical field.

I assume that a direct object (DO) is generated in the complement position of the VP, as depicted in (2). This head-complement relation is derived by the first application of External Merge, assuming as in Chomsky 1998 that arguments must be initially merged in thematic positions, and as in Di Sciullo and Isac 2008a that items lacking unvalued features are merged as soon as possible in a derivation. The representation in (3) illustrates the configurational difference between direct objects (DO) and subjects (SU). The SU is generated in the specifier of the functional category v.

(2) $[_{VP}\ V\ DO]$

(3) $[_{vP}\ SU\ [v\ [_{VP}\ DO\ [V\ \overline{DO}]]]]$

The DO is generated in the lexical field at a given point in the derivation, whereas the SU never is,[10] even though both DO and SU are in Spec-head relation after Internal Merge has applied.[11] Codeswitching is unlikely to occur at the juncture of V and DO in the lexical field. In contrast, codeswitching may occur in the functional field where parametric feature valuation may take place. This is the case, for example at the juncture of the subject and the T head hosting the internally merged V in languages such as French and Italian, (4). This is also the case at the juncture of an adverbial adjunct and the vP it modifies, (5).

(4)　[TP SU [V-T [vP ~~SU~~ [v [vP DO [V ~~DO~~]]]]]]

(5)　[TP SU [V-T [FP ADV [F [vP ~~SU~~ [v [vP DO [~~V~~ ~~DO~~]]]]]]]]

Given the properties of the operations of LF, while External Merge derives head-complement relations, Internal Merge targets noncomplement positions. Furthermore, the complement (object) of a lexical head is derived by the first application of External Merge; while the complement of a functional head is generated by a further application of External Merge. The complement/non-complement asymmetry relativized to the lexical/functional fields has empirical consequences for codeswitching, as evidenced in section 3.

In sum, according to the asymmetry-based approach, codeswithching may take place when G-features, say the G-features of Italian, are substituted for other G-features, say the G-features of French, at a certain point in the derivation, via the operations of LF, Merge and feature valuation. Assuming that parametric features are unvalued functional features and that code switching is one case of variation, subsumed under feature valuation, codeswitching sites are likely to be located in functional feature valuation sites and not in sites where there is no parametric feature-valuation. This follows from the Asymmetry Hypothesis, according to which asymmetric relations are core relations of LF.

In the following sections, I provide evidence to show that intrasentential codeswitching is a manifestation of the complement/noncomplement asymmetry. This predicts the following three striking facts that emerge from our Italian-French-English conversation corpus. The first fact is that objects generally have the same G-features as the verbs they are dependent on. The second fact is that adverbs and adjectival modifiers need not share the same G-features with the category they are related to. The third fact is that functional heads, including determiners and complementizers, may differ in G-features from the categories they are associated with. I consider these facts in turn.

3.3　Consequences of the Asymmetry Hypothesis

The consequences of the Asymmetry hypothesis for the analysis of codeswitching are both theoretical and empirical.

The theoretical consequence is that it simplifies previous accounts of the phenomena and extends their empirical coverage. For example, there are basic similarities as well as basic differences between the proposed asymmetry approach and the government approach of Di Sciullo, Muysken, and Singh 1986 to codeswitching. While both approaches are configurational and capitalize on the difference between the lexical field versus the functional field, the notions of government and L(anguage)-carrier are dispensed with in the current asymmetry approach. Di Sciullo, Muysken, and Singh 1986 proposed a configurational constraint on codeswitching based on the notion of L-carrier. This notion determines the configurational site of the switch, and it is proposed to capture the fact that, within a sentence, elements bearing a certain type of relation to each other (government) must be drawn from the same lexicon, or have the same language index. In the asymmetry-based approach to codeswitching, no additional constraint, including government is required to account for the difference between subjects and objects with respect to codeswitching. The asymmetry-based approach captures the generalization expressed in terms of the notions of government and L-carrier without appealing to these notions or to any additional constraint, given the independently needed notion of G-features including valued and unvalued functional features. Differences between possible and impossible switch sites are reduced to the derivational asymmetry between External Merge and Internal Merge relativized to the lexical/functional fields. Furthermore, the independently needed notion of feature valuation is used in the asymmetry-based approach to identify the possible switching sites, which is not the case in the government approach. Moreover, given that feature-valuation can be achieved by Merge, either Internal or External, it is possible to account for variation between codeswitching grammars, that is grammars where switches do occur in head-complement (government) relations, as well as grammars where switching does not occur in such relations, as detailed below. This result is beyond the scope of the government approach.

The Asymmetry Hypothesis also has empirical consequences for codeswitching in head-complement as well as in noncomplement sites. I consider them in turn in the following paragraphs.

3.3.1 Head Complement

I discuss two cases of head-complement sites originating within the VP with respect to whether or not they qualify as possible codeswitching sites. The first is the verb-direct object configuration and the second is the verb-cognate object configuration, which is a configuration where the object is morphologically related to the verb.

According to my hypothesis, the juncture of a verb and its object is not a likely codeswitching site, because there is a point in the derivation of a verb-object configuration, in fact the initial point derived by the first application of External Merge, where a parametric feature valuation, and thus a possible G-feature change, is unlikely to take place.

3.3.1.1   Head Complement in the VP

3.3.1.1.1   Verb Object   A striking fact that emerges from our multilingual conversation corpus is the absence of codeswitching between a V and its DO. Thus, expressions such as the ones in (6) and (7) are excluded by our Italian-English-French informants in elicitation judgment tasks.

(6)   a. *Gianni beve *le vin.*
     b. *Gianni beve *(the) wine.*
        'Gianni drinks (the) wine.'
     c. *Maria ascolta *la musique.*
     d. *Maria ascolta *to (the) music.*
        'Maria listens to the music.'

(7)   a. *John drinks *le vin.*
     b. *John drinks *(il) vino.*
        'Gianni drinks (the) wine.'
     c. *Mary listens *la musique.*
     d. *Mary listens *musica.*
        'Maria listens to (the) music.'

In the examples in (6), the verb is in Italian and the DP object is in French in (6a) and in English in (6b). In (6a–b), the Italian verb selects a DP complement. In the examples in (6c–d), the verb *to listen* takes a DP object in French and a PP object in English. The examples in (7) are parallel cases with the verb in English and the object in Italian or French. Interestingly, the judgments are constant, whether or not the object differs in categorical selection (DP vs. PP) in the grammar of the languages under consideration. This suggests that configurational relations, such as the head-complement relation, override differences in lexical selection and thus brings empirical support to the asymmetry approach to codeswitching.

The absence of codeswitching at the juncture of a verb and its object follows from our proposal, because an object is merged with a verb and is part of a head-complement configuration derived by the first application of External Merge. All things being equal, no parametric feature valuation, and possibly parametric feature change, takes place in that configuration.

3.3.1.1.2   Verb-Cognate Object   The Italian-English-French corpus does not include cases of codeswitching in cognate object contexts. This is exemplified with the Italian-English examples in (8), where the cognate object [*a song*] shares the G-features of the verb, contrary to the DP [*Un Piccolo Topo*] (I), which is an appositive DP and not a complement of the verb. Cognate objects can be passivized, questioned and relativized, like objects, e.g. *a song has been sung, what did you sing?, a song that you sang.* This is not the case for appositive DPs, **Three Nice Mice has been sang a song, *what did you sing a song?, *Three Nice Mice that you sang a song.*

(8) a. *Well, sing a ... song,* Un Piccolo Topo.
      'Well, sing a song, A Small Mouse."
     b. *Yeah, sing it,* Un Piccolo Topo.
      'Yeah, sing it, A Small Mouse.'

Codeswitching may not occur at the juncture of a verb and its cognate object. This fact is corroborated by our informants, as the following examples illustrate.

(9) a. *Gianni ha vissuto *sa vie.*
     b. *Gianni ha vissuto *his life.*
     c. *John lived *la sua vita.*
     d. *John lived *sa vie.*
     e. *Jean a vécu *sua vita.*
     f. *Jean a vécu *his life.*
      'John lived his life.'

(10) a. Gianni ha vissuto la sua vita, *une bonne vie.*
     b. Gianni ha vissuto la sua vita, *a good life.*
     c. John lived his life, *una buona vita.*
     d. John lived his life, *une bonne vie.*
     e. Jean a vécu sa vie, *una buona vita.*
     f. Jean a vécu sa vie, *a good life.*
      'John lived his life, a good life.'

These data further illustrate that the juncture between a head and its complement generated in the VP is not a possible codeswithching site. They also illustrate the effect of the complement/noncomplement asymmetry on codeswithching: according to our informants, codeswitching is impossible in head-complement configurations, including V-cognate object sites, and possible in non-complement configurations, including appositive contexts.

3.3.1.2 *Head Complement External to the VP*

Because functional projections are the locus of feature valuation, including parametric feature valuation, we expect purely functional head-complement sites—that is, configurations derived by the application of External Merge in the functional domain—to be possible sites for codeswitching. This is in fact what is observed in our corpus, which includes several cases of switches between a functional head and its complement. The examples below illustrate this point.

Considering the extended projection of V, the examples in (11) show that codeswitching may occur at the juncture of a C head and its TP complement. In (11a) the C head has French G-features, and its TP complement has English G-features. In (12), codeswitching occurs between the DP subject *lu fatore* (I) 'the postman' and the adverbial phrase *demain* (Fr) 'tomorrow' in its complement domain.

(11) a. Il   me   dit   que   *it's*   *hard*   *to*   *fix*   *it.*
        he   me   said   that   it's   hard   to   fix   it
        'He tells me that it's hard to fix it.'
     b. Mo   ti   dicco   mo   io la   trovo   che *watch, you know.*
        now (I) (to) you   say-1sg-Pres   now   I   her find   that (she) watch,
        you know
        'Now I am telling you now I find her that she watches, you know.'

(12) Lu   factore,   *demain,*   *pas*   *de*   *malle,*   *porte*   *pas*   *de*   *chèques.*
     The   postman   tomorrow   no   of   mail,   brings   no   of   checks.
     'The postman, tomorrow, no mail, he brings no checks.'

Considering the extended projection of N, codeswitching is possible between a D head and a constituent in its complement domain. Examples from our corpus include the cases in (13) where codeswitching occurs between the D head and its nominal complement, as well as cases such as (14), where the switch occurs between a quantifier and its nominal complement.

(13) a. C'era   il   *blé d'inde.*
        there was   the   corn
        'There was corn.'
     b. Li   voglio   lu   *juice.*
        it   want-1sg-Pres   the   juice
        'I want the juice.'
     c. Perche   a   mezzi   giorn ciud   la   *shop.*
        because   at   noon   closes   the   shop
        'Because the shop closes at noon.'

(14) C'   era   troppo   *noise* e   nu   realiza le   pareccie   che e   troppe quete.
     there was   too much noise   and   NOT   realize the   plane   that is too   quiet
     'There was too much noise and one does not realize that the plane is too quiet.'

These facts from our Italian-English-French corpus, corroborated by acceptability judgments from our informants, point to the correctness of the proposed hypothesis according to which head-complement sites in the functional field, because they are part of the feature valuation sites, are likely to allow codeswitching.

3.3.2 Noncomplement Sites

The asymmetry approach also predicts that codeswitching may occur in specifier-head relations in the functional field, which may host noncomplements. The following paragraphs provide evidence that this is indeed the case.

3.3.2.1 *Spec-Head Relation*

3.3.2.1.1 Subjects Subjects are generated by External Merge in the functional field, in a specifier-head relation within the vP and they may be displaced in the specifier of TP by Internal Merge for feature valuation.

As predicted, our corpus presents cases where codeswitching occurs between the subject, in Spec TP, and the T head. This is the case in (15), where codeswitching occurs at the juncture of the pro subject, which occupies the specifier of TP in pro-drop languages such as Italian, and T the head of TP. T includes the verb and the French accusative clitic *le*, assuming that object clitics are adjoined to V, which has been merged to T, given that the unvalued features of T attract V in Romance languages (V-to-T parameter), as represented in (16).

(15) È   buon perche *si le   laisse tranquille* nin gi   sta quest odio.
     (it) is good because if them leave alone   NOT there is   this hate
     'It is good because if we leave them alone there is not this hate.'

(16) [$_{CP}$ C [$_{TP}$ pro [$_T$ [[cl V]T] [$_{vP}$ ...

Specifier-head relations derived in the functional field are canonical configurations for parametric feature valuation, and according to our hypothesis, possible sites for G-features changes.

The example in (17) also points in the same direction. The verb *dit* (Fr) 'to say' and its CP complement *que fait la même chose* (Fr) 'that it does the same' have the same G-features, as predicted. This is also the case for the dative complement of the verb, which takes the form of the clitic pronoun *m'* (Fr) 'to me'. Codeswitching occurs in the matrix clause between the subject pronoun *lu*, a reduced form of Italian *lui* 'he' in Spec TP, and T. It also occurs in the embedded clause, between the covert pro subject and T. This is possible in a pro-drop language such as Italian, but not in a non-pro-drop language such as French, where the pronoun *ça* 'it' would be pronounced in this position.

(17) Lu *m'a*   *dit*   *que*   *fait*   *la*   *même*   *chose.*
     he to me have   said   that   does   the   same   thing
     'He told me that it does the same thing.'

This example illustrates further that G-feature changes may occur in the functional field where unvalued parametric features are valued.

Judgments from our informants point in the same direction. Codeswitching is possible at the juncture of a DP subject and a T head hosting a clitic pronoun, as in (18a), but not at the juncture of the clitic and the T head hosting the object clitic as in (18b).

(18) a. Questo   studente   *le*   *lit*   *souvent.*
         this   student   it   read   often
         'This student reads it often.'
     b. *Questo   studente lo   *lit*   *souvent.*
         this   student   it   read   often
         'This student reads it often.'

These facts point to the correctness of my hypothesis, according to which codeswitching is likely to occur in a specifier-head configuration, at the juncture of a subject and a verb, but not at the juncture of a verb and its object, in a configuration derived by the first application of External Merge. Because the subject is in a functional specifier-head relation through the derivation, parametric feature valuing, including G-feature changes, may occur between the subject and the head of its TP complement.

3.3.2.1.2 Modifiers I assume that adverbial and adjectival modifiers occupy the specifier position of a functional (F) category asymmetrically c-commanding the lexical projections it modifies. The lexical heads V and N are displaced in the domain of a functional projection for feature valuation. Given the copy theory of movement, configurations such as the ones in (19) and (20) can be generated in the derivation of adverbial and adjectival modifications.

(19) [$_{FP}$ ADV [$_F$ V-F ... [$_{vP}$ [V̶

(20) [$_{FP}$ ADJ [$_F$ N-F ... [$_{nP}$ [N̶

Codeswitching is correctly predicted to be possible in these sites, as attested by the following expressions observed in our corpus. The examples in (21)-(24) show that VP adverbs may have different G-features than the verbal head they are related to. The examples show that temporal adverbs (21) and (22), as well as subject-oriented (23) and speaker-oriented (24) adverbs, may also have different G-features than the projection they are associated with. This suggests that codeswitching is independent of semantic features, but is dependent on functional feature valuation.

(21) La   lascia   *toujours*   sulla   tavola.
     it   leave   always   on the   table
     'She always leaves it on the table.'

(22) *Addesso,*   will   sing   for   Christmas.
     now,   will   sing   for   Christmas
     'Now, we will sing for Christmas.'

(23) *Spontagnamente,*   tu   vas   parler   français.
     spontaneously,   you   going   speak   French
     'Spontaneously, you are going to speak French.'

(24) *Naturalmente,*   la   plupart   des   Canadiens
     naturally,   the   most   of   Canadians'
     'Naturally, most Canadians'

PP modifiers, generated in the functional field by External Merge, do not differ from other modifiers with respect to codeswitching, as evidenced in examples (25)-(28) from our corpus. Here again the facts indicate that codeswitching is not dependent on semantic features. In the example in (25) the PP modifier has temporal features; in (26), it has locative features; in (27), directional features; and in (28), manner features.

(25) Tu   mangi   quelle   piccole   cose   *in*   *between*   *meals.*
     you   eat   those   little   thing   in   between   meals
     'You eat those little things between meals.'

(26) a. Ma,   *in*   *Italy*   anche
        but,   in   Italy   as well
        'But, in Italy as well'
     b. C'era   un,   *à*   *la*   *radio,*   un'   a   la   radio   italiana,
        there was   one,   at   the   radio,   one   at   the   radio   Italian
        'There was one, on the radio, someone on the Italian radio,'
     c. E   vo   sciar   all'   *Ice Follies.*
        and   go   skiing   at   *Ice Follies*
        'And (I) go skiing at the Ice Follies.'

(27) Tony,   va   piglia   la   frutta   *en*   *bas.*
     Tony,   go   take   the   fruit   in   down
     'Tony, go take the fruit downstairs.'

(28) La   pizza   la   faccio   *all*   *dress.*
     the   pizza   it   make-3sg-Pres   all   dress
     'The pizza, I make it all dress.'

AP modifiers, like adverbial and prepositional modifiers, are noncomplements. As predicted, the expressions in (29) from our corpus illustrate that switching may occur at the juncture of an Adj and an N, as Adj are generated by External Merge in the specifier of a functional category.

(29) a. Little   *topo*   was   going   away,   another   one,   then   another   one.
        small   rat   was   going   away,   another   one,   the   another   one
        'A small rat was going away, another one, then another one.'
     b. *Un*   *hotel*   pulito ... non era   lussuoso   ah.
        an   hotel   clean ... it was not   luxurious   eh.'
        'A clean hotel ... it was not luxurious eh.'
     c. Puo   fa   le   belle   *party.*
        (she) can give   the   nice   parties
        'She can give nice parties.'
     d. Ma   ci stanno dei   *smart*   italiani.
        but   there are some   smart   Italian
        'But there are smart Italians.'

That similar facts are observed in other corpora, including English-Spanish, brings further empirical evidence to the phenomenon, which follows from the Asymmetry Hypothesis without further stipulation.

(30) a. Es eso color come [[muy dark] maroon].
        'It's that color like very dark maroon.'
        (Pfaff 1979, 256)
     b. Uno no podia comer carne *every day.*
        'One cannot eat meat every day.'
        (Sankoff and Poplack 1981)

According to Mahootian and Santorini 1996, all possible codeswitching combinations are attested in noun-adjective contexts. This generalization has been disputed in several works including MacSwan 1999, where it is suggested that it is the language of the determiner that sets possible and impossible switches between adjectives and nouns. I will not try to resolve this question here. However, I will make the following observation that bears on the issue.

There is a parameter differentiating Italian and English with respect to the distribution of modifying adjectives. This parameter involves aspectual features, because we observe that in Italian, individual-level adjectives may precede or follow the nominal head, as illustrated in (31), whereas stage-level adjectives follow the noun, as exemplified in (32). In English all adjectives are prenominal.

(31) a. Una persona brava/intelligente
     'A person good/intelligent'
  b. Una brava/intelligente persona
     'A good/intelligent person'

(32) a. Una persona pronta/disponibile
     'A person ready/available'
  b. *Una pronta/disponibile persona
     'A ready/available person'

If MacSwan is right, it is predicted that the expressions in (33), where the determiner is in Italian and where a stage-level adjective precedes the noun, should be impossible, as well as expressions such as (34), where the determiner is in English and the stage-level adjective follows the noun. In contrast, expressions such as the ones in (35), where the determiner is in Italian and the individual-level adjective precedes or follows the noun, as well as cases such as (36), where the determiner is in English and the adjective, whether individual or stage, precedes the noun, are possible. The elicited judgments obtained from my informants indicate that this is correct.

(33) a. *Il *available* professore
     'The available professor'
  b. *Il *ready* professore
     'The ready professor'

(34) a. *The   professor   *pronto*
     the   professor   ready
     'The ready professor'
  b. *The   professor   *disponibile*
     the   professor   available
     'The available professor'

(35) a. Il *nice* professore
  b. Il *bright* professore
  c. Il professore *nice*
  d. Il professore *bright*

(36) a. The *bravo* professor
  b. The *intelligente* professor
  c. The *pronto* professor
  d. The *disponibile* professor

In the asymmetry-based approach, nothing requires codeswitching to occur in a specifier-head configuration; this configuration is however a possible locus for G-feature changes which may give rise to codeswitching.

The facts presented in this section provide further evidence for the Asymmetry Hypothesis, one consequence of which is that codeswitching is possible in modification sites. The features of the modified category are valued in the specifier of a functional projection. According to our proposal, this site is a possible codeswitching site, because it is a point in the derivation where a change may arise in G-features.

3.3.2.1.3 Extractions Evidence from the Italian-English-French corpus shows that codeswitching may occur in relative clauses and in wh-questions at the juncture of the extracted constituent and the CP or TP it has been extracted from. The examples in (37) and (38) are cases where the extracted constituent originates from a specifier position, viz., the subject position in (37), and from an adjunct position in (38). Thus, in (37a), *la strega* (I) 'the witch' originates in the subject position of the verb *scared* (E), in (37b) *la persona* (I) 'the person' originates from the subject position of the verb *parle* (Fr) 'speak'. In (38), the wh-constituents originate in adjunct positions.

(37) a. È   la   strega ...   *who   scared   the   mouse.*
       is   the   witch ...   who   scared   the   mouse.
      'It is the witch who scared the mouse.'

    b. *La musique* è trope forte e   la   persona *qui   parle   je peux pas la comprendre.*
      the music is too   loud and the person who speaks I cannot   CL understand
      'The music is too loud and I cannot understand the person who is speaking.'

(38) a. *Pourquoi   sonne   cosi?*
      why   rings   like that
      'Why does it ring like that?'

    b. Frank,   *quand*   finishe?
      Frank,   when   finishes
      'Frank, when does he finish?'

    c. *Come*   disons   en   italien?
      how   say-1pl-Pres   in   Italian
      'How do we say in Italian?'

There are no cases of *wh*-extraction from the complement position in our corpus. The elicited judgments obtained from our informants indicate that codeswitching is not possible in these contexts, as it is the case in the examples in (39), using italic for Italian:

(39) a. *Qu'est-ce   que   *dici*?
         what is it   that   say
         'What are you saying?'
     b. *Que   *fai*?
         what   do
         'What do you do?'
     c. *Cosa   dis?
         (what) thing   say
         'What do you say?'
     d. *Che   dit   Marie?
         what   say   Mary
         'What is Mary saying?'

Our corpus also includes cases of switching within an extracted constituent. In (40a), *compound* (E) is the complement of the functional head *quel* (I) in the PP *con quel compound* (I) originating in an adjunct position. Similarly, in (40b) *street* (E) is the complement of the functional head *questu* (I) in the DP *questu street* (I), extracted from the subject position of the verb *piace* (I).

(40) a. Io,   con   quel   *compound*   che   dico   faccio   tutti   questi   piedi   qua.
         Me, with   that   compound   that   say   do   all   these   legs   here
         'Me, with that compound that I am saying I do all these (table) legs here'
     b. Come   si   chiame   questu   *street*   che   ti   piace   a   te,   Angelo?
         how   SELF   called   his   street   that   CL   like   at   you, Angelo
         'What is the street called that you like, Angelo?'

There are no clear cases of codeswitching in the context of extraction of a complement of a lexical V in our corpus. In (41), *fanno* (I) can be both a causative verb and a light verb.[12] As a light verb, it is a functional head, and thus, the DP *l'échantillon* (Fr) would not be extracted from a lexical complement position.

(41) *l'échantillon*   che   fanno ...
      the sample   that (they)   do-3pl-Pres
      'the sample that they do ...'

These facts provide further evidence that codeswitching is sensitive to the complement/noncomplement asymmetry relativized with respect to the functional/lexical field. Codeswitching is, in my view, a particular manifestation of the asymmetry of the operations of the grammar. In the next section, I consider variation between codeswitching grammars.

3.4 Variation

In Belazi, Rubin, and Toribio (1994), the Functional Head Constraint is proposed to account for Tunisian Arabic-French and Spanish-English bilingual intuitions about possible versus impossible codeswitching.

(42) *Functional Head Constraint*
   The language feature of the complement f-selected by a functional head, like all other relevant features, must match the corresponding feature of that functional head. (Belazi, Rubin, and Toribio 1994, 228)

The Functional Head Constraint predicts that switching is disallowed between C and TP, between D and NP, between Num and NP, between Neg and VP, as well as between ADV and VP. In contrast, switching between a lexical head and its complement occurs quite freely. According to Belazi and colleagues, switching is possible between a verb and its complement, as well as between a preposition and its complement. Some examples are given below.

(43) a. Ktib   *dix*   *livres.*
        wrote-he   ten   books
        'He wrote ten books.'
     b. *Ktib   *ʒasra*   *livres.*
        wrote-he   ten   books
        'He wrote ten books.'
        (Belazi, Rubin, and Toribio 1994, 229)

(44) The   police   officers   have   seen   *un*   *ladron.*
      *the   police   officers   have   *visto*   *un*   *ladron*
      'The police officers have seen a thief.'
      (Belazi, Rubin, and Toribio 1994, 230)

(45) They   used   to   serve   *bebidas*   *alcholicas*   *en*   *ese*   *restaurante.*
      they   used   to   serve   drinks   alcoholic   in   that   restaurant
      'They used to serve alcoholic beverages in that restaurant.'
      (Belazi, Rubin, and Toribio 1994, 230)

As we have seen above, codeswitching is impossible in these sites for Italian-English-French speakers. These sharp differences between possible and impossible switch sites, if correct, have to be accounted for. Moreover, if, as they assume, inflectional affixes are functional categories, Belazi, Rubin, and Toribio predict that switching is not possible under the word level, at the site between what they analyze as a functional head and its complement. Some examples of under the word-level impossible switch sites are illustrated below:

(46) *Suf-t   da:r-s.
      saw-I   house-PL
      'I saw the houses.'
      (Belazi, Rubin, and Toribio 1994, 231)

(47) *We   dance-*amos*   cha-cha.
      we   dance-1pl   cha-cha
      'We dance cha-cha.'
      (Belazi, Rubin, and Toribio 1994, 231)

The Functional Head Constraint, proposed to account for the nonoccurrence of switching between a functional head and its complement, makes the wrong predictions with respect to the Italian-English-French facts. Our hypothesis makes the wrong predictions with respect to the Tunisian Arabic-French and Spanish-English codeswitching data, because it predicts that a complement has the same G-features as the lexical head on which it is dependent.

If as I propose, codeswitching is one manifestation of the asymmetry of the operations of LF, it is possible to reconcile the apparently contradictory facts above by assuming that LF includes the following parameter.

(48) Parametric feature valuation is done by operation X.

I propose that LF does not specify the operation X by which feature valuation is performed. It leaves this choice to individual grammars, as a parametric option. This choice however is very limited, because there are only two core operations, Internal Merge and External Merge. Parameter (58) is a possible parameter in our model, which is based on a limited set of configurational asymmetries, including the head-complement configurations, lexical and functional, derived by External Merge and the specifier-head configurations derived by Internal Merge. Given (48), feature valuation can be done by an operation X, either External Merge, Internal Merge, both, or none. The last option is that X is not a syntactic operation and thus feature valuation would not be performed by syntactic operations, but by operations applying in another plane of the grammar, such as the morphological or the phonological planes of the computational space. See Di Sciullo, 2005 and 2011 for discussion.

I thus identify four sorts of codeswitching situations according to the value attributed to X in parameter (48). Consider the following chart.

X	G1	G2	G3	G4
Internal Merge	+	−	+	−
External Merge	−	+	+	−

In G1, purely lexical Merge does not give rise to possible head-complement switch sites, but purely functional Merge does, as well as the specifier-head relation derived by Internal Merge. Thus, switching is impossible between a verb and its complement, but it is possible between Comp and TP as well as between Neg and VP, D and NP, and Num and NP. This is the case with our Italian-English-French grammar. In contrast, in G2, purely functional head-complement relations would not constitute possible switch sites. Thus switching between Comp and TP, Neg and VP, D and NP, as well as Num and NP is impossible. However, switching between a lexical head and its complement would be possible. This would be the case with the Tunisian Arabic–French grammar discussed in Belazi, Rubin, and Toribio (1994). In G3, codeswitching may occur between a head, lexical or functional, and its complement, derived by Internal Merge, as well as in specifier-head configurations derived by External Merge. In G4, switching is, in addition, not possible between a lexical or functional head and its complement, the facts reported in MacSwan 1999.

It might be the case that basic morphosyntactic properties could allow us to predict which language pair would fall under which setting of the parameters. These basic properties would possibly give rise to differences in the derivation of lexical and functional relations with respect to feature valuation. It is well known that Romance and Semitic languages differ in this respect, just as languages with very poor morphology such as Chinese differ from languages with very rich morphology such as Turkish. I leave this conjecture open to further research.

3.5 Summary

I have discussed three striking facts that emerge from a spontaneous Italian-English-French conversation corpus as well as from data obtained by elicited judgments. The facts suggest that the complement/noncomplement asymmetry, relativized with respect to the functional/lexical domain, also manifests itself in codeswitching grammars.

In the proposed view, the complement/noncomplement asymmetry follows from the basic asymmetry of the operations of the grammar. The asymmetry also has consequences for differentiating possible from impossible codeswitching sites, given the setting of parameter (48). The Asymmetry Hypothesis accounts for the facts in a unified way.

Notes

I thank Jeff MacSwan, Dan Finer, and Helena Halmari for detailed comments on an earlier version of this chapter. This work has been supported in part by funding from the Social Sciences and Humanities Research Council of Canada for the Major Collaborative Research Initiative (MCRI) on Asymmetries in Natural Languages, grant number 214-97-0016 and by funding from the Fond de Recherche du Québec (FQRSC) for the Dynamic Interface Research project, grant number 137253, www.interfaceasymmetry.uqam.ca.

1. Asymmetry, as a property of the configurations underlying the linguistic expressions, is expressed in terms of the asymmetrical c-command relation, as defined in Kayne 1994.

2. Asymmetry, as a property of the features associated to the elements undergoing the operations of the language faculty, is expressed in terms of the proper subset relation, as defined in Di Sciullo 2005.

3. The Asymmetry Hypothesis has consequences for the understanding of the resetting of parameters in language development, where periods of fluctuating asymmetry are followed by periods of directional asymmetry. See Di Sciullo 2011 and related works for discussion.

4. The corpus is the one I gathered by recording spontaneous conversations between three groups of four Italian-English-French multilingual speakers in 1973 and 1974, as part of a research program on multilingual interaction funded by the Social Sciences and Humanities Research Council of Canada (cf. Di Sciullo et al. 1975). This is one of the corpora used in Di Sciullo, Muysken, and Singh's 1986 study on government and code-mixing. Furthermore, for the present study, six Italian-English-French multilingual speakers participated in the judgment tasks. I will use the following abbreviations for expressions Italian (I), French (Fr) and English (E) when necessary.

5. The valued features include categorial features (+/−N, +/−V, D, T, etc.), the φ-features of N (person, number, gender), and the [+wh] feature of *wh*-phrases. The unvalued features include the φ-features and the Case features of T, and the EPP feature.

6. Lexical items are bundles of features, and they may enter the derivation with valued or unvalued features. For example, the functional head T carries unvalued person, number and gender features, and DPs are unvalued for Case. The principle of Full Interpretation ensures that unvalued features are valued before Spell-Out, to be legible by the external systems. Unvalued features are valued by entering into an Agree relation with valued features. The Agree relation is generally followed by movement (pied-piping), and is defined as follows:

Agree: α Agrees with β iff: a. α and β are non-distinct for some formal feature F;

b. α and β are active (i.e. have at least one unvalued feature); c. α asymmetrically c-commands β; there is no γ, an active goal, which is both asymmetrically c-commanded and asymmetrically c-commands β.

7. External Merge applies to two syntactic objects that have not been merged before. Internal Merge remerges a syntactic object that has already been merged in the derivation.

8. Spell-Out is the point in the derivation where linguistic expressions are no longer subject to syntactic operations leading to the semantic interface, while they are subject to phonological operations leading to the phonetic interface.

9. Several constraints were proposed to account for the properties of codeswitched grammars, see Pfatt 1979, 1982; Poplack 1980, 1993; Joshi 1982; Di Sciullo, Muysken,

and Singh 1986; Belazi, Rubin, and Toribio 1994; Mahootian and Santorini 1996; Treffers-Daller 1997; Halmari 1993, 1998; Muysken 1995, 2000 a.o. The asymmetry-based approach I propose here does not require codeswitching-specific constraints, an approach also taken in McSwan 1999, 2000, 2013.

10. The projection of subjects has been discussed in various works, see Arab 1998, Chomsky 1998, Koopman and Sportiche 1991, and Williams 1980, a. o. The projection of a constituent within or outside of the minimal argument structure projection of a lexical head has been implemented in various ways, see Di Sciullo and Williams 1987, Jackendoff 1977, Kayne 1994, Chomsky 1998, as well as Hale and Keyser, 2002, a.o. In the Minimalist framework, the subject is generated within the vP.

11. The effects of the copy theory of movement are represented in the structures by crossing out the copy of the moved constituent.

12. Light verbs have defective argument structure properties (Grimshaw and Mester 1988, Di Sciullo and Rosen 1990, a.o.). They are generally analyzed as functional heads, and thus they are not part of the canonical lexical head-complement relations. See Muysken (2000) Hok-Shing Chan (2008) a.o. for discussion on codeswitching in light verbs contexts.

References

Arab, Maya. 1998. VP structure and the syntax-lexicon interface. Doctoral Dissertation, University College London.

Belazi, Helena, Edward Rubin, and Almeida Jaqueline Toribio. 1994. Code switching and X-bar theory. *Linguistic Inquiry* 25:234–235.

Chomsky, Noam. 1970. Remarks on nominalizations. In R. Jacobs and P. Rosenbaum, eds., *Readings in English Transformational Grammar*. Waltham, MA: Ginn.

Chomsky, Noam. 1981. *Lectures on Government and Binding*. Dordrecht: Foris.

Chomsky, Noam. 1995. *The Minimalist Program*. Cambridge, MA: MIT Press.

Chomsky, Noam. 2000. Minimalist inquiries. In Roger Martin et al., eds., *Step by Step. Essays on Minimalist Syntax in Honor of Howard Lasnik*, 89155. Cambridge, MA: MIT Press.

Chomsky, Noam. 2001. Derivation by phase. In Michael Kensowicz, ed. *Ken Hale: A Life in Language*, 1–52. Cambridge, MA: MIT Press.

Chomsky, Noam. 2005. Three factors in language design. *Linguistic Inquiry* 36(1):1–22.

Chomsky, Noam. 2008. On phases. In R. Freidin, C. P. Otero and M. L. Zubizarreta, eds., *Foundational Issues in Linguistic Theory. Essays in Honor of Jean-Roger Vergnaud*, 133–166. Cambridge, MA: MIT Press.

Chomsky, Noam. 2013. Problems of projection. *Lingua* 130:33–49.

Cinque, Guglielmo. 1999. *Adverbs and Functional Projections: A Cross-Linguistic Perspective*. New York: Oxford University Press.

Cinque, Guglielmo. 2010. *The Syntax of Adjectives. A Comparative Study*. Cambridge, MA: MIT Press.

Di Sciullo, Anna Maria. 1996. Modularity and X/XP asymmetry. *Linguistic Analysis* 26:3–28.

Di Sciullo, Anna Maria. 1997. Prefixed verbs and adjunct identification. In A. M. Di Sciullo, ed., *Projections and Interface Conditions: Essays on Modularity*, 52–74. New York: Oxford University Press

Di Sciullo, Anna Maria. 1998. Features and asymmetrical relations in morphological objects. *21st GLOW Newsletter* 42:68–89.

Di Sciullo, Anna Maria. 1999. Local asymmetry. In L. Pylkanen, A. van Hout, and H. Harley, eds., *MIT Working Papers in Linguistics 35: Papers from the UPenn/MIT Roundtable on the Lexicon*, 25–49. Cambridge, MA: MITWPL, Department of Linguistics and Philosophy, MIT

Di Sciullo, Anna Maria. 2000. Local asymmetries and their consequences for morphological configurations and paradigms. *Acta Linguistica Hungarica* 47:81–101.

Di Sciullo, Anna Maria. 2004. Morphological phases. In Jong-Yuri Yoon, ed., *Generative Grammar in a Broader Perspective. The 4th GLOW in Asia*, 113–137. The Korean Generative Grammar Circle and Cognitive Science, Seoul National University.

Di Sciullo, Anna Maria. 2005. *Asymmetry in Morphology*. Cambridge, MA: MIT Press.

Di Sciullo, Anna Maria. 2006. Grammar and the Shortest Path. *World Scientific and Engineering Academy and Society* 9:1781–1788.

Di Sciullo, Anna Maria. 2009. Why are compounds part of natural languages: A view from asymmetry theory. In Rochelle Lieber et Pavol Štekauer, eds., *Handbook of Compounds*, 145–177. Oxford: Oxford University Press.

Di Sciullo, Anna Maria. 2011. A biolinguistic approach to variation. In A. M. Di Sciullo and C. Boeckx, eds., *The Biolinguistic Entreprise: NewPerspectives on the Evolution and Nature of the Human Language Faculty*, 305–328. Oxford: Oxford University Press.

Di Sciullo, Anna Maria. 2014. Minimalism and I-Morphology. In P. Kosta, S. Franks and T. Radeva-Bork, eds., *Minimalism and Beyond: Radicalizing the interfaces*, 267–286. Amsterdam: John Benjamins.

Di Sciullo, Anna Maria, and Roberta D'Alessandro. 2008. Proper Subset Relation and Concord: Agreement in Abruzzese Possessive Copular Constructions. *North East Linguistic Society 38*. University of Massashussets, Amherst.

Di Sciullo, Anna Maria, and Dana Isac. 2008a. The Asymmetry of Merge. *Biolinguistics* 2:260–290.

Di Sciullo, Anna Maria, and Dana Isac. 2008b. Movement chains at the interfaces. *Revue Canadienne de Linguistique. Édition spéciale sur les Interfaces* 53:181–217.

Di Sciullo, Anna Maria, and Meredith Landman. 2009. On the Morphological Compositionality of Determiners. *Revista Letras* 73:203–222.

Di Sciullo, Anna Maria, Pieter Muysken, and Rajendra Singh. 1986. Government and code-mixing. *Journal of Linguistics* 22:1–24.

Di Sciullo, Anna Maria, and Marco Nicolis. 2011. Third factor in the development of P. Paper presented at the *North East Linguistic Society* 42. University of Toronto.

Di Sciullo, Anna Maria, Ileana Paul, and Stanca Somesfalean. 2003. The clause structure of extraction asymmetries. In A. M. Di Sciullo, ed., *Asymmetry in Grammar: Syntax and Semantics*, 279–300. Amsterdam: John Benjamins.

Di Sciullo, Anna Maria and Sara Thomas Rosen 1990. Light and semi-light verb constructions. In K. Dziwirek, P. Farrel and E. Mejias-Bikandi, eds., *Grammatical Relations: A Cross-Theoretical Perspective*, 109–112. Stanford, CA: Center for the Study of Language and Information.

Di Sciullo, Anna Maria, and Roumyana Slabakova. 2005. Quantification and aspect. In A. van Hout, H. de Swart and H. Verkuyl, eds., *Perspectives on Aspect*, 61–80. Dordrecht: Springer.

Di Sciullo, Anna Maria, and Stanca Somesfalean. 2013. Variation in the Position of the Definite Determiner in Romanian: A Biolinguistic Perspective. *Romance Linguistics in the Pacific: Variation in Time and Space. Special Issue of the Australian Journal of Linguistics* 33(2):121–139. Taylor & Francis.

Di Sciullo, Anna Maria, and Carol Tenny. 1997. Modification, event structure, and the word/phrase asymmetry. In K. Kusumoto, ed., *NELS 28*: 375–389. Amherst: GLSA, University of Massachusetts.

Di Sciullo, Anna Maria, Arie Van Amerongen, Herietta Cedergreen, and Paul Pupier, 1975. Etude de l'interaction verbale chez les montréalais d'origine italienne. In *Cahiers de Linguistique de l'Université du Québec*, V.

Di Sciullo, Anna Maria, and Edwin Williams. 1987. *On the Definition of Word*. Cambridge, MA: MIT Press.

Grimshaw, Jane, and Armin Mester. 1988. Light verbs and (theta)-marking. *Linguistic Inquiry* 19: 205232.

Hale, Ken, and Samuel Jay Keyser. 2003. *Prolegomenon to a Theory of Argument Structure*. Cambridge, MA: MIT Press.

Halmari, Helena. 1993. Structural relations and Finnish-English bilingual code-switching. *Linguistics* 31:1043–1068.

Halmari, Helena. 1998. Case assignment and adverbials in Finnish-English bilingual sentences. In J. Niemi, T. Odlin, and J. Heikkinen (eds.), *Studies in Languages 32: Language Contact, Variation and Change*, 98–110.

Hok-Shing Chan, Brian. 2008. Code-switching, word order and the lexical/functional category distinction. Lingua 118(6):777–809.

Huang, C.-T. Jim. 1982. Logical relations in Chinese and the theory of grammar. Doctoral dissertation, MIT.

Jackendoff, Ray. 1977. *X' Syntax*. Cambridge, MA: MIT Press.

Jakab, Edith. 2003. Asymmetry in case: Finnish and Old Russian nominative objects. In A. M. Di Sciullo, ed., *Asymmetry in Grammar: Syntax and Semantics*. Amsterdam: John Benjamins, 51–84.

Joshi, Aravind, 1982. Processing of sentences with intersentential code switching. COLING 1982: 145–150.

Kayne, Richard. 1994. *The Antisymmetry of Syntax*. Cambridge, MA: MIT Press.

Koopman, Hilda, and Dominique Sportiche. 1991. The position of subjects. *Lingua* 85:211–258.

MacSwan, Jeff. 1999. *A Minimalist Approach to Intersentential Codeswitching*. New York: Garland Press.

MacSwan, Jeff. 2000. The architecture of the bilingual language faculty: Evidence from codeswitching. *Bilingualism: Language and Cognition* 3, 1:37–54.

MacSwan, Jeff. 2013. Code-switching and grammatical theory. In T. Bhatia and W. Richie. *Handbook of Multilinguslism* (2nd ed.). Cambridge: Blackwell.

Mahootian, Shahrzad, and Beatrice. Santorini. 1996. Code-switching and the complement/adjunct distinction. *Linguistic Inquiry* 27:464–479.

Muysken, Pieter. 1995. Code switching and grammatical theory. In L. Milroy and P. Muysken (eds.), *One Speaker, Two Languages*, 177–198. Cambridge: Cambridge University Press.

Muysken, Pieter. 2000. *Bilingual Speech: A Typology of Code-Mixing*. Cambridge, MA: Cambridge University Press.

Pfaff, Carol. 1979. Constraints on language mixing: Intrasentential code-switching and borrowing in Spanish/English. *Language* 55:291–318.

Poplack, Shana. 1980. "Sometimes I'll start a sentence in Spanish y termino en Espanol": Towards a typology of code-switching. *Linguistics* 18:581–618.

Poplack, Shana. 1993. Variation theory and language contact. In D. Preston, ed., *American Dialect Research*. Amsterdam: Benjamins, 251–286.

Rizzi, Luiggi. 1990. *Relativized Minimality*. Cambridge, MA: MIT Press.

Rubin, Edward, and Almeida Jacqueline Toribio. 1995. Feature checking and the syntax of language contact. In J. Amastae, G. Goodall, M. Montalbetti, and M. Phinney, eds., *Contemporary Research in Romance Linguistics*, 177–185. Amsterdam: John Benjamins.

Sankoff, David, and Shana Poplack. 1981. A formal grammar for code-switching. *Papers in Linguistics* 14:3–45.

Toribio, Almeida Jacqueline, and Edward J. Rubin. 1996. Code-switching in generative grammar. In J. Jensen and A. Roca, eds., *Spanish in Contact*, 203–226. Somerville, MA: Cascadilla Press.

Treffers-Daller, Jeanine. 1997. Variability in codeswitching styles: Turkish-German codeswitching patterns. In R. Jacobson, ed., *Codeswitching Worldwide*, 277–297. Berlin: Mouton de Gruyter.

Williams, Edwin. 1980. Predication. *Linguistic Inquiry* 11:203–238.

4 Operator Movement in English-Spanish and German-Spanish Codeswitching

Almeida Jacqueline Toribio and Kay E. González-Vilbazo

4.1 Overview

This chapter investigates the syntactic-theoretical constructs and conditions on well-formedness that underlie the word-order patterns applicable to operator movement in English, German, and Spanish, with an eye toward explicating the coherence and co-occurrence restrictions relevant to operator movement and concomitant word order in English-Spanish and German-Spanish bilingual codeswitching. The monolingual and codeswitching patterns of constituent extraction and Infl/V2 in *wh*-interrogatives, negative fronting, and relative clauses are shown to owe to the interaction of invariant principles and the individual properties of the functional projections Infl and C of the languages under study. The analysis offered is developed and advanced within the Principles and Parameters framework, as articulated in the Government-Binding model (Chomsky 1981, 1986) and more recently in the Minimalist Program (Chomsky 1993, 1995, 2000, 2001, 2005, 2006). In taking account of codeswitching patterns by reference to universal principles and the language-specific properties that interact with these, the codeswitching data are revealed to be predicted by, and at once lend evidence to, linguistic-theoretical precepts.

4.2 Preliminaries: Codeswitching and Generative Grammar

Bilinguals may be shown to exhibit a shared knowledge of what constitutes appropriate codeswitching—that is, speakers will agree that some alternating sequences represent possible codeswitches, whereas others do not, although they may be unable to articulate exactly what accounts for this differential judgment. In research on monolingual codes, the linguistic knowledge reflected in speakers' awareness of linguistic well-formedness is considered to constitute part of a speaker's genetic endowment, or Universal Grammar, a set of abstract and general principles assumed to be adequate for characterizing core grammars of all natural languages (cf. Chomsky 1981, 1986). The question arises as to whether the syntactic constraints attested in bilingual codeswitching should be characterized by reference to this same innate system (cf. Toribio 2001b). As expressed by Bhatia and Ritchie (1996, 645), then, the challenge in research on codeswitching "is not whether or not it is subject to grammatical constraints but how best to capture these constraints and how to make deeper claims about human language in general and bilinguals' mixing competence and their language acquisition in particular."

To be sure, the past decades have witnessed considerable attention devoted to exploring codeswitching in generative frameworks. These investigations have sought an explanatory adequacy that was lacking in earlier, more descriptive formulations (cf., e.g., Gingràs 1974; Timm 1975; Pfaff 1979; Poplack 1981), by exploiting universal principles and relations hypothesized to characterize monolingual competence. This line of inquiry into language contact was followed by Woolford (1983), who proposes a generative model for English-Spanish bilingual codeswitching (cf. also the formal analyses of Sankoff and Poplack 1981). According to Woolford, the two component grammars of the bilingual remain separate, just as they do in monolingual speech, but when a bilingual generates a codeswitched utterance, each grammar contributes part of the sentence. Thus, the lexicons of English and Spanish maintain their autonomy, precluding word-internal switching, and both lexicons have access to terminal nodes in syntactic constructions common to both English and Spanish. In contrast, whenever a phrase structure rule unique to one language is used to expand a node, the terminal positions must be filled from the lexicon of that language, predicting the ill-formedness of codeswitching where the phrase structures of English and Spanish differ (e.g., as with the placement of attributive adjectives and clitic pronouns).[1]

Finally, of relevance to the present discussion, Woolford notes that while the grammars of English and Spanish share the phrase structure rule for expanding the sentence, the question-formation data in (1) are ill formed. On Woolford's view, such data may be accounted for by appeal to differences between English and Spanish with respect to inversion in matrix contexts: English requires subject-auxiliary inversion, whereas Spanish allows main verb inversion. And when neither language requires inversion, as with subject extraction, switching between the *wh*-phrase and the remainder of the sentence is permitted, as in (2).[2]

(1)   a. *How *lo hizo*?
          'How did s/he do it?'
          (Peñalosa 1980, cited in Woolford 1983)

b. *When *vino*?
  'When did s/he come?'
  (Peñalosa 1980, cited in Woolford 1983)
c. *Why *lloras*?
  'Why are you crying?'
  (Woolford 1983)
d. *Cómo *did he do it*?
  'How did he do it?'
  (Woolford 1983)

(2) Which of these men *es tu padre*?
  'Which of these men is your father?'
  (Woolford 1983)

While Woolford's model goes a long way toward accounting for codeswitching patterns, a closer examination reveals that it is insufficiently restrictive, allowing the grammar to overgenerate. For example, switching is disallowed in (3), although the two grammars share the same phrase structure rules in the switched components (cf. Belazi, Rubin, and Toribio 1994). And Woolford's proposal is in other respects too restrictive, because matrix nonsubject *wh*-extraction is in fact allowed, on the condition that the switched segments are of sufficient heaviness. Thus, while the data in (1) are ruled out, the corresponding data in (4) are acceptable. Because our study does not address heaviness of constituents (but see Arnold et al. 2000), we will seek to explain the acceptability of the data in (4), rather than rule out that in (1).

(3) a. *The boy had *visto la nueva película de Disney*.
      **El niño había* seen the new film by Disney.
      'The boy had seen the new film by Disney.'
    b. *The doctor warned the patient that *el fumar hace daño*.
      **El médico le aviso al paciente que* smoking is hazardous.
      'The doctor warned the patient that smoking is hazardous.'

(4) a. *¿Con cuánta frecuencia* does the bell chime?
      How often *suena la campana*?
      'How often does the bell chime?'
    b. *¿A qué hora* did the mayor arrive?
      At what time *llegó el alcalde*?
      'At what time did the mayor arrive?'
    c. *¿Con qué motivo* did he pose that question?
      With what aim *hizo esa pregunta*?
      'For what reason did he pose that question?'

The counterexamples in (3) and (4) notwithstanding, we recognize the import of Woolford's contribution in introducing codeswitching data into linguistic theorizing. In subsequent work (Woolford 1984), she further pursues this aim, taking account of the constraints on long-distance subject extractions by reference to the proper government condition on the application of *wh*-movement in English and Spanish. In this analysis, (5a) is ill formed because the complementizer blocks proper government of the subject trace (cf. Chomsky 1981); inversion is blocked in the lower clause because, following Torrego 1984, only Spanish *wh*-words trigger it. In turn, (5b) is ill formed because the Spanish *wh*-word triggers inversion, but the lower clause is English and cannot permit it.

(5) a. *Who do you think that *va a venir*?
        'Who do you think will come?'
        (Woolford 1984)
     b. *¿*Quién piensas tú que* will come?
        'Who do you think will come?'
        (Woolford 1984)

Motivated by similar interests, D'Introno (1996) also suggests that the patterns of grammaticality in *wh*-extraction in English-Spanish codeswitching may be accounted for by appeal to the Empty Category Principle (Chomsky 1981). It merits noting that D'Introno's account is indistinguishable from the Government Constraint proposed in Di Sciullo, Muysken, and Singh 1986, which disallows codeswitching between elements that stand in a government relation:

(6) *Government Constraint* (Di Sciullo, Muysken, and Singh 1986)
     i. If Lq carrier has index q, then $Y^{max}q$.
     ii. In a maximal projection Y^{max}, the Lq carrier is the lexical element which asymmetrically c-commands the other lexical elements or terminal phrase nodes dominated by Y^{max}.

In particular, D'Introno proposes that a *wh*-trace and its governor must bear the same language index—that is, they must be drawn from the same lexicon. On this view, switching in examples such as (7) induces ill-formedness because the *wh*-trace and the verb, which serves as a proper governor, are drawn from distinct lexicons. However, as we have already observed, data such as in (7) may be ruled out because of insufficient length of the *wh*-phrase. As the corresponding data in (8) demonstrate, codeswitching with expanded segments is acceptable, despite the fact that the *wh*-trace and the governing verb do not share a language index.

(7)   a. *What *quieres tú* ?
         'What do you want?'
         (D'Introno 1996)
      b. **Yo no sé quién* arrived.
         'I don't know who arrived.'
         (D'Introno 1996)
      c. *Who *llegó*?
         'Who arrived?'
         (D'Introno 1996)

(8)   a. Which game *quieren jugar tú y tu amigo*?
         'Which game do you and your friend want to play?'
      b. *Yo no sé qué pariente* just arrived.
         'I don't know which relative just arrived.'
      c. Which guests *llegaron tarde*?
         'Which guests arrived late?'

Nevertheless, while neither Woolford's nor D'Introno's Government-Binding accounts are tenable, it is desirable to maintain, with these authors, that codeswitching is constrained by principles of Universal Grammar and the parameter settings of the component languages—that is, by constructs extant in the grammars (cf. Belazi, Rubin, and Toribio 1994; González-Vilbazo 2005; Rubin and Toribio 1995; Toribio and Rubin 1996). As formally stated by MacSwan (2000, 43), "Nothing constrains codeswitching apart from the requirements of the mixed grammars." To that end, the ensuing discussion presents a careful consideration of the syntax of operator movement constructions in English, Spanish, and German, by way of unveiling the constraints on such constructions in English-Spanish and German-Spanish codeswitching. The discussion commences with a more traditional approach to operator movement, and subsequently turns to an analysis of operator constructions couched within the minimalist framework.

4.3   Word Order in *Wh*-Extraction in English, Spanish, and German

As noted, in Government-Binding Theory, structural relations such as government played an important role in defining structural positions and licensing conditions. As the theory developed, agreement emerged as a central relationship for syntactic processes. Thus, for example, c-command was extended to the less restrictive m-command, and nominative Case licensing proceeded within the local specifier-head agreement relation established by Infl and [Spec, I]. Parallel proposals were offered for the licensing of *wh*-phrases:

wh-operators are locally licensed under agreement, as instantiated in the specifier-head configuration (as in Chomsky's 1995 Minimalist Program).[3]

4.3.1 *Wh*-Questions in English

As a point of departure, consider the English *wh*-questions in (9). As shown, the *wh*-phrase moves to clause-initial position and the auxiliary element in these structures occurs to the left of the subject, in a pattern referred to as residual V2 or subject-Infl inversion (9a); when no auxiliary element is available, a form of the expletive verb *do* appears (9b). However, inversion does not apply when the questioned element is the subject of the clause (9c), though the corresponding "inversion" structure may be acceptable with a marked emphatic reading. Finally, inversion in English is restricted to matrix sentences; it does not apply in embedded environments (9d).

(9) a.   How many articles has Chomsky written?
          *How many articles Chomsky has written?
     b.   At what time did the students hand in the assignment?
          *At what time the students handed in the assignment?
     c.   Which French actress won the international prize?
          *Which French actress did win the international prize?
     d.   I don't know how many articles Chomsky has written.
          *I don't know how many articles has Chomsky written.

The above data indicate that the inversion characteristic of *wh*-extraction in matrix contexts should not be analyzed merely by reference to the trace of the movement; if that were the case, we would predict an object/adjunct asymmetry.[4] These facts should instead be analyzed by making reference to the landing site for the extracted *wh*-phrase. Accordingly, Rizzi (1990b) invokes May's (1985) Wh-Criterion, a condition on well-formedness, reproduced in (10). While the Wh-Criterion is an LF criterion, the general patterns of overt movement suggest that the [wh] feature is strong in English and thus the criterion must be satisfied at S-structure.

(10) Wh-Criterion
     a. Each +wh X° must be in a specifier-head relation with a *wh*-phrase.
     b. Each *wh*-phrase must be in a specifier-head relation with a +wh X°.

The [wh] feature may be specified on an embedded C by the selectional properties of verbs such as *wonder*, and *wh*-movement ensures that the *wh*-phrase moves to the embedded [Spec, C]; Infl-to-C movement is excluded in (11a) because the head C is filled—it bears a [wh] feature, and therefore movement into C would result in a violation of the Projection Principle (cf. Rizzi and Roberts 1989). For main clauses such as (9a–b), where selectional properties are unavailable to license a [wh] feature, Rizzi suggests that Infl can be specified [wh], a claim that finds evidence in the special form that a [wh] Infl may take in some languages, such as Kikuyu, Chamorro, Palauan, Moore, and Hausa (cf. Rizzi 1990a and references cited there). Then, the role of inversion in matrix contexts in English, as in (11b), is to carry the [wh] feature to a position where it can satisfy principle (10a). The [wh] Infl is moved to C and the empty verb *do* is inserted to support the stranded Infl. Finally, according to Rizzi, inversion is suspended with subject extraction because the requirement on the [wh] feature of Infl is satisfied by the tail of the *wh*-chain, as shown in (11c).

(11) a. I wonder [$_{CP}$ who$_i$ C$_{+wh}$ [$_{IP}$ John saw t_i?
    b. Who$_i$ did$_{j+wh}$ [$_{IP}$ John t_j see t_i?
    c. Who$_i$ [$_{IP}$ t_i Infl$_{+wh}$ saw John?

However, such an account of subject extraction leaves unexplained the facts of contraction, shown in (12a–b). Contraction, which is disallowed across a subject trace, is permissible between the *wh*-subject and the auxiliary, suggesting that the subject and Infl must be contiguous. Because there is no *do* support, we assume the *wh*-subject and Infl are adjacent in IP (rather than CP), in a structure illustrative of Chomsky's (1986) Vacuous Movement Hypothesis. On such an account, the matrix subject *wh*-phrase remains in [Spec, I] and satisfies the Wh-Criterion by specifier-head agreement with Infl, as in (12c).

(12) a. Who$_i$ did John want to see t_i →Who did John wanna see?
    b. Who$_i$ did John want t_i to win →*Who did John wanna win?
    c. Who has seen John → Who's seen John?

4.3.2 *Wh*-Questions in German

German is a true V2 language because the initial position in matrix clauses is occupied by any maximal projection—including *wh*- and non-*wh*-arguments, adverbials, and adjuncts—and the verb appears in second position, as shown in the data below, drawn from Vikner 1990.[5]

(13) a. Die   Kinder   sahen   den   Film.
       the   children   saw   the   film
      'The children saw the film.'
    b. Diesen   Film   haben   die Kinder gesehen.
       this   film   have   the children seen
      'The children have seen this film.'
    c. Gestern   sahen   die   Kinder   den   Film.
       yesterday   saw   the   children   the   film
      'The children saw the film yesterday.'

Like English, German demonstrates a matrix-versus-embedded contrast with respect to word patterns in *wh*-extraction. In matrix *wh*-clauses, the *wh*-constituent and the finite verb raise to CP, as in (14);[6] in embedded contexts, the *wh*-phrase moves to clause-initial position, but the verb remains in final position, as in (15). (It merits noting that German is OV, head final in Infl, and likely in VP as well.)

(14) a. Wieviele Artikel hat Chomsky geschrieben?
       'How many articles has Chomsky written?'
   b. Um wieviel Uhr haben die Studenten die Hausaufgaben abgegeben?
       'At what time have the students handed in the assignment?'
   c. Welche französische Schauspielerin gewann den internationalen Preis?
       'Which French actress won the international award?'

(15) a. Ich weiß nicht, wieviele Artikel Chomsky geschrieben hat.
       *Ich weiß nicht, wieviele Artikel hat Chomsky geschrieben.
       'I don't know how many articles Chomsky has written.'
   b. Ich weiß nicht, um wieviel Uhr die Studenten die Hausaufgaben abgegeben haben.
       *Ich weiß nicht, um wieviel Uhr haben die Studenten die Hausaufgaben abgegeben.
       'I don't know at what time the students have handed in the assignment.'
   c. Ich weiß nicht, welche französische Schauspielerin den internationalen Preis gewann.
       *Ich weiß nicht, welche französische Schauspielerin gewann den internationalen Preis.
       'Which French actress has won the prize?'

In the view espoused here, a [wh] feature resides on C in German, consistent with the approach taken by Lohnstein (2000), who proposes that the CP (he names it Modus Phrase, hence MP) rules the clause mode. The [wh] feature in C attracts the *wh*-constituent to [Spec, C], where it enters a Spec-head agreement relation, ensuring that the Wh-Criterion is satisfied. As already mentioned, in embedded *wh*-questions in German the finite verb does not move up to C, as it does in matrix sentences. This asymmetry regarding the surface position of the verb has been related to the Doubly Filled Comp Filter, although more recent approaches seek to explain this fact by means of feature design. For example, one candidate solution elaborated in Müller (2007) consists in assuming a Q-feature on C that has to be licensed (in current terms, checked or valued) by a Q-feature on Infl. If the Q-feature on C is strong it attracts Infl and hence the verb incorporates into it. If the feature on C is not strong, then movement of Infl to C is precluded. An alternative is found in Struckmeier (2007a, 2007b), which propose that uninterpretable features in C render the clause dependent, whereas interpretable features in C render it independent. In our analysis we would have to assume that [wh] is an uninterpretable feature that has to be licensed by either of two means: by movement of the finite verb to C or by entering a licensing (Agree) relation with a *wh*-selecting matrix verb in an upper clause.

4.3.3 *Wh*-Questions in Spanish

Spanish demonstrates a paradigm of *wh*-movement and subject-Infl inversion that is distinct from what is observed for English and German. First, unlike in English (but similar to German), Spanish also shows movement of full verbs into Infl. Moreover, unlike the subject/nonsubject and main/embedded asymmetries of English and German, Spanish demonstrates an argument/adjunct asymmetry. Extraction of arguments triggers obligatory Infl + V-subject order in main and embedded clauses alike, while extraction of adjuncts does not (cf. Torrego 1984; Groos and Bok-Bennema 1986; Goodall 1991, 1993; Toribio 1990, 1993c; Suñer 1994).[7] As shown in (16), the same patterns are maintained in embedded contexts.

(16) a.   ¿Cuántos artículos ha escrito Chomsky?
           *¿Cuántos artículos Chomsky ha escrito?
           'How many articles has Chomsky written?'
      b.   ¿A qué hora entregaron los estudiantes la tarea?
           ¿A qué hora los estudiantes entregaron la tarea?
           'At what time did the students hand in the assignment?'
      c.   ¿Qué actriz francesa ganó el premio internacional?
           'What French actress won the international award?'
      d.   No sé cuántos artículos ha escrito Chomsky.
           *No sé cuántos artículos Chomsky ha escrito.
           'I don't know how many articles Chomsky has written.'
      e.   No sé a qué hora entregaron los estudiantes la tarea.
           No sé a qué hora los estudiantes entregaron la tarea.
           'I don't know at what time the students handed in the assignment.'
      f.   No sé qué actriz francesa ganó el premio nacional.
           'I don't know what French actress won the international award.'

To understand how the Wh-Criterion is satisfied in the Spanish constructions exemplified above, it is instructive to identify the final position of the [wh] Infl and the landing site of *wh*-phrases. Suñer (1994) provides convincing evidence from adverbial placement and sentential negation that the verb always raises into Infl, but does not move into C. The position of the *wh*-phrase is a more contested issue. In her well-known work on inversion in Spanish, Torrego (1984) claims that subject-verb inversion takes place in Spanish when a *wh*-argument or its trace appears in Comp. In such cases, she claims, the verb preposes to the S-adjunction position. Of course, in the X-bar theoretic framework of Chomsky (1986 and following), Comp must consist of two positions—a head C and a specifier. Thus, Torrego's proposal is consistent with *wh*-movement to [Spec, C] and verb raising to C, and since adjuncts are not arguments of the verb, inversion is not obligatorily triggered. Further evidence of the position of the *wh*-phrase may be found in the position of the subject, because these are inextricably related in the phrase structure view adopted, in which the subject is base generated within the projection of VP (cf. Zagona 1982; Contreras 1987; Koopman and Sportiche 1991; Toribio 1993b, 1993c). From this perspective, [Spec, I] is a non-θ position. Less clear, however, is whether [Spec, I] should additionally serve as a potential A′ position.[8]

Goodall (1991, 1993) assumes that [Spec, I] is a potential A′ position to which a *wh*-phrase or the subject may move, resulting in the complementarity observed (cf. Groos and Bok-Bennema 1986). However, Goodall additionally provides evidence, drawn from Torrego 1985, that *wh*-phrases are in [Spec, C].[9] Given the apparent contradiction that *wh*-phrases and subjects compete for the same position, and that they occupy different positions, Goodall's solution is to propose that movement of *wh*-arguments is first to [Spec, I] and then to [Spec, C].[10] In doing so, he predicts the existence of three types of *wh*-movement—movement into [Spec, C], into [Spec, I], or into both through a cyclic process. As for *wh*-adjuncts, Goodall assumes that *wh*-words such as *por qué* 'why' are base generated in [Spec, C], as proposed for French by Rizzi (1990a); since there is no *wh*-movement, [Spec, I] is available for the subject.[11]

Suñer (1994) asserts that *wh*-movement in Spanish is uniform: all *wh*-phrases—argumental and adjunct alike—move to [Spec, C]. The question that becomes central to Suñer's work is why the non-*wh* subject is prohibited from appearing in [Spec, I] when a *wh*-argument occupies [Spec, C]. In answer to this query, Suñer proposes that a special relation of Argumental Agreement, a subtype of Relativized Minimality[12] (cf. Rizzi 1990a), holds between the *wh*-argument in [Spec, C] and the predicate in Infl.[13] In accordance with Argumental Agreement Licensing, C will bear the feature [argumental] by virtue of being in a specifier-head relation with a fronted *wh*-argument. This feature must be locally licensed by a selecting predicate; thus, no other arguments may intervene between C and the Infl + V complex. In other words, her claim is that argumentals must meet a strict locality condition that holds between C and the position that V (or Aux) occupies. Thus, subject preposing in nonsubject interrogatives would result in a violation of Argumental Agreement Licensing; a subject in [Spec, I] would violate minimality in terms of the feature [argumental]. Of course, when an adjunct-*wh* occupies [Spec, C], the locality condition is not operative since C does not inherit the [argumental] feature; therefore, the subject may move to [Spec, I]. In Suñer's analysis, then, Move-α carries the *wh*-phrase to [Spec, C] and the verb remains in Infl. In embedded clauses, the *wh*-phrase is in a specifier-head relation with a selected [wh] C and the Wh-Criterion is satisfied. For matrix clauses, however, Suñer must assume that movement of the *wh*-phrase into [Spec, C] induces a [wh] feature on the head C that is otherwise unspecified for this feature, a process unavailable in English (cf. Rizzi 1991).

Finally, Toribio (1993c) develops an account that reconciles the contradictions in the characterizations offered by Goodall and Suñer. That work aims to explain the argument/adjunct asymmetry by positing distinct landing sites for the two phrase types, a distinction that is based on the specifications on Infl and the concomitant nature of [Spec, I].[14] Specifically, the claim is that only *wh*-arguments will move through [Spec, I], as achieved by one of two means. In the spirit of Rizzi 1990b, Toribio proposes that in matrix clauses, where selection is not available as a licenser of the feature [wh], Infl may be specified [wh] only when an argument nominal in the clause is so marked— that is, the [wh] specification will result from feature checking between Infl (as a projection of V) and *wh*-arguments.[15] Since [Spec, I] may be a potential landing site for arguments only, we assume that adjunct-*wh* elements must move directly into [Spec, C] and will be licensed via the only means possible, namely, by inducing agreement on the head C via "dynamic agreement" (Rizzi 1991).[16] As outlined, Toribio's account is consonant with Goodall's claim that argument *wh*-extraction may proceed via [Spec, I]. This account is also compatible with Suñer's proposal in that the argumental feature of the *wh*-phrase must be matched or checked by the feature on the licensing head. This means that the Wh-Criterion will be satisfied in one of two projections in Spanish argument *wh*-extraction. It may be satisfied in IP: in matrix clauses, the *wh*-phrase raises to [Spec, I], a potential A′ position, where it is in a specifier-head relation with the [wh] Infl. And it may be satisfied in CP: in embedded clauses, the *wh*-phrase undergoes subsequent movement to [Spec, C], where it is in a specifier-head relation with the [wh] feature that resides on the selected C. Adjunct *wh*-phrases demonstrate disparate behavior, which is explained, in part, by restricting the specifications on Infl to reflect only the features of its arguments, as in Suñer 1994.

4.4   Word Order in *Wh*-Extraction in English-Spanish and German-Spanish Codeswitching

The data discussed in the foregoing sections have foregrounded crosslinguistic asymmetries with respect to word-order patterns in *wh*-movement constructions. Nonetheless, the Wh-Criterion has been shown to be operative in English, German, and Spanish alike, with language-specific differences ascribed to the locus of the [wh] feature on structural projections, and the concomitant differences in the configurations in which the criterion is satisfied. This characterization of *wh*-operator movement in English, German, and Spanish is essential to an understanding of the constraints on *wh*-movement in English-Spanish and German-Spanish codeswitching. On the premise that codeswitching is constrained by the constructs of the component grammars, we predict that *wh*-movement in codeswitching is likewise characterized by reference to the Wh-Criterion, an invariant principle, together with the noted language-specific characters of the nodes C, Infl, and V. To be clear: the operations implicated in specific derivations are the same for all languages, but a particular language is defined by its lexicon and the feature bundles of lexical and functional heads that enter the derivation (cf. Simpson 2000 for discussion of parameterization in *wh*-movement).

4.4.1   *Wh*-Questions in English-Spanish Codeswitching

Consider first the patterns of codeswitching grammaticality attested in the English-Spanish matrix *wh*-extractions in (17–19).[17]

(17) *Matrix wh-object extractions*
    a.   *¿Cuántos artículos* has Chomsky written?
    a.′ *¿Cuántos artículos* Chomsky has written?
    b.   How many articles *ha escrito Chomsky?*
    b.′ *How many articles *Chomsky ha escrito?*

(18) *Matrix wh-adjunct extractions*
    a.   *¿A qué hora* did the students hand in the assignment?
    a.′ *¿A qué hora* the students handed in the assignment?
    b.   At what time *entregaron los estudiantes la tarea?*
    b.′ At what time *los estudiantes entregaron la tarea?*

(19) *Matrix wh-subject extractions*
    a.   *¿Qué actriz francesa* won the international award?
    b.   What French actress *ganó el premio internacional?*

In (17a), the *wh*-phrase is extracted to [Spec, C] ([Spec, I] is unavailable since it is the position in which the subject receives nominative Case in English), and the movement of Infl to C ensures that the Wh-Criterion is met in CP. Example (17a′) is ill formed because the [wh] Infl is not in a specifier-head relation with the *wh*-phrase, and therefore the Wh-Criterion is not satisfied. In (17b), [Spec, I] is available for A′ movement and as such, the Wh-Criterion is observed in IP, precluding subject preposing, as in the ungrammatical (17b′). Similar contrasting word-order patterns are effected by the operation of the Wh-Criterion with *wh*-adjunct extraction in (18), as consistent with the preceding discussion. Lastly, the subject *wh*-extraction data in (19) demonstrate that the Wh-Criterion is satisfied in [Spec, I] in matrix subject extraction, because it is in both English and Spanish.

Consider next the patterns of grammaticality attested in the embedded extractions in (20).

(20) *Embedded wh-object and wh-adjunct extractions*
    a.   I don't know *cuántos artículos* Chomsky has written.
    a.′ *I don't know *cuántos artículos* has Chomsky written.
    b.   I don't know *a qué hora* the students handed in the assignment.
    b.′ *I don't know *a qué hora* did the students hand in the assignment.
    c.   *No sé* how many articles *ha escrito Chomsky.*
    c.′ **No sé* how many articles *Chomsky ha escrito.*
    d.   *No sé* at what time *entregaron los estudiantes la tarea.*
    d.′ *No sé* at what time *los estudiantes entregaron la tarea.*

In taking account of the patterns in (20a–b), we assume that the matrix verb selects a [wh] CP and the embedded *wh*-argument and *wh*-adjunct phrase moves to [Spec, C], where the Wh-Criterion is satisfied; Infl raising in the English embedded clause is unnecessary and therefore excluded, as shown in (20a′–b′). In (20c, c′), the Spanish main verb likewise selects a [wh] CP and the embedded Spanish Infl bears the [wh] feature in agreement with its *wh*-argument. Therefore, the embedded [Spec, I] (a potential A′ position) is available only for the *wh*-phrase, because it passes on to [Spec, C], but not for the non-*wh*-subject. When the embedded Spanish clause Infl is not marked with the [wh] feature, as with *wh*-adjunct extraction, [Spec, I] is available for subject preposing, as in (20d).

The generalization that emerges from the English-Spanish codeswitching data in (17–20) is that differential patterns of *wh*-movement and subject-Infl(+V) inversion in codeswitching are determined not by the language of the *wh*-phrase, but by the properties associated with the functional heads C and Infl + V of the clause from which *wh*-movement has taken place. For example, an English *wh*-object may be licensed in [Spec, I] by the [wh] Infl of a Spanish clause, and a Spanish *wh*-phrase may be licensed in [Spec, C] by the [wh] C

+ Infl of an English clause. Thus, the Wh-Criterion interacts with language-specific differences in the locus of the [wh] feature in constraining the form that codeswitched *wh*-questions take.

4.4.2　*Wh*-Questions in German-Spanish Codeswitching

The data from German-Spanish codeswitching parallel those of English-Spanish codeswitching in the sense that they respect the Wh-Criterion. Consider the data on matrix *wh*-extraction in (21–23):[18]

(21) *Matrix wh-object extractions*
    a.　*¿Cuántos artículos* hat Chomsky geschrieben?
    a.′ *¿Cuántos artículos* Chomsky hat geschrieben?
    a.″ *¿Cuántos artículos* Chosmky geschrieben hat?
    b.　Wieviele Artikel *ha escrito Chomsky*?
    b.′ *Wieviele Artikel *Chomsky ha escrito*?

(22) *Matrix wh-adjunct extraction*
    a.　*¿A qué hora* haben die Studenten die Hausaufgaben abgegeben?
    a.′ *¿A qué hora* die Studenten die Hausaufgaben abgegeben haben?
    a.″ *¿A qué hora* die Studenten haben die Hausaufgaben abgegeben?
    b.　Um wieviel Uhr *entregaron los estudiantes la tarea*?
    b.′ ?Um wieviel Uhr *los estudiantes entregaron la tarea*?

(23) *Matrix wh-subject extractions*
    a.　*¿Qué actriz francesa* hat den internationalen Preis gewonnen?
    a.′ *¿Qué actriz francesa* den internationalen Preis gewonnen hat?
    a.″ *¿Qué actriz francesa* den internationalen Preis hat gewonnen?
    b.　Welche französische Schauspielerin *ganó el premio internacional*?
    b.′ *Welche französische Schauspielerin *el premio internacional ganó*?

The data in (21a, 22a, 23a) demonstrate matrix extraction of a Spanish *wh*-phrase from a "German" clause, and the corresponding (b) data demonstrate matrix extraction of a German *wh*-constituent from an otherwise "Spanish" clause. Because the argument-versus-adjunct status of the extracted *wh*-constituent is of no consequence for word-order patterns in *wh*-extraction in German, there are no attendant asymmetries with extraction of a Spanish *wh*-constituent in (21a) versus (22a); hence, the data in (21–23) will be treated at once. In (21a) the German C bears a [wh] feature that is checked with the fronting of the *wh*-constituent to [Spec, C], and the verb raises to second position, as it does in all matrix clauses. (21a′) and (21a″) confirm that movement of the verb to second position is obligatory; it cannot remain in V or in Infl (though the latter is available in embedded clauses). More interesting are the data in which a German *wh*-constituent is fronted in a Spanish clause; recall that Spanish demonstrates an argument/adjunct asymmetry. In (21b) the German *wh*-phrase stands in a Spec-head relation with the Spanish [wh] Infl; accordingly, subject preposing to [Spec, I] is precluded, as in (21b'). However, adjunct phrases, such as *Um wieviel Uhr* in (22b), move directly to [Spec, C] and allow for the subject to move to [Spec, I], consistent with the analyses put forth above.[19] Finally, subject extraction likewise patterns as expected: the *wh*-subject moves to [Spec, C] in the German clause, where it enters a Spec-head agreement relation with the [wh] marked C; the finite verb must raise to C (23a, a', a''). In the corresponding Spanish clause, we observe that the German *wh*-subject agrees with the [wh] feature of Infl, and the verb obligatorily raises to Infl.

The data from German-Spanish embedded *wh*-questions are likewise as predicted:[20]

(24) *Embedded wh-objects and wh-adjunct extractions*
    a.   Ich weiß nicht, *cuántos artículos* Chomsky geschrieben hat.
    b.   Ich weiß nicht, *a qué hora* die Studenten die Hausaufgaben abgegeben haben.
    c.   *No sé* wieviele Artikel *ha escrito Chomsky.*
    c.' *No sé* wie viele Artikel *Chomsky ha escrito.*
    d.   *No sé* um wieviel Uhr *entregaron los estudiantes la tarea.*
    d.' *No sé* um wieviel Uhr *los estudiantes entregaron la tarea.*

The Spanish *wh*-object in (24a) moves to [Spec, C] of the German clause, where it stands in an agreement relation with the [wh] C. The finite verb stays in Infl, as is the norm in German subordinate clauses. Note that the account remains the same for adjunct fronting in German subordinate clauses. In contrast, extraction of a German phrase from a Spanish embedded clause does demonstrate the anticipated argument/adjunct asymmetry. If the *wh*-constituent is an argument, it moves through [Spec, I] and thus subject preposing is illicit (24c'), but extraction of the adjunct is compatible with the preposed subject (24d').

4.5 From the Government-Binding Operator Criterion to the Minimalist Program Feature Checking

At this juncture, it is worth pointing out that while Rizzi's Wh-Criterion can adequately characterize the patterns of word order previously considered, it was not intended to account for all instances of inversion or *wh*-movement. Similar patterns of inversion are observed in constructions that do not relate to *wh*-movement, and some *wh*-movement is not accompanied by inversion. Consider the negative fronting of English, Spanish, and English-Spanish codeswitching, shown in (25–27). In (25), the subject/nonsubject asymmetry observed for English matrix *wh*-questions is evident; in (26), the argument/adjunct asymmetry now familiar from Spanish *wh*-extraction is present; in (27) subject extraction does not trigger inversion.

(25) *Object negative-operator extraction*
    a.   Ni un alma vio Juan en el cementerio.
         *Ni un alma Juan vio en el cementerio.
    b.   Not a soul did John see at the cemetery.
         *Not a soul John saw at the cemetery.

(26) *Adjunct negative-operator extraction*
    a.   Por ningún motivo viajaría mi padre al extranjero.
         Por ningún motivo mi padre viajaría al extranjero.
    b.   For no reason would my father travel abroad.
         *For no reason my father would travel abroad.

(27) *Subject negative-operator extraction*
    a. Ni un paciente llegó a tiempo esta mañana.
    b. Not one patient arrived on time this morning.

And, as with *wh*-movement, we predict that English-Spanish and German-Spanish codeswitching data will be consistent with these language-specific patterns. The data in (28–30) confirm this prediction.

(28) *Object negative-operator extraction*
    a.   *Ni un alma* did John see at the cemetery.
    a′ *Ni un alma* John saw at the cemetery.
    b.   Not a soul *vio Juan en el cementerio.*
    b.′ *Not a soul *Juan vio en el cementerio.*
    c.   Keine Seele *vio Juan en el cementerio.*
    c.′ *Keine Seele *Juan vio en el cementerio.*

(29) *Adjunct negative-operator extraction*
    a.   *Por ningún motivo* would my father travel abroad.
    a.′ *Por nigún motivo* my father would travel abroad.
    b.   For no reason *viajaría mi padre al extranjero.*
    b.′ For no reason *mi padre viajaría al extranjero.*
    c.   Aus keinem Grund *viajaría mi padre al extranjero.*
    c.′ Aus keinem Grund *mi padre viajaría al extranjero.*

(30) *Subject negative-operator extraction*
    a. *Ni un paciente* arrived on time this morning.
    b. Not one patient *llegó a tiempo esta mañana.*
    c. Nicht ein Patient *llegó a tiempo esta mañana.*

Thus, negative operators, irrespective of whether they correspond to English, Spanish, or German, appear to be licensed in the same agreement configurations as *wh*-elements. Note that since such operators are not specified for a [wh] feature, the attested patterns of inversion cannot be accounted for by the Wh-Criterion; an adequate characterization should additionally incorporate a condition that is particular to negative-operator movement (cf. Haegemann and Zanuttini 1991). A more parsimonious solution would seek to unify these constructions. With this in mind, Rizzi (1990b, 1991) later proposes, based on Klima 1964, that "affective operators must be in a specifier-head configuration with a head marked with the relevant affective feature" (1991, 11). However, as we will observe in the ensuing paragraphs, such a criterion cannot be extended to account for the facts of word order with *wh*-movement in relative clauses.[21]

Consider the English, Spanish, and English-Spanish codeswitched relative clauses in (31). (Parallel German-Spanish codeswitching data is unavailable since it is ruled out on independent grounds; cf. González-Vilbazo 2005 for an account based on Case agreement in codeswitching.)

(31) a.   The children to whom Mary gave the gift
         *The children to whom did Mary give the gift
     b.   Los niños a quienes María hizo un regalo
         Los niños a quienes hizo María un regalo
     c.   The children *a quienes* Mary gave the gift
         *The children *a quienes* did Mary give the gift
     d.   *Los niños* to whom *María hizo un regalo*
         Los niños to whom *hizo María un regalo*

As shown, inversion is not triggered (though it is optional in Spanish). *Wh*-movement in relative clauses, then, circumvents the inversion required to satisfy the Wh-Criterion in *wh*-questions; it must be satisfied by some other means. However, it would be desirable to link these movements and licensing mechanisms under a single criterion.

In accounting for the data in (31), we assume relative operators quantify over a set delimited by the head noun, and yet, as adjunct modifiers, they do not bear a relation of selection with the head noun. The feature-sharing relation that holds between the relative operator and the head noun is one of predication; predication coindexation is obligatory for the interpretation of the relative operator. In fact, relative operators, unlike the other operators considered in this work, cannot remain in situ; they must move to [Spec, C] to be in a predication relation with the heads N and D of the relative construction, such as in (32).[22] Because the relative operator must be licensed via predication agreement, considerations of economy dictate that Infl/V will not be specified for [wh] features. Therefore, Infl raising to C is precluded in English, and [Spec, I] is available for fronting of the subject in Spanish.

(32)

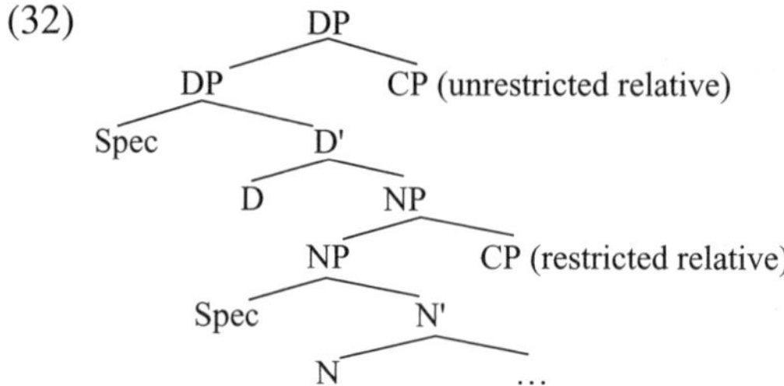

In unifying the constellation of patterns presented in the previous paragraphs, Toribio (1993c) proposes a basic principle, namely, the core structural notion of agreement in (33). In particular, the claim rests on the assumption that operators, broadly defined in (34), must obey a locality condition in (35), in the ways outlined in (36).[23] Thus, an operator can be licensed by specifier-head agreement with an appropriate head, where [α] ranges over different operator types.

(33) Agreement is a local relationship between two nodes α and β such that α and β share features.

(34) An operator is a phrase that occupies an A′ specifier, which heads an A′ chain and binds a variable.

(35) The Operator Criterion: operators must be properly licensed.

(36) An operator [α] is properly licensed if it stands in an agreement relation with an [α] head.

The application to *wh*-questions and negative fronting is straightforward: the operator is licensed by the checking of [α]-features in the specifier-head relation.[24] For relative clauses, the *wh*-phrase (or its null counterpart) is licensed by the head of the relative clause, with which it bears a predication relation, thereby obviating the need for movement of Infl to C. Thus, though similar in spirit to Rizzi's Wh-Criterion, the Operator Criterion is arrived at independently (cf. Toribio 1989), and it differs markedly from Rizzi's Affect Criterion in uniting the licensing conditions held to constrain various types of operator movement under one agreement condition.[25]

Summarizing, the well-formedness of operator movement constructions rests on universal principles (e.g., the Operator Criterion) and structural relations (e.g., specifier-head agreement and predication agreement), in interaction with language-specific feature specifications of $X°$ elements (e.g., the features of C, Infl, and V). This holds true of English, Spanish, German, English-Spanish, and German-Spanish codeswitching as well. Thus, the codewitching data receive a natural account within the theory of linguistic competence—a set of general principles and particular parameters that characterize natural languages.

The analysis of operator movement in codeswitching that has been motivated thus far is empirically adequate and is theoretically sound, as articulated in a preminimalist framework that developed over nearly a decade. As will be shown, the analysis is also in line with the general approach set forth in Chomsky's (1995) Minimalist Program. Chomsky proposes a simple and constrained conception of the grammar of human language, comprised of minimal assumptions dictated by conceptual grounds alone. The language faculty consists of two central components: a lexicon, acquired by experience, and an invariant computational system. The computational system is composed of principles (e.g., recalling the feature-checking Operator Criterion), with language-specific variation restricted to functional elements (recalling the properties of C and Infl noted throughout) and general properties of the lexicon (recalling the scopal features of interrogative and negative phrases).

In the Minimalist Program, the derivation of a particular linguistic expression involves a choice of items from the lexicon and a computation that constructs the articulatory-perceptual and conceptual-intentional interface representations, corresponding to PF and LF, respectively. The computational system is purely derivational, involving successive operations leading to a linguistic expression of a particular language, with PF and LF representations consisting of legitimate objects. Conditions on well-formedness determine which derivations and derived objects are licit and interpretable at the interface levels. A derivation converges at an interface level if it yields a representation satisfying Full Interpretation, otherwise it crashes. Given this system, syntactic structures are built derivationally from the bottom up, through the construction of syntactic objects drawn from a numeration (by Select) or from objects already formed (by Merge and Move).[26]

It has been noted above that in earlier models, lexical items were envisioned as being introduced in their base form and moving in the course of derivation to acquire morphological markings (e.g., NP movement for Case marking;

verb movement for affixation). In articulating the minimalist assumptions, Chomsky proposes that lexical items are selected from the lexicon fully endowed with their inflectional features, including φ-features, Case features, and scopal features. These features, collectively referred to as Case features, must be checked or matched against the specifications on functional nodes. This process of checking is represented as a generalized form of the Case Filter: all Case features must be checked. However, unlike the traditional Case Filter, which was assumed to hold at S-structure, checking may occur at any point in the derivation up to LF, as required by the principle of Full Interpretation. Whether checking takes place in overt syntax or in the LF component depends on the strength attributed to features. Strong features must be checked and eliminated prior to Spell-Out, but weak features remain after Spell-Out— in fact, by the economy principle Procrastinate, they must remain—and are checked instead at the level of LF. (Chomsky would subsequently propose that with covert movement, only the features that need checking move.) For checking and convergence to occur, an element with some feature must be in a specific structural relation with a checker for that feature. The Checking Domain of a head comprises all elements included in its maximal projection, where inclusion is understood in the sense of Chomsky 1986, and thus includes adjuncts and specifiers, but excludes elements contained within complements of the head. Unchecked features will be uninterpretable at the output levels (in violation of Full Interpretation) and the result will be a crash.

By way of example, consider the checking of verbal features. Following Pollock 1989, Chomsky articulates the Infl node into Agr and Tense.[27] In order for a derivation to converge, Agr and Tense must contain the same φ-features that appear on the verb. To check its agreement and tense features, the verb will raise to adjoin to Agr and Tense before or after Spell-Out.[28] In English, the verbal features of Tense and Agr are weak and hence may survive into PF without ill effect. Thus, as consistent with the principle Procrastinate, overt raising prior to PF is barred, and as a consequence, English main verbs are realized within the VP. This is not the case in Spanish. As noted, data concerning the placement of adverbs and negative markers provides evidence of overt verb raising in Spanish. Because movement is triggered by strong features, we assume that the verbal features of Agr and Tense are strong, ensuring that the verb will raise into these functional projections prior to Spell-Out. When the verbal features of these inflectional heads have checked the features on the lexical item, they disappear. If the verb does not raise to Agr and Tense overtly, the strong verbal features survive to PF, rendering the derivation illicit. Therefore, overt verb raising is a prerequisite for convergence in Spanish.

The functional nodes Agr and Tense also contain nominal features—the φ-features and Case features—that will be checked off against the corresponding inflectional features of DPs. To check its Agr and Tense features, the subject DP will raise to the specifier positions of these functional projections. In English, the nominal features of Agr are weak and therefore may appear at PF. In contrast, the nominal features of Tense are strong, and therefore raising of the subject DP to [Spec, Tense] occurs prior to Spell-Out. Spanish differs from English in this respect. In Spanish, the nominal Agr features are strong (a prerequisite for the licensing of null subjects), and subject DPs must raise to [Spec, Agr] prior to Spell-Out to ensure convergence. In contrast, the nominal features on Tense are weak in Spanish (licensing postverbal subjects) and may appear at PF without causing a crash. Since convergence is compatible with Procrastinate, raising of the subject is delayed until LF and the subject DP may be realized in post-verbal position, as determined by discourse information.[29] (Note that since all movement is motivated by feature checking, and hence there is no optional movement, we must assume that strong features relating to Focus and Topic are responsible for triggering movement of constituents to initial position (cf. Zubizaretta 1998).)

In this approach, crosslinguistic pairings of Spanish and English verbs and Agr/Tense specifications will be illicit (cf. Poplack 1980; Woolford 1983; Belazi, Rubin, and Toribio 1994), owing to the resultant conflict in features. However, as shown in (37), a derivation in which the subject DP bears φ- and Case features that are appropriately paired with those specified on Agr and Tense will be well formed, irrespective of whether the expression is English, Spanish, or a combination of the two; when there is a feature nonmatch, the derivation crashes. Subject-Infl agreement, then, is merely a subcase of feature checking.

(37) a. The students are/*is very hardworking.
     b. Los estudiantes son/*es muy trabajadores.
     c. The students *son/*es muy trabajadores*.
     d. *Los estudiantes* are/*is very trabajadores.

Turning to the formal features of *wh-* and negative phrases, we assume that they are assigned to lexical items and are themselves syntactic objects that are accessible in the course of a derivation. Like the φ-features and nominal features previously discussed, these features establish a checking relation with features of the same type and are checked as a prerequisite for convergence. The important positions in the Checking Domain of X are the specifier and adjunct positions, where operators will check formal features against an appropriate X. In an English matrix operator movement derivation, we assume that the operator is drawn from the lexicon bearing strong formal features. For checking and convergence, the operator must raise to [Spec, C], where it is in the Checking Domain of C + Infl; because the scopal morphological features are strong in English, these movements must apply prior to Spell-Out. In a Spanish matrix operator movement derivation, the operator is likewise drawn from the lexicon bearing strong features that motivate movement in the overt syntax; however, the Checking Domain for operator features may be TP (equivalent to Infl). This same configuration, schematized in (38), licenses operator constructions in codeswitching, as anticipated.[30]

(38)
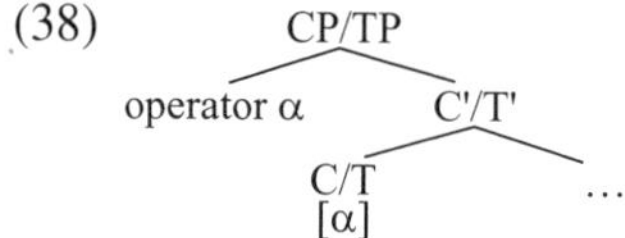

Moreover, recall that like specifiers, adjuncts are also contained within the Checking Domain of a head. Schematically, the nodes circled in the tree below constitute the Checking Domain of the head H in (39).[31]

(39)
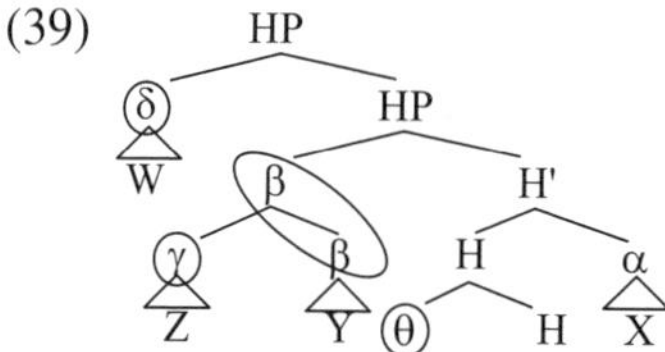

Therefore, the adjunct CP in (40) stands within the Checking Domains of the heads N and D of which the relative clause is predicated. (We leave open the question of whether the operators that occupy [Spec, C] of the adjunct clause are directly checked against by D and N, or whether this checking relation is mediated by C, which acquires its features from these functional heads.)

(40)
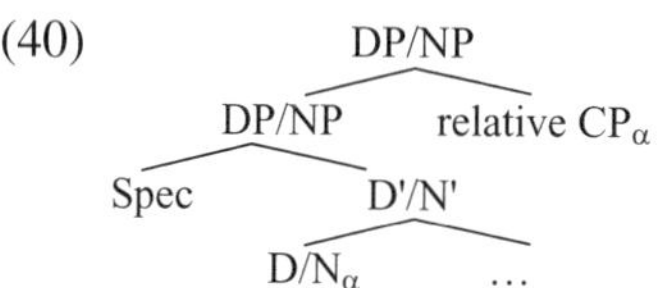

All movements thus receive a uniform treatment, all motivated by the requirement that features be checked and that all checking be achieved in a uniform configuration.

Having considered the issue of operator movement from a minimalist perspective, we conclude that crosslinguistic variation (English vs. German vs. Spanish) with regard to phenomena such as operator raising and subject-auxiliary inversion should be accounted for in terms of formal licensing conditions, specifically, the checking of operator features. Thus, the Operator Criterion in (35) is best viewed as a specific instantiation of a general feature-matching process—checking—in the computational component. On this view, then, the lexically encoded features [α] will induce derivations and produce derived objects that pertain to one particular language, or to both. This examination of the patterning of operator movement in Spanish-English codeswitching data has also been shown to further support the proposal of MacSwan (2000, chapter 1), who asserts that the well-formedness of a linguistic expression rests on its interpretability at the interface levels, regardless of whether the set of lexical items is associated with one or both languages.

We will not attempt to adapt our proposal to be consistent with recent minimalist developments (Chomsky 2000, 2001, 2005, 2006), because so far the program remains largely a sketch of a desired system. However, it should be clear that in further developing this program, it would prove worthwhile to consider not only monolingual data, but bilingual codeswitching data, since the latter can often reveal otherwise obscured details of the characteristics of the languages involved.[32]

4.6 Conclusions

To recapitulate, the data reviewed converge in demonstrating that English, German, and Spanish differ in significant respects and that these language-specific properties are mirrored in English-Spanish and German-Spanish codeswitched derivations. Specifically, we have observed that the patterns of word order attested in *wh*-questions, negative fronting, and relative clauses in English, Spanish, German, English-Spanish, and German-Spanish codeswitching may be characterized by reference to a core principle, Checking, and by appeal to the locus of the [α] feature specifications of the component languages that interact with this universal principle. Such a conceptualization not only succeeds in capturing the observed patterns of word order in operator movement in unilingual and codeswitched data, but it does so in a fashion consistent with general considerations of theoretical syntax. In sum, the analysis offered here has strong empirical and theoretical validity. More importantly, however, the foregoing discussion has made evident the potential benefits of the study of codeswitching for linguistic theory in elucidating aspects of Universal Grammar. As demonstrated, the analysis of operator movement in codeswitching reveals patterns of derivations that bolster syntactic-theoretical argumentation and corroborate the structures and principles of the Minimalist Program. Thus the study of codeswitching competence can both be informed by, and can contribute to, the continued advancement of linguistic theory.

Notes

This work was begun in 1997 as a study of word-order patterns in Spanish-English codeswitching (supported in part by a National Endowment for the Humanities Fellowship to the first author) and was resuscitated ten years later, encouraged by Jeff MacSwan and inspired by the work on German-Spanish codeswitching by the second author. We would like to express our gratitude to Teresa Satterfield, Hector Campos, Verónica González, Luis López-Carretero, Volker Struckmeier, and Dennis Ott for comments at distinct stages and on distinct parts of the chapter; the work has been much improved by their valuable comments and suggestions. Any remaining errors are ours.

1. Woolford's model represents an early generative reformulation of two constraints previously proposed in the literature: Poplack's (1981) Free Morpheme Constraint and Equivalence Constraint. The Free Morpheme Constraint accounts for the non-occurrence of word-internal switching; and the Equivalence Constraint predicts that codeswitching will be permitted where the grammars of Spanish and English coincide, but not where they diverge.

2. Throughout the text, italics will be employed to represent Spanish language segments of code-switched sentences.

3. Recent years have witnessed vigorous efforts to "map" the left periphery of the clause. Readers are referred in particular to "cartographic" approaches inspired by Rizzi's (1997) cartographic approach.

4. Recall that in Government-Binding Theory, movement is restricted by the Empty Category Principle, which requires that traces be properly governed. Proper-government is a subset of government, a conjunctive or disjunctive formulation of lexical (or θ)-government and coindexation (cf. Chomsky 1986 versus Rizzi 1990a). Object traces are properly governed (by the verb), but adjunct traces are not.

5. The position of the topic and its relation to the CP has been widely discussed. Rizzi (1997) proposes a split CP that would include a specific position for topics and Frey (2004a, 2004b), Fanselow (2004), and others discuss this possibility for German.

6. It is not clear, however, what position on a layered left periphery the *wh*-constituent has to move to. See Grewendorf 2002, 234ff for discussion of the landing (or merging) sites of short and long *wh*-extraction.

7. One reviewer suggests that the notion of discourse linking may be relevant. Although this suggestion is not explored here, it is worth pursuing in view of contrasts such as the following:

(i)   *Qué Juan compró en la librería?
      'What did Juan buy in the bookstore?'

(ii) ?Cuál de los nuevos libros de Chomsky Juan compró en la librería?
      'Which of Chomsky's new books did Juan buy in the bookstore?'

Consult Goodall 2004 for the development of such an analysis.

8. Koopman and Sportiche (1991) reject this possibility, defining as A-positions specifiers or complements of the θ-marking categories Infl, V, N, P, and A. In contrast,

Diesing (1991) suggests that in Yiddish [Spec, I] may be an A-position when occupied by the subject, or an A′ position when other elements occupy it.

9. Citing Torrego 1985, Goodall notes that a PP can be extracted out of a fronted *wh*-phrase, but not out of a preverbal subject because the PP trace is antecedent-governed, as in (ii), since the *wh*-phrase is in [Spec, C]; the subject, in (i), is in [Spec, I], so the trace it contains is not properly governed.

(i) *Esta es la autora de la que [varias traducciones *t*] han ganado premios.
     'This is the author whose various translations have won prizes.' (Torrego 1985)

(ii) ¿De qué autora no sabes [qué traducciones *t*] han ganado premios?
     'Which author don't you know what translations have won prizes?' (Torrego 1985)

10. This claim is rooted in the work of Kuroda (1988), who argues that in some languages the null [wh] C must agree with its specifier, and in the work of Rizzi (1990a), who proposes that a head may agree with its specifier, with the specifier of its complement, or with both.

11. But Goodall fails to consider data that demonstrate that the subject-Infl inversion pattern is also markedly absent from other types of adjunct extraction. On his account, these *wh*-phrases would also be base generated in [Spec, C]. Alternatively, Goodall would have to propose that *wh*-adjuncts, unlike *wh*-arguments, do not move through [Spec, I].

12. Minimality conditions guarantee that there will be one governor for each governee. Following Rizzi's (1990a) Relativized Minimality, minimality is relativized to the type of category involved such that, in a minimality configuration, proper government of an XP can only be blocked by an intervening XP and proper government of an $X°$ can only be blocked by an intervening $X°$.

13. According to Suñer's Argumental Agreement Licensing, (a) Argumental *wh*-phrases must be licensed through symmetric Arg-agreement between α (=[Spec, C]) and β (=C); (b) β Arg-agrees with γ (=V) only if β and γ are Arg-marked and no other Arg-marked element is closer to γ.

14. Corroborating evidence for this analysis is found in Welsh, a language that exhibits an argument/adjunct asymmetry similar to that observed in Spanish. In Welsh, argument extraction is accompanied by an agreeing complementizer, *a*. In contrast, nonargument extraction demonstrates the ordinary declarative complementizer *yr*, realized as *y* below, drawn from Sadler 1988. These data find a straightforward explanation if one assumes that only *wh*-arguments substitute into [Spec, C], where they are licensed by the head C, which agrees with the argument by specifier-head agreement. The *wh*-adjunct adjoins to [Spec, C], where it is licensed by the head C; crucially, the agreeing complementizer is excluded since [Spec, C] remains empty, and hence the default complementizer appears.

(i) Pwy   <u>a</u>   welodd   Mair?
     who   COMP-agr   saw   Mair
     'Who did Mair see?'

(ii) Pad   bryd   <u>y</u>   daw   ef?
     what   time   that   will-come   he
     'What time will he come?'

15. Such an account is consistent with both Rizzi 1990b, which assumes that Infl in English carries the requisite feature for operator licensing, and Suñer 1994, which assumes that V is responsible for said licensing.

16. The alternatives, whereby *wh*-adjuncts are base generated in [Spec, C] (cf. Rizzi 1990a), or base generated in or moved into an IP-adjunction position (cf. Travis 1991), are untenable on this analysis.

17. The codeswitched sentences were prepared by A. J. Toribio. The judgments reflect the author's intuition, and corroborating judgments have been elicited from naive and informed Spanish-English bilinguals in a variety of contexts, including informal interview settings, freshman seminars, pedagogical workshops, and syntax courses.

18. The codeswitching data have been constructed by K. E. González and have been corroborated by other bilingual German-Spanish codeswitchers.

19. K. E. González-Vilbazo, the main informant for this set of data, does not speak a Spanish dialect that includes this kind of optional subject movement with *wh*-adjunct extraction. We have only found one informant who speaks such a Spanish dialect and is bilingual in German. She accepted the datum without hesitating.

20. Ungrammaticality in codeswitched utterances can be due to a number of factors, in addition to those discussed in this chapter. The embedded sentences in (24) might sound somewhat marked, but this markedness strongly depends on the context and intonation of the utterance. For prosody, information structure, and codeswitching see González-Vilbazo and López-Carretero 2007.

21. See Kayne 1994 for a nonmovement account of relative clauses in which the relative clause is a complement of D (not N or N′), with clause-internal raising of the relativized noun:

(i)   The [CP photograph [C that John took [e]

(ii) La [CP fotografía [C que Juan tomó [e]

22. We assume that restrictive relatives adjoin to NP, whereas unrestrictive relatives adjoin to DP, a claim that has long been implicit in the literature (cf. Jackendoff 1977), and that was made explicit in Fabb 1987 and Murasugi 1991.

23. This characterization supersedes that proposed in Toribio 1990, where it is suggested that operators are licensed under government. However, the proposal developed in Toribio 1993c is rooted in that earlier work, where it is proposed that operator chains must be licensed by coindexation with a lexical head, on the well-founded assumption that theory allows for two types of coindexation: specifier-head agreement and predication agreement. It also supersedes Toribio 1993a, where it is suggested that argument and nonargument operators have distinct landing sites—Spec and an adjoined position, respectively.

24. Like Rizzi's Wh-Criterion, the Operator Criterion is an invariant, universal condition on LF well-formedness. However, it will apply to the syntax in English, German, and Spanish, the languages considered here.

25. We additionally note that the Operator Criterion only makes reference to the requirement on the operator. Recall that the Wh-Criterion had reciprocal requirements on a [wh] head: "Each +wh $X°$ must be in a specifier-head relation with a *wh*-phrase."

Operators need not be forced by the Operator Criterion to move to the specifier of an [op] head—considerations of scope will effect this movement (cf. May 1985; Chomsky 1986).

26. It should be pointed out that Move in the Minimalist Program differs markedly from its predecessor Move-α in Government-Binding Theory. First, Move is incorporated into the structure-building process; it changes the structure it operates on. In contrast, Move-α was structure-preserving, merely relocating objects in an existing structure. Second, Move takes a copy of the moved element and inserts it into another position, subsequently deleting the phonetic content of the original. Move-a displaces an element and leaves a trace. Finally, in the Minimalist Program, restrictions on movement fall out of Full Interpretation and economy measures such as the Last Resort Principle and the Minimal Link Condition. In Government-Binding, constraints such as the Empty Category Principle were proposed to operate alongside the movement process.

27. Chomsky would subsequently propose that Agr projections should be discarded on conceptual grounds.

28. This minimal assumption has its antecedents in Chomsky and Lasnik 1993. Whereas in traditional Government-Binding analyses the verb and the associated inflectional morphology were united by verb raising or affix lowering, in the Minimalist Program, the movement of verbs to Infl is separate from morphological processes. Verbs enter into a syntactic derivation fully formed. Thus, verb raising/lowering is not understood as supporting morphological affixes, but as checking morphological features.

29. We make the crucial assumption that Tense dominates Agr in Spanish; a similar proposal is set forth by Pollock (1989) for French. Such a reordering of the functional nodes is straightforward and consonant with minimalist assumptions: feature strength on functional nodes is one element of language variation, and relative positioning of these functional nodes is another (cf. Toribio 2000a, 2000b).

30. Of course, as noted, movement is an application of a Generalized Transformation, and therefore this structure is built from the bottom up, as elements are selected and moved to positions in which their features can be checked.

31. The relevant definitions are found in Chomsky 1995, pp. 177–178.

32. These papers alter previous assumptions quite considerably. First, the only structure-building operation is Merge. Movement is reduced to Merge, a desirable change, since Move had been considered a costly operation, a flaw in the system. Merge takes an internal part of a structure and merges it with the whole structure, cost free, and banned solely by interface conditions. Second, feature valuation is substituted for feature checking. Uninterpretable features are unvalued features that have to be valued by an agreement process in a local configuration, "phase." Third, the derivation of a sentence consists of different phases or computational units. The specifier of the phase head and the head itself are the only parts of the phase that will make it into the next phase. Thus, for a constituent to raise to the next phase it has to move through the specifier

position of the phase head. (Multiple specifiers are in principle allowed, since, following Chomsky 2006, 6, "Complement and specifier mean nothing more in this framework than first-merged and later-merged.") The two phases are CP and *v*P, being their heads C and *v* respectively. TP (formerly IP) is not a phase because its head T (formerly Infl) only inherits its features from C. All grammatical relations start at the phase head. Its unvalued (uninterpretable) features "probe" into its phase in search of a "goal" that shares its features and might be able to value them. In this system, *wh*-movement results from a phase head probing into the head's complement.*

References

Arnold, Jennifer E., Anthony Losongco, Thomas Washow, and Ryan Grinstrom. 2000. Heaviness vs. newness: The effects of structural complexity and discourse status on constituent ordering. *Language* 76:28–55.

Belazi, Hedi, Edward Rubin, and Almeida Jacqueline Toribio. 1994. Code switching and X-bar theory: The Functional Head Constraint. *Linguistic Inquiry* 25:221–237.

Bhatia, Tej, and William Ritchie. 1996. Bilingual language mixing, Universal Grammar, and second language acquisition. In W. Ritchie and T. Bhatia, eds., *Handbook of Second Language Acquisition*, 627–688. New York: Academic Press.

Chomsky, Noam. 1981. *Lectures on Government and Binding*. Dordrecht: Foris.

Chomsky, Noam. 1986. *Barriers*. Cambridge, MA: MIT Press.

Chomsky, Noam. 1993. A Minimalist Program for linguistic theory. In K. Hale and S. J. Keyser, eds., *The View from Building 20*, 1–52. Cambridge, MA: MIT Press.

Chomsky, Noam. 1995. *The Minimalist Program*. Cambridge, MA: MIT Press.

Chomsky, Noam. 2000. Minimalist inquiries: The framework. In R. Martin, D. Michaels, and J. Uriagereka, eds., *Step by Step: Essays on Minimalist Syntax in Honor of Howard Lasnik*, 89–156. Cambridge, MA: MIT Press.

Chomsky, Noam. 2001. Derivation by phrase. In M. Kenstowicz, ed., *Ken Hale: A Life in Language*, 1–52. Cambridge, MA: MIT Press.

Chomsky, Noam. 2005. On phases. Ms., MIT.

Chomsky, Noam. 2006. Approaching UG from below. Ms., MIT.

Chomsky, Noam, and Howard Lasnik. 1993. The theory of Principles and Parameters. In J. Jacobs, A. von Stechow, W. Sternfeld, and T. Vennemann, eds., *Syntax: An International Handbook of Contemporary Research*, 506–569. Berlin: Walter de Gruyter.

Contreras, Heles. 1987. On the position of subjects. In S. Rothstein, ed., *Perspectives on Phrase Structure: Heads and Licensing*, 63–79. New York: Academic Press.

Den Dikken, Marcel. 2003. On the morphosyntax of wh-movement. In C. Boeckx, ed., *Multiple Wh-Fronting*, 77–98. Philadelphia: John Benjamins.

Diesing, Molly. 1991. Verb movement and the subject position in Yiddish. *Natural Language and Linguistic Theory* 8:41–79.

D'Introno, Francesco. 1996. English-Spanish code-switching: Conditions on movement. In J. Jensen and A. Roca, eds., *Spanish in Contact*, 187–201. Somerville, MA: Cascadilla Press.

Di Sciullo, Anna Maria, Peter Muysken, and Rajendra Singh. 1986. Government and code-mixing. *Journal of Linguistics* 22:1–24.

Fabb, Nigel. 1987. Nonrestrictive relative clauses and D-structure adjunction. Paper presented at the Annual Meeting of the Linguistic Society of America, San Francisco.

Fanselow, Gisbert. 2004. Cyclic phonology-syntax-interaction: Movement to first position in German. In I. S. Ishihara, M. Schmitz, and A. Schwarz, eds., *Interdisciplinary Studies on Information Structure 1*, 1–42. Potsdam: University of Potsdam.

Frey, Werner. 2004a. A medial topic position for German. *Linguistische Berichte* 198:153–190.

Frey, Werner. 2004b. Notes on the syntax and the pragmatics of German Left Dislocation. In H. Lohnstein and S. Trissler, eds., *The Syntax and Semantics of the Left Sentence Periphery*, 203–233. Berlin: Mouton de Gruyter.

Gingràs, Rosario. 1974. Problems in the description of Spanish/English intrasentential code-switching. In G. Bills, ed., *Southwest Areal Linguistics*, 167–174. San Diego: University of California Institute for Cultural Pluralism.

González-Vilbazo, Kay-Eduardo. 2005. Die Syntax des Code-Switching. Esplugisch: Sprachwechsel an der Deutschen Schule Barcelona. Dissertation, Universität zu Köln.

González-Vilbazo, Kay-Eduardo, and Luis López-Carretero. 2007. The little v hypothesis: Evidence from code-switching. Ms., University of Illinois at Chicago.

Goodall, Grant. 1991. On the status of Spec of IP. In D. Bates, ed., *Proceedings of the Tenth West Coast Conference on Formal Linguistics*, 175–182. Stanford, CA: Stanford Linguistics Association.

Goodall, Grant. 1993. Spec of IP and Spec of CP in Spanish Wh-Questions. In W. Ashby, M. Mithun, G. Perissinotto, and E. Raposo, eds., *Linguistic Perspectives on the Romance Languages* (*Current Issues in Linguistic Theory 103*), 199–209. Amsterdam: John Benjamins.

Goodall, Grant. 2004. On the syntax and processing of wh-questions in Spanish. In B. Schmeiser, V. Chand, A. Kelleher, and A. Rodríguez, eds., *WCCFL 23 Proceedings*, 101–114. Somerville, MA: Cascadilla Press.

Grewendorf, Günther. 2002. *Minimalistische Syntax*. Tübingen/Basel: Francke.

Grohmann, Kleanthes K. 2006. Top issues in questions: Topics-topicalization-topicalizability. In Lisa Lai-Shen and Norbert Corver, eds., *Wh-Movement: Moving On*, 249–288. Cambridge, MA: MIT Press.

Groos, Anneke, and Reineke Bok-Bennema. 1986. The structure of the sentence in Spanish. In I. Bordelois, H. Contreras, and K. Zagona, eds., *Generative Studies in Spanish Syntax*, 67–80. Dordrecht: Foris.

Haegemann, Liliane, and Raffaella Zanuttini. 1991. Negative heads and the Neg Criterion. *Linguistic Review* 8:233–251.

Jackendoff, Ray. 1977. *X-Bar Syntax: A Study of Phrase Structure*. Cambridge, MA: MIT Press.

Kayne, Richard. 1994. *The Antisymmetry of Syntax*. Cambridge, MA: MIT Press.

Klima, Edward. 1964. Negation in English. In J. Fodor and J. Katz, eds., *The Structure of Language: Readings in the Philosophy of Language*, 246–323. Englewood Clifts, NJ: Prentice Hall.

Koopman, Hilda, and Dominique Sportiche. 1991. The position of subjects. *Lingua* 85:211–258.

Kuroda, S.-Y. 1988. Whether we agree or not: A comparative study of English and Japanese. *Linguistic Investigations* 12:1–47.

Lohnstein, Horst. 2000. *Satzmodus—kompositionell: Zur Parametrisierung der Modusphrase im Deutschen*. Studia grammatica 49. Berlin: Akademie Verlag.

MacSwan, J. 2000. The architecture of the bilingual language faculty: Evidence from codeswitching. *Bilingualism: Language and Cognition* 3 (1): 37–54.

May, Robert. 1985. *Logical Form*. Cambridge, MA: MIT Press.

Müller, Gereon. 2007. Einführung in die Syntax: w-Bewegung. http://www.uni-leipzig.de/~muellerg/mu611a.pdf.

Murasugi, Keiko. 1991. Noun phrases in Japanese and English: A study in syntax, learnability, and acquisition. Doctoral dissertation, University of Connecticut, Storrs.

Peñalosa, Fernando. 1980. *Chicano sociolinguistics. A brief introduction*. Rowley, MA: Newbury House.

Pfaff, Carol W. 1979. Constraints on language mixing: Intrasentential code-switching and borrowing in Spanish/English. *Language* 55:291–318.

Pollock, Jean-Yves. 1989. Verb movement, Universal Grammar, and the structure of IP. *Linguistic Inquiry* 20:365–424.

Poplack, Shana. 1981. Sometimes I'll start a sentence in Spanish y termino en español: Toward a typology of code-switching. In J. Amastae and L. Elías-Olivares, eds., *Spanish in the United States: Sociolinguistic Aspects*, 230–263. Cambridge: Cambridge University Press.

Rizzi, Luigi. 1990a. *Relativized Minimality*. Cambridge, MA: MIT Press.

Rizzi, Luigi 1990b. Speculations on Verb Second. In J. Mascaró and M. Nespor, eds., *Grammar in Progress*, 375–386. Dordrecht: Foris.

Rizzi, Luigi. 1991. *Residual Verb Second and the Wh-Criterion*. Technical Reports in Formal and Computational Linguistics, 2. Geneva, Switzerland: Faculté des Lettres, Université de Genève.

Rizzi, Luigi. 1997. The fine structure of the Left Periphery. In L. Haegeman, ed., *Elements of Grammar: Handbook in Generative Syntax*, 281–337. Dordrecht: Kluwer.

Rizzi, Luigi, and Ian Roberts. 1989. Complex Inversion in French. *Probus: International Journal of Latin and Romance Languages* 1:1–30.

Rubin, Edward, and Almeida Jacqueline Toribio. 1995. Feature checking and the syntax of language contact. In J. Amastae, G. Goodall, M. Montalbetti, and M. Phinney, eds.,

Current Issues in Linguistic Theory 123: Contemporary Research in Romance Linguistics, 177–185. Amsterdam: John Benjamins.

Sadler, L. 1988. *Welsh Syntax: A Government-Binding Approach*. London: Croom Helm Linguistics Series.

Sankoff, David, and Shana Poplack. 1981. A formal grammar for code-switching. *Papers in Linguistics* 14: 3–45.

Simpson, Andrew. 2000. *Wh-Movement and the Theory of Feature-Checking*. Amsterdam: John Benjamins.

Struckmeier, Volker. 2007a. *Attribute im Deutschen: Zu ihren Eigenschaften und ihrer Stellung im grammatischen System*. Berlin: Akademie Verlag.

Struckmeier, Volker. 2007b. Towards a typology of phase heads: Subordinating D. Presentation in UIC Talks in Linguistics at the University of Illinois at Chicago, November 14.

Suñer, Margarita. 1994. V-movement and the licensing of Argumental wh-phrases in Spanish. *Natural Language and Linguistic Theory* 12: 335–372.

Timm, L. A. 1975. Spanish-English code-switching: El porque and how-not-to. *Romance Philology* 28:473–482.

Toribio, Almeida Jacqueline. 1989. Subject-Auxiliary Inversion in English: Licensing Operators. In P. Branigan, J. Gaulding, M. Kubo, and K. Murasugi, eds., *MIT Working Papers in Linguistics 11*, 240–256. Cambridge, MA: MITWPL, Department of Linguistics and Philosophy, MIT.

Toribio, Almeida Jacqueline. 1990. A-bar movement in Spanish: Wh-questions, focalization, and relative clauses. In Y. No and M. Libucha eds., *ESCOL '90: Proceedings of the Seventh Eastern States Conference on Linguistics*, 286–294. Columbus, OH: Ohio University Press.

Toribio, Almeida Jacqueline. 1993a. α to α: Constraining the landing site of movement. Paper presented at the Annual Meeting of the Linguistic Society of America.

Toribio, Almeida Jacqueline. 1993b. Lexical subjects in finite and non-finite clauses. In E. Rubin and M. Bernstein, eds., *Cornell Working Papers in Linguistics 11*, 149–178. Ithaca, NY: Department of Modern Languages and Linguistics, Cornell University.

Toribio, Almeida Jacqueline. 1993c. Parametric variation in the licensing of nominals. Doctoral dissertation, Cornell University.

Toribio, Almeida Jacqueline. 2000a. Minimalist ideas on parametric variation. In M. Hirotani, A. Coetzle, N. Hall, and J.-Y. Kim, eds., *NELS 30*, 627–638. Amherst: GLSA, University of Massachusetts.

Toribio, Almeida Jacqueline. 2000b. Setting parametric limits on dialectal variation in Spanish. *Lingua* 110:315–341.

Toribio, Almeida Jacqueline. 2001a. Accessing Spanish-English code-switching competence. *International Journal of Bilingualism* 5:403–436.

Toribio, Almeida Jacqueline. 2001b. On the emergence of code-switching competence. *Bilingualism: Language and Cognition* 4:203–231.

Toribio, Almeida Jacqueline, and Edward J. Rubin. 1996. Code-switching in generative grammar. In J. Jensen and A. Roca, eds., *Spanish in Contact*, 203–226. Cambridge, MA: Cascadilla Press.

Torrego, Esther. 1984. On inversion in Spanish and some of its effects. *Linguistic Inquiry* 15:103–129.

Torrego, Esther. 1985. On empty categories in nominals. Ms., University of Massachusetts, Boston.

Travis, Lisa 1991. Parameters of phrase structure and verb-second phenomena. In R. Freidin, ed., *Principles and Parameters in Comparative Grammar*, 339–364. Cambridge, MA: MIT Press

Vikner, S. 1990. Verb movement and the licensing of NP positions in the Germanic languages. Doctoral dissertation, Université de Genève.

Watanabe, Akira. 1991. Wh-in-situ, subjacency, and chain formation. Ms., MIT.

Woolford, Ellen. 1983. Bilingual code-switching and syntactic theory. *Linguistic Inquiry* 14:520–536.

Woolford, Ellen. 1984. On the application of wh-movement and inversion in code-switching sentences. *Revue Québécoise de Linguistique* 14:77–86.

Zagona, Karen. 1982. Government and proper government in verbal projections. Doctoral dissertation, University of Washington, Seattle.

Zubizarreta, María Luisa. 1998. *Prosody, Focus, and Word Order*. Cambridge, MA: MIT Press.

5 Categorial Mismatches in the Syntax and the Lexicon: Evidence from Language Contact Research

Pieter Muysken

Most researchers assume that the lexical categories of a language are also its syntactic categories, and that there is a one-to-one correspondence between the two. In many ways, this is a reasonable assumption. Thus, if a language has adjectives in its lexicon, these can be inserted into adjective positions made available in the phrase structure rules of the language, and so on. For many linguists, it would be difficult to imagine a different setup: adjectives in the lexicon that could not be inserted, or adjective positions in the syntax that could not be filled lexically.

This chapter explores the possibility that the match between syntactic and lexical categories is not perfect, nonetheless, and in particular, adduces evidence from language contact research that makes the case for mismatches even stronger.

There are a number of general phenomena hinting at a potential categorial mismatch. These phenomena are discussed in section 5.1. In section 5.2 I discuss cases from the contact between the Otomanguean language Popoloca on the one hand and Spanish on the other. In section 5.3 I consider more general theoretical implications of the approach taken in this chapter and suggest some avenues for further research.

5.1 Potential Mismatches between Lexical and Syntactic Categories

The categories characterizing the lexicon of a language need not always be relevant syntactically, and syntactically relevant categories do not always have a lexical expression. A number of cases come to mind.

5.1.1 Dutch Gender and Definiteness

Dutch nouns are characterized by a neuter/nonneuter distinction, which is expressed by the choice of the definite article (*de* vs. *het*) and shows up in the ending of the preposed adjective in indefinite noun phrases:

(1) *Dutch*
> a. de koe 'the cow'
> b. een witt*e* koe 'a white cow'

(2) Dutch
> a. het paard 'the horse'
> b. een wit paard 'the white horse'

The distinction is pervasive in the lexicon: for any noun, you have to know its gender. However, it does not play a role elsewhere in the grammar, beyond the already-mentioned adjective agreement. Andrew Carstairs-McCarthy (2000) has drawn attention in this respect to the conjugation classes in many languages. It is important to know the conjugation class of a verb in Romance (to produce the right verb form), but there are no syntactic rules that refer to a conjugation class.

In contrast, the definiteness distinction plays a role in Dutch syntax for noun phrases, but not in the lexicon. Dutch definite and indefinite noun phrases do not have the same distribution (cf. e.g. Hoekstra 1984):

(3) *Dutch*
> a. Er loopt een wit paard.
>   'There walks a white horse.'
> b. *Er loopt het witte paard.
>   'There walks the white horse.'

(4) *Dutch*
> a. Ik heb de man gisteren in Parijs gezien.
>   'I saw the man in Paris yesterday.'
> b. ?Ik heb een man gisteren in Parijs gezien.
>   'I saw a man in Paris yesterday.'

However, this distinction, which is crucial in the syntax/semantics interface, plays no role in the lexicon. In fact, definiteness is also a feature of proper names (5a) and personal pronouns (5b):

(5) *Dutch*
> a. Ik heb Jan gisteren in Parijs gezien.
>   'I saw John in Paris yesterday.'
> b. Ik heb haar gisteren in Parijs gezien.
>   'I saw her in Paris yesterday.'

5.1.2 Null Subjects

A second mismatch between the lexicon and the syntax is evident in the fact that null elements can occur in some languages as subjects. The two creole languages Sranan and Papiamentu have many similar syntactic structures. But with verbs like 'seem' Papiamentu has a null element, while Sranan has a lexical pronoun:

(6) Papiamentu
    Parse   ku   e   ta   bin.
    seem   that   3sg   PR   come
    'It seems that he is coming.'

(7) *Sranan*
    A   gersi   dati   a   e   kon.
    3sg   seem   that   3sg   PR   come
    'It seems that he is coming.'

However, this difference has no known syntactic effects. Thus extraction out of the complement subject position is blocked in both languages (see Rizzi 1982):

(8) *Papiamentu*
    *Ken   parse   ku   ta   bin?
    who   seem   that   PR   come
    'Who does it seem that is coming?'

(9) *Sranan*
    *Suma   gersi   dati   e   kon?
    who   seem   that   3sg   PR   come
    'Who does it seem that is coming?

In other words, Papiamentu behaves like a non-pro-drop language in this respect, even though it allows a null subject in some contexts (see e.g. Muysken and Law 2001; see also DeGraff 1993, which takes a different perspective). Significantly, however, it does not allow null subjects in argument positions:

(10) *Papiamentu*
    *Ta bin.
    PR come
    'I/you/(s)he comes.'

5.1.3 Predicate Adjectives in Creoles

A third categorial mismatch concerns partially overlapping categories, such as adjective and predicate verb. In the maroon creole language Saramaccan, to give a well-researched example, adjectives can occur both in attributive position (11a), and in predicative position (11b) (spelling is given as in the original sources):

(11) *Saramaccan* (De Groot 1977, 93)
    a. Kó gaán páu ku donú njanjá
       'Becomes [a] big tree with yellow fruit'
    b. Di boto baáka.
       'The boat [is] black.'

In predicative position, adjectives (12a) pattern with verbs (12b) and allow no copula (12c):

(12) a. *Saramaccan* (Rountree 1992, 37)
       Di möön gaan hanse mujëë u di köndë
       'The more great beautiful (most beautiful) woman in the village'
    b. *Saramaccan* (Alleyne 1987b)
       Di mujee hanse.
       DET woman beautiful
       'The woman is beautiful.'
    c. *Saramaccan* (Alleyne 1987b)
       *Di mujee dë hanse

Notice now that with reduplicated predicates copula *de* is obligatory:

(13) *Saramaccan* (Bakker 1987, 25)
     mi de tjalitjali.
     1sg COP sad.REDUP
     'I am sad.'

This suggests that the nonreduplicated forms are true verbs, and the reduplicated forms are derived adjectives. Often the reduplicated form has a derived, more specific meaning in Saramaccan (Bakker 1987, 25), suggesting its lexicalized status:

(14) a. Di   mii   bunu.
       DET   child   good
       'The child is good.'
    b. Di   mii   de   bunbunu.
       DET   child   COP   good-REDUP
       'The child is fine.'

(15) a. A   satu.
       3sg   salt
       'It has been salted.'
    b. *Saramaccan* (Bakker 1987, 25)
       A   de   satusatu.
       3sg   COP   salt.REDUP
       'It is salty.'

The reduplicated forms can also occur in prenominal attributive position:

(16) Di   lailai   goni
     DET   load.REDUP   gun
     'The loaded gun'

(17) *Saramaccan* (Bakker 1987, 25)
     Di   dåå-dåå   koosu
     DET   dry.REDUP   cloth
     'The dried cloth'

The lexicon/syntax mismatch arises in examples such as (11) and (12), where color terms and predicates such as *hanse* 'beautiful' have two overlapping distributions: as adjectives and as verbs.

5.1.4 For Prepositions to Become Complementizers

Creole prepositions meaning 'for' are often related to other categories. A typical example is the status of Haitian *pou* (< Fr. *pour*), which can function as a preposition, complementizer, and mood marker. As a preposition, *pou* is used mostly as a benefactive:

(18) *Haitian* (Koopman and Lefebvre 1980, 203)
     Pote   sa   pou   mwen.
     carry   this   for   me
     'Bring this for me.'

As a mood marker, *pou* marks obligation or irrealis:

(19) *Haitian* (Koopman and Lefebvre 1980, 209)
     Nou   pa   te   pou   wè   sa.
     1pl   NEG   ANT   MD   see   this
     'We did not have to see this.'

Finally, as a complementizer, *pou* marks purposives or oblique complement clauses:

(20) *Haitian* (Hall 1953, 192)
     Li   pa-jam   tro   ta   pou   chen   anraje.
     3sg   NEG-ever   too   late   for   dog   go.mad
     'It is never too late for a dog to go mad.'

Confronted with this state of affairs, which is much more general, creolists have adopted two approaches: (a) they have assumed a considerable number of homonyms, so that there are three synchronically unrelated forms *pou* in Haitian, or (b) they have assumed a grammar for Haitian in which the category of mood is very different from that of Western European languages, in that there is no real distinction between complementizers and mood markers.

Here I will suggest a third possibility: the lexical entry is underspecified with respect to distinctions the syntax makes. In fact, this may be a more general phenomenon in prepositions. Thus, Spanish *a* 'to, animate accusative' or Afrikaans *vir* 'for, to, animate accusative' shows behavior uncharacteristic of typical prepositions, in being deletable in certain contexts—for example, when their complement appears in clause-initial position.

5.1.5 Adjectives versus Adverbs

A fifth mismatch involves cases where languages differ in their marking of distinctions in the lexicon, though not in the syntax. Thus in English, most adjectives are marked with -*ly* when they occur in adverbial position, while in Dutch generally adjectives are not formally distinguished from adverbs:

(21) *Dutch*
   a. Een mooi lied
      'A beautiful song'
   b. Zij zingt mooi.
      'She sings beautifully.'

Thus, the class of adverbs and the class of adjectives are not sharply delineated in the Dutch lexicon, while they often are in English (though not always, particularly in informal spoken English).

5.1.6 Limited Sets of Adjectives

Ordinarily, the major categories constitute open lexical classes. This holds for nouns in most if not all languages, and possibly for verbs. However, it does not hold fully for adpositions (the status of which as a major category is subject to discussion), and interestingly not for adjectives either. While in Indo-European languages, the adjective class is open, in languages belonging to widely different language families, the class of adjectives is quite limited and may consist of only a handful of elements (Dixon, 1977).

These six bits of evidence suggest that the categorial match between the lexicon and the syntax is much less neat than is often assumed. The two systems interact, of course, but the correspondence between them is approximate rather than perfect. The mismatches between them can be classified into several types: (a) different features are relevant in the syntax and in the lexicon (Dutch determiner phrases in section 5.1.1); (b) null/non-null realization of elements occurs without syntactic consequences (impersonal subjects in Papiamentu and Sranan in section 5.1.2); (c) there are overlapping categories of adjective and predicate verbs (Saramaccan in section 5.1.3); (d) preposition-like elements are underspecified for the syntactic position they can occur in (Haitian in section 5.1.4); (e) a similar set of syntactic categories is morphologically distinguished in one language, English, but not in another, Dutch (section 5.1.5); and (f) what can be inserted into a major category position may or may not be an open-class item. Thus the version of the lexicalist position that suggested that syntactic structures are simply projected from the lexicon through category-neutral X-bar rules has lost much of its appeal. It seems that syntactic structures exist separately from the lexicons that are meant to fill these structures.

This result gains particular saliency in light of language contact, where the lexicon of one language is brought into contact with the syntax of another: lexical borrowing. In the next section I focus on this phenomenon as yet another source of evidence for lexicon/syntax mismatches.

5.2   Otomanguean-Spanish Language Contact

Together with most other Mexican Amerindian languages, languages belonging to the Otomanguean language family have been in intimate contact with Spanish for several centuries at a minimum. From the perspective of the present chapter, the borrowing patterns in these languages are particularly interesting.

Consider the material from texts in Popoloca de Mezontla presented in Veerman-Leichsenring 1991, using Norberto Bautista Cortés (born in 1923) as an informant. The Otomanguean language Popoloca is spoken by 11,200 people (age 55 and older) in eleven villages near Tehuacán in the state of Puebla, Mexico; there are virtually no monolinguals in Mezontla, and the process of language shift has been going on since the 1930s. The texts are traditional and comprise the following topics. Six texts are given, labeled A–F. For each text the number of lines and subject matter are specified:

A	31	How pottery is made
B	79	How we lived before
C	60	Riddle (Adivinación) [more traditional]
D	46	My grandfather's school
E	64	The teacher Juan Pérez Rosales
F	159	How to ask for the hand of a girl

I have analyzed the Spanish elements in these texts and split them up into the broad categories of content words (table 5.1) and function words (table 5.2).

In table 5.1 the content elements are further divided into adjectives and verbs; the nouns (and a few fixed expressions) are divided into clusters along the lines of semantic fields. For these semantic fields only a few illustrative examples are given, as well as the totals per text. For the verbs and adjectives all types are given, with their distribution, and for the noun categories a few illustrative examples. The first number in parentheses after a category heading refers to the number of types, and the second to the number of singly occurring types, also termed hapaxes, nonce borrowings, or singletons.

In table 5.2 functional items are listed with their distribution, and totals are given as well. Again, the first number in parentheses after a category heading refers to the number of types, and the second to the number of singly occurring types.

Comparing the two tables, several things are apparent. The borrowed content words have a quite specific distribution, depending on the topic of the text they occur in. The number of nonconcrete words is rather limited. The total number of tokens borrowed is not much higher for the content words than for the function words (172 vs. 131), but the number of nonce borrowings is double (45 vs. 22). Consequently, the type/token ratio for the content-word borrowings is higher than for the function-word borrowings, with 79/172 = 0.46as compared to 42/131 = 0.32.

Most important, however, is the simple fact that the number of function words borrowed (in tokens) is almost comparable to that of content words (tokens, 172 vs. 133; types, 79 vs. 42). In general, when we compare borrowing patterns around the world, far fewer function words are borrowed than content words, as is clear from the borrowability hierarchies in the recent literature (see Van Hout and Muysken 1994 for an overview of the issues). To take a simple example, Treffers-Daller (1994, 99, 179) shows that in Brussels Dutch (taking the category of function words to include adverbs except for the *-ment* class, *juste* 'precisely', and adverbially used adjectives), the ratio of content words to function words is 3263/725 (four and a half times as great) on the token level and 1008/79 (over twelve times as great) on the type level. Asymmetries between content-word and function-word borrowing for Strasbourg (Gardner-Chloros 1991) and Ottawa (Poplack, Sankoff, and Miller 1988) are quite similar to, or even more extreme than, those of Brussels.

The fact that there is this large a difference between Popoloca and the other cases cited suggests that the borrowing process itself may have different features in the Popoloca case for some categories. For interjections the two language setttings may be the same. The latter are also a frequently borrowed category in the Brussels case: while in the native lexicon interjections constitute only 5% of the tokens, in the borrowed lexicon they constitute over 12%.

Table 5.1
Borrowed content words in the Popoloca texts

	A	B	C	D	E	F	tot.	gloss
Household items: (17, 10)								
karru								car
servesa								beer
platu								plate, dish
	2	**12**			**13**	**11**	**38**	
Abstract words: (7, 3)								
ladu								side
kosa								thing
	3	**3**		**2**	**3**	**5**	**16**	
Courtship and ritual: (14, 10)								
konsentimyento								agreement
Dio								God
			2			**22**	**24**	
Government and education: (11, 2)								
gubyernu								government
skwela								school
		4	**1**	**20**	**9**	**1**	**35**	
Natural world: (4, 4)								
leu								puma (mountain lion)
klavelina								carnation
					2	**2**	**4**	
Social and family relations: (7, 2)								
señor								sir, mister
be:lu								grandfather
			3	**5**		**15**	**23**	
Numbers, dates, times, measures: (8, 5)								
veintisiete								27
madrugada								dawn
litru								liter
	1	**5**			**5**	**3**	**14**	
Adjectives: (3, 3)								
finu					1			fine
potable		1						drinkable
sufisiente		1						sufficient
		2			**1**		**3**	
Verbs: (8, 6)								
tú- mantener	1	5						maintain
kú- sùfrĭč?ā		1						suffer
tú- yuda		1						help
čē- kompara						3		compare
tú- kompara						1		compare
č?ē-kompone						1		compose
č?ē-kompaña						1		accompany
sentrega						1		hands over
	1	**7**				**7**	**15**	
Total (79, 45)	**7**	**32**	**6**	**27**	**34**	**66**	**172**	

Table 5.2
Borrowed function words in the Popoloca texts

	A	B	C	D	E	F	tot.	gloss
Discourse organizers: (6, 5)								
pues						3	**3**	then
X si fuera						1	**1**	... it were
solo					1		**1**	only
a ve						1	**1**	let's see
sea	1						**1**	it were
sí						1	**1**	indeed
	1				**1**	**6**	**8**	
Prepositions and conjunctions: (14, 4)								
pero/u	1	6	6	6	2	2	**23**	but
asta		6	1	4		5	**16**	until
porke	2			2	2	2	**8**	because
ke		1	2		2	2	**7**	that
para i:ši:	1	3			1	1	**6**	for
desde			4				**4**	since
por					2		**2**	by
despwe (de)		1				1	**2**	after
lo ke						2	**2**	the that
sino			2				**2**	but
ya ke		1					**1**	now that
de ke					1		**1**	of that
asta ke						1	**1**	until that
a		1					**1**	to
	4	**19**	**15**	**12**	**10**	**16**	**76**	
Temporal expressions: (11, 7)								
ante		2		1		3	**6**	before
una ve(z)	1	1				1	**3**	once
tyempu		2					**2**	time
ora						2	**2**	hour
repente					1		**1**	suddenly
a veces		1					**1**	sometimes
komo syempre		1					**1**	as always
syempre						1	**1**	always
semana	1						**1**	week
primero						1	**1**	at first
prinsipio						1	**1**	beginning
	2	**7**		**1**	**1**	**9**	**20**	
Quantifiers: (11, 6)								
puru	1	6		2	1		**10**	pure(ly)
no mas					1	1	**2**	only
tanto		5			1		**6**	so much
mero				1		1	**2**	merely
ni					2		**2**	neither
kwantu						1	**1**	how much
tal						1	**1**	such
kada						1	**1**	each
algo					1		**1**	something
mismo						1	**1**	same
klase						1	**1**	type
	1	**11**		**3**	**6**	**7**	**28**	
Total (42, 22)							**131**	

This may be explained by assuming that interjections are borrowed via alternational codeswitching (Muysken 2000), and that this is a quite productive route. In the Brussels case conjunctions and prepositions are not borrowed very much (together they constitute 1% of the borrowed tokens). In this respect Popoloca is different, with 76 out of a total of 303 borrowed tokens (25%), and I want to propose that evidence may be found here for a lexicon/syntax asymmetry.

Several arguments may be adduced for the claim that prepositions and conjunctions were also originally borrowed via alternational switching. First, sometimes we have *doubling*:

(22) *Popoloca* (Veerman-Leichsenring 1991, 393)

cùnda ngē   thèé   ná   ngū   karru   nà   *para īšī*   mē ...
have-1   that   PR-look.for-1ex   one   car   for   that   then ...
'We have to look for a car so that then ...'

(23) *Popoloca* (Veerman-Leichsenring 1991, 400)

mé   tʔayá-šā   ná   ndaʔ   khí   *para īšī*   kʔué-kʔiá ná.
thus   cart-INS-1pl   water   far   for   that   IM-drink-1pl
'Thus we carted the water from afar in order to drink it.'

Here the Spanish preposition/conjunction *para* 'for' is combined with the Popoloca conjunction *ī:šī:*, even though either could have been used (Veerman-Leichsenring 1991). Doubling in itself suggests a paratactic structure, typical of alternational code mixing.

Second, note that *para* is *external* to *īšī*, with respect to the complement clause. This external doubling is an extra argument for alternation. The Spanish element is simply added or adjoined to the clause here, and adjunction is always external.

However, all or most of the borrowed conjunctions and prepositions are *not equivalent* to Popoloca elements, as becomes clear from Veerman-Leichsenring's grammatical description. The precise relation between constituents is often left unspecified by overt elements in Popoloca, and it seems as if Popoloca fills empty positions in the syntax with elements from a nonnative lexicon. If this is correct, lexical borrowing may lead to very rapid syntactic change.

5.3   Research Program: Nouns and Verbs

In several North American languages, particularly in Salish, it is unclear how to distinguish nouns and verbs (Mithun 1999). Jelinek and Demers (1994) present data from Straits Salish illustrating the problem:

(24) *Straits Salish* (Jelinek and Demers 1994, 697–736)
    a. t'iləm-lə-sx^w
       sing-PST-2sg
       'You sang.'
    b. sey'si'-lə-sx^w
       afraid-PST-2sg
       'You were afraid.'
    c. si'em-lə-sx^w
       noble-PST-2sg
       'You were a chief.'

In (24) elements that in English correspond to verbs (24a), adjectives (24b), and nouns (24c) all occur in the same predicate position. This characteristic has led some researchers to conclude that those categories are not distinct in Salish.

However, Van Eijk and Hess (1986) have argued that there is clear evidence in the realm of morphology for a distinction between nouns and verbs. Some affixes are limited to one of these classes; however both occur in predicate position. This can be represented as follows:

(25) *Salish*
    a. Nouns and verbs are *distinct* in the *lexicon*, through suffixation of possible suffixes.
    b. Nouns and verbs are *nondistinct* in the *syntax*: both function as predicates.

The mirror-image situation may be found in the Polynesian language Tongan, as analyzed by Broschart (1997). Here again there is doubt about the categorial distinction between nouns and verbs:

(26) *Tongan* (Broschart 1997, 123–165)
    a. Na'e   lele   e   kau   fefiné.
       PST   run   DET   pl   woman
       'The women were running.'
    b. Na'e   fefine   kotoa   e   kau   lelé.
       PST   woman   all   DET   pl   run
       'The ones running were all female.'

What makes Tongan distinct from Salish is that there is a clear difference between the verbal position (following the tense marker) and the nominal position (following the determiner and the plural marker). In addition, morphology is poor, and nouns and verbs are hard to keep apart by suffixes. We can summarize this in the following schema:

(27) *Tongan*
    a. Nouns and verbs are *nondistinct* in the *lexicon.*
    b. Nouns and verbs are *distinct* in the *syntax*, through different
       structural positions in the clause.

In the analysis given in (25) and (27), Salish and Tongan, in occupying two opposite positions on the typological spectrum, illustrate the relative autonomy of the syntax and the lexicon. The fact that such radical mismatches are typologically relatively rare should not daunt us. This is to be expected given that the lexicon/syntax interface is subject to optimalized matching tendencies.

Where language contact research should come in is to provide independent evidence for these interface mismatches. The analysis given predicts (but this is no more than a prediction so far) that in Salish borrowing is sensitive to lexical restrictions, but that in Tongan any category can be borrowed.

For Lillooet, the Salishan language studied by Van Eijk (1985, 209), borrowing is extremely limited in any case. Only proper nouns (Bill, Mary) can be borrowed felicitously. There are not many studies of borrowing in North American Indian languages, and most focus on cultural aspects. Huot (1950) and Bonvillain (1978) focus on Mohawk, while Prunet (1992) deals with Carrier. The available evidence suggests very strong noun-verb asymmetries, but a more comprehensive typological-comparative study is needed. The same is true of the Polynesian languages of the South Pacific.

Note

I am grateful to Michael Cysouw for earlier discussions of this topic and for useful references. Abbreviations used: ANT = anterior; COP = copula; DET = determiner; IM = imperative; INS = XX; MD = irrealis mood; NEG = negation; PR = progressive; PST = past; REDUP = reduplication; sg = singular; pl = plural; 1ex = first-person exclusive plural.

References

Alleyne, Mervyn C., ed. 1987a. *Caribbean Culture Studies 2: Studies in Saramaccan Language Structure.* Amsterdam/Mona, Jamaica: University of Amsterdam / University of the West Indies.

Alleyne, Mervyn C. 1987b. Predicate structures in Saramaccan. In Mervyn C. Alleyne, ed., *Caribbean Culture Studies 2: Studies in Saramaccan Language Structure,* 71–88. Amsterdam/ Mona, Jamaica: University of Amsterdam / University of the West Indies.

Bakker, Peter. 1987. Reduplications in Saramaccan. In Mervyn C. Alleyne, ed., *Caribbean Culture Studies 2: Studies in Saramaccan Language Structure,* 17–40. Amsterdam/Mona, Jamaica: University of Amsterdam / University of the West Indies.

Barner, David, and Alan Bale. 2002. No nouns, no verbs: Psycholinguistic arguments in favor of lexical underspecification. *Lingua* 112:771–791.

Bonvillain, Nancy. 1978. Linguistic change in Akwesasne Mohawk: French and English influences. *IJAL* 44:31–39.

Broschart, Jürgen. 1997. Why Tongan does it differently: Categorial distinctions in a language without nouns and verbs. *Linguistic Typology* 1:123–165.

Carstairs-McCarthy, Andrew. 2000. *The Origins of Complex Language*. Oxford: Oxford University Press.

DeGraff, Michel. 1993. Is Haitian Creole a *pro*-drop language? In Frank Byrne and John Holm, eds., *Atlantic Meets Pacific*, 71–90. Amsterdam: John Benjamins.

De Groot, A. 1977. *Woordregister Nederlands-Saramaccan*. Paramaribo: Summer Institute of Linguistics.

Dixon, R. M. W. 1977. Where have all the adjectives gone? *Studies in Language* 1:19–80.

Gardner-Chloros, Penelope. 1991. *Language Selection and Switching in Strasbourg*. Oxford: Clarendon Press.

Hall, Robert A. 1953. *Haitian Creole: Grammar—Texts—Vocabulary*. Philadelphia: American Folklore Society.

Hoekstra, Teun. 1984. *Transitivity*. Dordrecht: Foris.

Huot, Martha Champion. 1950. Some Mohawk words of acculturation. *IJAL* 14:150–154.

Jelinek, Eloise, and Richard D. Demers. 1994. Predicates and pronominal arguments in Straits Salish. *Language* 70:697–736.

Koopman, Hilda, and Claire Lefebvre. 1980. Haitian Creole Pu. In Pieter Muysken, ed., *Generative Studies on Creole Languages*, 25–34. Dordrecht: Foris.

Mithun, Marianne. 1999. *The Languages of Native North America*. Cambridge: Cambridge University Press.

Muysken, Pieter. 2000. Bilingual Speech. The Typology of Code-Mixing. Cambridge: Cambridge University Press.

Poplack, Shana, David Sankoff, and Christopher Miller. 1988. The social correlates and linguistic processes of lexical borrowing and assimilation. *Linguistics* 26:47–104.

Prunet, Jean François. 1992. The origin and interpretation of French loans in Carrier. *IJAL* 56:484–502.

Rizzi, Luigi. 1982. *Italian Syntax*. Dordrecht: Foris.

Rountree, S. Catherine. 1992. *Saramaccan Grammar Sketch*. Paramaribo: Summer Institute of Linguistics.

Rountree, S. Catherine, and Naomi Glock. 1977. *Saramaccan for Beginners*. Paramaribo: Summer Institute of Linguistics.

Treffers-Daller, Jeanine. 1994. *Mixing Two Languages: French-Dutch Contact in a Comparative Perspective*. Berlin: Mouton de Gruyter.

Van Eijk, Jan. 1985. The Lillooet language: Phonology, morphology, syntax. Doctoral dissertation, University of Amsterdam.

Van Eijk, Jan, and Thom Hess. 1986. Noun and verb in Salish. *Lingua* 69:319–331.

Van Hout, Roeland, and Pieter Muysken. 1994. Modelling lexical borrowability. *Language Variation and Change* 6:39–62.

Veerman-Leichsenring, Annette. 1991. *Gramática del popoloca de Mezontla*. Amsterdam: Rodopi.

6 Argument Licensing in Optimal Switches

Rakesh M. Bhatt

6.1 Introduction

This chapter presents an Optimality-Theoretic account of the linguistically significant generalizations of bilingual codeswitching in argument positions in different language pairs. Several studies on intrasentential codeswitching have appealed to the idea that codeswitches are subjected to certain well-formedness conditions that, however, appear to be true only of certain language pairs and not others (cf. Clyne 1987; Bokamba 1989).[1] But recently, with the introduction of "soft" constraints, as in Optimality Theory (OT), it has become possible to express certain crosslinguistic generalizations on codeswitching that have been theoretically recalcitrant. In this chapter, I claim that the constraint interaction and satisfaction approach of OT (Prince and Smolensky 1993; Grimshaw 1997) yields a straightforward account of the distribution of bilingual codeswitching in argument positions in different language pairs making use of mainly two conflicting constraints, *Spec and Comp (see Bhatt 1997), both violable under appropriate conditions. The difference in codeswitching outcomes in different language pairs turns out to be, as expected under OT, how these constraints are ranked relative to each other.

This chapter is organized in the following manner: section 6.2 presents crosslinguistic data and empirical generalizations on codeswitching mainly from Kashmiri-English, Hindi-English, Spanish-English, and Swahili-English; section 6.3 presents a brief overview of the Optimality-Theoretic framework of assumptions; section 6.4 discusses how OT can be used to capture the linguistically significant generalizations noted in section 6.2; section 6.5 presents an OT account of argument licensing in codeswitching; and section 6.6 presents conclusions and summarizes the main arguments.

6.2 The Generalizations

The data reported in this study come from the following sources: (i) recordings of spontaneous speech, (ii) printed sources, such as English newspapers and weekly magazines, and (iii) grammaticality judgments from survey questionnaires. Roughly ten hours of spontaneous speech were recorded, seven of which are from a series of conversations among twelve adult speakers, six men and six women. Only those topics that lend themselves to codeswitching were initiated to elicit casual conversations, which vary in length from ten to thirty-five minutes. Subjects' permission to use the recorded material in an anonymous fashion was obtained. The other three hours of recordings are from various news items and sociocultural programs from Indian television and radio, programs known to use Hindi and English rather inextricably. The conversations that showed codeswitched utterances were selected and transcribed.

Further, grammaticality judgments were elicited on a variety of Hindi-English codeswitching data. The sentences were constructed specifically to check whether some grammatical constraints proposed earlier and/or the ones proposed in this study hold. This was done to estimate the range of what is not possible in Hindi-English codeswitching. There were forty items designed to cover most of the syntactic constraints proposed in the literature, such as the Government Constraint (Di Sciullo, Muysken, and Singh 1986), the Functional Head Constraint (Belazi et al. 1994), the Equivalence Constraint (Poplack 1981), and the System Morpheme and the Embedding Language-Island constraints (Myers-Scotton 1993). Test items were randomized and an additional eighteen items were added to serve as distractors. Subjects were given three choices to express their responses (relative acceptability) for each item: [√] good, acceptable; [?] odd, but perhaps acceptable; and [*] bad, completely unacceptable. Since societal attitudes toward codeswitching are sometimes negative (Mahootian and Santorini 1996), the subjects were given relatively more freedom in choosing the acceptability option [√ or ?] in order to give them a chance to include, even if marginally, socially unacceptable or marked—low-frequency, low-exposure—codeswitched structures. The calculations of grammaticality [√ or ?] or ungrammaticality [*] were based on the score of 80% agreement or more for an item. Items that scored less than 80%, one way or another, were assumed to be data for which no clear, robust intuition exists, and were, therefore, discarded under the assumption that subjects' knowledge of the syntactic generalization about those items is not secure.

6.2.1 Subject Switches

The data from Kashmiri-English and Hindi-English show that the entire subject constituent is prohibited from appearing in the embedding (host) language.[2] In (1a–b), Kashmiri subject DP in an English clause results in ungrammaticality. Similarly, in (2a–b), English subject DP in a Hindi clause results in ungrammaticality.

(1) a. *Con zaamtur* sat on the floor.
         your son-in-law
         'Your son-in-law sat on the floor.'
     b. *Akh laRkI* got up and left.
         one boy
         'One boy got up and left.'

(2) a. *Your sister*   aajkal   kyaa   paRhaatii   hai?
                         these days   what   teaches   is
         'What does your sister teach these days?'
     b. *Some diplomats*   kal   dilii   ja   rahee   haiN.
                            tomorrow   Delhi   go   prog   are
         'Some diplomats are going to Delhi tomorrow.'

These data pose a problem for a variety of constraints proposed in the literature. They violate the Equivalence Constraint proposed by Poplack (1981), since the Kashmiri and Hindi syntax coincides perfectly with the English syntax at the point of the switches, and, accordingly, should be licit. The data also violate Belazi at al.'s (1994) Functional Head Constraint, since the constraint incorrectly predicts that switches such as (1) and (2) are licit. Finally, the ungrammaticality of (1) and (2) does not follow from Myers-Scotton's (1993) EL-Island Constraint; the EL island—switching of the entire constituent—is incorrectly predicted to be produced as a well-formed switch. A minimalist (MacSwan 1999, 2013) account does not block the derivations of (1) and (2) above, since neither the structure-building operations (Merge, Move) nor any checking (Case, EPP), Computational (Last Resort, Minimal Link Condition), or Economy (Full Interpretation, Procrastinate, Shortest Derivation Condition) principles are violated by the switched items in (1) and (2).[3]

Surprisingly, the Government Constraint proposed by Di Sciullo, Muysken, and Singh (1986) and refined by Halmari (1994, 1997)—codeswitching cannot occur where a government relation holds—correctly bans codeswitching options such as (1) and (2) where the subject position is governed (under m-command). This theory is further supported by the grammaticality contrast between (2) and (3). Notice, in contrast to (1) and (2) above, that the switching of the entire subject constituent to English is well formed, but only if there is a distinct pause after the subject constituent giving an "As for" topic reading, as shown in Kashmiri-English (3a) and Hindi-English (3b).[4] What this suggests is that the antigovernment relation permits codeswitching, as in the case of the subject phrases in (3) that appear in an ungoverned topic position.

(3)   a. *Con zaamtur* [PAUSE] sat on the floor.
         your son-in-law
         'Your son-in-law sat on the floor.'
     b. *Your sister* [PAUSE]   aajkal   kyaa   paRhaatii hai?
                         these days what   teaches   is
         'What does your sister teach these days?'

The data above shows that switching the entire constituent in the subject position, [Spec, IP], is penalized, but members of the constituent are switchable only if they appear in positions that are licensed to switch, not otherwise. Consider again the data in (4), Kashmiri-English codeswitching, and (5), Hindi-English codeswitching, corresponding to (1a) and (2a), respectively. The grammaticality contrast between (4a) and (4b) and between (5a) and (5b) clearly shows that the Spec of DP inside [Spec, IP] is not permitted to switch.

(4)   a. **Con* son-in-law sat on the floor.
         Your
         'Your son-in-law sat on the floor.'
     b. Your *zaamtur* sat on the floor.
          son-in-law
         'Your son-in-law sat on the floor.'

(5)   a. **Your*   behan   aajkal   kyaa   paRhaatii   hai?
               sister   these days what   teaches   is
         'What does your sister teach these days?'
     b. Aapkii *sister*   aajkal   kyaa   paRhaatii   hai?
         your   these days what   teaches   is
         'What does your sister teach these days?'

The grammaticality contrasts between (4a) and (4b) and between (5a) and (5b) do not, however, follow from the Government Constraint on codeswitching since all of the switched elements appear in subject position, which is governed by Infl. The data observed so far can instead be understood in terms of the generalization (6) about the licensing condition on subject DP codeswitching, which encodes the robust empirical observation, given in (7), about Kashmiri-English and Hindi-English codeswitching.

(6)   The language of the Case checker (e.g., I^0) must match the language of the Spec of the XP (DP) within its checking domain (e.g., IP).[5]

(7)   Codeswitching cannot occur between [Spec, IP] and I^0 in Kashmiri-English and Hindi English.

6.2.2   Object Switches

6.2.2.1   Direct Object Switches

Direct object DPs follow the same pattern of codeswitching as the subject DPs. The ungrammaticality of the Hindi-English codeswitching data presented in (8a–c) shows this most clearly. These data find a straightforward account under the Government Constraint, discussed earlier: object DPs are governed by the verb and therefore cannot be codeswitched.

(8)   a. *MaiN *his handwriting*   nahiN   paRh   saktaa.
      I   not   read   can
      'I cannot read his handwriting.'
    b. *I heard   *tumharii*   *burii*   *khabar* today.
          your   bad   news
      'I heard your bad news today.'
    c. *Maine *his new critique* paRhaa.
      I   read
      'I read his new critique.'

Notice, however, that the ungrammaticality of (8a–c) disappears when the specifier of the switched DP carries the same language index as that of the governor, or Case checker, as shown in (9a–b). Notice also that the grammaticality of (9a–b) does not follow from the Government Constraint: object DPs are also sensitive to the same licensing conditions of codeswitching that were observed earlier for subjects, stated in (6). The grammaticality contrast between (8) and (9) supports the hypothesis that as long as the specifier of the object DPs carries the same language index as that of the governor—for example, the Case checker—the (rest of the) object DP is free to switch to another language.

(9)   a. I heard your   *burii*   *khabar* today.
             bad   news
     'I heard your bad news today.'
    b. Maine   uska *new critique*   paRhaa.
      I   his   read
     'I read his new critique.'

If, as the data seem to suggest, the statement in (6) is the correct hypothesis on codeswitching, then it follows that there must be some language production data that uniquely follows only as a consequence of this hypothesis. In (10a–b), Hindi-English codeswitching, I present such data. The curious nature of these data is that although the codeswitched object complement DP of the English verbs "give" and "finish" exhibit the Hindi DP order (Possessive pronoun + Quantifier + Noun), the first (highest) specifier must nevertheless carry the language index of the governor/Case checker. It appears as though the entire object complement in (10a–b) is switched, but in order for the switch to be legal the highest specifier is forbidden to switch, by hypothesis (6).

(10) a. He gave [his   *saarii   jaaydaad*]   to his youngest son.
                       all   fortune
     'He gave (away) all his fortune to his youngest son.'
   b. First, you finish [your   *saaraa   kaam*].
                                 all   work
     'First, you finish all your work.'

The data observed so far leads to the postulation of a specific hypothesis on argument licensing in codeswitching that captures the linguistically significant generalizations of both the subject and the object codeswitching. The hypothesis is presented in (11) and its structural instantiation is given in (12). The hypothesis in (11) captures the crosslinguistic generalization that Spec-XP in an A-position is forbidden to codeswitch.[6]

(11) *Spec Constraint: *XP iff:
     a. XP is in an A-position;
     b. [Spec, XP] is drawn from Language α, and
     c. XP is in the checking domain of Y^0, Y^0 drawn from Language ß.

(12)

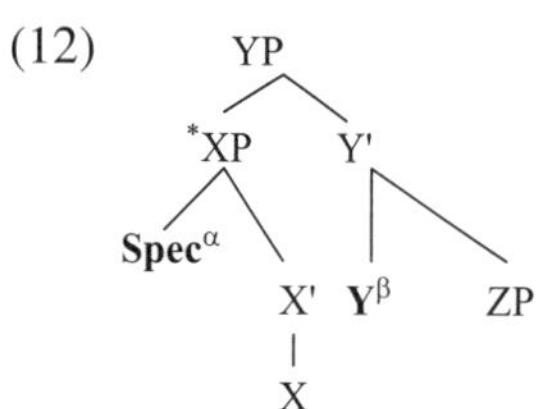

Given (11), and assuming (13) as the X'-theoretic structure of the object complement in (10), the grammaticality of codeswitching in (10a–b) follows from the fact that only [Spec, XP] but not [Spec, X']—the lower Spec in (13)—is required to match the Language feature of the Case assigner/checker (V, AgrO). The Language matching is satisfied by the upper Spec, yielding the legitimate codeswitches in (10).[7]

(13)

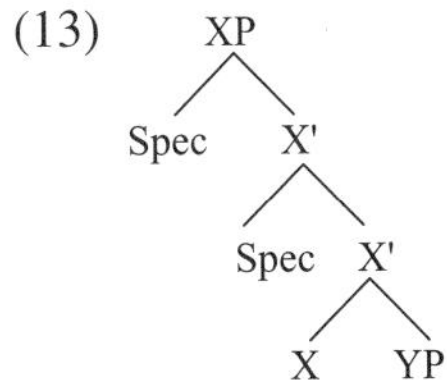

The generalizations about subject switches—the grammaticality contrast between (5a) and (5b)—follow, similarly, from hypothesis (11). In (5a) there is a mismatch between the Language of I^0 (Hindi) and [Spec, DP] (English) in [Spec, IP]. Thus, it is correctly ruled out by the *Spec Constraint (11).

6.2.2.2 *Indirect Object Switches*

In contrast to the patterns observed for subject and direct object codeswitches, entire indirect objects are permitted to switch, as shown by the Kashmiri-Hindi codeswitching in (14). In (14a), the entire indirect object is codeswitched to Hindi; the switched constituent, however, appears in a noncanonical, clause-final position. In Hindi-Kashmiri codeswitching (14b), the entire indirect object is switched to Kashmiri and appears in the canonical indirect object position, preceding the direct object.

(14) a. Pat *pro* dyutun suyi patluun *bimla ke sabse   chote bete ko.*
        then   gave that pant Bimla of from-all small son to
        '(And) then she gave those pants to Bimla's youngest son.'
    b. *pro panyis baayis khatr* gilaas le   gayii (question intonation)?
          your brother for   glass take went
        '(Did you) take a glass for your brother?'

English-Hindi codeswitching also permits the pattern found above in (14). Both (15a–b) are well-formed indirect object codeswitches to Hindi.

(15) a. Ramesh bought an expensive watch   *apne bhaaii ke liye.*
                                             his   brother for
        'Ramesh bought an expensive watch for his brother.'
    b. I gave your book   *is   laRke   ko.*
                           this   boy   to
        'I gave your book to this boy.'

So, a corollary of hypothesis (11) can now be stated as in (16).

(16) A constituent outside the Case domain of a governing/checking head is allowed to switch all its elements.

Interestingly, however, (16) makes incorrect empirical predictions for those cases of codeswitching where the codeswitched element, the indirect object, is English, not Hindi, as shown by the ungrammaticality of (17a) and (17b).

(17) a. *Vah   laRka *for his sister*   phuul   laayaa.
       that   boy   flowers   brought
       'That boy brought flowers for his sister.'

    b. *Kal   Ramesh-ne   *to his teacher*   kitaab   dii.
       yesterday   ERG   book   gave
       'Yesterday Ramesh gave a book to his teacher.'

One plausible explanation for the ungrammaticality of (17a–b) can be offered by following Kayne's (1994) proposal of Specifier-Head-Complement as universal order. Under that proposal, we can argue that Hindi allows left movement—scrambling feature checking—of its complements, but English does not allow such (scrambling) movements, and, therefore, any left movement will be an "Economic" liability. Thus, whereas Hindi complements may left-move [maine (I) khaanaa (food) khaayaa (ate)] or may not left-move [maine (I) khaayaa (ate) khaanaa (food)], English complements remain in situ; they cannot left-move since there is no scrambling feature that needs to be checked.[8] This nonmovement property of English complements may be responsible for ungrammatical mixed structures, such as (17a) and (17b), where the English complement (indirect object) has been moved in each instance to the left of the head (verb). Hindi, a language with scrambling properties, can afford to have a codeswitched complement well formed even to the right of the verb, interpreted semantically-pragmatically as "tail" (Vallduví 1992), which explains why in English-Hindi codeswitching, indirect objects can appear codeswitched to Hindi.

Codeswitching data within the indirect object constituent provides further support for hypothesis (11). The Hindi-English codeswitching data in (18) support hypothesis (11): the direct complement DP of the preposition is forbidden to switch since the DP is within the Case domain of the preposition.

(18) *Suresh bought flowers for   *apnii   behan.*
                          his   sister
      'Suresh bought flowers for his sister.'

However, the above example can be salvaged if the Language of the Spec of the complement of the preposition matches the Language of the preposition. This is shown by (19a). Contrasting (19a) with unacceptable cases like (19b–c), where the preposition and the Spec of the complement belong to different languages, further supports the claim that the [Spec, XP] and the head that assigns/checks Case to XP must belong to the same language.[9]

(19) a.   Suresh bought flowers for his   *behan.*
                                          sister
     b. *Suresh bought flowers for   *apnii*   *behan.*
                                          his   sister
     c. *Suresh bought flowers for   *apnii*   sister.
                                          his

The contrast between (20a) and (20b–c), using Hindi postposition, provides further support for (11): the language of [Spec, DP] and the language of the head in whose Case domain the DP is must be the same.

(20) a.   Suresh bought flowers   *apnii* sister   *ke liye.*
                                    his   for
     b. *Suresh bought flowers   his sister   *ke liye.*
                                                      for
     c. *Suresh bought flowers   his   *behan*   *ke liye.*
                                            sister   for

Finally, there is a curious, albeit subtle, contrast that indirect object codeswitching displays, shown in (21). It turns out that the well-formed instances of indirect object codeswitching such as (21a) seem to be preferred (shown below as √) over other well-formed instances of indirect object codeswitching such as (21b), where everything except the noun has switched. This contrast is based on our subjects' stronger preference (96%) for (nearly perfect) switches in (21a) compared to (slightly degraded) switches (82%) in (21b). Finally, also compare the contrast between (21c) and (21a–b); the Hindi-English codeswitching option in (21c) is ungrammatical; it is also illicit, by hypothesis (11).

(21) a.   √Ramesh bought an expensive watch   *apne*   *bhaaii*   *ke liye.*
                                                his   brother   for
          'Ramesh bought an expensive watch for his brother.'
     b.   Ramesh bought an expensive watch   *apne* brother   *ke liye.*
                                               his   for
     c. *Ramesh bought an expensive watch   his brother   *ke liye.*
                                                              for

6.2.2.3 Noun Switches

One generalization I have not yet considered in dealing with codeswitching in argument position is one for which there is overwhelming crosslinguistic evidence: among all the grammatical categories, nouns switch most freely (Kachru 1978; Pfaff 1979; Poplack 1981; McClure 1981). All of the data considered so far shows the robustness of this empirical generalization. I will not discuss it further, but will, in section 6.5, show how this generalization is captured by the interaction of the two proposed constraints, neither appealing directly to the codeswitching status of the noun.

6.2.3 Spanish-English, Swahili-English

Compared to the patterns observed above for Hindi-English and Kashmiri-English codeswitching, Spanish-English and Swahili-English codeswitching behave differently.[10] Observe, for example, the grammaticality of Spanish-English codeswitching in (22a–b), where the entire subject constituent appears in Spanish.

(22) a. *Pocos   estudiantes*   finished the exam.
         few   students
         'Few students finished the exam.'
     b. *The water*   esta   *boil*-ando.
                        is   boiling
         'The water is boiling.'

These data seem to suggest that hypothesis (11) makes incorrect predictions for Spanish-English codeswitching of subject constituents. More counterexamples to (11) come from codeswitching of objects, as shown by the grammaticality of (23).

(23) a. I saw   *la*   *casa*.
                  the   house
         'I saw the house.'
     b. Los policías   han   visto *a thief*.
         the police officers have   seen
         'The police officers have seen a thief.'
     c. Esto ano en P.E.   ha ganado   *three ribbons*   ya.
         this year in   I have won   already
         'This year I have won three ribbons already.'

The Spanish-English data observed so far seem to force the conclusion that hypothesis (11) does not have crosslinguistic generalizability. On closer inspection of the Spanish-English data, however, we find support for our hypothesis. First, consider codeswitching in the subject position. Notice the contrast in (24): (24a) is grammatical when both the Spec and the head codeswitched to Spanish, but when only the specifier is switched (24b), the result is ungrammaticality.

(24) a. *Pocos*   *estudiantes*   finished the exam.
      few   students
   b. **Pocos*   students finished the exam.
      few   students

The grammaticality contrast in (25) is revealing, because it is controversial. Belazi et al. (1994) do not accept (25b–c) as possible codeswitching, which are ruled out by the Functional Head Constraint they have proposed. For several other scholars, (25b) is acceptable codeswitching (cf. Pfaff 1979; McClure 1981; MacSwan 1999). Our bilingual Spanish-English informants have pointed out that (25b) is slightly degraded compared to (25a), whereas (25c) is completely unacceptable. The contrast between (25b–c) provides more evidence for the claim that even Spanish-English codeswitching respects hypothesis (11): the [Spec, DP] and I^0 match in the Language feature.[11]

(25) a. I saw   *la*   *casa.*
         the house
   b. ? I saw the *casa.*
               house
   c. *I saw   *la*   house.
         the

The contrast between (25a) and (25c) suggests that *Spec violations in Spanish-English codeswitching can only occur in those cases when both the Spec and its head switch. This generalization—that if [Spec, XP] switches, then the head X also switches—is formalized in (26). Notice that the constraint in (26) only imposes a language-matching restriction on Specs, not heads.[12]

(26) *Complaisance (Comp) Constraint*
    [Spec, XP] of a codeswitched constituent must match in Language feature, α, with the head X^0 (a reflex of a more general process of Spec-head agreement).

The *Spec Constraint, (11), imposes external (to XP) Language matching requirements whereas the Comp Constraint, (26), imposes internal (to XP) Language feature-matching requirements. And, in all those instances when the Language matching requirements of the two constraints are in conflict with each other, Spanish-English chooses, as shown by (24a), the internal (to XP) requirements, (26), to override the external (to XP) requirements, (11). Kashmiri-English and Hindi-English favor external requirements (11) over the internal requirements (26).

Even in Hindi-English codeswitching, there is evidence of the presence of the Comp Constraint. Since *Spec will forbid any legitimate expression of Comp, it is necessary to find evidence where *Spec does not conflict with Comp. Such instances are presented in (27) and (28), where the visibility of the Comp Constraint becomes apparent since it does not conflict with the *Spec Constraint: *Spec is inoperative since XP is not in an A-position.

(27) a. Ham *every year* garmiyoN kii chuTiyoN meN kashmiir jaate t^he.
         we   summer of holidays in   Kashmir go   was
         'We used to go to Kashmir every year during summer holidays.'
     b. *Ham *every* saal garmiyoN kii chuTiyoN meN kashmiir jaate t^he.
         we   year summer of holidays in   Kashmir go   was

(28) a. Tumhaaraa bhaaii *two years in a row* ham-se   milne   aayaa.
         your brother   us-with meet   came
         'Your brother came two years in a row to meet us.'
     b. *Tumhaaraa bhaaii *two* saal *in a row* ham-se   milne   aayaa.
         your   brother years   us-with meet   came
         'Your brother came two years in a row to meet us.'

Turning now to Swahili-English data, we notice that it patterns much like Spanish-English codeswitching, as the data in (29) shows. The ungrammaticality of (29a) results from violations of both *Spec and Comp, but the grammaticality of (29b) shows that violations of *Spec are tolerated as long as Comp is satisfied.

(29) a. *Sikuona   *your* barua   ambayo   uliipoteza.
         I didn't see   letter   which   you lost
     b. Wache mimi nielekeee tauni, tukutane *this evening at the usual place.*
                                     let us meet
         'Let me go so that I may reach town, let's meet this evening at the usual place.'

6.2.4 The Linguistically Significant Generalization

The difference between the Spanish-English/Swahili-English type of codeswitching and the Hindi-English/Kashmiri-English type of codeswitching reduces to the relative prominence of the two constraints in the grammar of codeswitching languages, *Spec (11) and Comp (26). The grammar of the Hindi-English/Kashmiri-English type of codeswitching prefers *Spec over Comp, when the two are in conflict, as shown in (30a). The grammar of Spanish-English/Swahili-English, on the other hand, shows the opposite preference, Comp over *Spec, when the two are in conflict, as shown in (30b).

(30) a.

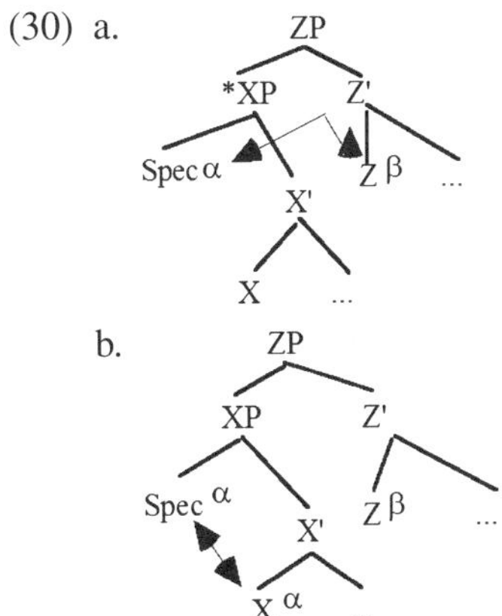

This linguistically significant generalization of conflict and its variable management by the different grammars can be straightforwardly captured within the Optimality Theory of constraint interaction and satisfaction, to which I turn next.

6.3 Optimality Theory (OT)

Optimality Theory (Prince and Smolensky 1993) is about how grammars are defined by constraint hierarchies. Universal Grammar in OT is expected to provide a finite set of potentially conflicting (violable) constraints on structural well-formedness. Languages differ from each other in terms of how their respective grammars rank the set of violable constraints. Thus, in essence, different configurations of constraint ranking yield, in principle, different grammars, as shown schematically in figure 6.1.

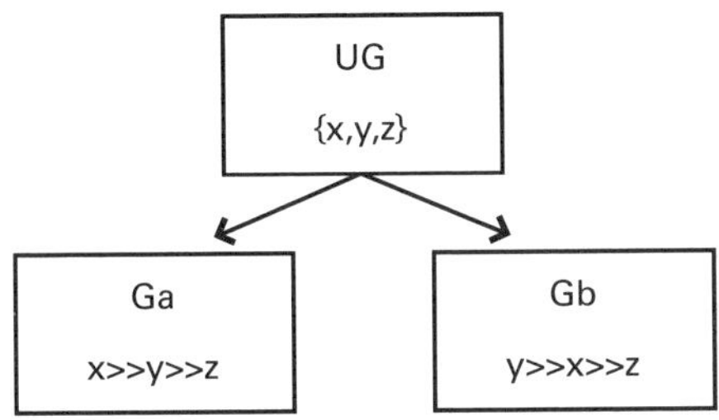

Figure 6.1
Universal Grammar and language variation

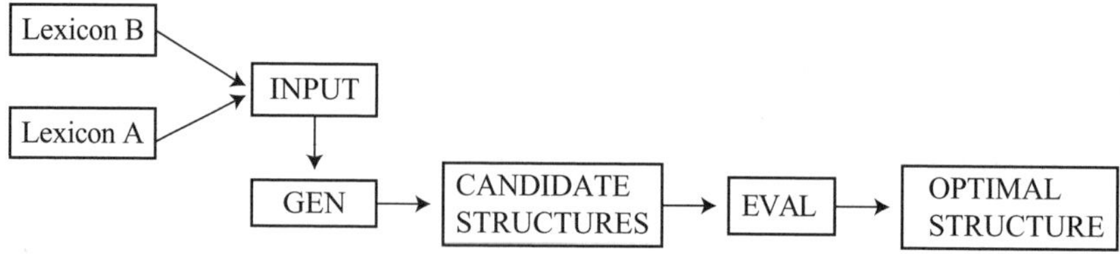

Figure 6.2
OT Grammar

Generative grammar consists of ranked constraints that examine (via *Eval*) all possible candidate structural descriptions freely generated by input-output function (*Gen*). This is illustrated in figure 6.2. The output that has the fewest violations (= 0, in the best-case scenario) is optimal—that is, grammatical. Inputs in OT syntax, according to Samek-Lodovici (1996,10), provide "the lexical items out of which extended projections are built, as well as the argument relations between them." Thus the input for a verbal extended projection is a lexical head and its argument structure and an assignment of lexical heads to its arguments, plus a specification of the associated tense and aspect (Grimshaw 1997, 375–376).

6.4   Optimality Theory and Codeswitching

The crosslinguistic observation that languages involved in codeswitching have "preferences" for what counts as "well formed" yields a plausible explanation that the syntax of codeswitched constructions strives toward well-formedness—that is, when elements from two languages appear within a clause, the syntax operates to optimize well-formedness. In other words, certain adjustments must naturally follow in the "mixed" grammars (cf. also Muysken 2000), when items (words, phrases) from one language with one set of well-formedness conditions appear with items from another language with another set of well-formedness conditions. The claim is that the optimal adjustment between items of the two languages is the grammatical (well-formed) option.

The constraints offered in the past to express distributional generalizations of codeswitching were categorical; their violations led to ungrammaticality. Instead of using categorical constraints to express empirical generalizations, the Optimality framework (à la Prince and Smolensky 1993) uses "violable" (soft) constraints, as discussed above. These soft constraints are defeasible in just those contexts in which they conflict with a higher-ranked constraint. The claim, then, is that there are no language pair-specific rules of codeswitching, as previously thought, but rather that the patterns of codeswitching emerge from the interactions among these (soft) constraints. For bilingual language use in codeswitching, the only assumption we must add to the standard accounts of OT is that lexical items from (at least) two languages are drawn to compose a set of competing candidates as long as the items drawn are translation equivalents (i.e., the competing candidates have nondistinct LFs).[13]

In this chapter, I use two constraints, *Spec and Comp, the interaction and satisfaction of which yield the distribution of codeswitching in argument positions. To recruit them in an explanation for codeswitching, a couple of theoretical assumptions need to be explicitly stated. First, these constraints are not necessarily "surface-true"; this is expected since the constraints that are always surface-true are going to be those that either do not conflict with any other constraint, or are always victorious in any conflict by virtue of the fact that they are always ranked higher than those with which they conflict. Second, and importantly, these constraints are universal (cf. Bhatt 1997); the grammar of every codeswitching language has them and all rankings of them are possible. This assumption follows a central metaprinciple of OT, called UNIV, which simply states that constraints are universal. Although the proposed constraints, *Spec and Comp, are universal, their operation is vacuously satisfied in monolingual grammars. In other words, because these constraints refer to two languages, say Language x and Language y, in a way that governs their interaction, they will have no effect in monolingual grammars of either Language x or Language y.[14]

The theory of bilingual codeswitching, under the assumptions discussed above, works as follows. All possible codeswitched output representations for a given bilingual input are examined by a set of (violable) ranked constraints that evaluate their well-formedness. The optimal, harmonic, codeswitched output representation is the one that has the least serious constraint violations. Thus, with the introduction of the idea that a grammar is a set of ranked constraints, it becomes possible, for the first time, to capture crosslinguistic generalizations of codeswitching within one theoretical framework.

Before I close the discussion in this section, let me give an illustration of how OT accounts for variation in the grammars of, for example, Hindi-English codeswitching and Spanish-English codeswitching. Assume that Grammar H-E and Grammar S-E have three constraints, $\{x, y, z\}$. Assume further that in Grammar H-E these constraints are ranked in such a way that $\{x\}$ dominates $\{y\}$ dominates $\{z\}$ [= x >> y, y >> z, x >> z]. In other words, Grammar H-E imposes a total order on the constraints: x >> y >> z. Now, assume that for a certain bilingual input we get two competing codeswitched output candidates: *cand 1* and *cand 2*. Tableau 6.1 shows the competition between the two candidates. *cand 1* violates the highest-ranking constraint $\{x\}$, which is lethal.

Table 6.1
Output = *cand2*

Candidates		x	y	z
a.	*cand1*	*!		*
b. ⇒	*cand2*		*	*

Table 6.2
Output = *cand1*

Candidates		y	x	z
a. ⇒	*cand1*		*	
b.	*cand2*	*!		*

Grammar H-E, therefore, chooses *cand 2* straightforwardly as the optimal, grammatical, option.

Now consider the other grammar, Grammar S-E. Assume that it, too, has the same three (universal) constraints, {x, y, z}. However, this grammar imposes slightly different ordering, namely, constraint {y} dominates {x} dominates {z}. Now for the similar bilingual input, as in Grammar H-E, we get two similar competing codeswitched outputs: *cand 1* and *cand 2*. The optimal output, as shown in tableau 6.2, is *cand 1*, because in this grammar *cand 2* violates a higher-ranked constraint {y}, leading to its rejection as optimal.

With this background, I turn to the optimization of well-formedness in codeswitching in argument positions, which I will show follows from the interaction and satisfaction of two constraints, *Spec and Comp, giving rise to at least a two-way typology of the grammars of codeswitching in argument position.

6.5   The OT Account

Maximally general constraints on codeswitching will inevitably be in conflict; the options chosen by different grammars to resolve the conflict give rise to a typology of codeswitching languages. From the vantage point of Optimality Theory, the question is how the proposed constraints, (11) and (26), are ranked in different codeswitching languages; the theory must specify the constraints and their rankings. As discussed above, Universal Grammar in OT is conceptualized as having a set of universal constraints, whereas particular grammars are instantiations of the way these constraints are ranked. Language variation arises when different ranking configurations yield different codeswitching grammars.

I claim that the grammar of Hindi-English and Kashmiri-English ranks *Spec above Comp: *Spec >> Comp. This ranking correctly predicts the distribution of the grammaticality patterns of codeswitching in these pairs of languages. Consider the grammaticality contrast between (31a) and (31b) in Hindi-English codeswitching. Given these two competing candidates of codeswitching, the EVAL (ranked constraints) function correctly picks out (b) as the optimal ($\Rightarrow$), grammatical output, as shown in tableau (32). Tableau (32) shows that candidate (b) violates a low-ranked constraint (Comp) compared to its competing candidate (a), which violates the hierarchically superior *Spec constraint, which is lethal (*!).

(31) a. *Maine *his new critique*   paRhaa.
         I   read
         'I read his new critique.'
     b. Maine   uska *new critique*   paRhaa.
         I   his   read
         'I read his new critique.'

(32) *Hindi-English argument codeswitching*

Candidates	*Spec	Comp
(a) Maine his new critique paRhaa	*!	
$\Rightarrow$(b) Maine uska new crtique paRhaa		*

The fact that the constraint Comp does empirical work in Hindi-English codeswitching can be evidenced in those instances of codeswitching where Comp is not in conflict with *Spec. In those cases, Comp plays a critical role in the grammar to weed out the ungrammatical codeswitching possibilities. This is shown in tableau (34), where the function Eval picks out the optimal output between the candidate set (33a) and (33b).

(33) a. Tumhaaraa bhaaii   *two years in a row*   ham-se milne aayaa.
         your brother   us-with meet came
         'Your brother came two years in a row to meet us.'
     b. *Tumhaaraa bhaaii *two* saal *in a row* ham-se milne aayaa.
         your   brother   years   us-with meet   came
         'Your brother came two years in a row to meet us.'

(34) *Hindi-English nonargument codeswitching*

Candidates	*Spec	Comp
⇒ (a) tumhaaraa bhaaii *two years in a row* ham-se milne aayaa.		
(b) tumhaaraa bhaaii *two* saal *in a row* ham-se milne aayaa.		*!

Another instance where the role of Comp becomes visible in argument position is provided by the data in (21), repeated below in (35). The data in (35) (and later in 39) point out the empirical generalization of degrees of grammaticality (gradient acceptability). This gradience in data is regularly experienced by linguists who use notations such as "?", "??", "?*" to mark subtle acceptability contrasts. Recent work in generative grammar has in fact argued against maintaining the categorical view of grammaticality (see Manning 2003, as well as Sternefeld 2001, Kolb 1997, and Abney 1996). Gradience, as opposed to categoricity, has been successfully captured in OT frameworks, especially in the work of Ralf Vogel, who uses a Stochastic OT model to relate empirical gradience to relative optimality of violation profiles (Vogel 2004, and see also Keller 2000).

Tableau (36) shows a way to capture, on the one hand, the grammaticality contrast between (35a–b) and (35c), and on the other hand, the subtle contrast between (35a) and (35b). Tableau (36) shows that candidate (a) is the optimal option, given the three competing candidates: (a), (b), and (c). Candidate (a) does not violate any constraint, whereas the other two violate one or the other constraint. However, the competition between the two suboptimal candidates results in the victory, indicated as [→], of candidate (b) since it only violates a low-ranked (Comp) constraint compared to candidate (c), which violates a high-ranked constraint (*Spec). Thus, in this way, Optimality Theory not only makes it possible to capture grammaticality contrasts in codeswitching, but it also allows us to capture some subtle contrasts that do not compartmentalize neatly into grammatical-ungrammatical distinctions.

(35) a. √Ramesh bought an expensive watch   *apne   bhaaii   ke liye.*
                                                         his   brother   for
           'Ramesh bought an expensive watch for his brother.'
      b. Ramesh bought an expensive watch   *apne* brother   *ke liye.*
                                                         his   for
      c. *Ramesh bought an expensive watch   his brother   *ke liye.*
                                                                          for

(36) *Comp in Hindi-English codeswitching*

Candidates	*Spec	Comp
⇒ (a) Ramesh bought an expensive watch *apne bhaaii ke liye*		
→(b) Ramesh bought an expensive watch *apne* brother *ke liye*		*!
(c) Ramesh bought an expensive watch his brother *ke liye*	*!	

Turning to Spanish-English codeswitching, I claim that its grammar ranks Comp over *Spec: Comp >> *Spec. This ranking correctly yields the codeswitching generalization in subject position, as shown by the grammaticality contrast between (37a) and (37b). Tableau (38) shows how this generalization is captured in OT.

(37) a. *Pocos estudiantes*   finished the exam.
         few students
     b. **Pocos* students finished the exam.
         few students

(38) Subject switches in Spanish-English codeswitching

Candidates	Comp	*Spec
⇒ *Pocos estudiantes* finished the exam		*
Pocos students finished the exam	*!	*

Next compare the subtle object codeswitching contrasts discussed earlier in (25), repeated in (39). These contrasts are captured neatly in tableau (40).

(39) a. I saw   *la*   *casa.*
                 the   house
     b. ? I saw   the   *casa.*
     c. *I saw   *la*   house.

(40) *Object switches in Spanish-English codeswitching*

Candidates	Comp	*Spec
⇒ (a) I saw *la casa.*		*
→(b) I saw the *casa.*	*!	
(c) I saw *la* house.	*!	*!

Tableau (40) captures the grammaticality contrast in (39) in a straightforward manner: the two candidates, (b) and (c), both violate the superior constraint, Comp, and are therefore out of the competition vis-à-vis candidate (a), which is the winner. The OT grammar of Spanish-English codeswitching can further tease out the different degrees of acceptability among the three candidates. Candidate (a) is the most acceptable, given that the grammar picks it out as the most optimal choice. To distinguish between the less acceptable candidate (b) and the unacceptable candidate (c), the OT grammar works in the following manner. The constraint Comp cannot decide between the two candidates (b) and (c) because both violate Comp. In this case, then, the computation proceeds to the next constraint lower down on the hierarchy, *Spec. Candidate (b) wins out [→] in this competition because candidate (c) violates *Spec and (b) does not, yielding the desired result that between (b) and (c), (b) is somewhat acceptable but (c) is not (compare 39a–c).

Finally, the interaction between the two constraints, *Spec and Comp, yields the crosslinguistic generalization about noun switches, discussed in section 6.2.2.3. Tableaux (32), (34), and (36) show how the ranking in Hindi-English (and Kashmiri-English) codeswitching guarantees noun switching, whereas the opposite ranking of the two constraints (tableaux (38) and (40)) in Spanish-English (and Swahili-English) also yields the same results. In other words, one of the favorable consequences of the Optimality view of codeswitching is that linguistically significant generalizations are captured most economically as a result of the interaction of violable constraints.

6.6 Conclusions

The specific proposal adopted in this chapter to account for the generalizations of codeswitching has evolved from one important crosslinguistic observation: that languages involved in codeswitching have "preferences" for what constitutes "well-formed" (Gumperz and Hernández-Chávez 1975; Shaffer 1977; Kachru 1978; Gumperz 1982; Poplack 1981; Singh 1985; among others). This observation motivates the theoretical content of this chapter, which is premised on the assumption that a linguistic structure (i.e., a codeswitched constituent) that violates a particular constraint has its well-formedness "reduced" by a certain amount. Using "violable" (soft) constraints on well-formedness, as in Optimality Theory (Prince and Smolensky 1993; Grimshaw 1997), and allowing them all to interact accounts for a large range of patterns of codeswitching, especially, as shown in this chapter, in argument positions.

I have presented evidence to claim that two universal constraints on the well-formedness of codeswitching, *Spec and Comp (see also Bhatt 1997), are in conflict with each other, and that different grammars resolve this conflict in different ways, giving rise to the grammatical variation observed in different codeswitching languages. Hindi-English and Kashmiri-English rank *Spec over Comp, whereas Spanish-English and Swahili-English rank Comp over *Spec. These two rankings correctly account for codeswitching in argument positions in the four pairs of languages investigated in this chapter.

Notes

I thank María Alvarez and Sam Mendoza for their help with Spanish-English codeswitching data. Thanks to Matt Ciscel, Larry Lafond, and Sharon Fellows for their help in the preparation of this chapter. My thanks also to the two reviewers, Jeff MacSwan and Marcel den Dikken, for their thoughtful comments and critiques.

1 Bentahila and Davies (1995) present an interesting account of the different patterns of codeswitching in terms of the different (sociohistorical and psychological) patterns of language contact.

2 This is true of an EL island—where the entire constituent is codeswitched—in the sense of Myers-Scotton 1993.

3 The data in (1a), for example, is both LF and PF convergent. There are no special lexical requirements of the Kashmiri subject DP that would lead the derivation to crash: the nominative (phonologically null) Case of the (Kashmiri) Subject DP, sitting in Spec-TP, is checked by T.

4 Crosslinguistic data from French-Dutch (Treffers-Daller 1994) and Finnish-English (Halmari 1994) have also shown that subjects do not readily switch unless followed by a pause. The interpretation of the sentences in these switched constituents is a contrastive ("As for") topic reading. If so, I claim that the switched constituents are dislocated constituents, therefore ungoverned and therefore switchable. There is, however, a problem for the Government Constraint with respect to the data in (3a), noted by Marcel den Dikken: if the italicized NP in (3a) is an "As for" topic, and if the actual subject is pro, then if this pro is taken to be a Kashmiri pro it will violate the Government Constraint, and if this pro is the subject of the English sentence, then the Government Constraint is satisfied but the English pro remains unlicensed.

5 I am assuming an X'-theory where Specs are sisters of X', as shown:

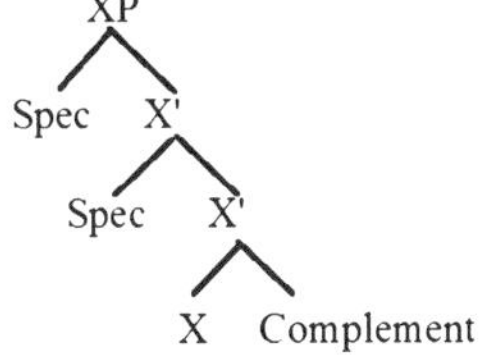

Further, I assume that all determiners (articles, demonstratives, quantifiers, possessives) are generated under the Spec positions.

6 The constraint (11) proposed here encodes the most robust crosslinguistic generalization in codeswitching (see, among others, the works of Di Scuillo, Muysken, and Singh (1986, formalized as the Government Constraint), Myers-Scotton (1993, formalized as the System Morpheme Principle), and Bhatt 1997.

7 The idea of "language matching" requiring formal compatibility between switched items has been previously discussed within the generative grammatical theory in slightly different terms in Di Sciullo, Muysken, and Singh 1986; Pandit 1986, 1990; Halmari 1994, 1997; and Belazi, Rubin, and Toribio 1994. However, MacSwan (1999) and Mahootian and Santorini (1996) have argued against this position, particularly the ideas in Belazi, Rubin, and Toribio 1994, where the "Language" feature is presumed to have the same formal status as other formal features {Case, Tense, etc.}. This controversial issue is noted here and its resolution is left to future research.

8 The functional heads in Hindi-English codeswitched utterances in (17) are endowed with grammatical ("featural") properties of Hindi, under theoretical assumptions explicitly or implicitly stated in Di Sciullo, Muysken, and Singh 1986; Myers-Scotton 1993; Belazi, Rubin, and Toribio 1994; Halmari 1994; Treffers-Daller 1994; and MacSwan 1997.

9 I will assume, for purposes of uniformity, that prepositions also check Case of their complements in a Spec-head configuration; the complement NP moves to the empty Spec-PP for Case checking with P. The alternative is to use the traditional case of Case assignment by prepositions directly to their complements, and this alternative too will account for the grammaticality contrasts in (19).

10 The data in this section comes from various sources: Belazi, Rubin, and Toribio 1994, Myers-Scotton 1993, Valdés-Fallis 1978, and McClure 1981.

11 The Functional Head Constraint cannot furnish an account of the data in (25).

12 The head, X^0, is free to switch without any obligation to the language of [Spec, XP].

13 I thank Marcel den Dikken for raising the issue of how to define the candidate set in bilingual language use.

14 I thank Jeff MacSwan for help in clarifying this issue.

References

Abney, Steven. 1996. Statistical methods and linguistics. In Judith L. Klavans and Philip Resnick, eds., *The Balancing Act: Combining Symbolic and Statistical Approaches to Language*, 1–26. Cambridge, MA: MIT Press.

Belazi, Hedi, Edward Rubin, and Almeida Toribio. 1994. Code switching and X-bar theory: The functional head constraint. *Linguistic Inquiry* 25 (2), 221–237.

Bhatt, Rakesh M. 1997. Code-switching, constraints, and optimal grammars. *Lingua* 102:223–251.

Bokamba, Eyamba G. 1989. Are there syntactic constraints on code-mixing? *World Englishes* 8:277–292.

Clyne, Michael. 1987. Constraints on code-switching: How universal are they? *Linguistics* 25:739–764.

Di Sciullo, Anna Maria, Pieter Muysken, and Rajendra Singh. 1986. Government and code-mixing. *Journal of Linguistics* 22:1–24.

Grimshaw, Jane. 1997. Projection, Heads, and Optimality. *Linguistic Inquiry* 28:373–422.

Gumperz, John J. 1982. The sociolinguistic significance of conversational code-switching. In John Gumperz, ed., *Discourse Strategies*, 55–99. London: Cambridge University Press.

Gumperz, John J., and Eduardo Hernández-Chávez. 1975. Cognitive aspects of bilingual communication. In Eduardo Hernández Chávez, A. Cohen, and A. Beltramo, eds., *El lengauje de los chicanos*, 154–163. Arlington, VA: Center for Applied Linguistics.

Halmari, Helena. 1994. A government approach to Finnish-English intrasentential code-switching. Doctoral dissertation, University of Southern California.

Halmari, Helena. 1997. *Government and Codeswitching: Explaining American Finnish.* Amsterdam: John Benjamins.

Kachru, Braj B. 1978. Toward structuring code-mixing: An Indian perspective. *International Journal of the Sociology of Language* 16:28–46.

Kayne, Richard. 1994. *The Antisymmetry of Syntax.* Cambridge, MA: MIT Press.

Keller, Frank. 2000. Gradience in grammar: Experimental and computational aspects of degrees of grammaticality. Doctoral dissertation, University of Edinburgh.

Kolb, Hans-Peter. 1997. Is I-language a generative procedure? In *GB-Blues: Two Essays*, no. 110 in Arbeitspapiere des Sonderforschungs-bereichs 340, 1–14. Tübingen: University of Tübingen

MacSwan, Jeff. 1999. *A Minimalist Approach to Intrasentential Code Switching.* New York: Garland Press.

MacSwan, J. 2013. Code switching and linguistic theory. In T. K. Bhatia & W. Ritchie (eds.), *Handbook of Bilingualism and Multilingualism*, 2nd edition, 223–350. Oxford: Blackwell.

Mahootian, Shahrzad, and Beatrice Santorini. 1996. Codeswitching and the complement/adjunct distinction. *Linguistic Inquiry* 27 (3): 464–479.

Manning, Christopher D. 2003. Probabilistic syntax. In Rens Bod, Jennifer Hay, and Stefanie Jannedy, eds., *Probabilistic Linguistics*, 289–341. Cambridge, MA: MIT Press.

McClure, Erica. 1981. Formal and functional aspects of the codeswitched discourse of bilingual children. In Richard P. Duran, ed., *Latino Language and Communicative Behavior*, 69–92. Norwood, NJ: Ablex.

Muysken, Pieter. 2000. *Bilingual Speech: A Typology of Code-Mixing.* Cambridge: Cambridge University Press.

Myers-Scotton, Carol. 1993. *Duelling Languages: Grammatical Structure in Codeswitching.* Oxford: Oxford University Press.

Pandit, Ira. 1990. Grammaticality in codeswitching. In Rodolfo Jacobson, ed., *Codeswitching as a Worldwide Phenomenon*, 15–32. New York: Lang.

Pfaff, Carol. 1979. Constraints on language mixing. *Language* 55:291–319.

Poplack, Shana, 1981. Syntactic structure and social function of codeswitching. In Richard P. Duran, ed., *Latino Language and Communicative Behavior*, 169–184. Norwood, NY: Ablex.

Prince, Alan, and Paul Smolensky. 1993. Optimality Theory: Constraint interaction in generative grammar. Ms., University of Colorado and Rutgers University.

Samek-Lodovici, Vieri. 1996. Constraints on subjects: An Optimality Theoretic analysis. Doctoral dissertation, Rutgers University.

Shaffer, D. 1977. The place of code-switching in language contact. In M. Paradis, ed., *Aspects of Bilingualism*, 265–274. Columbia, SC: Hornbeam Press.

Singh, Rajendra. 1985. Grammatical constraints on code-mixing: Evidence from Hindi-English. *Canadian Journal of Linguistics* 30:33–45.

Sternefeld, Wolfgang. 2001. Grammatikalität und Sprachvermögen: Anmerkungen zum Induktionsproblem in der Syntax. In Josef Bayer and C. Römer, eds., *Von der Philologie zur Grammatiktheorie: Peter Suchsland zum 65*, 15–44. Tübingen: Niemeyer.

Treffers-Daller, Jeanine. 1994. *Mixing Two Languages: French-Dutch Contact in Comparative Perspective*. Berlin: Mouton De Gruyter.

Valdés-Fallis, Guadalupe. 1978. *Code-Switching and the Classroom Teacher*. Washington, DC: Center for Applied Linguistics.

Vallduvi, Enric 1992. *The Informational Component*. New York: Garland Publishers.

Vogel, Ralf. 2004. Correspondence in OT syntax and Minimal Link effects. In Arthur Stepanov, Gisbert Fanselow, and Ralf Vogel eds. *Minimality Effects in Syntax*, 401–441. Berlin: Mouton de Gruyter.

Part II

Codeswitching, Morphology, and the PF Interface

7 Light Switches: On *v* as a Pivot in Codeswitching, and the Nature of the Ban on Word-Internal Switches

Shoba Bandi-Rao and Marcel den Dikken

7.1 The Background: Telugu Causatives

Classical Telugu (a South-Central Dravidian language) makes its causatives with the aid of the freestanding lexical verb *cees* 'do/make', which takes an infinitival complement (ending in *-a(n)*, the infinitival suffix) whose subject is marked accusative by the matrix verb (ECM) and whose object is ACC-marked by the infinitive (cf. (1b)). Informal modern Telugu instead employs the suffix *-inc*, which we will gloss as 'DO' (cf. Murti 1973; Krishnamurti and Gwynn 1985, 202, for discussion of Telugu causatives). This suffix attaches to the transitive verb stem and gives rise to a *faire-par* type causative, with the causee marked with *ceeta* 'INST, by means of' (cf. (2b)). (Note that South Asian languages have been transcribed in several ways by linguists; since there is no standard approach, we utilize one commonly used in linguistic literature.)

(1) a. paapa   pustakamu-nu   caduwu-nu.
        child   book-ACC   read-AGR
        'A child reads a book.'

     b. siita   paapa-nu   pustakamu(-nu) caduw-a   *ceeyu*-nu.
        Sita   child-ACC   book-ACC   read-INFIN   make-AGR
        'Sita makes a child read a book.'

(2) a. kamala   niiLLu   kaacindi.
        Kamala   water   boil-PST-AGR
        'Kamala boiled the water.'

     b. raamu   kamala-ceeta   niiLLu   kaay-*inc*-EEDu.
        Ramu   Kamala-INST   water   boil-DO-PST-AGR
        'Ramu made Kamala boil the water.'

We have glossed neither *cees* nor *-inc* as causative elements because neither is in fact intrinsically causative: both *cees* and *-inc* can be used, alongside their causativizing uses, as light verbs serving as hosts for inflection in Sanskrit loans, as illustrated in (3a–b).[1]'they chanted'

(3) a. pooja   'worship' →   pooj *cees*   'to worship'
     b. preema   'love'   →   preem-*inc*   'to love'

Both *cees* and *-inc* are multipurpose light verbs, therefore—the former differing from the latter in taking an infinitivally inflected complement. Selection of a full-fledged infinitival complement is a property of lexical verbs—*cees*, therefore, is a V, with both "heavy" and "light" incarnations. In its "heavy" guise, *cees* behaves like garden-variety transitive verbs and is capable of taking a nominal complement (as in *siita vankai palyam cees-indi* 'Siita eggplant dish make-3PST'). As a "light" verb, it behaves essentially like the types of verbs discussed by Grimshaw and Mester (1988), such as English *make*, *give*, and *do* (cf. *siita pani cees-indi* 'Siita work make-3PST', where *pani* is a Telugu noun, not a Sanskrit loan).

By contrast, *-inc* selects a stem—either a bare stem or a transitive stem. Whenever *-inc* is attached to a transitive stem, the output is causative. But when the stem hosting *-inc* is not a transitive stem, the result of *-inc* affixation is not causative; it may be transitive, but it does not have to be: (4a) is an unaccusative inchoative construction with *-inc*, itself eligible as input to causativization with the aid of *cees*, as shown in (4b).

(4) a. nadi   prawah-*inc*u-nu.
        river   flow-DO-AGR
        'A river flows.'
     b. gangadevi   nadi-ni   prawah-*inc*-a   ceeyu-nu.
        Ganges goddess   river-ACC   flow-DO-INFIN   make-AGR
        'The Goddess Ganges makes the river flow.'

What (4) shows very clearly, then, is that *-inc* is not itself a causativizer. As a matter of fact, its sole function in the example in (4a) is to serve as a bridge between the Sanskrit loan *prawah* 'flow' and the subject agreement inflection *-nu*. Similarly, in (4b) *-inc* attaches to *prawah* to mediate between it and the infinitival inflection, *-a*. This makes *-inc* a "light verb" in the sense of Chomsky 1995, 2000, 2001—a connective *v* between the predicative root and the inflectional structure of the clause.[2]

Thus, we have identified two types of "light verb" in Telugu, a *lexical* "light V" (*cees* 'do/make') and a nonlexical "light *v*" (*-inc*), the former selecting a full-fledged infinitival complement, and the latter a projection of the lexical verb, yielding a verbal but not necessarily transitive output. This is summarized in (5).

(5) a. "Light V" (*cees*): takes a full infinitival complement

    b. "Light *v*" (*-inc*): takes a projection of the lexical verb as its complement

7.2 The Problem: A Codeswitching Asymmetry

7.2.1 The Use of *-ify* as a Pivot in Codeswitching

English *-ify* is a close match for Telugu *-inc* as far as syntactic distribution is concerned (cf. (6a–b)): it likewise functions as a go-between for lexical roots and inflectional morphology, producing an output that is verbal but not necessarily transitive.

(6) a. They are trying to diversify/gentrify/pacify/ ... the neighborhood.

    b. This neighborhood has diversified/gentrified/pacified/ ...
dramatically over the past few years.

It is precisely the fact that *-ify* connects things that could not otherwise host verbal inflectional morphology—such as the adjective *diverse* or the noun *gentry*—that makes *-ify* an ideal "pivot" in codeswitching. From this perspective, it does not come as a surprise that it is *-ify* that helps out in codeswitches at the juncture between English verbal inflection and a Telugu root.[3] Indeed, the apparently completely vacuous use of *-ify* is extremely common in this context. Some illustrative examples are provided in (7).[4]

(7) a. My sister **kal(i)p**-*ified* the curry.   *kalp* 'stir'

    b. You have to **kar(i)g**-*ify* the butter.   *karg* 'melt$_{\text{TRANS}}$'

    c. The butter that I left outside **kar(i)g**-*ified*.   *karg* 'melt$_{\text{INTRANS}}$'

    d. The teacher made the child **Ed(i)c**-*ify* in school.   *Edc* 'cry'

    e. I **kaTT-inc-kon**-*ified* this house.   *katti* 'build'+-*inc*
                                                      'DO'+-*kon* 'REFL'

      'I had the house built for myself.'

That *-ify* does not add any causative or inchoative semantics here is particularly clear from (7c), where *-ify* attaches to a Telugu unaccusative inchoative and delivers an unaccusative inchoative output, as well as from (7d–e), where the English causative verb *make* and Telugu *-inc*, respectively, bring in the semantics of causation, entirely independently of *-ify*, which appears to be semantically vacuous.[5] All that *-ify* does in these English/Telugu codeswitching cases is ensure that the inflectional heads can get their uninterpretable features checked. In this regard, *-ify* is directly similar to Telugu *-inc*. We are thus led to postulate the same analysis for *-ify* that we set up for Telugu *-inc*, as an instance of the generalized Chomskyan "light *v*." The use, within English, of *-ify* as an intermediary between a noun or adjective and verbal inflection seen in (6) is a facilitator for its use as a "little light verb" in codeswitching contexts—but arguably, the English-internal *-ify* in (6) and its incarnation in the codeswitching examples in (7) are not exactly identical. Thus, note the fact that the vacuous *-ify* of (7) does not behave as a stress shifter, unlike the Level I suffix *-ify*, which on standard assumptions attaches to its host in the lexical morphological component. This can perhaps be seen particularly clearly in the context of the vacuous use of *-ify* found in varieties of English spoken in the Southern United States. Thus, for Smoky Mountain English (spoken in the Tennessee/North Carolina border region), Montgomery and Hall (2004) note the use of "*-ify* on verbs redundantly to form verbs" in such cases as *argufy* (cf. *argue*) and *blamify* (cf. *blame*). This vacuous *-ify* seems to have precisely the same profile as the *-ify* seen in our codeswitching examples. Now notice that in the pair *árgue/árgufy*, stress remains on the initial syllable, while in *héro/heróify*, where *-ify* changes category and is standardly taken to be attached in the lexicon, we see the stress shifting rightward.[6]

In not triggering stress shift, vacuous *-ify* behaves like a phrasal affix and quite unlike the Level I suffix familiar from Standard English. The fact that *-ify* qua pivot behaves like a phrasal affix confirms, it seems to us, that this *-ify* is a "little light verb" (*v*) mediating between the lexical root and the inflectional system.[7] For Standard English Level-I *-ify*, we would not want to claim that it should be reanalyzed as a "little light verb." But the very fact that Standard English *-ify* can be used in contexts such as (6), where it seems to be a mere intermediary between the lexical root and the verbal inflection, makes *-ify* an ideal model from which to *create* a pivot for codeswitches at the juncture of the root and the verbal inflection. Thus, *-ify* is being recruited, from the vocabulary of Standard English, to perform a function, absent from Standard English, that is essential in the context of codeswitching: that of a pivot between the lexical and functional domains, a juncture where the two "codes" would otherwise clash head-on. Simply put, therefore, *-ify* is called upon in (7) to avoid a collision between the Telugu verb and the English Infl. We call these kinds of switches *"light switches"*—switches made at the "light *v*" stage, for inflectional purposes.

7.2.2 The Asymmetry

While the use of *-ify* to facilitate a switch at the juncture of English inflection and a Telugu root, as illustrated in (7), is now straightforward, with *-ify* analyzed as a "light *v*," what is entirely unexpected in this light is that *-inc*, the Telugu "light *v*," *cannot* help out in codeswitches in the opposite direction, at the juncture of Telugu inflection and an English root. Thus, (8a) is entirely impossible; instead, to make the switch, a token of the "light V" *cees* must be used, as in (8b).

(8)   a.   *vaaDu   nanni   **love**-*inc*-EEDu
            he-NOM   me-ACC   love-DO-PST-AGR
      b.   vaaDu   nanni   **love**   *cees*-EEDu
            he-NOM   me-ACC   love   do-PST-AGR
            'He loved me.'

There are two ways in which these examples are significant. First of all, (8a) highlights a striking difference between codeswitching and borrowing: in our earlier examples in (3b) and (4), *-inc* attaches to a Sanskrit loan (*preem, prawah*) perfectly grammatically, showing that what we have on our hands in (8a) is *not* an instance of borrowing. Second, the contrast between (7) and (8a) presents a prima facie surprising *asymmetry* in English/Telugu codeswitching—"light switches" with *-ify* of the type in (7) are extremely common, but "light switches" in the opposite direction, with *-inc* (cf. (8a)), are out of the question.

This, then, is the conundrum that this chapter seeks to shed "light" on: why is it that English *-ify* can serve as an intermediary in codeswitching at the inflectional juncture while what appears to be its direct counterpart in Telugu cannot do the same.

7.3   The Light: How and When the Twain Shall Meet

7.3.1   The Ban on Word-Internal Switches: A Quick Review of the Literature

The contrast between (8a), with affixal *-inc*, and (8b), with freestanding *cees*, recalls the familiar ban on word-internal switches, well documented in the literature in works as early as Poplack 1980 for English/Spanish codeswitching:

(9)   *estoy   **eat**-*iendo*   (Poplack 1980, 586)
       I-am   eat-ing

Poplack's (1980) account of the ungrammaticality of switches of the type in (9) was in terms of what she called the Free Morpheme Constraint, reproduced in (10):

(10)   *Free Morpheme Constraint*   (Poplack 1980)
        A switch may occur at any point in the discourse at which it is possible to make a surface constituent cut and still retain a free morpheme.

It should be plain that this constraint readily captures the Telugu facts in (8) as well: in (8b), nothing goes wrong since *cees* is a free morpheme, but (8a) is problematic because *-inc* is a bound morpheme, and we are not allowed to make the cut between two languages at a bound-morpheme juncture. By the same token, English/Telugu switches of the type in (11) are ungrammatical as well:

(11) a. *vaaDu   nanni   **love-D**-u
         he-NOM   me-ACC   love-PST-AGR
     b. *vaaDu   nanni   **love**-EEDu
         he-NOM   me-ACC   love-PST-AGR
     c. *My sister **kalp**-ed the curry.

But though (11c) is ill formed, recall from (7) (of which (7a) is repeated below) that it is not *categorically* impossible to make a switch at a bound-morpheme juncture:

(7a) My sister **kalp**-*ified* the curry.   *kalp* 'stir'

So although it readily captures (8) and (9), the Free Morpheme Constraint is ultimately empirically untenable.[8]

   Belazi, Rubin, and Toribio's (1994) Functional Head Constraint in (12) is an alternative attempt at capturing the ungrammaticality of things like (9): with *-iendo* a representative of Infl and *eat* the lexical V-head, (9) involves a switch between I and VP, disallowed by (12).

(12) *Functional Head Constraint* (Belazi, Rubin, and Toribio 1994)
     The language feature of the complement f-selected by a functional
     head, like all other relevant features, must match the corresponding
     feature of that functional head.

Once again, the English/Telugu facts in (8) readily fall into place, as do the ones in (11). But for the same reason that the Free Morpheme Constraint fails for English/Telugu codeswitching, the Functional Head Constraint fails as well: it will not take care of (7). For we have come to the conclusion that *-ify* in English is a lexicalization of the "light verb" head *v*, a functional (or "nonsubstantive") head that takes the lexical VP as its complement. Thus (12) would lead us to expect that switches between functional/nonsubstantive *-ify* and a Telugu lexical verb should be impossible, which is incorrect, as (7) shows. Therefore, (12) will not do for our purposes. It is also problematic for its conceptually quite awkward outlook on codeswitching couched in terms of "language features," and because of the fact that it makes a variety of incorrect empirical predictions outside the realm of English/Telugu switches as well (radically ruling out, for instance, any switches between D and NP, which turn out not to be infrequent; see MacSwan 1997 for Nahuatl/Spanish switches at that juncture). This leaves little to recommend (12), which we hereby set aside.

In this chapter, we focus on MacSwan's (2000) claim in (14), which he takes to follow from his PF Disjunction Theorem in (13).

(13) *PF Disjunction Theorem*   (MacSwan 1997)
>   (i)   the PF component consists of rules/constraints which must be (partially) ordered/ranked with respect to each other, and these orders/rankings vary cross-linguistically
>   (ii) code switching entails the union of at least two (lexically-encoded) grammars
>   (iii) ordering relations are not preserved under union
>   (iv) therefore, code switching within a PF component is not possible

(14) code switches below X^0 are ill-formed

We will argue that (14) stands the best chance of making sense of the English/Telugu codeswitching facts in (7) and (8). But while the discussion in the remainder of this section will thus lend support to (a modified version of) the constraint in (14), we will also argue (in section 7.4) that MacSwan's particular way of arriving at the conclusion on (14) is not correct, and provide an alternative rationale for it. (See MacSwan and Colina, chapter 8, this volume, where some of our criticisms are addressed.)

7.3.2 The Key Difference between *-inc* and *-ify*: To Incorporate or Not to Incorporate

The key question to ask is why there should be a difference between (7a) on the one hand, and (8a) on the other.[9]

(7a) my sister **kalp**-*ified* the curry *kalp* 'stir'

(8a) *vaaDu   nanni   **love**-*inc*-EEDu
     he-NOM   me-ACC   love-DO-PST-AGR

What these examples share is that they both instantiate a switch at the v–VP juncture: *-ify* and *-inc* both represent the "little light verb" v. But where they differ, we would like to argue, is that, while *-inc* incorporates the verbal head of its complement and forms a complex X^0 with it, *-ify* qua v does not:

(15) a. Telugu *-inc*=v is an incorporator
     b. English *-ify*=v is NOT an incorporator

That is, we analyze Telugu constructions featuring *-inc* as incorporation constructions in which the lexical verb V is raised to the "little light verb" v, while for English constructions with *-ify* we reject a head-incorporation analysis. If we can motivate this distinction between English *-ify* and Telugu *-inc* (which is something to which the rest of this section will be devoted), it will be immediately clear that the contrast between (7) and (8a) follows from (14) as a matter of course. In the derivation of (8a), a complex X^0 is formed via incorporation of *love* into *-inc*, and this complex X^0 contravenes (14); in (7), by contrast, no X^0 complex including *kalp* and *-ify* is formed at any point in the derivation, and (14) is respected.

Let us now proceed to motivating (15). The background for our key distinction between *-inc* and *-ify* lies in the fact that, as is well known, English entirely rules out all incorporation into verbal heads. While languages such as Mohawk, which feature incorporation profusely, allow nouns and other dependents of V to incorporate into the verb, forming things like (16a) and (16b) (with the appropriate language-specific lexical items, of course; cf. Baker 1988), English systematically rejects such constructions, producing (17a–b) instead.

(16) a. John meat-eats.
     b. John up-looked the number.

(17) a. John eats meat.
     b. John looked up the number.

This is not because English does not have head movement—nor even because English lacks head *incorporation*. Arguably, English and Mohawk (and all other languages in the world) treat constructions in which there is a bare noun phrase or a bare particle in the complement of the verb in precisely the same way in syntax, forcing the bare noun or particle to incorporate into the verb in order to get licensed. That is, in *all* languages, the head of a bare noun phrase complement like *meat* in *John eats meat* must incorporate into the verb because it cannot be licensed in any other way. It is impossible to license the nominal head within its own extended projection: the quintessential property of a bare noun phrase is precisely the *absence* of an extended projection to the noun; the noun projects up to NP and is not associated with functional projections of its own. The absence of functional heads in the noun's extended projection makes it impossible for the noun to be licensed within the verb's complement unless it incorporates into V, being licensed by what Baker (1988) calls "morphological licensing." This is a universal fact about bare NP complements (see especially Van Geenhoven 1998 and Dayal 1999 for detailed discussion from a semantic point of view). But languages differ with respect to whether the output of incorporation is morphophonologically realized—there is a morphological Well-Formedness Condition (19) at work that determines whether the incorporated head is spelled out inside the complex verb (as in (18a)) or outside it (i.e., in the head position of its syntactic phrase, as in (18b)):[10]

(18) a. $[_{VP} [_V N_i V] [_{NP} \cancel{N_i}]]$

    b. $[_{VP} [_V \cancel{N_i} V] [_{NP} N_i]]$

(19) $*[_V L_i V]$ where $L \in \{A, N, P, V\}$

Since English does not incorporate anything "physically" into something of category V (i.e., in English, constructions of the type in (16) are systematically impossible), we are led to conclude—on the standard assumption that v has the same category as V—that material that surfaces to the left of the English bound morpheme *-ify*, when base generated in v, *does not form a complex head with it*. That is, there is no X^0 that contains both *-ify* and its host in cases where *-ify* lexicalizes v. To be sure, there *is* always something physically to the left of *-ify* that provides a host for the bound morpheme—we obviously are not contesting that *-ify* is a bound morpheme. But our point is that the host of *-ify* qua v does not amalgamate with *-ify* via morphosyntactic incorporation. Instead (although little depends on the details of this for the remainder of the discussion), we will assume that the (remnant) syntactic *projection* of the host of *-ify* is maneuvered into a specifier position local to v.[11] The "little light verb" *-ify* and its host come together to form a phonological unit only in the phonological component.

So the essence of our account of the difference between (7) and (8a) is the way in which, and the point at which, "the twain shall meet"—that is, how and when the root and the affix come together. While (8a) is bad because of a violation of the ban on head-internal switches (14) (since *-inc* amalgamates with its host via incorporation), the switches in (7), with *-ify* attached to a Telugu root, come out well formed because English *-ify*, in perfect agreement with all other English verbal morphology, is not an incorporator. In (7), therefore, the Telugu root and English *-ify*=v do *not* form a complex word—that is, **kalp**-*ify* in (7a) is not formed via V-to-v raising, nor in the lexicon; the vacuous *-ify* seen in these codeswitching cases is a syntactically autonomous, freestanding head, coming together with its host only in the phonological component.

Our discussion of the way that (7) is reconciled with a constraint of the type in (14) resembles the brief discussion by MacSwan (2003, 7) of Treffers-Daller's (1994, 152) Brussels-Dutch/French codeswitching case in (20).

(20) da's   ne   **sympathiqu**-*e*

      that's   a   sympathetic-AGR (one)

The thing to look at here is the italicized *-e* (pronounced as schwa), an agreement morpheme from Dutch, attached to the French host *sympathique* (whose final orthographic *-e* is mute). MacSwan capitalizes on Zwart's (1996) claim that the schwa of Dutch adjectival agreement is a phrasal affix, triggering *phrasal* movement (not *head* movement) across it, thus avoiding a collision with (14). This is directly in line with what we said about (7).

But notice that for both (7) and (20) it is undeniably the case that the suffix does form a phonological (PF) unit with its host. Thus, MacSwan's (2003, 7) assertion that the phrasal affix approach to *-e* in (20) makes this example conform to the criteria of his PF Disjunction Theorem (13) is actually false— something that leads us to a discussion of the role of phonology in the licensing of apparent word-internal switches, and the roots of (14).

7.4   The Phonology: Where Are the Roots of the Ban on Head-Internal Switches?

MacSwan (1997) takes (14) to follow from (13iv), the ban on codeswitching within PF. Clearly, *-ify* does end up forming a phonological unit with its host, eventually, in the phonological component. It just does not happen "under one and the same X^0." But whether or not a complex X^0 is created is a matter of morphosyntax, not of phonology (on the assumption that there is no syntactic movement at all in the PF component[12]). So it cannot be the phonology per se that is responsible for the ban on word-internal codeswitching.

Nonetheless, the phonology does have a key role to play. To appreciate this, it will be advantageous to return to our earlier point about bare noun phrase complements. We said, in the discussion of (16a) and (17a), that the head of a bare noun phrase complement *must* incorporate into V in order to be licensed: it would not be able to survive on its own. We also pointed out that there may be no PF reflex to N-incorporation: in languages in which there is a morpho-logical Well-Formedness Condition banning the verb-internal realization of nouns (a specimen of (19)), the noun will be lexicalized outside the complex verb. But the complex verb is *always* formed, whenever there is a bare noun phrase in V's complement. Now suppose that we perform a codeswitch between the lexical verb and its bare noun phrase complement, for instance between Spanish and English, or between English and Telugu. The result will be (21a–b), which are well formed, just as good as any switch between V and its object.[13]

(21) a. **comio**   *meat*

             eat-1SG.PST

   b. *meat/chicken*   **tinTini**

             eat-1SG-PST

Now, if we were to *categorically* block switches within X^0, we would wrongly rule out examples of the type in (21). After all, complex V^0s are formed in the course of the derivation of these examples, for the simple reason that the nominal head of the bare noun phrase complement *meat* must incorporate into V in order to be licensed. Plainly, the reason why the complex X^0s formed in (21) do not contravene the ban on head-internal switches must be that the incorporated noun *is not actually spelled out inside the complex head.*

So phonology plays a role and it doesn't—it accepts head-internal switches that do not give rise, in the PF component, to "schizophrenic" phonological words, but it does not reject "schizophrenic" phonological words that were never a complex X^0 in the morphosyntax. The conclusion that presents itself, then, is that it is not bad, in and of itself, to have a phonological word featuring components from different languages: this is bad if and only if those components are subparts of a morphosyntactic X^0 complex. So (14) is correct *and* it applies in the PF component (i.e., it rejects complex X^0s of the type in (18a) but has nothing to say about (18b), where the morphosyntactically incorporated element is not spelled out at PF inside the complex V). But (14) is *not* a *consequence* of a general ban on codeswitching within a PF component (13iv), as MacSwan (1997) would have it. That is all for the better: it would be quite absurd, when one thinks about it, to take (13iv) literally and ban all codeswitching at PF, for that would de facto rule out codeswitching categorically. Let us show why.

MacSwan arrives at (13iv) by way of the observed ordering/ranking of rules/constraints in the phonology (13i). But as is well known, phonological rules do not just operate *within* words: there are phonological rules that apply *between* words as well—many postlexical rules, such as the English *wanna* contraction or the Italian *raddoppiamento sintattico*, are of this type. Now, if one were to literally prevent codeswitching from applying in domains in which phonological rules apply, then, given that phonological rules apply not only within words but across words as well, we would be led to conclude that codeswitching is prohibited, period.

Notice that this critique of MacSwan's (1997) proposed way of deriving (13iv) and, concomitantly, (14) is entirely independent of the question of what counts as a "phonological unit." All that is needed is the realization that phonological rules/constraints that plainly belong to the phonological component can apply across word boundaries, which leads one to define the domain of phonological rules as something substantially *larger* than the word. If the fact that the PF component consists of rules/constraints that must be ordered/ranked vis-à-vis each other (13i) is ultimately is responsible for (13iv), as MacSwan argues it is, then what follows (in light of the well-established fact that phonological constraints are at work not only below X^0 but at the juncture of different X^0s as well) is not actually (14) but the much broader conclusion that codeswitching is altogether ruled out. Since, clearly, codeswitching does exist, it seems unlikely that we would be able to profitably exploit MacSwan's (1997) line of reasoning based on (13) to arrive at the conclusion in (14).

We therefore reject MacSwan's *rationale* for (14), but we do not reject (14) per se—on the contrary, we have *supported* (14) and made it more specific by confirming in an interesting way that switches within X^0 are indeed ill formed (as shown by the contrast between (7) and (8a)), as long as X^0 is *physically* (i.e., *phonologically*) "schizophrenic" (recall the discussion of (21)). So to summarize, our conclusion is that (22) is a descriptively adequate restriction on codeswitching:

(22) Codeswitching within phonological words that are morphosyntactic heads (X^0s) is illicit.[14]

But of course, we would like to elevate our analysis beyond the level of descriptive adequacy to level the playing field with MacSwan 1997. So it is incumbent on us to ask why there should be a constraint like (22).

What we would like to suggest is that a "late spell-out" analysis of the type championed by Distributed Morphology (Halle and Marantz 1993; Marantz 1997) and espoused in recent minimalism (Chomsky 2000, 2001) may allow us to derive (22). The syntactic derivation proceeds solely on the basis of bundles of morphosyntactic features, which lead to the projection of syntactic structures in which these features can be checked. The result of the syntax is handed over to the interpretive components at spell-out, at which point, on the PF wing of the grammar, the structure gets its phonological shape. The phonology then "forgets" (as Chomsky 2001, 13, puts it) the earlier stages of the derivation: the result is a morphosyntactic monolith.[15] For complex categories of type X^0, such as those in (18a) and (19), this means that, after spell-out, they become *single, simple words* for the purposes of the phonology. So when it comes to providing such X^0s with a phonetic form, it follows that we have to recruit that form *in its entirety* from a *single* language: by the time X^0 is spelled out, it has become a single unanalyzed unit, hence it cannot be realized as a mix of morpholexical material from two different languages. A switch inside a morphologically complex X^0, viewed from this perspective, is entirely on a par with a situation in which, for some simplex head, we recruit some syllables or individual segments from one language and the other syllables or segments from another. Such situations are not instances of codeswitching; codeswitching within phonological words, regardless of whether they are morphologically simple or complex, is systematically ruled out. The constraint in (22) may thus be derived from a theory that adopts the "late spell-out" perspective on the phonological realization of morphosyntactic constructs. The fact that nothing bans codeswitching in situations of the type in (18b), where we *are* dealing with a morphologically complex X^0 but the incorporated element and its host, recruited from different languages, are *not* both spelled out inside that X^0, follows as well.

7.5   The Economy: On Switching with *cees* and *do*

In the examples in (8), the switch at the juncture of Telugu inflection and an English root could be successfully made only with the aid of the freestanding "light V" *cees*, not with the affixal "light *v*" *-inc*. We have just supplied an account for why switching from English to Telugu with *-inc* is impossible, while switching in the other direction, with *-ify*, is perfect (as we saw in (7)). It is incumbent on us now to cast some light on another asymmetry in English/ Telugu codeswitching: the fact that, while the "light V" *cees* 'do/make' is perfectly happy to help out in (8b), English *do* will not serve as a go-between.

To see this, contrast the examples in (23a) (which repeats our earlier (8b)) and (23b–b').

(23) a.   vaaDu   nanni   **love** *cees*-EEDu (= (8b))

          he-NOM me-ACC   love do-PST-AGR

      b. *My sister {**kalp** did/did **kalp**}   the curry. *kalp* 'stir'

      b'. *My sister {**kalp-*edi*** did/did **kalp-*edi***} the curry. *kalp-edi* 'stir-INF'

Regardless of whether we place English *did* to the left or to the right of the Telugu root (i.e., regardless of whether we follow English or Telugu word-order rules), (23b) is impossible, whether we construe *do* as a main verb or as the dummy support morpheme. (23b'), which differs from (23b) in featuring infinitival morphology on the verb, is likewise ungrammatical—it does not matter, therefore, whether what combines with *do* is a bare root or a full-fledged infinitive.

The fact that (23b), with *do* construed as the dummy, is ungrammatical would seem to suggest that switching between T (occupied by the dummy *do*) and *v*P is impossible. That would of course be a straightforward consequence of Belazi, Rubin, and Toribio's (1994) Functional Head Constraint in (12), above. But we have already discarded (12) as a descriptively and explanatorily adequate constraint, so we cannot resort to it here. Nor can we get any mileage this time out of the ban on X^0-internal switches: there are no such switches anywhere in (23). But there is nonetheless an entirely straightforward way of understanding the ban on switching between T and vP in (23b), one focused on morphology.

As a result of making the switch between T and vP in (23b), and having the only inflectional features present in the clause borne by the dummy *do*, we end up with a naked Telugu stem in the complement of T. Naked stems cannot surface, however: a Telugu stem always needs to be adorned with some appropriate morphology, whether inflectional or derivational. Since there is nothing to adorn the stem with in (23b), however, the resulting codeswitching construction is ill formed—this time not as a result of a ban on switching within X^0 (nor of a ban on switching between T and vP per se) but because of a general morphophonological restriction:

(24) Bare stems cannot surface on their own.

This morphophonological restriction has nothing to do with codeswitching at all: it is an entirely general fact holding for "pure" Telugu as well (and not just for Telugu but presumably universally). It automatically rules out (23b) as a viable codeswitch,[16] but it is not violated in the legitimate codeswitches in (7): *kalp* in (7a) serves as host to *-ify*, a phrasal affix that, in the PF component, comes to form a phonological word (though *not* a morphosyntactic word, X^0) with *kalp*.

The fact that (23b′), with *do* construed as a lexical light verb (as in *to do a dance*) with a full-fledged Telugu infinitive in its complement, is also ungrammatical indicates that "light switches," whenever available, are cheaper than switches that call on the projection of an additional lexical verb (main verb *do*). The fact that "light switches" are apparently cheaper than switches that call on an additional lexical verb (main verb verb *do* in the case at hand, in (23b′)) can be thought of in terms of *economy* (or "blocking," in some extended sense of this Aronovian notion; cf. Aronoff 1976).[17] Faced, at the point in the derivation at which the root VP is complete, with the choice of merging a "little light verb" v or a "lexical light verb" V, one will take the former tack if one can get away with it—that is, if merging a "little light verb" v will lead to a converging derivation.

(25) Merging the "little light verb" v is cheaper than merging the "lexical
      light verb" V.

As we have seen, merging the English "little light verb" *-ify* with the projection of Telugu *kalp* 'stir' leads to a perfectly well-formed output—thanks to the fact that no violation of (22) presents itself. The grammaticality of merging the "little light verb" *-ify* then effectively blocks (essentially in the Aronovian sense of the term, applied here beyond the confines of morphology proper) the merger of the "lexical light verb" *do* (the *do* of *do a dance*), so that (23b′)

will never arise.[18] It is all a matter of economy: merging the "lexical light verb" V with the projection of *kalp* 'stir' still requires the merger of *v* on top of the "light" VP, so the "lexical light verb" route takes two applications of Merge while the "little light verb" route gets to its destination via just one instance of Merge, that of *v* with the VP of *kalp*.

Note that this line of thought with respect to (23b′) leaves (23a) entirely unaffected. For when it comes to a switch from an English lexical verb to a Telugu continuation of the clause structure, there simply is no choice. While in the opposite case, a switch with the aid of *-ify* yields a grammatical output, in the case at hand it is impossible to resort to the Telugu "little light verb" *-inc* to make the switch. Telugu *-inc* is an overt incorporator—that is, it attracts the V-head of its complement up to it and thus creates a complex X^0 that is not "language uniform," in violation of (22). And the very fact that (23a) has no "cheaper" competitor then makes a switch with the aid of a "lexical light verb," Telugu *cees*, perfectly legitimate. This is exactly what an approach in terms of economy leads one to expect.

So basically, (23a) is good because (8a) is bad (i.e., there is no competition, no "cheaper" option, in the case of a switch from an English lexical root to a Telugu environment), and conversely, (23b′) is bad because things like (7) are well formed. Economy will force the codeswitcher to make the switch at the "little light verb" (*v*) level *unless* such a "light switch" is excluded for independent reasons (in particular, by (22)).

While this takes care of the English/Telugu codeswitching facts discussed in this chapter, let us add a little postlude here to show that the economy approach also allows us to understand the facts of English/Hindi codeswitching reported in Bhatia and Ritchie 1996, which are highly germane to the foregoing discussion since they involve the use of a "lexical light verb," *kar* 'do'. Bhatia and Ritchie show that the light verb *kar* is called on in two contexts by Hindi speakers: (i) in monolingual Hindi (26a) as well as in the English/Hindi codeswitching case in (26b), *kar* serves as an intermediary between verbal morphology (*-egii* in (26)) and an adjectival or nominal root (*pasand* and *choice* in our examples); in addition, (ii) in English/Hindi codeswitching but not in monolingual Hindi, *kar* also mediates between (English) *verbal* roots (*choose* in (26b)) and (Hindi) verbal morphology.

(26) a. merii patnii saaRii {kii pasand/ *cun(-naa)} *kar*-egii
   my wife saree of liking$_N$ choose$_V$-INF do-FUT.3SG.FEM
   'My wife will take a liking to/*choose a saree.'
  b. merii patnii saaRii {kii **choice/ choose**} *kar*-egii
   my wife saree of choice$_N$ choose$_V$ do-FUT.3SG.FEM
   'My wife will choose a saree.'

Bhatia and Ritchie (1996, 58) take an approach to these facts that is congruent with ours, arguing that "grammatical theory within the economy framework and the Minimalist Program provide natural answers" to the questions posed by (26) (but recall our note 17). The upshot of their approach is that *kar* will be called on only if its presence is necessary for convergence. In both the monolingual and the codeswitching context, *kar* is needed in the examples featuring a *non*verbal lexical root to provide a verbal host for the inflectional morphology.[19] In the codeswitching case with an English *verbal* root, *kar* will still be required despite the fact that the lexical root is now verbal, because that lexical root, taken from English, is unable to form a morphosyntactic (X^0) complex with the Hindi inflectional morpheme *-egii*. But in the *monolingual* example in which the lexical root is *verbal*, there is no need for *kar*, and consequently no *kar* can be inserted.

This approach to (26) strikes us as entirely reasonable. And if it is correct, it further underscores the importance of economy considerations in the use of "light" elements—both in monolingual and in codeswitching contexts.

7.6 The Wrap: Concluding Remarks

In this chapter we have endeavored to show that English *-ify*, in its capacity as a "little light verb" *v* that does not (in fact, cannot) incorporate the head of its complement, is an ideal "pivot" in codeswitching. It serves as an intermediary between the root and the inflectional domain of the clause, connecting things that could not otherwise host verbal inflectional morphology. The Telugu suffix *-inc*, while occupying the same structural position in the tree (*v*), does not manage to play the same pivotal role—it incorporates the V-head, thus creating a complex X^0 category that is not "language uniform," in violation of the ban on head-internal codeswitching. We have shown, in agreement with MacSwan, that this ban on head-internal switches is a phonological constraint on codeswitching—there is no general ban on head incorporation in switching contexts, but the incorporated element from L1 must not be spelled out under the same X^0 as the incorporator from L2. We have also shown, in disagreement with MacSwan, that switching within a phonological word is not disallowed: switches of the type in (7) instantiate precisely this. What makes these cases different from ungrammatical cases of word-internal switches is that the subparts of the phonological words in (7) do not form a morphosyntactic X^0 unit. Thus, there is no ban on switching inside phonological words per se (cf. (7)), nor is there a ban on switching inside morphosyntactic X^0s per se (cf. (21)). What *is* disallowed, however, is switching inside phonological words that are morphosyntactic heads (X^0s). As we have shown, the restriction in (22) follows straightforwardly from a theory that adopts the "late spell-out" perspective on the phonological realization of morphosyntactic constructs. In the final section of the chapter, we showed that economy considerations play an important role in adjudicating between "light switching" options: when a switch at the "little light verb" level is legitimate (as in (7)), it will block the structurally more complex alternative of switching at the "lexical light verb" level.

Notes

We would like to thank the audience at the Fourth International Symposium on Bilingualism, Tempe, Arizona, April/May 2003, for their feedback, and especially Dan Finer and Jeff MacSwan for their detailed written comments.

1. The form *pooj* preceding *cees* in (3a) is seemingly a bare stem. In actual fact, however, what we are dealing with here is a *phonological* reduction of *pooja cees* to *pooj cees*; in syntax, therefore, we do in fact have an infinitive in the complement of *cees*. Three things support this interpretation of the facts. First, when adverbial material follows the left-hand verb, as in (i), we see the infinitival suffix *-a* showing up overtly. Second, those (few) consonant-final words that serve as input to the *cees* construction, such as *bajan* 'religious chant', do indeed show up in their infinitival form (cf. (ii)). And third, in Kannada the phonological reduction of the counterpart of Telugu *pooja* to *pooj* does not take place in the context at hand: cf. *pooje* 'worship' and *poojemaaDide* 'to worship' (not *poojmaaDide*).

(i) pooja   baaga   ceesiri.
worship   well   make-3PL-PST
'They worshipped well.'

(ii) bajanceesiri
chant-make-3PL-PST
"They chanted."

2. On *-is*, the Kannada counterpart of Telugu *-inc*, as the spell-out of the Chomskyan light verb *v*, see Lidz 1998.

3. All the codeswitching data reported in this chapter are based on native speaker judgments collected by the first author. The use of *-ify* as a "pivot" in codeswitching is by no means peculiar to the English/Telugu case. It is in fact used profusely on the Indian subcontinent—there is evidence of the use of *-ify* in codeswitching constructions featuring Kannada, Malayalam, and Tamil as well (for their judgments, we thank Sudha Gowda, Prem Panikar, and Latha Narayan, respectively), with *-ify* being necessary (as in the Telugu case) to link the verb to the English inflection. Bhatia (1989) argues that in "Filmi English," a specific form of English/Hindi codeswitching, English *-ify* (reduced to *-fy* and obligatorily separated from the stem by the vowel *-o-*, which Bhatia (1989, 271) claims is a functional morpheme of sorts) attaches exclusively to *nominal* stems (cf. e.g. *you **mask-o-fied** him* 'you joke$_N$-*o*-*ify*-PST (joked with) him'); when the Hindi stem is *verbal*, English verbal morphology may be added directly to the

combination of the Hindi stem and the -o- morpheme (cf. *I manaa- -o-ed her* 'I con-soled her'). But for the English/Telugu -*ify* cases discussed in this chapter, it is entirely clear that the Telugu root is verbal. (In fact, switches between Telugu nouns or adjec-tives and English -*ify*+INFL are impossible: the "lexical light verb" *cees* will always mediate between Telugu N/A and English -*ify*—something that will follow if (i) -*ify* is a lexicalization of *v* (as we are claiming) and (ii) *v* must have a VP in its complement.)

4. The -*i*- in forms like *kal(i)pify* is subject to elision, the syncopated forms being particularly common in the spoken language. The fact that, when it does show up, the vowel surfaces as -*i*- provides an interesting piece of evidence for the claim that the Telugu base verb and the suffix -*ify* form a phonological unit. Telugu has a vowel harmony process by which a /u/ in the final syllable of the stem changes to /i/ under the influence of a high-vowel suffix (see Babu 1981). Roots like *kalupu* 'stir' undergo this process not just in the context of an indigenous suffix (cf. *kalip-indi* 'she stirred') but also under the influence of -*ify* (cf. (7a–d)).

5. The fact that -*inc* and -*ify* co-occur in (7e) may prima facie seem to compromise an analysis of these elements as lexicalizations of the "little light verb" *v* (as Rakesh Bhatt, personal communication, points out): in a simplex clause, there would appear to be but a single *v* present in the structure. Two possible replies suggest themselves. One would be to deny that there is at most one *v* in a simplex clause—a possibility that seriously presents itself once one abandons the idea that *v* necessarily introduces an external thematic role (cf. Chomsky 2000, 2001). Alternatively, on the assumption that there is indeed at most one *v* per simplex clause, the co-occurrence of -*inc* and -*ify* in (7e) may be accommodated by assigning this sentence a biclausal structure. We will not address the choice between these two options here, noting merely that the co-occurrence of -*inc* and -*ify* in (7e) does not necessarily threaten the text approach to these formatives.

6. The obligatory elision of the *i* of -*ify* in *argufy*, seen also in the Filmi English examples mentioned in note 3 above (cf. *maskofy* 'joke with'), is another respect in which -*ify* qua *v* differs from -*ify* qua Level I suffix (cf. *heroify* ~*herofy*).

7. The claim that -*ify* qua pivot is a spell-out of *v* and not a lexical Level I suffix does not make it ineligible for Level I affixation——*ify* qua light verb is itself a lexical item that is a possible host for Level I affixes. Thus it is not a problem for our analysis that in Southern U.S. English we find words like *twistification* or *argufication* (cf. e.g. *Vent yer spleen here, but expect some serious argufication!*, at http://www.thesagebrushsa-loon.com/forum/, provided by Dan Finer, personal communication) and in Telugu/English codeswitching we find *kalpification*. We thank Dan Finer for instrumental discussion of the issues raised in this paragraph.

8. Further underpinning the empirical inadequacy of (10), MacSwan (1997) notes that there are grammatical Nahuatl/Spanish codeswitches involving Nahuatl bound mor-phemes attaching to a Spanish verb, in clear breach of (10).

9. We leave (8b) aside for now: it does not present any particular trouble from the perspective of (14). We return to it in section 7.5.

10. Note that the WFC in (19) refers specifically to complexes of category V—complex heads of other categories may behave differently. Thus, in English, while N-incorpo-

ration into *verbs* is impossible (cf. (16a)), N-incorporation into *nouns* is fine (cf. *John is a meateater*). Note also that different languages pick out different subsets of the set {L}: thus, in Dutch, while nouns will not incorporate, particles do, under specific circumstances. See Den Dikken 2003 for detailed discussion, irrelevant here.

11. A remnant movement account is readily devised, with all nonverbal material vacating the VP (raising to specifier positions below *v*) prior to movement of the remnant VP to a specifier position immediately above *v*. Adjacency of V and *v* then follows as a matter of course. Execution of the remnant movement analysis is not necessarily trivial, but we will not pursue this here since it is essentially orthogonal to our concerns in this chapter.

12. This is not an entirely uncontroversial issue—in fact, in Chomsky's (2000, 2001) recent work, it is suggested that head movement, to the extent that it exists, occurs exclusively in the PFcomponent. We do not follow Chomsky on this point, firmly believing that (i) there is robust evidence for syntactic head movement (all the evidence originally advanced by Travis 1984, Baker 1988, and Pollock 1989, among many others), and (ii) there is no convincing evidence for the existence of head movement at PF.

13. Jeff MacSwan (personal communication) asks what accounts for the OV/VO contrast in (21a–b), and in particular, how a bare NP object comes to surface to the left of the verb, as in (21b). The text discussion below (17) argued (in line with the literature) that the head noun of bare NP objects cannot be licensed in its own extended projection, because it has none. And the fact that it has no extended projection makes it ineligible for EPP-driven raising.—if, as seems plausible, the EPP is recastable as a D-feature of the probe (Chomsky 1995). The fact that bare NPs cannot be preverbal subjects in languages like Spanish, while in others (such as Dutch) they get a "strong," DP-type interpretation, strongly suggests a link between the EPP and D. These two things combined entail that preverbal placement of bare NP objects cannot be the result of EPP-driven movement, nor can it be the result of overt incorporation (which would contravene (14)). We are thus led to assume, by logical elimination, that OV order is *base generated*: contra Kayne 1994 but following, for example, Haider 1997 and Barbiers 2000, we assume that the VP is underlyingly head *final*, with VO order resulting from movement of the verb around its object (cf. Pesetsky 1989, Johnson 1991, Costa 1996, and Haider 1997, among others, for evidence that the lexical verb can indeed be shown to move leftward in English; and see Haider 1997 and Barbiers 2000 for a detailed plea for an underlyingly head-final VP in Dutch and German). The combination of (i) the absence of an extended projection for the bare noun, (ii) the standard hypothesis that phrasal movement is EPP-driven, and (iii) the empirically supported assumption that the EPP is linked to D inevitably leads to the conclusion that (bare-object) OV orders must be basegenerated, entirely independently of (21b).

14. Note that (22) will allow codeswitching to obey Myers-Scotton's (1993, 83) System Morpheme Principle (which says that all grammatical morphemes come from the dominant/matrix language) only for those grammatical morphemes that do not form morphosyntactic (X^0) units with their hosts from the embedded language. For morphosyntactically affixal grammatical morphemes, the SMP is false—as a consequence, Myers-Scotton's (1993, 82) Matrix Language Hypothesis (which says that "the matrix language provides the morphosyntactic frame" for codeswitches) is refuted as well.

For relevant critical discussion of the Matrix Language Hypothesis, see also Bhatia and Ritchie 1996, with reference to English/Hindi codeswitching data, and MacSwan 2004, 2005.

Though we will not have the opportunity here to explore them in detail, it should be clear that (22) makes predictions well beyond the specific case of codeswitching with *-ify/-inc*. One interesting domain to investigate is the switch between determiners and nouns, especially for a language pair of which both members have postnominal determiners but one of them (L1) derives those by raising the noun to an affixal D, adjoining it to the left of the determiner (thus forming a complex D^0 overtly), and the other (L2) makes them by raising the NP (or some extended projection of N) into SpecDP. For such a pair, we would expect a switch at the D/NP juncture to be legitimate if the determiner is from L2 but not if it is from L1. We thank Jeff MacSwan for suggesting that switches at the D/NP juncture would be a fruitful testing ground for (22); we have to leave the actual verification for future research.

15. The recent phase-based cyclic spell-out approach to the interface between syntax and the interpretive components (cf. Chomsky 2001) has potentially interesting consequences for codeswitching between morphosyntactically autonomous elements as well: if, at spell-out, all morphosyntactic structure inside (the domain of) the spelled-out phase literally gets erased, with a monolithic chunk as the result, one might expect codeswitching between, say, V and its complement to be impossible if both stay inside the root VP, which would make both of them subparts of an unstructured VP "chunk" when the *v*P is handed over to PF. If this is correct, codeswitching between V and its complement is expected to be possible only if either V or the complement (or both) leave the root VP prior to spell-out of *v*P. For the *kalpify* cases in (7), a phase-based cyclic spell-out perspective would have no adverse consequences: the Telugu lexical verb is in VP, in the domain of the *v*P phase, while *-ify* is in *v*, not "frozen" on spell-out of *v*P; V and *v* can hence be lexicalized by material recruited from different languages, as desired. The broader consequences of the tentative remarks in this note are open to further exploration.

16. Notice that the ungrammaticality of (23b), as well as that of (11c) (**my sister kalp-ed the curry*), is another indication that the root *kalp* has not simply been borrowed into English: if it had been borrowed and hence adopted into the English lexicon of Telugu speakers, it ought to have been perfectly eligible for suffixation with *-ed*, as in (11c), or for surfacing on its own (given that English makes no bare root/infinitive distinction), as in (23b) (or its negative or emphatically affirmative counterparts).

17. We added the reference to "blocking" because, although there is an intuitive sense in which economy considerations adjudicate between using a "little light verb" and a "lexical light verb" to make a switch, it may be best to conceive of this in blocking terms. Note that economy in minimalism (Chomsky 1995 and more recent work) compares only derivations built on the same *numeration* (array of elements from the lexicon); obviously, in the cases at hand, the numerations involved are different (*-ify* vs. *do*, *-inc* vs. *cees*).

18. The question of why *to dance* and *to do a dance* do in fact alternate freely is relevant in this context. Two lines of thought present themselves here. The first would capitalize on Hale and Keyser's (1993) claim that unergative verbs like *to dance* are in

fact transitive, taking a "cognate object" as their complement—that is, *to dance* would effectively be represented underlyingly as *to dance a dance*, or (if the verb is not underlyingly specified) as *to do a dance*. If this is the right way of looking at unergative *to dance*, then there is no structural alternation between *to dance* and *to do a dance* at all: the two actually have exactly the same structures, both featuring a "lexical light verb" (which in *to dance* receives no phonological matrix). Looked at this way, then, the alternation between *to dance* and *to do a dance* does not bear on the text discussion in any way. Alternatively, one may assume (in line with the tradition but in disagreement with Marantz 1997 and subsequent work in Distributed Morphology that espouses the view that lexical roots are underlyingly unspecified for category) that *dance* in *to dance* and *dance* in *to do a dance* are categorially distinct: the latter often is a noun. That very fact will then prevent it from merging directly with v (with v combining only with VPs). By the logic of the text discussion, we may then understand why the inclusion of a "lexical light verb" is forced whenever nominal *dance* is selected as the predicate head: there is no "cheaper" option; merger of the "little light verb" v is illicit in the context at hand, so merger of the "lexical light verb" V is the only possibility. We will not make a choice between the two approaches to the alternation of *to dance* and *to do a dance* here; for us it will suffice to simply note that this alternation in no way compromises the text discussion.

19. Recall from the brief discussion in note 3 that according to Bhatia 1989, in Filmi English, *-ify* serves basically the same purpose, in the other direction, as Hindi *kar* does in the variants of (26) in which the root is nonverbal: in Filmi English, *-ify* is used *only* when the Hindi root is nonverbal. We have made a point of showing that the distribution of *-ify* in English/Telugu codeswitching cannot be understood in quite the same terms: category does not play the key role here (since the Telugu root to which *-ify* is attached may very well be verbal itself). But mediation between the lexical and the inflectional domains is what underlies all cases, throughout.

References

Aronoff, M. 1976. *Word Formation in Generative Grammar*. Cambridge, MA: MIT Press.

Babu, P. B. A. 1981. Vowel harmony in Telugu. *International Journal of Dravidian Linguistics* 10:1.

Baker, M. 1988. *Incorporation*. Chicago: University of Chicago Press.

Barbiers, S. 2000. The right periphery in SOV languages: English and Dutch. In P. Svenonius, ed., *The Derivation of VO and OV*, 181–218. Amsterdam: John Benjamins.

Belazi, H., E. Rubin, and A. J. Toribio. 1994. Code switching and X-bar theory: The functional head constraint. *Linguistic Inquiry* 25:221–237.

Bhatia, T. K. 1989. Bilinguals' creativity and syntactic theory: Evidence for emerging grammar. *World Englishes* 8:265–276.

Bhatia, T. K., and W. C. Ritchie. 1996. Light verbs in code-switched utterances: Derivational economy in I-language or incongruence in production? In A. Stringfellow, D.

Cahana-Amitay, E. Hughes & A. Zukowski , eds., *Proceedings of the Twentieth Annual Boston University Conference on Language Development*, vol. 1, 52–62. Somerville, MA: Cascadilla Press.

Chomsky, N. 1995. *The Minimalist Program*. Cambridge, MA: MIT Press.

Chomsky, N. 2000. Minimalist inquiries: The framework. In R. Martin, D. Michaels, and J. Uriagereka, eds., *Step by Step: Essays on Minimalist Syntax in Honor of Howard Lasnik*, 89–115. Cambridge, MA: MIT Press.

Chomsky, N. 2001. Derivation by phase. In M. Kenstowicz, ed., *Ken Hale: A Life in Language*, 1–52. Cambridge, MA: MIT Press.

Costa, J. 1996. Adverb positioning and verb movement in English: Some more evidence. *Studia Linguistica* 50:1.

Dayal, V. 1999. Bare NP's, reference to kinds, and incorporation. In T. Matthews & D. Strolovitch, eds., *SALT IX Proceedings*, 34–51. Ithaca: Cornell University Press

Den Dikken, M. 2003. When particles won't part. Ms., CUNY Graduate Center.

Grimshaw, J., and R. A. Mester. 1988. Light verbs and theta-marking. *Linguistic Inquiry* 19:205–232.

Haider, H. 1997. Extraposition. In D. Beermann, D. LeBlanc, and H. van Riemsdijk, eds., *Rightward Movement*, 115–152. Amsterdam: John Benjamins.

Hale, K., and S. J. Keyser. 1993. On argument structure and the lexical expression of syntactic relations. In K. Hale and S. J. Keyser, eds., *The View from Building 20*, 55–109. Cambridge, MA: MIT Press.

Halle, M., and A. Marantz. 1993. Distributed Morphology and the pieces of inflection. In K. Hale and S. J. Keyser, eds., *The View from Building 20*, 111–176. Cambridge, MA: MIT Press.

Johnson, K. 1991. Object positions. *Natural Language and Linguistic Theory* 9:577–636.

Kayne, R. 1994. *The Antisymmetry of Syntax*. Cambridge, MA: MIT Press.

Krishnamurti, B. H., and J. P. L. Gwynn. 1985. *A Grammar of Modern Telugu*. Delhi: Oxford University Press.

Lidz, J. 1998. Valency in Kannada: Evidence for interpretive morphology. In A. Dimitriadis, H. Lee, C. Moisset & A. Williams, eds., *Penn Working Papers in Linguistics 5.2*, 37–63. Philadelphia: University of Pennsylvania.

MacSwan, J. 1997. A minimalist approach to intrasentential code switching: Spanish-Nahuatl bilingualism in central Mexico. Doctoral dissertation, UCLA.

MacSwan, J. 2000. The architecture of the bilingual language faculty: Evidence from intrasentential code switching. *Bilingualism: Language and cognition*, 3(01), 37–54.
MacSwan, J. 2003. Minimalism and the derivation of basic word orders in codeswitching. Paper presented at the Fourth International Symposium on Bilingualism, Arizona State University, Tempe, May 2003.

MacSwan, J. 2004. Code switching and linguistic theory. In T. K. Bhatia and W. C. Ritchie, eds., *Handbook of Bilingualism*. Oxford: Blackwell.

MacSwan, J. 2005. Code switching and generative grammar: A critique of the MLF model and some remarks on "modified minimalism." *Bilingualism: Language and Cognition* 8:1.

Marantz, A. 1997. No escape from syntax: Don't try morphological analysis in the privacy of your own lexicon. In Dimitriadis et al., eds., *Penn Working Papers in Linguistics 4*, 201–225. Philadelphia: University of Pennsylvania.

Montgomery, M. B., and J. S. Hall. 2004. *A Dictionary of Smoky Mountain English.* Knoxville: University of Tennessee Press.

Murti, K. V. S. 1973. Causative forms in Telugu. *Linguistics* 107:23–37.

Myers-Scotton, C. 1993. *Duelling Languages: Grammatical Structure in Codeswitching.* Oxford: Clarendon Press.

Pesetsky, D. 1989. Language-particular processes and the Earliness Principle. Paper presented at the Twelfth GLOW Colloquium, Utrecht, April 5. Abstract in *GLOW Newsletter.*

Pollock, J.-Y. 1989. Verb movement, Universal Grammar, and the structure of IP. *Linguistic Inquiry* 20:365–424.

Poplack, S. 1980. "Sometimes I'll start a sentence in English y termino en Español": Toward a typology of code-switching. *Linguistics* 18:581–618.

Travis, L. 1984. Parameters and effects of word order variation. Doctoral dissertation, MIT.

Treffers-Daller, J. 1994. *Mixing Two Languages: French-Dutch Contact in a Comparative Perspective.* Berlin: Mouton de Gruyter.

Van Geenhoven, V. 1998. *Semantic Incorporation and Indefinite Descriptions.* Stanford, CA: CSLI.

Zwart, C. J.-W. 1996. On the status and position of PPs inside APs in Dutch. Ms., University of Groningen.

8 Some Consequences of Language Design: Codeswitching and the PF Interface

Jeff MacSwan and Sonia Colina

The Minimalist Program (MP) took the basic structure of the Principles and Parameters framework for granted and posed an intriguing question: How much of the structure could be the direct result of optimal, computationally efficient design? The strong hypothesis formed in response to the question is that Universal Grammar is perfectly designed, providing an optimal solution with minimal design specifications: Merge builds structures that are handed over to the conceptual-intentional (CI) interface and the articulatory-perceptual (AP) interface, corresponding to Logical Form (LF) and Phonetic Form (PF) respectively.

Further, one might reasonably conjecture, as we do here, that substantially many of the grammaticality facts observed in the codeswitching (CS) literature fall out of a related assumption: ill-formedness in CS occurs as a consequence of design features of the human language faculty encountered at the interface levels (PF, in particular), as one instance. To motivate our analysis, we present findings of a phonologically focused study of CS at word boundaries, and motivate a revision of MacSwan's (1999, 2009) PF Disjunction Theorem (PFDT) as the PF Interface Condition (PFIC) (Colina and MacSwan, 2005; MacSwan and Colina, 2007; MacSwan, 2013). Our basic proposal is that, as Spell-Out hands over chunks of PF-relevant material to the phonological system to be readied for the AP Interface, each chunk must be no smaller than a syntactic head and may be parsed by only one phonological system in the bilingual's repertoire, all for reasons which follow from the nature of the phonological system and its interface.

8.1 Codeswitching and Phonology

8.1.1 The Basic Intuition: Codeswitching Is Phonological Switching
Einar Haugen claimed original use of the term *codeswitching* (Benson 2001). Haugen was a pioneer in sociolinguistics, where the term *code* had emerged

in the discussion of distinctions in registers and speech styles revolving around social variables. While the term *codeswitching* persists among sociolinguists as well as formal linguists interested in the topic, it may at times be more useful for linguists who study the grammatical characteristics of CS to conceptualize the phenomenon as *language switching*. Doing so forces us to engage two closely related questions: What is a language, and how do we identify a switch between languages?

Language, of course, is a multiply ambiguous term and may be conceptualized at a community or individual level, among other distinctions. Chomsky (1965, 8) famously defined linguistic theory as concerned with "an ideal speaker-hearer, in a completely homogeneous speech community," a suggestion that raised some complaints among researchers concerned with language variation at the community level (see Newmeyer 1986 for discussion). The idea, however, went back at least as far as the early structuralists for whom Bloomfield (1928) had defined a language as "the totality of utterances that can be made in a speech community," where language was understood as a homogeneous construct for the purposes of scientific study. However, as Chomsky (1986) has stressed, "speech communities" in this sense "do not exist in the real world." Rather, "each individual has acquired a language in the course of complex social interactions with people who vary in the ways in which they speak and interpret what they hear and in the internal representations that underlie their use of language" (p. 16). In Chomsky's terms, knowing a language L entails that the language faculty of the knower's mind/brain is in a certain state. This sense of language Chomsky termed I-language, or "internalized language," as distinct from "externalized language" (E-language), or language conceived as a set of externalized objects and behaviors. These external characteristics of language do not enter into the theory of grammar: "What we call 'English,' 'French,' 'Spanish,' and so on, even under idealizations to idiolects in homogeneous speech communities, reflect the Norman Conquest, proximity to Germanic areas, a Basque substratum, and other factors that cannot seriously be regarded as properties of the language faculty" (Chomsky, 1995, 11).

Hence, the notion of "a language" in the E-language sense should play no role in the formal system employed to account for the data under analysis. When we study CS formally, we must be concerned with language not as a sociopolitical entity, or as an externalized set of utterances, but rather as a state of an individual's human language faculty. A grammar G for a particular language L—that is, $G(L)$—is a set of statements depicting exactly what properties L has, that is, what an individual has learned from a particular speech community, supplemented by innate principles. In CS, we are concerned with the need to identify when one language ends and another begins in a given utterance. Thus, we identify an element e with a language L by its syntactic, morphological, and phonological properties: e is a member of L if and only if it has the properties defined by $G(L)$ for e.

The need to define language membership carefully in CS research is significant both theoretically and empirically (MacSwan and McAlister, 2010). From a theoretical point of view, it protects us against equivocation, the fallacy of using an ambiguous term (like *language*) differently as an argument proceeds. A central argument against CS-specific constraints, for instance, has been the tendency in such proposals to use language labels, which are artifacts of E-language, as grammatical constructs—that is, elements of $G(L)$, L an I-language (see MacSwan, chapter 1, this volume). From an empirical point of view, the need for a careful definition of language membership forces us to respond to the observable characteristics of our data. For example, some have defined *borrowing* in a way that does not entail phonological integration, making it empirically indistinguishable from CS and precluding any meaningful discussion of grammatical mechanisms at play in language mixing.[1]

As mentioned, e is a member of L if and only if it has the properties defined by $G(L)$ for e. If e is a lexical item, then, in minimalist terms, it may be of two types: *lexical*, with substantive content, or *functional*, without substantive content. Each lexical item is a feature set. Chomsky (1995, 54) cataloged four specific kinds of features encoded in lexical items:

(1)   a. Categorial features (N, V, A, P, T, C, and others)
       b. Grammatical features (φ-features, and others relevant to syntactic derivations)
       c. Inherent semantic and syntactic features
       d. A phonological feature matrix

Note that (1a–c) are largely universal in nature. All languages appear to share substantially the same set of substantive categories such as N, V, and A. While languages differ with regard to the value functional categories assign to grammatical features, feature types relevant to syntactic variation do not appear to substantially vary crosslinguistically. In addition, inherent semantic properties that have consequences for semantic interpretation and certain specific syntactic behaviors associated with classes of items (verbs of speaking, for instance) similarly do not appear to substantially vary across languages.

However, the phonological matrices (features of type (1d)) of lexical items do vary substantially crosslinguistically, and so do the respective phonological components responsible for mapping the structure to PF, readying it to be handed over to the articulatory-perceptual interface. In considering, for instance, the linguistic properties distinguishing English *tree* from German *Baum* (apart from Saussurean arbitrariness), phonological contrast is the most prominent. Similarly, Italian *albero* has the same meaning and gender as Spanish *árbol* as well as a common ancestry, but they differ only with respect to their phonological features. Indeed, as a practical matter, CS researchers take for granted that these phonological differences define language switching in CS data, and use *italics* to typographically signal a shift from one language to another in the written presentation of data.

In an important respect, then, language switching *is* phonological switching. When we stop speaking one language and begin speaking another, the shift is prominently characterized by a change in the way we say words. So conceived, the relevant research question would appear to revolve around discovering the conditions under which one can switch from one phonological system to another.

Of course, we are not suggesting that there are no syntactic effects of CS. There are. However, syntactic explanations have more typically focused on word order outcomes in mixed-language utterances rather than on ill-formedness per se. For instance, feature types (1a–c) are useful in explanations of basic word order differences in CS (chapter 1, this volume; MacSwan 2013) as well as adjective/noun order in Germanic-Romance mixing (Cantone and MacSwan 2009), but have very infrequently been charged with explaining ill-formedness per se (see chapter 9 for a compelling example). On the other hand, phonological explanations have tended to play a significant role in constraint-free accounts of CS, and much more frequently are featured as the culprit in explanations of ill-formedness in CS (MacSwan, 1999, 2013).

This tendency is not surprising considering that features relevant to the syntactic derivation generally do not differ much crosslinguistically. While their values and abstract properties may differ, and these clearly have consequences for word order in CS, the differences rarely relate directly to an account of ill-formedness in CS. Rather, ill-formedness in CS is more typically the result of a crash at PF, for reasons related to language design and the special character of phonology.

8.1.2 What's Special about Phonology?

Recent developments in phonology in the form of Optimality Theory (OT) have come under sustained criticism by derivationalists favoring traditional serial approaches (e.g, Halle 1995). Despite these objections, OT has become the dominant theoretical framework within phonology. While efforts have been made to extend the OT framework to syntax (Legendre, Grimshaw, and Vikner

2001), the Minimalist Program (MP) remains the clear dominant research program among syntacticians (Bermúdez-Otero and Honeybone 2006).

Chomsky (1991) noted that his work on the phonology of modern Hebrew (Chomsky 1951) originally led him to consider whether some of the devices used there might usefully extend to syntax. He concluded, in work crystallized in Government-Binding Theory and later in the MP, that phonology and syntax differ in fundamental respects as rule systems—in particular, as Bromberger and Halle (1989) claim, phonology appears to be structured as "a system of intrinsically ordered rules," whereas syntax, since Chomsky 1981, does not.

Because phonology and syntax operate as independent systems, divergence in the nature of the rule systems has no negative effect on the integrity of the general system. Indeed, in the MP, Chomsky offered a "radically autonomous" view of syntax, as Bermúdez-Otero and Honeybone (2006) put it, permitting the systems to operate independently and meet only at Spell-Out, when features relevant to PF are handed over to the phonological system. Chomsky (1995, 229) described the relationship in this way, using π for the computation to PF, λ for the computation to LF:

The computation splits into two parts, one forming π and the other forming λ. The simplest assumptions are (1) that there is no further interaction between computations and (2) that computational procedures are uniform throughout: any operation can apply at any point. We adopt (1), and assume (2) for the computation from N to λ, though not for the computation from N to π; the latter modifies structures (including the internal structure of lexical entries) by processes very different from those that take place in the N $\rightarrow$ λ computation.

Like Bromberger and Halle (1989), Chomsky sees phonology as involving "processes very different" from those of the syntax. In the terms of the MP, phonology is the most pervasively language-particular component of the grammatical system, and an imperfection:

Probably the entire phonology is an imperfection. Furthermore the phonological system has, in a way, bad computational properties. For example, one reasonable computational optimality condition is the Inclusiveness Condition, which holds that the computation shouldn't add anything new; it just takes the features that it has and rearranges them; that is the best system, it doesn't add junk along the way. The phonology violates it, wildly. The whole narrow phonetics is new, metrics is new, everything is just added along the way. If you look at the phonetics, it seems to violate every reasonable computational principle that you can think of. (Chomsky 2002, 118)

Phonology violates Inclusiveness and other computational principles perhaps because, by doing so, it may serve as the best solution to a difficult problem.

Is the phonology just a kind of ugly system? Or is it like what inflectional morphology might be, that is, the optimal solution to some problem? Well, there *is* a problem that the phonology has to satisfy, that an engineer designing the language would have to address. There are syntactic structures being generated, and they are being generated the way they are to satisfy the LF conditions, the thought conditions; there is a sensorimotor system, it has its own properties. The syntactic structures have to interact with this "external" system. So, the engineer would be forced to find some way of relating the given syntactic objects to the given sensorimotor system. (Chomsky 2002, 118–119)

OT was developed to handle a number of intriguing phonological puzzles that appeared to defy earlier serial approaches. Departing from the notion of partially ordered rules, OT posited a system of constraints ranked with respect to one another with regard to their relative importance in the derivation: "OT hypothesizes that constraints are prioritized with respect to each other on a language-specific basis. If a constraint A is prioritized above B, we will write A>>B and say that A is ranked above or dominates B. A ranking of the constraint set—*a constraint dominance hierarchy*—allows the entire set to evaluate alternatives" (Prince and Smolensky 1993, 3). Each set of internally ranked constraints is a constraint dominance hierarchy, and a language-particular phonology is a set of constraint dominance hierarchies. Since language-particular phonologies differ with respect to their internal rankings, we might reasonably posit that bilinguals have a separately encapsulated phonological system for each language in their repertoire in order to avoid *ranking paradoxes* resulting from the availability of distinct constraint dominance hierarchies with conflicting priorities. This property of the bilingual language faculty emerges as a result of the *design constraints* imposed by the linguistic system; a learner must establish separate phonological systems in order to preserve the respective ranking requirements for each language under analysis, lest a ranking paradox emerge.

Furthermore, OT posits that lexical form (input) is mapped to the surface form (output) in one step, with no intermediate representations, another dramatic departure from earlier approaches. Moreover, in order to have a sensorimotor interpretation, all phonological material must be parsed—minimally, at the word level. Thus, we are led to anticipate that phonological systems may be switched between syntactic heads but not within them, since every syntactic head must be phonologically parsed at Spell-Out, and the mapping of phonological structure occurs in a single step, with no intermediate representations. There are therefore no opportunities for switching from one phonological system to another within words.

The properties relevant to the ban on word-internal CS are summed up in (2), the PF Interface Condition. Importantly, (2) is not a principle of a grammar in any sense, but an epiphenomenon resulting from independent design features of the grammatical system.

(2) *PF Interface Condition*

    i. Phonological input is mapped to the output in one step with no intermediate representations.

    ii. Each set of internally ranked constraints is a constraint dominance hierarchy, and a language-particular phonology is a set of constraint dominance hierarchies.

    iii. Bilinguals have a separately encapsulated phonological system for each language in their repertoire in order to avoid *ranking paradoxes*, which result from the availability of distinct constraint dominance hierarchies with conflicting priorities.

    iv. Every syntactic head must be phonologically parsed at Spell-Out. Therefore, the boundary between heads (words) represents the minimal opportunity for codeswitching.

Note that the formalization in (2) is intended as a refinement of MacSwan's (1999, 2000) PF Disjunction Theorem (PFDT), which was based on segmental phonology, and intended as a theoretical implementation of a description generalization due to MacSwan (1999), that CS is banned head-internally.

The PFIC reconceptualizes the fundamental problem associated with word-internal mixing as one related to the interface of syntax and phonology and refines the restriction in terms of word boundaries, on the supposition that words are inputs to phonology and must be phonologically parsed. Hence, "the boundary between heads (words) represents the minimal opportunity for codeswitching," as noted in the PFIC. Moreover, the generalization that word boundaries represent the minimal opportunity for CS can and should be subject to empirical verification. To examine how phonology behaves at the edges of words involved in CS, we conducted two experiments.

8.2 Studies of Phonological Switching

Previous studies of phonological aspects of CS have focused on phonetic effects. For instance, on the basis of Voice Onset Time (VOT) measurements in French-English, Grosjean and Miller (1994) found that what they termed the "base language" had no impact on the production of CS for VOT, and that the shift from one language to the next was total and immediate. In contrast with these results, Botero and colleagues (2004) found a trend toward convergence in the VOT values of voiceless stops in Spanish-English CS, and concluded that there are persistent phonetic effects in CS contexts. Although Grosjean and Miller (1994) and Botero and colleagues (2004) differ as to the type of data under investigation (lexical vs. sentential switches), both studies coincide in focusing on phonetic, gradient phenomena (i.e., VOT).

Bullock and colleagues (Botero et al., 2004; Bullock et al., 2004; Bullock and Toribio, 2009) also focus on phonetics (phonetic convergence), despite the introduction of allophonic distribution in their data. They hypothesized that the English allophones /l/ and /r/ (/l/ realized as a dark /l/ in English) may be substituted for the Spanish ones (contrast neutralized in coda position in Puerto Rican Spanish) or vice versa in the speech of bilinguals. Their hypothesis was not borne out because they found no allophonic substitution and no convergence at the phonological level of representation. Phonetic convergence was found instead: the acoustic values of [l] in CS are closer to those of an English dark /l/ than those of monolingual Spanish, but still below the threshold level necessary to be perceived as dark. Although subjects show coda neutralization of the *l/r* contrast in Spanish (lambdacism), no such process was found for CS into English.

Adopting a theoretical framework for the formulation of the hypothesis, more specifically, an Optimality-Theoretic (OT) account of the phonological system, and on the general framework expressed in (2), one would have no reason to believe that coda /l/ will be velarized in Spanish as it is in English. Under an OT account, velarization in English is the result of the domination of a constraint requiring coda laterals to have a velar point of articulation (or similarly penalizing any other point of articulation for coda laterals) over the identity constraints demanding preservation of underlying contrasts/specifications. Spanish (with no velar /l/) would have the opposite ranking of the same universal constraints. Given that the phonological system of a language consists of a set of universal constraints ranked in a language-specific fashion, it is not possible for bilinguals to apply English rankings in general and then switch to the Spanish ranking only with regard to velar /l/. Doing so in this case is especially problematic because a ranking paradox would result.

Previous studies of the phonology of CS have focused on phonetic, gradient phenomena and have formulated hypotheses mostly on the basis of descriptive facts. By contrast, we seek to examine categorical, phonological phenomena that could provide more conclusive results than those of gradient, phonetic processes with regard to the question of crosslinguistic phonological effects. Our research should help to inform the question of whether a sudden switch of phonological systems is possible—and if so, in what contexts.

8.3 Optimality Theory and CS

As mentioned, OT makes certain predictions with regard to CS that are worthy of empirical investigation. In OT, crosslinguistic variation (language typology) is the result of language-specific ranking of universal constraints. Two languages can and often do have opposite rankings of the same constraints—for instance, languages with consonant epenthesis have the ranking ONSET >> DEP, and those without it, DEP >> ONSET.[2] However, opposite rankings of the same universal constraints should not exist within one language, or ranking paradoxes will result. This theoretically motivated stipulation is also supported empirically from a wide range of phonological research.

In what follows we present the results of two experiments designed to study the predictions made by the OT framework. Before presenting the experiments and results, we introduce the descriptive data and the OT analyses on which the hypotheses are based. The first set of data and analysis are those of intervocalic voiced obstruents in Spanish and English; they were selected because the OT analysis reveals that their allophonic distribution responds to opposite rankings in English and Spanish. The second set consists of /s/ voicing assimilation data and analysis, with no conflicting rankings. Due to space considerations and to the scope of this research, only the parts of the analysis crucial to the current proposal will be introduced here.

To sum up, we seek to explore the relationship among specific phonological attributes of English and Spanish, and to discover whether there is a sudden switch from one phonological system to another at word boundaries. Furthermore, we will examine whether a ranking paradox specific to the phonological process in question affects the efficacy of the process itself. We now turn to the relevant phonological phenomena in English and Spanish.

8.4 Voiced Obstruents in Spanish and English

8.4.1 Data

Spanish /b, d, g/ are usually realized as [−continuant] when following a stop, a pause, or /l/ in the case of /d/.

(3) cuando   [kwaṇdo]   'when'
     tengo   [teŋgo]   'I have'
     cambio   [kambjo]   'change'
     caldo   [kaḷdo]   'broth'

In most normative varieties of Spanish an approximant appears in all other contexts. Some dialects also have stops in postconsonantal positions (Lipski 1994) or even after an approximant. Yet all dialects with [+continuant] allophones of the voiced stops have a [+continuant] [−vocalic] segment in intervocalic contexts. As a result, and to avoid the confounding effect of contextual and dialectal variation, the current study focuses exclusively on intervocalic position, the one exhibiting the least variation.

(4)   haba   [aßa]   'bean'
      hada   [aða]   'fairy'
      haga   [aɰa]   'do-subj.3sg'

Although traditionally these segments were considered fricatives, presently there is almost universal agreement on their approximant nature. Notice that the difference is only in the degree of aperture and/or the [+/−consonantal] nature of the sound (fricatives are, of course [+consonantal], while approximants are [−consonantal]. In English the intervocalic allophones of /b, d, g/ are always [−continuant].

8.4.2   OT Analysis and Hypothesis[3]

We propose that in Spanish the approximant allophones of /b, d, g/ are the result of the domination of the constraint AGREE (stricture), which requires adjacent segments to agree in degree of stricture, over Identity constraints demanding preservation of underlying +/− specification for [continuant] and for [sonorant].[4] In other words, it is more important for an intervocalic consonant to be like the surrounding vowels in terms of aperture than for it to preserve its underlying [−continuant] and [−sonorant] specification. Note that the current analysis does not crucially depend on voiced obstruents being underlyingly specified for the features [continuant] and [sonorant]. OT places no restrictions on the form of the input. Underlying representations are a natural consequence of the constraints and constraint ranking (cf. Richness of the Base (ROTB); McCarthy 2002). What we refer to here in traditional terms as underlying velar nasals are in fact an epiphenomenon of constraint ranking.

(5)   *Relevant constraints*
      AGREE(stricture): Adjacent segments must agree in degree of stricture (Díaz-Campos and Colina 2006; Steriade 1993).
      IDENTITY-IO(continuant): Corresponding segments are identical with regard to their [+/− continuant] specification (i.e., the [+/− continuant] specification of the output must match that of the input and vice versa).
      IDENTITY-IO(sonorant): Corresponding segments are identical with regard to their [+/− sonorant] specification (i.e., the [+/− sonorant] specification of the output must match that of the input and vice versa).
      FAITHFULNESS: Any segment present in the input must also be present in the output (MAX-IO); any segment present in the output must have a correspondent in the input (DEP-IO).

IDENTITY-IO(consonantal): Corresponding segments are identical with regard to their [+/–consonantal] specification.

Under stricture theory (Streriade 1993), noncontinuants (stops, nasals, and laterals) have the greatest degree of stricture, and approximants and vowels exhibit minimal stricture. Fricatives have medium aperture.

(6) *Stricture theory* (cf. Steriade 1993)
A_0: maximal stricture (noncontinuants, stops, nasals, and laterals)
A_f: medium aperture (fricatives)
A_{MAX}: minimal stricture (approximants and vowels)

The relevant ranking for Spanish is (7).

(7) AGREE(stricture) >> IDENT-IO(continuant), IDENT-IO(sonorant)

As seen in the tableau in (8), the voiced stop in (b) (A_0) disagrees in stricture with the preceding and following vowels (A_{MAX}), thus violating the top-ranked AGREE(stricture). The approximant in (a) agrees in stricture with the adjacent vowels, all being A_{MAX}. Under the assumption that voiced obstruents are underlyingly stops, (a) incurs IDENT-IO(continuant) and IDENT-IO(sonorant) violations, both lower in the hierarchy than AGREE(stricture). (a) is therefore the winner and the optimal candidate. Positing an input with a different specification of [continuant], namely an underlying approximant or fricative, has no consequences for the analysis: the optimal candidate would continue to satisfy AGREE(stricture), and it would incur fewer IDENT-IO marks.

(8) Monolingual Spanish
/lagala/ [lauɣala] 'the gala'

	AGREE(stricture)	IDENT-IO(continuant)	IDENT-IO(sonorant)
☞ a. [lauɣala]		*	*
b. [lagala]	*!		

Since in Spanish only voiced (not voiceless) obstruents have [+continuant] allophones, a constraint against voiceless approximants must be undominated.

The relevant ranking for English has to be the opposite of that found in Spanish, because /b,d,g/ are always realized as [–continuant].

(9) *English ranking*
IDENTITY-IO(continuant), IDENT-IO(sonorant) >> AGREE(stricture)

(10) *Monolingual English*
     /eigoust/ [ejgowst] 'a ghost'

	Ident-IO(continuant)	Ident-IO(sonorant)	Agree(stricture)
☞ [ejgowst]			*
b. [ejɰowst]	*!	*	

As (10) shows, although the stop in (a) violates Agree(stricture), the low ranking of this constraint guarantees selection of (a) over a candidate with an approximant, such as (b), because (b) violates the dominating Ident-IO(continuant) and Ident-IO(sonorant). If we were to posit an approximant in the underlying representation), candidate (10b) would not violate Identity-IO(continuant) or Ident-IO(sonorant), yet it would incur a violation of the constraint banning velar approximants (*ɰ), which is undominated (i.e., never violated) in English.

In a codeswitched utterance, as seen in (11), the Spanish and English rankings (11i–ii) show that Ident-IO(continuant) and Ident-IO(sonorant) are ranked above and below Agree(stricture). Since the union of both rankings results in a ranking paradox, the prediction is that codeswitched utterances will exhibit a sudden switch of phonologies (rankings) at the point of switch.

(11) *Codeswitched utterance (Spanish > English)*
     /mi ‖ goust/ [mi gowst] 'my ghost'
     i. *Spanish ranking*   ii. *English ranking*

	Agree (stricture)	Ident-IO (continuant)	Ident-IO (sonorant)	Ident-IO (continuant)	Ident-IO (sonorant)	Agree (stricture)
a. [mi‖gowst]	*!					*
b. [mi ‖ ɰowst]		*	*	*!	*	

‖ = Point of switch

8.4.3 Experiment

The experiment described below was designed to test the hypothesis that English voiced obstruents that are switch-initial will be realized as stops regardless of the contact with Spanish and of the presence of the context favoring an approximant realization in Spanish. This result would constitute evidence for a sudden switch in phonological system at word boundaries.

Methods. The participants were five simultaneous Spanish-English bilinguals from Central Arizona enrolled at Arizona State University. The task consisted in pronouncing twenty-seven sentences three times each in nonsequential order using Presentation, a stimulus-delivery software package, in a sound booth. The items involved codeswitches from Spanish into English (voiced stop-initial English noun at the onset of the switch, preceded by a vowel-final Spanish determiner).

(12) Hablamos de mi *ghost yesterday.*
  'We talked about my ghost yesterday.'
  Hablamos de mi *disk yesterday.*
  'We talked about my disk yesterday.'
  Hablamos de mi *book yesterday.*
  'We talked about my book yesterday.'

The intervocalic context was selected because it is not affected by dialectal variation, with the voiced obstruents consistently being realized as [+continuant] segments.

It could be argued that the word-initial position of the switch could affect the realization of the voiced obstruent since pauses favor a stop realization in a monolingual Spanish context. For this reason sentences were designed that contained DP-internal (Determiner + Noun) codeswitches; the selected DPs constituted one prosodic word because monosyllabic articles and determiners are usually considered phonological clitics.

The sentences were recorded, transcribed, and subjected to spectrographic analysis using Praat to determine the continuancy (stop vs. approximant) of /b, d, g/. A total of 275 tokens were obtained for analysis (between 52 and 61 per subject).[5] The codeswitched samples were compared to approximantization in contexts that did not involve a switch to rule out convergence toward English in participants' Spanish phonology. These were contained in the Spanish portion of the test sentences, before the switch (e.g., *hablamos* / ablamos/).[6]

Findings. As figure 8.1 shows, the hypothesis was clearly borne out, with a high percentage of the English stops being realized as [−continuant] and

	Total tokens	Stops	Approximants	Per cent stops	Other
s2	52	50	2	96.15%	
s3	55	49	4	89.09%	2
s4 (excluded)*	54	52	2	96.29%	
s5	53	52	1	98.11%	
s6	61	48	1	78.68%	2

Figure 8.1
Results for Spanish-English bilingual speech sample

	Total Tokens	Stops	Approximants	Per cent approximants	Other
s2	50	3	29	91%	18 (deletion)
s3	55	0	47	100%	8 (deletion)
s4*	54	51	0	0%	1 (deletion); 3 (stops induced by pause)
s5	53	1	49	98%	3 (unintelligible)
s6	61	5	27	84%	13 (deletions); 16 (unintelligible)

Figure 8.2
Results for Spanish speech sample

therefore indicating that the switch to the English ranking/phonology is immediate and sudden. In other words, there was no effect of Spanish phonology
on English. The results for subject 4 were excluded because, as seen in figure
8.2, this subject does not appear to have [+continuant] allophones of the
Spanish voiced obstruents in intervocalic position, all being realized as stops.
Results for this subject cannot therefore be interpreted in regard to our research
question.

8.5 /s/-Voicing Assimilation

8.5.1 Data

In Spanish /s/ is realized as [z] when followed by a voiced consonant.

(13) desde   [dezðe]   'from'
      mismo   [mizmo]   'same'
      las dos   [lazðos]   'the two'
      tres manos   [trezmanos]   'three hands'
      tres osos   [tresosos]   'three bears'

Although the process is known to be somewhat gradient and variable (Navarro
Tomás 1977), the presence of at least some /s/-voicing in a CS context, in
particular when /s/ is followed by an English word that starts with a voiced
consonant, would indicate that the feature [+voice] can serve as a trigger for
the Spanish process independently of its belonging to an English lexical item.
Note that it is not necessary to have voice assimilation in all cases or in a
significantly high number of cases. The presence of at least some assimilation
would mean that the feature [+voice] can trigger the process regardless of the
language of the lexical item it is part of.

8.5.2   OT Analysis and Hypothesis

It seems reasonable to assume that the CS facts could be different if ranking paradoxes were not involved. In other words, we want to find out whether an cross-linguistic effect could exist in the absence of conflicting rankings; in segmental terms, can a feature of language X be used to meet the structural description of a phonological rule of language Y? To investigate this type of situation a small experiment was designed that involved no conflicting rankings. More specifically, the process under investigation, /s/ voicing in Spanish, will speak to the question of whether a word-initial English segment may serve as a trigger for a Spanish process that has as its target a word-final consonant.

An OT analysis of /s/-voicing in Spanish necessitates the following constraints:

(14) AGREE(voice): Adjacent segments must agree in voicing.
      IDENTITY-IO CODA(voice): Corresponding coda segments are identical
      with regard to their [+/−voice] specification (i.e., the [+/−voice]
      specification of the output must match that of the input and vice versa).
      IDENT-IO ONSET(voice): Corresponding onset segments are identical
      with regard to their [+/−voice] specification. (i.e., the [+/−voice]
      specification of the output must match that of the input and vice versa).

IDENT-IO(voice) must be divided into IDENT-IO CODA(voice) and IDENT-IO ONSET(voice) because voicing contrasts are often preserved in the onset and neutralized in the coda. This indicates that IDENT-IO ONSET(voice) dominates AGREE(voice) since there is no voice neutralization in the onset. Although onset voicing neutralization does not need to be ruled out for /s/, since Spanish has no [z] in its underlying inventory, the distinction is still necessary given that it affects other obstruents whose voicing is neutralized in the coda (e.g., [p]*ata* 'leg' vs. [b]*ata* 'gown', but *ecli*[p]*se* ~ *ecli*[b]*se* 'eclipse'). Voicing neutralization in the coda is the result of the domination of AGREE (voice) over IDENT-IO CODA(voice).[7]

(15) *Spanish ranking*
      IDENT-IO ONSET(voice) >> AGREE(voice) >> IDENT-IO CODA(voice)

(16) Monolingual Spanish
      /mismo/ [mizmo] 'same'

	IDENT-IO ONSET(voice)	AGREE(voice)	IDENT-IO CODA(voice)
☞ a. [mizmo]			*
b. [mismo]		*!	

In (16) (a) is the optimal candidate because (b), with no assimilation, violates Agree(voice), which is more highly ranked than the constraint violated by (a)—Ident-IO Coda(voice).

For a codeswitching context such as the one in (17), the prediction is that the English ranking would be irrelevant, since the English segment is a trigger rather than a target of the process and no conflicting constraints are involved. In order to satisfy Agree(voice), evaluation would look for agreement with the voice specification of the adjacent consonant (i.e., /g/ in (17)). Evaluation in a codeswitched utterance then would proceed as in monolingual Spanish.

(17) Codeswitched utterance (Spanish > English)
     /mis ‖ gousts/ [miz gowsts] 'my ghosts'

	Ident-IO Onset(voice)	Agree(voice)	Ident-IO Coda(voice)
☞ a. [miz gowsts]			*
b. [mis gowsts]		*!	

We hypothesize that a switch-initial voiced English consonant can trigger voicing assimilation of a switch-final Spanish consonant.

8.5.3 Experiment

Methods. The methods were similar to those of Experiment 1, with the data being collected simultaneously with those for Experiment 1. The participants were the same five simultaneous Spanish-English bilinguals from Central Arizona (students at Arizona State University). The task consisted of pronouncing nine sentences three times each in nonsequential order using Presentation, a stimulus-delivery software package, in a sound booth.[8] The items involved codeswitches from Spanish into English (a voiced stop-initial English noun at the onset of the switch, preceded by an /s/-final Spanish determiner). See the examples in (12).

The sentences were recorded, transcribed, and subjected to spectrographic analysis (using Praat) to determine the voiced-versus-voiceless status of /s/. A total of 138 tokens were obtained for analysis (between 25 and 32 per subject).[9] The codeswitched samples were compared to voicing in contexts that did not involve a codeswitch to rule out convergence toward English in participants' Spanish phonology. These were contained in the Spanish portion of the test sentences, before the switch (e.g., *hablamo[z] de*).

Findings. Experiment 2 confirmed the peculiar phonology of subject 4, since she again behaved in a way atypical for most varieties of Spanish (figure

	Total tokens	[s]	[z]	Per cent [z]	Other
s2	28	18 (64.28%)	6	21.42%	4 (14.28%)
s3	26	5 (19.23%)	18	69.23%	3 (11.53%)
s4	27	26 (96.29%)	1	3.70%	
s5	25	13 (52%)	8	32%	4 (partial voicing) (16%)
s6	32	5 (15.62%)	16	50%	11 (34.37%)

Figure 8.3
Results for Spanish-English bilingual speech sample

	Total tokens	[s]	[z]	Per cent [z]	Other[i]
s2	28	14 (50%)	13	46.42%	1
s3	26	1(3.84%)	15	57.59%	10
s4* excluded	27	26 (96.29%)	0		1
s5	25	2(8%)	21	84%	2
s6	32	0	29	90.62%	3

---

[i]Includes deletion, pauses and unintelligible forms.

Figure 8.4
Results for monolingual Spanish speech sample (e.g., hablamos de)

8.4). In this case her Spanish did not exhibit voice assimilation; as in Experiment 1, her codeswitching results were excluded from the study. All other subjects exhibited voicing assimilation within the normal parameters (variable, around 50% or higher).

In Experiment 1, the trigger consisted of a Spanish vowel to the right and an English vowel to the left, but the Spanish process was not triggered on English words, providing evidence of a sudden shift in phonologies. In Experiment 2, we see that a word-initial English voiced consonant can trigger voicing assimilation in Spanish. Hence, while the phonological processes appear to accept triggers from another language, they cannot be stimulated to modify word structure across word boundaries. This generalization is true regardless of whether the specific process involves a ranking paradox (as in Experiment 1) or not (as in Experiment 2). This is as expected if we view crosslinguistic rankings to be phonology-wide, so that crosslinguistic differences among constraints relevant to specific phonological processes are sufficient to constitute a ranking paradox for the purpose of the PFIC in (2). These findings are consistent with those of Bullock and colleagues (Botero et al., 2004; Bullock et al., 2004; Bullock and Toribio, 2009). Furthermore, they are consistent with Schindler, Legendre and Mbaye's (2008) Wolof-French data, which show that a French vowel may trigger vowel harmony on a Wolof stem much as an English vowel may trigger voicing on a Spanish segment in Experiment 2.

The PFIC extends nicely to the case of complex heads. As we show in the next section, these farther reaching consequences explain a number of syntactic facts as well.

8.6   Syntactic Reflexes

Poplack (1981, 5), and others since, have noted a prohibition against CS between a stem and its bound morpheme, her Free Morpheme Constraint: "A switch may not occur between a bound morpheme and a lexical item unless the latter has been phonologically integrated into the language of the bound morpheme." Consider, for example, (18), where the restriction is illustrated with English-Spanish examples.

(18) a. *Juan está *eat*-iendo.
          Juan be/1Ss eat-DUR
          'Juan is eating.'
      b. *Juan *eat*-ó.
          Juan eat-PAST/3Ss
          'Juan ate.'
      c. *Juan *com*-ed.
          Juan eat-PAST
          'Juan ate.'
      d. *Juan eat-*ará*.
          Juan be/1Ss eat-FUT/3Ss
          'Juan will eat.'

Sankoff and Poplack (1981) further noted that phonological integration will change matters. When the stem is phonologically integrated into the language of the inflectional morpheme, as in (19), where the English stem *park* is borrowed into Spanish, no ill-formedness results.

(19) a. Juan está parqueando su coche.
          Juan be/3Ss park-DUR his car
          'Juan is parking his car.'
      b. Juan parqueó su coche.
          Juan park-PAST/3Ss his car
          'Juan parked his car.'

    c. Juan parqueará su coche.

      Juan park-FUT/3Ss

      'Juan will park his car.'

While the restriction on word-internal switching has been widely attested, it has also been somewhat controversial in the CS literature. It has been attested in numerous corpora (Bentahila and Davis 1983; Berk-Seligson 1986; Clyne 1987; MacSwan 1999), but questioned by some apparent counterexamples in others (Bokamba 1989; Myers-Scotton 1993; Nartey 1982; Halmari 1997; Chan 1999; Hlavac 2003). In some cases, researchers have not adequately documented the phonological characteristics of items to permit us to judge their level of integration, and in others assumptions about the morphological status of elements have not been made explicit.

The PFIC predicts the facts represented in (18) and (19), as it prohibits word-internal switching for reasons associated with the phonological system. The PFIC has a significant advantage over the Free Morpheme Constraint in that it follows from independently motivated principles of grammar and is not stipulative, like the Free Morpheme Constraint. It therefore adheres to the CS research principle outlined in MacSwan (1999; chapter 1, this volume) prohibiting the use of CS-specific mechanisms in our analysis of mixed-language data.

Because heads are inputs to the phonological system, the PFIC also predicts that switching within a complex head is prohibited. The prediction is borne out, as illustrated by the negation facts in (20) (MacSwan, 1999).

(20) a. *No *nitekititoc.*

         no ni-tekiti-toc

         not 1S-work-DUR

         'I'm not working.'

     b. Amo *estoy trabajando.*

         amo estoy trabaja-ndo

         not be/PRES/1Ss work-DUR

         'I'm not working.'

Although Spanish and Nahuatl have the same basic word-order requirements with respect to negation, and the same basic functional and semantic properties are common to both examples, Spanish negation does not permit a Nahautl verb in its complement position in (20a), but Nahuatl negation followed by a Spanish verb is fine in (20b).

Zagona (1988) argues that Spanish *no* is a syntactic clitic and forms part of the Spanish verbal complex as a result of head movement. To make a case for this analysis, Zagona points out that Spanish *no* must be fronted with the verb in (21), unlike the adverbs in (22).

(21) ¿Qué no dijo Juan?
     what not say/1Ss/PAST Juan
     'What didn't Juan say?'

(22) a. *¿Qué sólo leyó Juan?
        what only read/1Ss/PAST Juan
        'What did Juan only read?'
    b. *¿Qué meramente leyó Juan?
        what merely read/1Ss/PAST Juan
        'What did Juan merely read?'

Zagona (1988) also points out that Spanish *no* cannot be contrastively stressed in (23a) as its English counterpart in (23b) can be, because clitics are inherently unstressable. The example in (23b) shows that in English, in contrast to Spanish, the negative element is not a syntactic clitic.

(23) a. *Juan no ha *no* hecho la tarea.
        Juan not has not done the task
        'Juan hasn't not done the task.'
    b. Juan hasn't *not* done the task.

These facts suggest that in Spanish, the verb is a host for negation. Nahuatl, on the other hand, behaves differently from French and Spanish with regard to negation. A test similar to the one Zagona uses in (23) shows that Nahuatl patterns with English:

(24) Amo nio amo niktati nowelti.
     amo ni-o amo ni-k-tati no-welti
     not 1S-go amo 1S-3Os-see my-sister
     'I'm not going to not see my sister.'

Since clitics are inherently unstressable, we may conclude from (24) that *amo* is not a clitic in Nahuatl.

Thus, we conclude that (20a) is ill formed because Spanish *no* forms a syntactic clitic (complex head) with a Nahuatl verb, a violation of the ban on head-internal switching expressed by the PFIC, and hence crashes at PF. In (20b), *amo* does not trigger head movement, and no violation of the PFIC occurs.

The head movement facts in (20) are illustrative of a general fact: CS in head movement contexts is prohibited (MacSwan, 1999, 2009, 2013). The PFIC derives these facts by stipulating that all heads, simple and complex (created by head adjunction), are inputs to phonology, and phonological derivations proceed by mapping lexical forms to surface forms in a single step, with no intermediate representations visible to other subsystems of the bilingual language faculty. However, the CS facts are also consistent with the view that head movement is itself a *phonological operation*, as suggested by Chomsky (2000, 2001) and Boeckx and Stjepanovic (2001), and recently discussed in Platzack (2013).

A few apparent counter-examples to the PFIC have surfaced, specifically focusing on the ban on word-internal mixing at affix boundaries. However, these proposed counter-examples appear to be cases of phrase-level affixes, and therefore do not submit to the PFIC. Jake, Myers-Scotton and Gross (2005), for instance, discuss cases involving Swahili agreement suffixes *m-* and *-tu-* on an English stem (but only if the English stem is bare), English genitive *-s* attached to a Croatian noun, Dutch agreement suffix *-e* attached to a French adjective, and Finnish inessive and partitive case marking on English nouns. Similarly, Schindler, Legendre and Mbaye (2008) offer counter-examples to the PFIC based on Wolof *-woon* affixation of a French stem. However, MacSwan (2005, 2008) notes that these specific morphological examples have frequently been analyzed, or may very plausibly be analyzed, as cases of phrase-level affixation, as Bandi-Rao and den Dikken (chapter 7, this volume) also conclude regarding *-ify* and *-inc* in English-Telugu CS. Furthermore, Jake, Myers-Scotton and Gross (2005) and Schindler, Legendre and Mbaye (2008) do not present alternative analytic frameworks in which their proposed counter-examples may be reconciled with the facts in (18)-(20). As Lightfoot (1979, 73) noted, it is not sufficient "simply to cite unanalyzed phenomena as alleged counterexamples to a theoretical claim," absent a viable alternative analysis.

Bandi-Rao and den Dikken (chapter 7, this volume) also correctly note that the restriction stated in the PF Disjunction Theorem (here replaced with the PFIC) was too strong. Specifically, they point out that phonology occurs not only within words (heads) but also between them, so the stipulation in the earlier formulation that CS "within a PF component is not possible" prohibited CS in all contexts. Bandi-Rao and den Dikken propose an alternative based on Distributed Morphology (DM). We believe the solution proposed here, which more clearly captures the word-bound nature of phonological parsing in an OT framework, adequately addresses these concerns, and has an important advantage over the DM framework for CS theory – namely, it overcomes the more general problem of late lexical insertion associated with earlier generative models and DM, discussed at length in MacSwan (chapter 1, this volume).

8.7 Conclusions

The phonological findings presented here suggests that phonological systems may be switched at word boundaries but not word-internally. A phonological operation of one language cannot affect another by changing its structure. These facts follow from independent properties of the phonological system, leading us to the conclusion that many cases of ill-formedness observed in the CS literature are a consequence of language design. Phonology is the locus of imperfection and arbitrariness and presents marked contrasts crosslinguistically. The phonological system operates independently of the syntax, and in a manner that is quite distinct. At Spell-Out, as features relevant to the phonological system are handed over to the PF component for processing, efforts to force phonological switching below the word level result in the formation of uninterpretable objects at PF, because every word (head) must be parsed by an internally coherent phonological system.

Notes

1. Jake, Myers-Scotton, and Gross (2002) erroneously attribute this view to MacSwan (1999, 2000) but subsequently acknowledged the error (Jake, Myers-Scotton, and Gross 2005).

2. DEP = No epenthesis; ONSET = all syllables must have onsets.

3. The experiments described in this paper and the formal analysis they are based on were originally carried out in preparation for Colina and MacSwan (2005) and MacSwan and Colina (2007). Since then, alternative analyses of the voiced obstruent allophony in Spanish have emerged. Most recently, Colina (2013) argues that the allophonic variation encountered in the standard dialects can be explained as the result of input and output underspecification; that is, the input contains a voiced obstruent underspecified for continuancy and this underspecification persists in the output of the phonology (cf. Hale and Kissock [2007] and references therein for the mechanism of output underspecification in OT). This means that the voiced obstruent is realized variably according to the surrounding segments in the phonetic component; in the intervocalic context under consideration here, the [+continuant] specification would be the result of phonetic implementation rather than the effect of the AGREE constraint. The consequences of input/output underspecification proposals for CS data remain to be investigated.

4. For alternative, detailed OT analyses of Spanish voiced obstruents, see Barlow 2003, Baković 1997, Díaz-Campos and Colina 2006; for derivational analyses, see Hammond 1976, Harris 1984, Lozano 1979, Mascaró 1984, Hualde 1989, as well as the references cited therein.

5. Some of the differences were due to repetitions and backtracking.

6. Although this example does not involve intervocalic position, a complex onset in postvocalic position is another context that favors the approximant realization of voiced obstruents across dialects.

7. See Colina (2009) for an alternative analysis that sees voicing assimilation as the result of the coda's inability to license voice specifications.

8. These sentences were the plural forms of the possessive + N sentences used for Experiment 1.

9. Some of the differences were due to repetitions and backtracking.

References

Bandi-Rao, S., and M. den Dikken. 2014. Light switches: On v as a pivot in codeswitching, and the nature of the ban on word-internal switches. In J. MacSwan, ed., *Grammatical Theory and Bilingual Codeswitching*. Cambridge, MA: MIT Press.

Baković, E. 1997. Strong onsets and Spanish fortition. *MIT Working Papers in Linguistics* 23:21–39.

Barlow, Jessica. 2003. The stop-spirant alternation in Spanish: Converging evidence for a fortition account. *Southwest Journal of Linguistics* 22(1): 51–86.

Bentahila, A., and E. E. Davis. 1983. The syntax of Arabic-French code-switching. *Lingua* 59:301–330.

Berk-Seligson, S. 1986. Linguistic constraints on intrasentential code-switching: A study of Spanish-Hebrew bilingualism. *Language in Society* 15:313–348.

Bermúdez-Otero, Ricardo, and Patrick Honeyboneb. 2006. Phonology and syntax: A shifting relationship. *Lingua* 116:543–561.

Bloomfield, L. 1928. A set of postulates for the science of language. *Language* 2.

Boeckx, C., and Stjepanovic, S. 2001. Head-ing toward PF. *Linguistic Inquiry*, 32(2): 345–355.

Bokamba, E. G. 1989. Are there syntactic constraints on code-mixing? *World Englishes* 8:277–292.

Botero, C., Barbara Bullock, Kristopher Davis, and Almeida Jacqueline Toribio. 2004. Perseverative phonetic effects in bilingual code-switching. Paper presented at the 34th Linguistic Symposium on Romance Languages, University of Utah, March.

Bullock, Barbara E., Almeida Jacqueline Toribio, Kristopher Allen Davis, and Christopher G. Botero. 2004. Phonetic convergence in bilingual Puerto Rican Spanish. In Benjamin Schmeiser, Vineeta Chand, Ann Kelleher and Angelo Rodriguez, eds., *WCCFL 23: Proceedings of the 23rd West Coast Conference on Formal Linguistic*, 101–113. Somerville, MA: Cascadilla Press.

Bullock, Barbara E., Almeida Jacqueline Toribio. 2009. Trying to hit a moving target: On the sociophonetics of code-switching. In L. Isurin, D. Winford, and K. de Bot, eds., *Multidisciplinary Approaches to Codeswitching*, 189–206. Amsterdam: John Benjamins Publishing.

Bromberger, S., and M. Halle. 1989. Why phonology is different. *Linguistic Inquiry* 20:51–70.

Cantone, K. F., and MacSwan, J. 2009. The syntax of DP-internal codeswitching, pp. 243–278. In L. Isurin, D. Winford, and K. de Bot, eds., *Multidisciplinary Approaches to Codeswitching*. Amsterdam: John Benjamins Publishing.

Chan, B. H.-S. 1999. Aspects of the syntax, production and pragmatics of codeswitching with special reference to Cantonese-English. Doctoral dissertation, University College London.

Chomsky, N. 1951. Morphophonemics of modern Hebrew. Master's thesis, University of Pennsylvania.

Chomsky, N. 1965. *Aspects of the Theory of Syntax*. Cambridge, MA: MIT Press.

Chomsky, Noam. 1981. *Lectures on Government and Binding*. Dordrecht: Foris.

Chomsky, N. 1986. *Knowledge of Language: Its Nature, Origins, and Use*. New York: Praeger.

Chomsky, N. 1991. Linguistics and cognitive science: Problems and mysteries. In A. Kasher, ed., *The Chomskyan Turn*. Cambridge, MA: Blackwell.

Chomsky, N. 1995. *The Minimalist Program*. Cambridge, MA: MIT Press.

Chomsky, N. 2000. Minimalist inquiries: The framework. In R. Martin, D. Michaels, and J. Uriagereka, eds., *Step by Step: Essays on Minimalist Syntax in Honor of Howard Lasnik*, 89–155. Cambridge, MA: MIT Press.

Chomsky, N. 2001. Derivation by phase. In M. Kenstowicz, ed., *Ken Hale: A Life in Language*, 1–51. Cambridge, MA: MIT Press.

Chomsky, N. 2002. *On Nature and Language*. Cambridge: Cambridge University Press.

Clyne, M. 1987. Constraints on code switching: How universal are they? *Linguistics* 25:739–764.

Colina, S. 2009. Sibilant voicing in Ecuadoran Spanish. *Studies in Hispanic and Lusophone Linguistics* 2: 3–29.

Colina, S. 2013. Spanish voiced obstruent alternation and underspecification in OT. Paper presented at the 43rd Linguistic Symposium on Romance Languages, City University of New York, April 19–21.

Colina, S., and MacSwan, J. 2005. Language mixing at the interface: How does phonology affect the syntax of codeswitching? Paper presented at the 5th International Symposium on Bilingualism (ISB5), Barcelona, Spain.

Díaz-Campos, M., and S. Colina. 2006. The interaction between faithfulness constraints and sociolinguistic variation: The acquisition of phonological variation in first language speakers. In Fernando Martínez-Gil and Sonia Colina (eds.), *Optimality-Theoretic Studies in Spanish Phonology*, 424–446. Amsterdam: John Benjamins Publishing Company.

Grosjean, François, and Joanne Miller. 1994. Going in and out of languages: An example of bilingual flexibility. *Psychological Science* 5 (4): 201–206.

Hale, Mark, and Madelyn Kissock. 2007. The phonetics-phonology interface and the acquisition of perseverant underspecification. In Gillian Ramchand and Charles Reiss eds., *The Oxford Handbook of Linguistic Interfaces*, 81–101. Oxford: Oxford University Press.

Halle, Morris. 1995. Feature geometry and feature spreading. *Linguistic Inquiry* 26:1–46.

Halmari, H. 1997. *Government and Code Switching: Explaining American Finnish.* New York: John Benjamins.

Hammond, Robert M. 1976. Phonemic restructuring of voiced obstruents in Miami Cuban Spanish. In Frances M. Aid, Melvyn C. Resnik, and Bohdan Saciuk, eds., *1975 Colloquium on Hispanic Linguistics*, 42–51. Washington, DC: Georgetown University Press.

Harris, James W. 1984. La espirantización en castellano y la representación fonológica autosegmental. *Estudis Gramaticals* 1:149–167.

Hlavac, J. 2003. *Second-Generation Speech: Lexicon, Code-Switching, and Morpho-Syntax of Croatian-English Bilinguals.* Berlin: Peter Lang.

Hualde, José Ignacio. 1989. Procesos consonánticos y estructuras geométricas en español. *Lingüística* 1:7–44.

Jake, J., C. Myers-Scotton, and S. Gross. 2002. Making a minimalist approach to codeswitching work: Adding the Matrix Language. *Bilingualism: Language and Cognition* 5 (1): 69–91.

Legendre, Géraldine, Jane Grimshaw, and Sten Vikner. 2001. *Optimality-Theoretic Syntax.* Cambridge, MA: MIT Press.

Lightfoot, D. 1979. *Principles of Diachronic Syntax.* Cambridge: Cambridge University Press.

Lipski, John. 1994. *Latin American Spanish.* London and New York: Longman.

Lozano, M. C. 1979. *Stop and Spirant Alternations: Fortition and Spirantization Processes in Spanish Phonology.* Bloomington, IN: Indiana University Linguistics Club.

MacSwan, J. 1999. *A Minimalist Approach to Intrasentential Code Switching.* New York: Garland Press.

MacSwan, J. 2000. The architecture of the bilingual language faculty: Evidence from codeswitching. *Bilingualism: Language and Cognition* 3 (1): 37–54.

MacSwan, J. 2005. Codeswitching and generative grammar: A critique of the MLF model and some remarks on "modified minimalism." *Bilingualism: Language and Cognition* 8 (1): 1–22.

MacSwan, J. 2008. Plenary address: Unconstraining codeswitching theories. *Proceedings from the Annual Meeting of the Chicago Linguistic Society*, 44(2): 151–168. Chicago: University of Chicago Press.

MacSwan, J. 2009. Generative approaches to codeswitching. In A. J. Toribio and B. E. Bullock, eds., *Cambridge Handbook of Linguistic Codeswitching I*, 309–335. Cambridge University Press.

MacSwan, J. 2013. Code switching and linguistic theory. In T. K. Bhatia and W. Ritchie, eds., *Handbook of Bilingualism and Multilingualism*, 2nd edition, 223–350. Oxford: Blackwell.

MacSwan, J., and K. McAlister. 2010. Naturalistic and elicited data in grammatical studies of codeswitching. *Studies in Hispanic and Lusophone Linguistics* 3 (2): 521–532.

MacSwan, J., and S. Colina. 2007. Interface conditions on language mixing. Paper presented at the 6th International Symposium on Bilingualism. Hamburg, Germany, May 30-June 2.

Martínez-Gil, Fernando. 2004. On the stop-spirant distribution of Spanish voiced obstruents. Paper presented at the 35th LSRL, University of Texas at Austin, February.

Mascaró, Joan. 1984. Continuant spreading in Basque, Catalan, and Spanish language sound structure. In Mark Aronoff and Richard T. Oehrle, eds., *Language Sound Structure: Studies in Phonology Presented to Morris Halle by His Teacher and Students*, 287–298. Cambridge, MA: MIT Press.

McCarthy, John J. 2002. *A Thematic Guide to Optimality Theory*. Cambridge: Cambridge University Press.

Myers-Scotton, C. 1993. *Dueling Languages: Grammatical Structure in Code Switching*. Oxford: Clarendon Press.

Nartey, J. S. 1982. Code-switching, interference or faddism? Language use among educated Ghanaians. *Anthropological Linguistics* 24:183–192.

Navarro Tomás, T. 1997. *Manual de pronunciación española*. Madrid: Consejo Superior de Investigaciones Científicas.

Newmeyer, F. J. 1986. *The History of Linguistics*. Chicago: University of Chicago Press.

Platzack, Christer. 2013. Head movement as a phonological operation. In Lisa Lai-Shen Cheng and Norbert Corver, eds., *Diagnosing Syntax*, 21–43. Oxford: Oxford University Press.

Poplack, S. 1981. The syntactic structure and social function of code-switching. In R. Durán, ed., *Latino Language and Communicative Behavior*. Norwood, NJ: Ablex.

Prince, Alan, and Paul Smolensky. 1993. *Optimality Theory: Constraint Interaction in Generative Grammar*. Rutgers University Center for Cognitive Science Technical Report 2. New Brunswick, NJ: Rutgers University.

Sankoff, D., and S. Poplack. 1981. A formal grammar for code-switching. *Papers in Linguistics* 14:3–145

Schindler, M., G. Legendre, and A. Mbaye. 2008. Violations of the PF Interface Condition in Urban Wolof. *Proceedings from the Annual Meeting of the Chicago Linguistic Society*, 44(2): 169–184.

Steriade, Donca. 1993. Closure, release and nasal contours. In Marie Huffman and Rena Krakow, eds., *Phonetics and Phonology*, 401–470. San Diego: Academic Press.

Zagona, K. 1988. *Verb Phrase Syntax: A Parametric Study of English and Spanish*. Boston: Kluwer Academic Publishers.

Part III

Codeswitching and the LF Interface

9 The Semantic Interpretation and Syntactic Distribution of Determiner Phrases in Spanish-English Codeswitching

Monica Moro Quintanilla

9.1 Introduction

There are many bilingual communities whose speakers use both of their languages in a single sentence:

(1) *English-Spanish in New York (Ramírez 1992, 199)*
So you *todavía* haven't decided *lo que vas a hacer* next week.
'So you haven't decided yet what you are going to do next week.'

(2) *German-English in Australia (Clyne 1987, 754)*
Ich les' gerade eins, das handelt von einem alten *secondhand dealer and his son.*
'I'm just reading one. It's about an old secondhand dealer and his son.'

(3) *French/Lingala in Central Africa (Bokamba 1988, 25)*
Est-ce que *o-tun-áki yé soko a-ko-zónga* le lendemain?
'Did you (sg.) ask him/her if (s)he will return the day after tomorrow?'

(4) *Catalan/Spanish in Spain (Blas Arroyo 1999, 103)*
Estem *de acuerdo.*
'We are in agreement.'

(5) *English/Marathi in India (Pandharipande 1990, 18)*
Building cya samor ubha raha.
'Stand in front of the building.'

All these sequences rest on elements taken from two languages that combine in different forms. Such sequences are normal—that is, they belong to the daily use of the individuals in question. I have deliberately taken a wide variety of language pairs to show that this phenomenon known as codeswitching probably appears in most bilingual communities on the five continents.

The codeswitching phenomena mentioned above have received extensive research treatment within the framework of generative grammar over the last thirty years (see MacSwan, chapter 1, this volume). MacSwan (1997, 1999, 2000, 2013), Huybregts and Boeschoten (1999), and Toribio (1999), among others, attempt to explain restrictions on codeswitching in terms of the most recent theory of linguistic competence: the Minimalist Program (Chomsky 1995, 1998, 1999). Their main claim is that "nothing constrains codeswitching apart from the requirements of the mixed grammars," as MacSwan (2000, 43) puts it. Adopting the minimalist approach to syntax (Chomsky 1995), they assume that all codeswitching samples can be analyzed in terms of mechanisms independently motivated for the analysis of monolingual data, and therefore codeswitching phenomena can be explained without appealing to ad hoc constraints specific to codeswitching.

The purpose of this chapter is to test the validity of the claim made by these authors. The phenomenon in question is the occurrence of determiner phrases (DPs) in Spanish-English codeswitching utterances. In section 9.2, I examine one of the syntactic sites where the contrast between English and Spanish is most salient, which is in the absence of determination, particularly focusing on the semantic interpretation and syntactic typology of determinerless nominals and adopting the theory of bare nouns presented in Longobardi 1994, 1999, 2000. Section 9.3 suggests some grammatical explanations for one of the most frequent codeswitches in the data, which is the alternation between the Spanish definite article and the English noun, following certain basic assumptions of the Minimalist Program developed by Chomsky (1995, 1998, 1999).

9.2 The Semantic Interpretation of Determiner Phrases in Spanish-English Codeswitching

It seems that natural languages use determiners with nouns because of the need to indicate which and how many entities speakers intend to refer to when they use a noun phrase. It is, therefore, a category intrinsically linked with the referential and quantificational operations, which relate the linguistic expressions to the extralinguistic entities represented by them (see Leonetti 1999). That's one of the reasons Abney's (1987) DP-analysis has been assumed in the generative grammar literature, since the noun itself cannot refer to any entity, and consequently only nominal expressions introduced by a determiner can be arguments.

Thus, the main function of determiners is to make possible the reference and quantification of noun phrases. This leads us to explore why some nouns that have no determiner are able to perform these tasks themselves, why this capacity varies from language to language, and how this affects codewitched determiner phrases. To answer these questions, I will first present and analyze the main differences between Spanish and English as regards the use of bare nouns, then we will see how these differences show up in codeswitching contact situations, and finally, I will propose an analysis of these facts.

9.2.1 Semantic Preliminaries: Bare Nouns

As I have already mentioned, the acceptability of a bare nominal phrase can vary from language to language—and even within the same language—depending on the kind of noun involved. For example, Romance languages like Spanish only admit bare nominal phrases in subject position when the noun is a proper noun or a pronoun. This is not the case with Germanic languages like English, in which the acceptability of a bare nominal phrase extends to mass nouns and plural nouns (see Lois 1996). Consider the contrast between English and Spanish illustrated in (6) and (7):

(6)　a.　Beavers are mammals.　　*(generic)*
　　　b. *Castores son mamíferos.

(7)　a.　Wine is made out of grape.　　*(generic)*
　　　b. *Vino se hace de la uva.

In Spanish, speakers use the definite determiner to express genericity:

(8)　a. Los castores son mamíferos.　　*(generic)*
　　　b. El vino se hace de la uva.　　*(generic)*

But bare nominal phrases can appear in object position with single-event verbs or the so-called stage-level predicates (see Kratzer 1988) in both languages. This is corroborated by examples (9) and (10):

(9)　a.　Bebo siempre vino.　　*(existential)*
　　　b.　I always drink wine.

(10) a.　Come manzanas todos los días.　　*(existential)*
　　　b.　He eats apples every day.

In both Spanish and English, the bare nominal phrases illustrated in (9) and (10) do not have a generic interpretation, but an indefinite or "existential" one. That is, the interpretation of these nominal phrases is similar to that of an indefinite, existentially quantified noun phrase, as for example *an apple*. However, in Spanish they do not combine well with permanent-state verbs or "individual-level predicates" (see also Kratzer 1988) like *love* or *hate*:

(11) a. *Me gusta/odio vino.　　*(generic)*
　　　b. *Me gusta/odio manzanas.　　*(generic)*

On the contrary, English does accept mass nouns and plural nouns with a generic interpretation, as we have seen in examples (6) and (7), so that sentences like (12) are acceptable:

(12) a. I love/ hate wine.   (*generic*)
     b. I love/ hate apples.   (*generic*)

On the basis of these observations, we can conclude that Spanish bare nouns are excluded from preverbal subject position, but admitted in internal argument position with the existential reading (see 9a and 10a). In English, bare plurals and bare mass nouns are less restricted; they may survive in subject position with the generic reading (see 6a and 7a) as well as in the object position with the existential reading (see 9b and 10b) and also the generic reading (see 12a and 12b).

In light of these data, I will now propose an analysis of these facts based on some of the hypotheses developed by Longobardi (1994, 1999, 2000) but adopting certain basic assumptions of Chomsky's Minimalist Program (see Chomsky 1995, 1998, 1999).

According to Longobardi (1994, 1999, 2000), natural languages contain only two types of entities: individual objects (denoted by proper names) and kinds (expressed by common nouns). The rest of the readings associated with DPs (e.g., the existential reading, the definite reading, etc.) follow from an operator-variable structure in which the different lexical determiners restrict the interpretation of nouns because they work as operators binding a variable whose range is always the extension of the natural kind referred to by the head noun. Consequently, only common nouns, being expressions for kinds, can provide a range to a lexical determiner understood as an operator, as opposed to proper nouns and personal pronouns, which cannot be interpreted this way in normal circumstances (they always refer to a specific and unique entity of the domain of discourse).

Therefore, in unmarked circumstances, nominals will refer to kinds (common nouns) or individual objects (proper names). These two basic semantic values are licensed, following Longobardi, via checking of the [+/- referential] features with which all D positions are universally generated and that are associated with individual objects and kinds respectively. Hence in all languages the noun head must raise to the empty determiner position in order to check those [+/- referential] features, so that the [+referential] value is checked only if the DP contains an object-referring expression (i.e., a pronoun or a proper name) and the [-referential] value is checked when the DP does not contain any object-referring expression. Consequently, no grammatical checking of the [+referential] value is ever possible if D selects a kind-referring expression (a common noun) and, conversely, no grammatical checking of the [-referential] value is possible if D selects a proper name.

In this light, Longobardi can easily explain the fact that in English the common nouns that appear without a determiner have a generic reading since D has no operator force, and therefore it forms a chain with a non-object-referring expression that checks the [-referential] value associated with kinds. In contrast, Spanish common nouns require the lexical realization of a determiner, a definite article. Following Longobardi I will admit that in these cases, the determiner is an expletive that has no real semantic content, so that it checks the [-referential] feature with which D is generated. Consequently, the N-raising to D is no longer necessary. English does not tolerate the use of the definite article with plural or mass nouns because it does not allow expletive occurrences of the article.

In minimalist terms, I will admit that D can have operator features (restricted to the presence of lexical determiners or event verbs), but also other features, like [+/- referential], that license the existence of the empty D as a functional category. I also assume that N raises to the checking domain of D to check those features by substitution—that is, N occupies the landing head position and checks the [+/- referential] features. In addition, when there is a lexical determiner with operator force, N raises to D by adjunction, preserving the independent content of the landing position and allowing the trace of the raised noun to provide the required quantificational range to the surviving D position.

I will also adopt Chomsky's (1998, 1999) hypothesis that the lexical insertion of an expletive is more economical than movement because the Move operation is considered a *last resort*; it is seen as a costly operation that must apply when nothing else is available. Therefore, I propose that the insertion of the Spanish expletive article *el/la/lo/las* is more economical than the raising of N. Because English does not have expletive *the*, N has to move obligatorily.

9.2.2   Generic and Existential Determiner Phrases in Codeswitching

Having established that parametric difference between English and Spanish, I will now describe the structures involving generic and existential readings of DPs in codeswitching contact situations.

First of all, I will present data obtained by Melissa Moyer from native bilinguals who alternate English and Spanish in the same sentence. These data were all recorded in naturally occurring speech situations in Gibraltar: ordinary situations at school, in a local bank office, at a hospital, at home, and so on.

Table 9.1

	Codeswitching form	No. of occurrences
Generic reading in subject position	Det [*el/los*] + N $_{\text{plural/mass}}$	4
	Det [∅] + N $_{\text{plural/mass}}$	0
Generic reading in object position	Individual-level predicate + Det [*el/los*] + N $_{\text{plural/mass}}$	1
	Individual-level predicate + Det [∅] + N $_{\text{plural/mass}}$	1
Existential reading	Stage-level predicate + Det [*el/los*] + N $_{\text{plural/mass}}$	0
	Stage-level predicate + Det [∅] + N $_{\text{plural/mass}}$	14
	TOTAL	20

Twenty instances of intrasentential codeswitching involving DPs with generic and existential readings form the database for the current analysis. Table 9.1 shows the distribution of the switch types investigated.

The codeswitching forms indicated in table 9.1 are illustrated in (13)–(17), from Moyer 1993:

(13) Los *employers* toman la persona.
      the *employers* take the person
      'Employers take the person.'

(14) El *self-rising flour* es para todo.
      the self-rising flour is for everything
      'Self-rising flour is suitable for everything.'

(15) Me encanta *cornflakes*.
      'I love cornflakes.'

(16) Criamos *mushrooms* en Gibraltar.
      'We grow mushrooms in Gibraltar.'

(17) Compramos *kitchen scales*.
      'We bought kitchen scales.'

Among the switch types investigated, we find the use of the Spanish determiner to be the most frequent way of expressing genericity, as opposed to the zero [∅] article, which is only used once in object position. On the other hand, the existential reading in object position is always expressed with the zero article, without causing any conflict in either language.

Now consider the application of the assumptions made in 9.2.1 to the particular linguistic cases we are analyzing here. In codeswitching contact situations, speakers show two different ways of expressing genericity: they use the Spanish expletive article with an English noun so that the N-raising to D is not obligatory. This is precisely what happens in examples (13) and (14), where speakers use the Spanish expletive article that does not have any substantive interpretation as semantic operator; therefore, the common noun, referring to a kind, checks the [-referential] feature with which the empty D is generated. Thus, the Spanish expletive article *los/el* licenses the structure with the generic reading of the English mass and plural common nouns *employers* and *flour*, the same as in Spanish. Alternatively, they may use no article, as shown in (15). In grammatical terms, this means that the raising of N to D is obligatory and the generic reading is attained by raising the head noun *cornflakes* to the empty D to check the [-referential] feature, as in English. However, data show that this is less frequent in both subject and object position (see table 9.1). Therefore, codeswitching data seem to suggest that bilingual speakers prefer the insertion of the expletive since it is more economical than N-raising to D.

As for the expression of the existential reading, no conflict arises in Spanish-English codeswitching, as illustrated in table 9.1 and its corresponding examples, (16) and (17). I argue that this existential quantification is determined to a great extent by the meaning of the verb (a stage-level predicate) that establishes a head-to-head relation with the empty D in both languages alike (see Lois 1996; Laca 1996). In other words, bilingual speakers of English and Spanish do not have problems expressing existential readings of DPs in object position due to the presence of a stage- or event-denoting verb like *eat* or *drink* that imposes the existential reading on the empty D. This is predictable, given that an event verb denotes stages that can be quantified. On the contrary, verbs like *love* or *hate* denote permanent states that cannot be decomposed.

9.3   The Syntactic Distribution of Spanish-English Codeswitched Determiner Phrases

One of the most frequent switches within determiner phrases found among Spanish-English bilingual speakers from Gibraltar is between the Spanish article and the English noun. Phrases (18)–(23) illustrate the prototypical models of codeswitching used by these speakers:

(18) El *employer* ve y conoce qué persona es.
      'The employer sees and knows what person is.'

(19) Los *employers* toman la persona.
      'The employers take the person.'

(20) Va a aumentar los *plates*.
      'He is going to increase the plates.'

(21) Y bebiendo con el *sailors*, con los marineros.
     'And drinking with the sailors, with the sailors.'

(22) Luego sale en la *chronicle*.
     'Then it appears in the chronicle.'

(23) Con la *washing machine*.
     'With the washing machine.'

Although the possibility of switching between a determiner and its NP complement is disputed in Belazi, Rubin, and Toribio 1994, it is well attested in a number of codeswitching corpora including Cajun-English, Arabic-French, Farsi-English, and Spanish-Nahuatl, as reported by Brown (1986), Bentahila and Davies (1983), Mahootian (1993), and MacSwan (1997) respectively. Besides, the majority of the studies on codeswitching in Spanish-English provide many examples of this kind (e.g., Pfaff 1979; Poplack 1980).

As we have just seen, this is a very frequent occurrence in the data analyzed for this work, contrasting with the absence of combinations between the English determiner and the Spanish noun.[1] This is an absence that Lipski (1978) and Aguirre (1976) report to be ungrammatical:

(24) *I see the *casa*.
     'I see the house.'

(25) *I gave it to the *vecina*.
     'I gave it to the neighbor.'

Consequently, I believe that the absence of DPs with English determiners and Spanish nouns can be attributed to grammatical factors that I will try to explain. I first propose and discuss different hypotheses about the structure of DPs and the nature of feature checking within this phrasal domain.

9.3.1 Syntactic Preliminaries: The Dp-Hypothesis

On the syntactic side, the analysis proposed in the present work builds on the work by Abney (1987) and many others, showing that noun phrases have a much greater similarity to sentences than previously believed. Abney was one of the first to propose that the different determiners and some quantifiers must be analyzed as heads of a higher hierarchical projection, rather than as elements that occupy the specifier of a nominal projection. Therefore, the determiner projection becomes the category that introduces the noun phrase, much like the IP introduces the sentence. This novel analysis has become generalized in recent years in the study of nominal structures in generative grammar.

Although this analysis has been subject to several modifications, the basic features that I have just noted have been preserved. Among others, Ritter (1991, 1993), Valois (1991), Bernstein (1991), Picallo (1991), Lorenzo (1995), and Roca (1996) have all argued for the existence of several functional projections below DP and above NP. (See also Haegeman and Gueron 1999, 417–439) For instance, in his analysis of Spanish Lorenzo (1995), building on Picallo's (1991) work, proposes that between DP and NP there are functional projections of Number and Gender whose order is determined by the order each holds with respect to the nominal root or lexical head. The presence of these functional projections is justified by the fact that in languages like Spanish both gender and number specifications can vary for the same root and have easily distinguishable meanings, or at least are not confused with the root in many of the lexical items inserted within the determiner projection:

(26) L-o-s   chic-o-s   solitari-o-s;   l-a-s   chic-a-s   solitari-a-s
      the$_{MPl}$ boy$_{MPl}$ lonely$_{MPl}$;   the$_{FPl}$ girl$_{FPl}$ lonely$_{FPl}$
      'The lonely boys; the lonely girls'

Therefore, it makes sense to propose that the formal features of gender and number are present in the checking domain of the Spanish determiner phrase as opposed to English, which lacks such a dual agreement. Rather than positing two different configurations for the two languages, I propose that the base structure is identical and that in both languages there is a D functional head that selects as its complement a projection of N. Therefore, the label DP refers to the full nominal projection. In Spanish D contains uninterpretable gender and number features, while in English D only contains uninterpretable number features.

Another important element of similarity between noun phrases and sentences is the possibility of N-movement, which parallels the idea of V-movement to Infl or TP. To account for the formal characteristics of the nominal structures in Spanish, Lorenzo (1995) proposes that the noun head moves to the functional projections of gender and number, just as the verb moves to the functional projections of the sentence. Evidence for N-to-D movement comes from the relative position of the N and its modifying adjectives. In Romance, the unmarked position for most adjectives is postnominal, between N and its complements as in (27a) (examples from Spanish; adapted from Cinque 1993); in Germanic (exemplified here by English) the unmarked case has adjectives preceding N and its complements, as in (27b). Adjectives expressing the thematic subject of a nominalization must appear postnominally in Romance and prenominally in Germanic ((27) vs. (29)):

(27) a. Un estudio detallado del genoma
      b. A detailed study of the genome

(28) a. La primera descripción chomskiana de la oración
      b. *La primera chomskiana descripción de la oración

(29) a. The first Chomskyan description of the sentence
     b. *The first description Chomskyan of the sentence

Cinque (1993) proposes that the base structure is the same for the two language groups (adjectives are hosted in the specifiers of multiple functional projections inserted between DP and NP) and that the ordering difference can be derived from the fact that Spanish raises lexical elements to functional heads in overt syntax while English does not.

Given the presence of visible morphological marks for gender and number on both the determiner and the noun in Romance languages like Spanish and the N-to-D movement attested by the position of modifying adjectives in these languages, I propose that Spanish determiners receive a complete set of φ-features (i.e., gender and number), which are uninterpretable and consequently need to be checked. In English, however, we exclude the gender feature from being a φ-feature on English extended nominal projections because, unlike the Number feature, gender is invariant in all the functional projections that accompany the noun. Consequently, the view that gender is an attribute that has to be checked in the derivation of the English nominal phrasal structure in which it is incorporated appears implausible.

9.3.2 Syntactic Analysis of Codeswitched DPs

Consider again the data presented in (18)–(23) and (24)–(25). From a syntactic point of view, there is no word-order violation since both languages share the same order—that is, determiner plus noun. On the other hand, we cannot focus on head-complement relations to derive these data either. In (18)–(23) a functional category D subcategorizes an N and the structures are well formed; in (24)–(25) also, a functional category D subcategorizes an N, but these structures are ill formed. It seems that the conflict resides in the absence of inflectional features in the English determiner and, in particular, in the absence of the gender feature in contrast to the Spanish determiner that appears with all the agreement features of number and gender.[2]

We have assumed that the φ-features on the Spanish determiner phrase are [-interpretable]. Therefore, they must be deleted so that the expression generated by the computational system converges to satisfy the Full Interpretation Principle (i.e., the performance systems can interpret the linguistic expression generated by the language).

We have further assumed that the deletion of [-interpretable] features takes place via the Move operation, which according to Chomsky (1995) is motivated by the checking and deletion of the [-interpretable] features of the functional categories. In addition, Chomsky (1998, 37–40 1999, 4) establishes that the φ-feature set is a *probe* with unvalued uninterpretable features that seeks a *goal*, namely "matching" features that establish agreement. Locating the goal, the probe erases under matching and its features receive a value. Then, the Agree operation erases and values the uninterpretable features of the probe. Moreover, Deletion is taken to be a "one-fell-swoop" operation, dealing with the φ-set as a unit. Its features cannot selectively delete: either all or none, and only a probe with a full set of φ-features is capable of deleting its uninterpretable features.

A natural explanation for the asymmetry found in codeswitched DPs follows from the syntactic proposals revised in section 9.3.1. and the minimalist assumptions made above. In (18)–(23) the number feature on the English noun (i.e., the goal) is activated by the matching probe (i.e., the number and gender features of the Spanish determiner), which contains a complete set of φ-features. Thus it is able to delete and value its uninterpretable φ-set. In (24)–(25), however, both number and gender features are activated, but in this case the English determiner is deficient, lacking the complete set of agreement features. Hence it is unable to check the φ-features of the Spanish noun and consequently Agree cannot delete the uninterpretable features that make the derivation crash. In other words, the Agree operation does not delete the uninterpretable or unvalued features that do not allow the expression to be legible for the performance systems of the bilingual speakers of Spanish and English. Given a minimalist perspective, deletion and valuation of uninterpretable features is a requirement imposed on the interface levels PF and LF by the interaction between the language faculty and the articulatory- perceptual and conceptual-intentional performance systems. Consequently, bilinguals reject the determiner phrases illustrated in (24) and (25). I assume, therefore, that the number and gender features of the determiner enter the derivation unvalued and have to be valued via Agree with the corresponding N. Accordingly, the unvalued features number and gender in the Spanish determiner can be valued via Agree with the English noun because the former bears the full set of these features (number and gender). On the contrary, the derivation crashes in the case of the English determiner and the Spanish noun because the feature set of the English determiner is incomplete (it lacks the gender feature). Therefore, only when the unvalued features of the determiner include the features of the noun will the functional-lexical mixing converge.

9.4 Concluding Remarks

In summary, I have argued that the phenomenon of DPs in Spanish-English codeswitching constructions receives a natural explanation within the MP. The major implication of such a model is that codeswitching involves the same principles formulated within the minimalist theory of monolingual linguistic competence. Thus, the data under analysis in this chapter have been accounted for in terms of the Full Interpretation Principle (i.e., all expressions generated by the computational system must be interpretable or legible to the interface levels) and a general principle of economy (i.e., simpler operations like the insertion of an expletive are preferred to more complex ones like Move). In so doing, I have assumed that the syntactic and semantic variation with respect to determiner phrases in Spanish and English can be reduced to the different properties of their functional category D and their inflectional morphology. In particular, I have assumed that the syntactic distribution of determiners in Spanish-English codeswitching can be attributed to the presence of an uninterpretable gender feature on the Spanish determiner, as opposed to its absence on the English determiner. The variation in the semantic interpretation and syntactic typology of bare nouns in Spanish and English is due to the presence of expletive occurrences of the article in Spanish in contrast to English, which does not tolerate their use.

Notes

This chapter is part of a research project funded by the FICYT, grant BP00-103, Ministry of Education and Culture, Spain. I would like to thank Ana Isabel Ojea for her comments on earlier drafts of the chapter.

1. I only found 2 examples of English determiners before Spanish nouns out of 243 cases, as illustrated in (i) and (ii):

(i)   Taking my share of the *vino*
      'Taking my share of the wine'

(ii) You are going to ruin the manzanita.
      'You are going to ruin the apple.'

This means an insignificant 0.8% of the total number of switches between determiners and nouns can be attributed to slips of the tongue due to performance factors.

2. Note that in the codeswitched examples the agreement morphology of gender that characterizes the Spanish noun phrase is lexically realized on the Spanish lexical item and not on the English one, since English does not distinguish gender in determiners or nouns. However, the agreement features of number between the determiner and the noun are lexically realized in the items of both languages, which is why speakers may make corrections like the one shown in (21).

References

Abney, S. P. 1987. The English noun phrase in its sentential aspect. Doctoral dissertation, MIT.

Aguirre, A. 1976. Acceptability Judgements of Code-Switching Phrases by Chicanos: Some Preliminary Findings. ERIC Document ED 129 122. Springfield, VA.

Belazi, H., E. Rubin, and A. Toribio. 1994. Code switching and X-bar theory: The Functional Head Constraint. *Linguistic Inquiry* 25:221–237.

Bentahila, A., and E. Davies. 1983. The syntax of Arabic-French code-switching. *Lingua* 59:301–330.

Bernstein, J. 1991. Nominal enclitics in Romance. In J. D. Bobaljik and T. Bures, ed., *MIT Working Papers in Linguistics 14*, 51–66. Cambridge, MA: MITWPL, Department of Linguistics and Philosophy, MIT.

Blas Arroyo, J. L. 1999. *Lenguas en Contacto: Consecuencias Lingüísticas del Bilingüismo Social en las Comunidades de Habla del Este Peninsular.* Madrid: Iberoamericana.

Bokamba, E. G. 1988. Code-mixing, language variation, and linguistic theory: Evidence from Bantu languages. *Lingua* 76:21–62.

Brown, B. 1986. Cajun/English code-switching: A test of formal models. In D. Sankoff, ed., *Diversity and Diachrony*, 399–406. Amsterdam: John Benjamins.

Chomsky, N. 1995. *The Minimalist Program.* Cambridge, MA: MIT Press.

Chomsky, N. 1998. Minimalist inquiries: The framework. *MIT Occasional Papers in Linguistics 15*, Cambridge, MA: MITWPL, Department of Linguistics and Philosophy, MIT.

Chomsky, N. 1999. Derivation by phase. *MIT Occasional Papers in Linguistics 18.* Cambridge, MA: MITWPL, Department of Linguistics and Philosophy, MIT.

Cinque, G. 1993. On the evidence for partial N movement in the Romance DPs. Ms., Università di Venezia.

Clyne, M. 1987. Constraints on code-switching: How universal are they? *Linguistics* 25:739–764.

Haegeman, L., and J. Guéron. 1999. *English grammar: A generative perspective.* Oxford: Blackwell.

Huybregts, M., and H. Boeschoten. 1999. Minimalist code-switching can do without switching codes. Paper presented at the Second International Symposium on Bilingualism, Newcastle upon Tyne, UK, April 14–17.

Kratzer, A. 1988. Stage level and individual level predicates. In M. Krifka, ed., *Genericity in Natural Languages*, 247–284. Tübingen: Universität Tübingen.

Laca, B. 1996. Acerca de la semántica de los plurales escuetos en español. In I. Bosque, ed., *El sustantivo sin determinación*, 241–268. Madrid: Visor.

Leonetti, M. 1999. *Los determinantes.* Madrid: Arco.

Lipski, J. 1978. Code-switching and the problem of bilingual competence. In M. Paradis, ed., *Aspects of Bilingualism*, 250–264. Columbia, SC: Hornbeam Press.

Lois, X. 1996. Los grupos nominales sin determinante y el paralelismo entre las oraciones y la frase nominal. In I. Bosque, ed., *El sustantivo sin determinación*, 201–238. Madrid: Visor.

Longobardi, G. 1994. Reference and proper nouns: A theory of N-movement in syntax and LF. *Linguistic Inquiry* 25:609–665.

Longobardi, G. 1999. How comparative is semantics?: A unified parametric theory of bare nouns and proper names. Ms., Università di Trieste.

Longobardi, G. 2000. How comparative is semantics? Paper presented at the Tenth Colloquium on Generative Grammar, University of Alcala, Madrid, Spain, April 12–14.

Lorenzo, G. 1995. *Geometría de las Estructuras Nominales: Sintaxis y Semántica del SDet*. Oviedo: Servicio de Publicaciones de la Universidad de Oviedo.

MacSwan, J. 1997. A minimalist approach to intrasentential code-switching: Spanish-Nahuatl bilingualism in Central Mexico. Doctoral dissertation, UCLA.

MacSwan, J. 1999. A minimalist approach to intrasentential code-switching. Paper presented at the Second International Symposium on Bilingualism, Newcastle upon Tyne, UK, April 14–17.

MacSwan, J. 2000. The architecture of the bilingual language faculty: Evidence from codeswitching. *Bilingualism: Language and Cognition* 3 (1): 37–54.

MacSwan, J. 2013. Code switching and linguistic theory. In T. K. Bhatia and W. Ritchie, eds., *Handbook of Bilingualism and Multilingualism*, 2nd ed., 223–350. Oxford: Blackwell.

Mahootian, S. 1993. A null theory of codeswitching. Doctoral dissertation, Northwestern University, Evanston, Ill.

Moyer, M. 1993. Analysis of code-switching in Gibraltar. Doctoral dissertation, Universidad Autonoma de Barcelona,.

Pandharipande, R. 1990. Formal and functional constraints on code-mixing. In R. Jacobson, ed., *Codeswitching as a Worldwide Phenomenon*, 15–31. New York: Peter Lang.

Pfaff, C. 1979. Constraints on language mixing: Intrasentential code-switching and borrowing in Spanish/English. *Language* 55:291–318.

Picallo, C. 1991. Possessive pronouns in Catalan and the Avoid Pronoun Principle. In A. Branchadell, B. Palmada, J. Quer, F. Roca and J. Solá, eds., *Catalan Working Papers in Linguistics* 1 211–234. Barcelona: Departamento de Filología Catalana y Filología Española, Universidad Autónoma de Barcelona.

Poplack, S. 1980. "Sometimes I'll start a sentence in Spanish y termino en Español": Toward a typology of code-switching. *Linguistics* 18:581–618.

Ramírez, A. G. 1992. *El Español de los Estados Unidos: El Lenguaje de los Hispanos*. Madrid: Mapfre.

Ritter, E. 1991. Two functional categories in NP: Evidence from modern Hebrew. In S. D. Rothstein, ed., *Syntax and Semantics 25: Perspectives on Phrase Structure: Heads and Licensing*, 37–62. San Diego: Academic Press.

Ritter, E. 1993. Where is gender? *Linguistic Inquiry* 24:795–803.

Roca, F. 1996. La determinación y la modificación nominal en español. Doctoral dissertation, Universidad Autónoma de Barcelona, Barcelona.

Toribio, J. 1999. Minimalist perspectives on bilingualism. Paper presented at the Second International Symposium on Bilingualism, Newcastle upon Tyne, UK, April 14–17.

Valois, D. 1991. The internal syntax of DP and the A placement in French and English. In T. Sherer, *NELS 21*, 367–381. Amherst: GLSA, University of Massachusetts.

10 Codeswitching and the Syntax-Semantics Interface: The Role of Aspectual Features in Constraining Intrasentential Codeswitching Involving the Verb

Sílvia Milian Hita

10.1 Introduction

Most of the syntactic constraints on codeswitching that have been proposed in recent years have dealt with word order (Poplack 1982), with syntactic points where switching is allowed (Di Sciullo, Muysken, and Singh 1986; Belazi, Rubin, and Toribio 1994, among others), or with the asymmetry in the role played by the participating languages in codeswitching and their syntactic categories (Myers-Scotton 1993, 1995; Jake and Myers-Scotton 1996, 1997; Joshi 1985). These approaches do not take into consideration differences in the semantic systems of the languages involved in codeswitching to account for possible constraints, thus ignoring the importance of the *syntax-semantics interface* (Tenny 1988 1994), or more specifically, how the mapping of verb arguments into syntactic positions takes place. Chomsky's Minimalist Program (1995) provides a new and useful window into the study of this mapping between conceptual and syntactic constructions, and into an understanding of how parameters specify different mappings in languages.

According to the Minimalist Program (1995), functional categories have their own projections in the phrase hierarchy of a sentence. These projections have features that must be pronounced or spelled-out (*-ed*, *-s*), and some others that are merely structural, like *Case*. Differences across languages are explained by assuming that the features of their functional projections have different semantic interpretability. Thus, while "semantically uninterpreted" features are required to cause syntactic operations like movement of lexical categories, "semantically interpreted" features are not. When a feature of a functional projection is uninterpreted, a lexical category in the sentence with the same feature must move to the functional projection in order to check it[1]

Following minimalist and lexical semantics assumptions,[2] this chapter will analyze the role played by uninterpreted aspectual or *aktionsart*[3] features[4] (or internal temporal organization properties of events) in constraining *intrasentential* Spanish-English codeswitching involving the verb and its arguments. The data analyzed comes from three different Spanish-English bilingual communities (Mexican-American, Puerto Rican, and Gibraltarian).

The goal of this chapter is to show that constraints on Spanish-English codeswitching are based on the grammars of these two languages. This argument follows from recent proposals within the minimalist framework (MacSwan 1997, 1999, 2000, 2013). MacSwan (2000, 43) concludes that "nothing constrains code switching apart from the requirements of the mixed grammars," and that codeswitchers have the same grammatical competence as monolingual speakers. Also, the fact that for minimalism there are no differences regarding the rules of syntax among different languages allows, as MacSwan suggests, for a great simplification in our conception of bilingualism. In other words, in minimalist terms, parametric variation among languages relies on their feature matrix.

If we assume, as minimalism does, that syntax is constrained by the features of functional projections, then the same claim can be made for codeswitching. More specifically, it is argued that codeswitching involving the verb and its arguments will be allowed as long as the aspectual requirements of the participating verbs are satisfied, and the speakers engaged in codeswitching know what features are uninterpreted in each of the participating languages. As will be shown, an adequate analysis of codeswitching needs to account for differences in the aspectual configuration of verbs in the languages engaged in codeswitching. This aspectual configuration, in turn, triggers different mappings of arguments into syntactic positions.

10.2 Sanz and Bever's "Event Phrase" and Its Consequences for Spanish and English

In their account of Spanish-English bilingual interference in language processing, Sanz and Bever (2001) take from Chomsky's Minimalist Program (1995) the role played by uninterpretable features of functional categories, and combine it with Tenny's *Aspectual Interface Hypothesis* (Tenny 1988, 1994), which states that aspectual features determine the number and position of syntactic arguments. However, these authors go beyond the Minimalist Program and hypothesize that "the features that distinguish events from states and other related features are embedded in the functional projection called Event Phrase" (Sanz and Bever 2001, 136)[5] These features, which they adopt from previous research (see Vendler 1967; Dowty 1979, 1991; Tenny 1988 1994 Davidson 1967; Carlson 1977; Parsons 1990; Higginbotham 1996, among others) are [+/−telic], [+/−eventive], [+/−permanent]. They can be

Table 10.1
Classification of Sentences According to Their Action Type

EVENTS [+eventive]	[+telic]	[+measure]	Write a letter	Accomplishment
		[−measure]	Cross the finish line	Achievement
NON-EVENTS [−eventive]	[−telic]	Write letters/run		Activity
	[+permanent state]	Know math / be tall		Individual-level property
	[−permanent state]	Be tired / be here		Stage-level property

semantically interpretable and uninterpreted, and characterize predicate types crosslinguistically. This is illustrated in table 10.1.

As table 10.1 shows, events (modes of action that can be ongoing in time) can be telic or atelic. Telic events are events that have an endpoint in time and that may therefore be accompanied by a prepositional phrase like "*in one day," whereas atelic events do not have an endpoint in time. Telic events can be divided into accomplishments and achievements. Accomplishments are telic events whose endpoint can be measured along a scale, for example by adding the adverb *halfway*, while achievements are telic events whose endpoint cannot be measured along a scale. Nonevents or states [−eventive] may be either [+permanent] or [− permanent]. This feature allows us to distinguish between *stage-level property states* (locations or psychological states, which affect entities in general), and *individual-level property states* (states that affect an entity in particular, e.g., *being short, tall*).

Classifying one of these features as uninterpreted in a language when it is interpretable and the other way around, as Sanz and Bever (2001, 137) observe, accounts for bilingual interference in language processing: "We predict that there might be some interference from L1 into L2 because the speaker may have classified the features in a certain place in the grammar of his native language."

For Spanish and English specifically, Sanz and Bever (2001) argue that the features of the Event Phrase are uninterpreted in Spanish and must therefore be spelled-out and checked in the course of the derivation, and interpretable in English, in which case no overt syntactic operations are needed. To support this claim, they provide evidence from different monolingual Spanish and English sentences and constructions. Thus, the fact that the distinction between telic and atelic events is relevant for the syntax of Spanish is shown in the obligatory use of the reflexive *se* to mark an event as having an endpoint in time with two argument predicates.

(1)   a. Mi   hermano   leyó   un   libro.   ([+/−*telic*])
          my   brother   read   a   book
          'My brother read a book.'
      b. My brother read a book.   ([+/−*telic*])
      c. Mi   hermano   **se**   leyó   un   libro.   ([+*telic*])
          my   brother   to   himself   read   a   book
          'My brother finished up reading a book.'

Examples (1a–b) are ambiguous and could be interpreted as either having
an endpoint in time ([+telic]) or not ([−telic]). The presence of the object *el
libro* is not enough to make this distinction clear. However, in (1c), through
the use of *se*, the sentence is definitely interpreted as a telic event. Sanz and
Bever provide further evidence from monadic telic predicates.

(2)   a. El   barco   se   hundió.   ([+*telic*])
           the   ship   itself   sank
           'The ship sank down.'
      b. *El barco hundió.
           the ship sank
           'The ship sank.'

According to these authors, the obligatory presence of *se* in (2a) and the
ungrammaticality of (2b) support the claim that telicity is uninterpreted in
Spanish and that the verb needs to be overtly marked as being telic through
se, since 'the ship' is only a delimiting object, not a measuring one.

Regarding the distinction between states and events, the following examples support the claim that the feature [+/−eventive] is uninterpreted in Spanish
(Sanz and Bever 2001, 153).

(3)   a. La   ciudad   fue   arruinada   (por   los   enemigos).   ([+*eventive*])
          the   city   was   ruined   (by   the   enemies)
          'The city was ruined.'
      b. La   ciudad   estaba   arruinada   (*por   los   enemigos).   ([−*eventive*])
          the   city   was   ruined   (*by   the   enemies)
          'The city was ruined (by the enemies).'
      c. The city was ruined. ([+/−*eventive*])

Spanish needs to use a different copula, *ser* or *estar*, to make a distinction
between an event, as in (3a), and a state, as in (3b). This is also supported by
the ungrammaticality of using 'by the enemies' in (3b), which bears the agent
role. In English though, as (3c) shows, the sentence is ambiguous, and only
the context helps us distinguish between an event and a nonevent.

Finally, the use of a different copula in Spanish to express a [+/−permanent] state provides evidence for the claim that this is an uninterpreted feature in Spanish. This is shown in (4).

(4) a. Mi   hermano   es   alto.
         my   brother   is   tall
         'My brother is tall.'
     b. Mi   hermano   está   aquí/está   cansado.
         my   brother   is   here/is   tired
         'My brother is here/is tired.'

Let us now see how the aspectual features of the Event Phrase are checked, and the consequences that their different interpretability in English (interpretable) and in Spanish (uninterpreted) have on the syntactic mapping. The tree for any derivation would be as illustrated in (5).

(5)

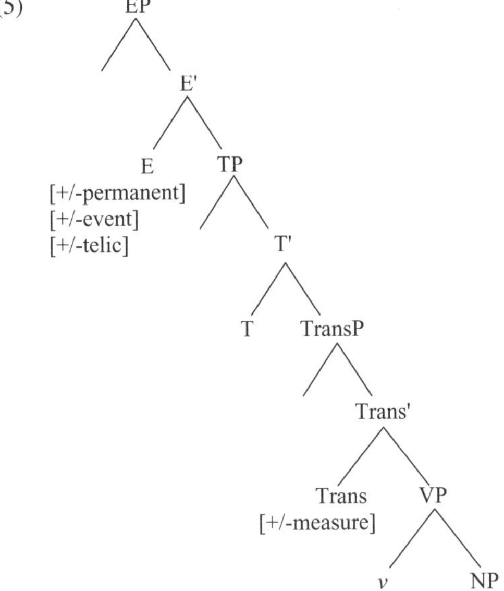

The tree in (6) shows the derivation of a [+telic] event in Spanish (Sanz and Bever 2001, 148).

(6)

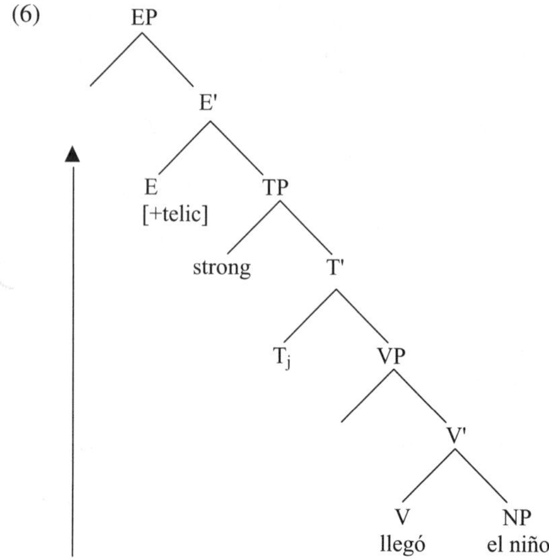

Telicity is an uninterpreted feature in Spanish, and therefore it must be checked overtly. *El niño* 'the boy' originates VP internally (as the internal direct argument of 'arrive'), and it delimits the verb 'arrive' (*llegó*). Then, *el niño* moves to the Spec position of Event Phrase, leaving a trace behind. Compare this with the derivation in (7).

(7)

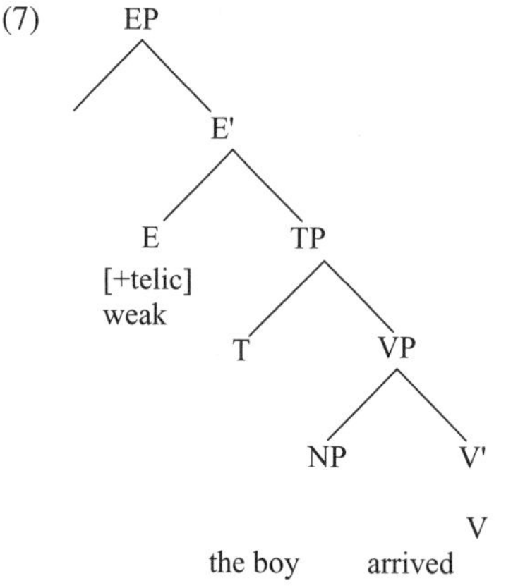

Since telicity is interpretable in English, the verb does not need to be delimited overtly. As a result of this, the argument *The boy*, which originates in the specifier position of VP, remains external throughout the derivation.

10.3   Hypothesis and Predictions for the Data

As was mentioned in the introductory section, the goal of this chapter is to provide evidence for the claim made by some researchers (MacSwan, chapter 1 of this volume) that codeswitching is subject to the same constraints governing monolingual grammars. The chapter argues that intrasentential codeswitching involving a verb and its arguments is subject to the constraints imposed by the aspectual features of the functional projection of the Event Phrase proposed by Sanz and Bever (2001): [+/–eventive], [+/–telic], [+/–permanent]. It is assumed that proficient bilinguals[6] engaged in codeswitching know what aspectual features are semantically uninterpreted for each language.

Bearing in mind Sanz and Bever's (2001) claim that the features contained in the Event Phrase are uninterpreted in Spanish and interpretable in English, the following predictions are made for Spanish-English intrasentential codeswitching. First, Spanish reflexive *se* is obligatory in the head of the Event Phrase when the main verb is in Spanish, and optional when the main verb is in English.

(8)   a.   El   barco   *sank.*
           the   ship   sank
           'The ship sank.'

      b.   El   barco   se   *sank.*
           the   ship   se   sank
           'The ship sank.'

      c.   *The*   *ship*   sehundió.
           the   ship   itself   sank
           'The ship sank down.'

      d. *The   ship   hundió.
           the   ship   sank
           'The ship sank.'

According to the constraint proposed earlier, the examples in (8) are grammatical because the aspectual requirements of both Spanish and English are met. In (8a–b) the main verb is in English. Since telicity is interpretable in English, it does not need to be checked, so the verb does not need to move overtly, even if the head of the Event Phrase is filled with *se*. This is shown in (9).

(9)

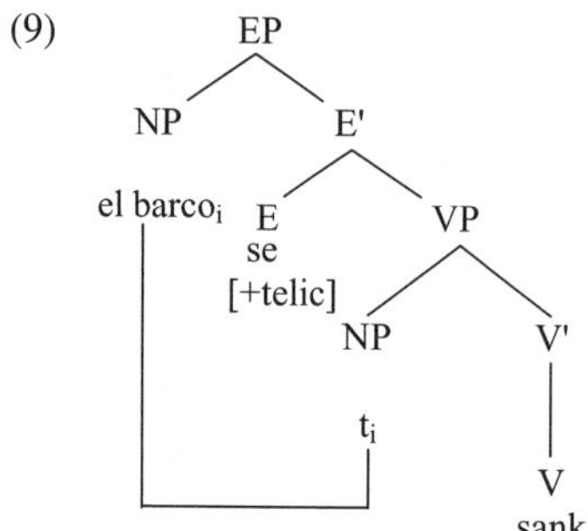

In (8c) the main verb is in Spanish. Telicity is uninterpreted in this language, and the verb needs to move to check this feature overtly. The derivation, as a result, converges.

(10)

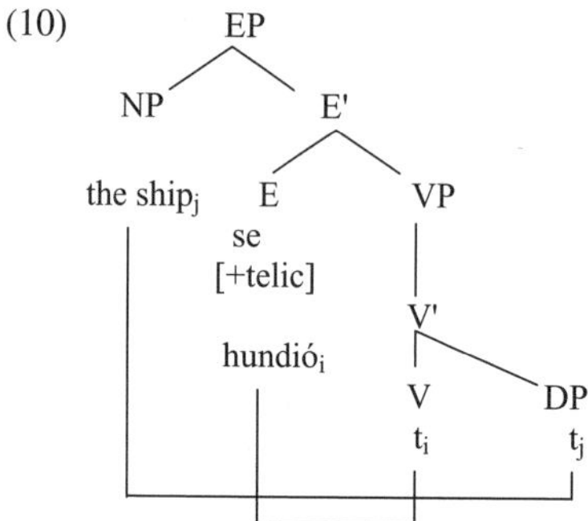

However, (8d) is ungrammatical because the verb is in Spanish and the only argument, *The ship*, delimits the event but does not measure it along a scale. It is *se* that measures the event, and in its absence the telic feature of *hundió* cannot be checked; hence its ungrammaticality.

Second, as far as stative ([−eventive]) verbs are concerned, we predict the Spanish copula *ser* will be used with an English individual-level property state, and *estar* with an English stage-level property state.

(11) a. *John*   *is*   aburrido.   ([+*permanent*])
     John   is   boring

     'John is boring.'

   b. Juan   es   *boring.*   ([+*permanent*])
     John   is   boring

     'John is boring.'

   c. Juan   está   *bored.*   ([−*permanent*])
     John   is   bored

     'John is bored.'

(12) a. *Juan es bored.

  b. *Juan está boring.

[+/−permanent] is an uninterpreted feature in Spanish, hence it is spelled out in the syntax through the use of different copulas: *ser* ([+permanent]) and *estar* ([−permanent]). All the mixed sentences in (11) fulfill the requirement that the copula and its attribute have the same "+/−" value regarding the [+/−permanent] feature.

(13)

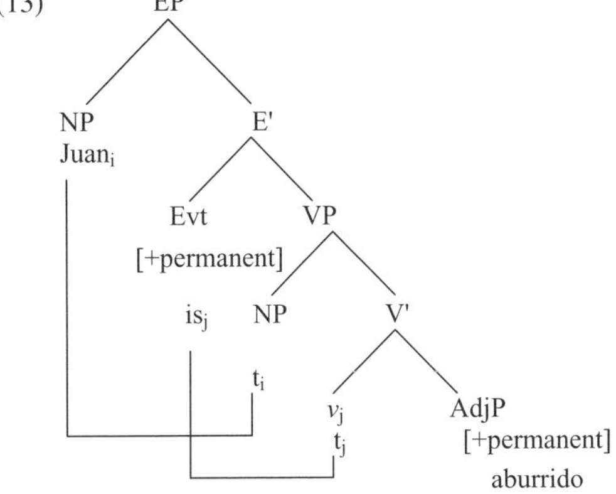

However, the examples in (12) are not expected to occur among proficient bilinguals, because there is a mismatch between the value of the feature of the copula and the value of the attribute complement. Thus, in (12a) *ser* ([+permanent]) is followed by a [−permanent] attribute, *bored*, whereas in (12b) *estar* ([−permanent]) is being used with a [+permanent] attribute, *boring*.

Finally, when codeswitching involves passive constructions with *ser* and *estar*, *ser* is predicted to occur to express a process ([+eventive]), and *estar* to express a result ([−eventive], [+permanent]). Therefore, while the examples in (14) are likely to be found, those in (15) are not.

(14) a. La ciudad/*The city*   *was*   arruinada.   ([+/−*eventive*])

    the city   was   ruined

    'The city was ruined.'

  b. La ciudad/*the city* fue *ruined* por los moros/*by the Moors*. ([+*eventive*])

    the city   was ruined by   the Moors

    'The city was ruined by the Moors.'

  c. La ciudad/*the city*   estaba   *ruined*. ([−*eventive*])

    the   city   was   ruined

    'The city   was   ruined.'

(15) a. *La ciudad/*the city* estaba *ruined* por los moros/*by the Moors*.

   b. *La ciudad/*the city* fue *ruined* (as a result of the bombings).

In (14a) the passive auxiliary verb is in English. The feature [+/−eventive] is interpretable and does not need to be checked overtly, so both interpretations are possible, as a state or as an event. When the verb is in Spanish, as in (14b) and (14c), the use of *ser* or *estar* allows us to clearly differentiate between a process and a result.

Unlike the examples in (14), the examples in (15) are ungrammatical. This ungrammaticality can be accounted for in minimalist terms. The derivations in (16) and (17) show this.

(16)

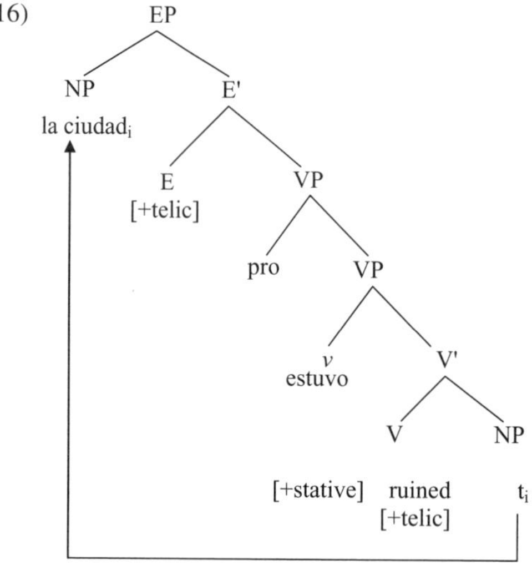

As we can see in (16), there is a mismatch between the [+telic] value of the head of the Event Phrase and the [−eventive] value of the verb. The speaker is trying to produce an eventive passive sentence (by using *By the Moors*), but he or she is using an auxiliary with a [−eventive] feature. This aspectual feature cannot be erased after checking, but telicity is uninterpreted in Spanish and needs to be checked. The same occurs in (17).

(17)

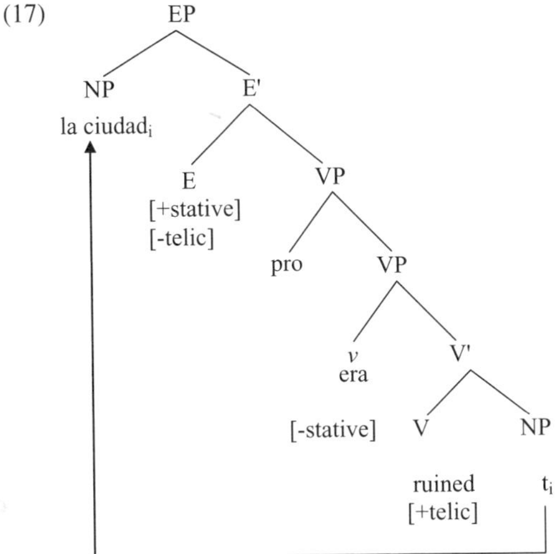

In (17), the context of the sentence "as a result of the bombings" tells us that the speaker's intention is to express the result of a bombing, "to be ruined." The auxiliary is in Spanish, and it carries a [+eventive] feature, which cannot be checked and erased with the [−eventive] feature of the Event Phrase.

10.4 Data and Presentation of Results

The data analyzed are instances of Spanish-English CS among proficient speakers from three different Spanish-English bilingual communities: the Mexican-American community from the Southwest of the United States and California (Coltharp 1970;[7] Jacobson 1977 1982 1990;[8] Lipski1995; Pfaff 1979;[9] Reyes 1982;[10] Silva-Corvalán 1994;[11] Valdés Fallis 1981[11]); the Puerto Rican community in New York (Language Policy Task Force 1984;[12] Poplack 1982[13] Zentella 1997[15]) and in Columbia, South Carolina (Milian 1996b[16]); and finally the Spanish-English community in Gibraltar (Moyer 1992). This corpus was extracted from sociolinguistic studies on Spanish-English codeswitching, as well as from studies on its grammatical constraints. No significant differences were found in the type of switches involving the verb and the direct argument among the three communities.[17] Nevertheless, it would be useful for future research to carry out a more detailed study to test the validity of this claim.

All of the data compiled for this study constitute a corpus of naturally occurring data,[18] as opposed to other data based on intuitions used especially by researchers working within the different Chomskyan frameworks (Belazi, Rubin, and Toribio 1994; Di Sciullo, Muysken, and Singh 1986; Toribio and

Rubin 1996, among others). After selecting Spanish-English codeswitching data from the authors mentioned above, only those instances involving a Spanish or an English main verb and its arguments were chosen. The following parameters were used to classify both Spanish and English verbs: (1) the language of the verb, and (2) the mode of action ([+/−telic], [+/−permanent], [+/−eventive]).

Predicates, on the other hand, were classified in the following manner: as [+eventive] if the verb could take the gerund form, and [−eventive] if the gerund form was banned; as [+telic] if the verb could be delimited by the prepositional phrase "in an hour," and [−telic] if such a possibility was disallowed; and as [+permanent] if the verb indicated an individual-level property state, and [−permanent] if it signaled a stage-level property state. Examples (18) through (20) show how these tests were performed.

(18) a. I am studying English.   ([+*eventive*])
     b. *I am knowing math.

(19) a. Write a letter in an hour/*for an hour.   ([+*telic*])
     b. Run *in an hour/ for an hour.   ([−*telic*])

(20) a. I know math.   ([−*eventive*], [+*permanent*])
     b. I am tired.

Table 10.2 summarizes in total raw numbers and percentages Spanish and English verbs classified according to aspectual features.

As we can see in table 10.2, 76 (61%) of the switches had to do with Spanish verbs, and 48 (29%) with English verbs. This can be explained if we take into account that in the data analyzed, Spanish happened to be the most frequently used language among the participating subjects. Also, whereas in Spanish the majority of the predicates involved the [+permanent] feature, in English most of the predicates (35%) were [+telic] events. Activities [−telic] happened almost as frequently in both English and Spanish.

Table 10.2
Percentages of Spanish and English Verbs According to Aspectual Features

Feature	Spanish	English
[−eventive] [+permanent]	30 (39%)	12 (25%)
[−eventive] [−permanent]	18 (24%)	2 (4%)
[+/−eventive] [+telic]	10 (13%)	17 (35%)
[+eventive] [−telic]	18 (24%)	17 (35%)
Total	76	48

Table 10.3
Percentages of Verbs in Spanish and English According to
Predicate Type

Predicate type	Spanish	English
Event	28 (36%)	34 (70%)
State	48 (64%)	14 (30%)
Total	76	48

Table 10.4
Percentages of verbs in Spanish and English with the feature
[+/−permanent]

Feature	Spanish	English
[+permanent]	30 (62%)	12 (85%)
[−permanent]	18 (38%)	2 (15%)
Total	48	14

On examining the predicate type for each language, there seems to be a
clear asymmetry between Spanish and English. This is shown in table 10.3.

While most of the predicates in Spanish (64%) were states ([−eventive]),
in English 70% of the predicates were events ([+eventive]). It could be argued
that even though the three features contained in the Event Phrase are uninterpreted in Spanish and interpretable in English, the feature [−eventive] seems
to play a more important role in constraining intrasentential Spanish-English
codeswitching when the main verb is in Spanish.

Table 10.4 summarizes the occurrences of the feature [+/−permanent] in
English and Spanish. As the table shows, for both English and Spanish the
percentages of the feature [+permanent] were higher than those of the feature
[−permanent]. Thus, when the main verb was in Spanish, 62% of the switches
involved [+permanent] predicates, and 38% [−permanent] predicates. Likewise, with an English main verb, 85% of the predicates contained the [+perma-
nent] feature, and only 15% were characterized by the [−permanent], feature.
This seems to indicate that the feature [+permanent] plays a more important
role in constraining intrasentential codeswitching involving the verb and its
arguments than the feature [−permanent], both when this feature is interpretable and uninterpreted in a given language.

10.5 The Role of Aspectual Features in Constraining Codeswitching

The data collected from several authors reveals that codeswitching can and in
fact does occur between a verb and its arguments in all types of predicates:

accomplishments and achievements ([+telic]), activities ([−telic]), individual-level properties ([+permanent]), and stage-level properties ([−permanent]), in both English and Spanish. A number of examples confirm this.

<u>Main verb in English</u>

(21) Va   a   *charter*   un   camion.
     go (3PS-Pres)   to   charter   a   truck
     'He/she is going to charter a truck.'
     (Pfaff 1979, 300)

(22) *If   I'm   talking   to   you*   en   español
     If   I'm   talking   to   you   in   Spanish
     'If I'm talking to you in Spanish'
     (Jacobson 1977)

(23) *It   was   the   day   you   went*   al parque.
     it   was   the   day   you   went   to the (contraction) park
     'It was the day you went to the park.'
     (Jacobson 1977, 185)

(24) Nos   va   a   *blackmail.*
     us   go-3PS   to   blackmail
     'He/she is going to blackmail us.'
     (Milian 1996b)

<u>Main verb in Spanish</u>

(25) Tú   estás   metiendo   *your   big   mouth*
     you   are   putting   your   big   mouth
     'You are putting your big mouth'
     (Zentella 1997)
     Se   sentó,   honey,   *away   from   us.*
     REFL-3PS sit-PAST,   honey,   away   from   us
     'He/she sat, honey, away from us.'
     (Poplack 1981, 598)

(26) VCEn   New   Orleans   se le   pone   *oyster   bread.*
     in   New   Orleans   one to it   put   oyster   bread
     'In New Orleans they serve it with oyster bread.'
     (Milian 1996b)

Let us now see if the predictions made for the set of Spanish-English intra-sentential codeswitching data were correct.

10.5.1 Codeswitching Involving One-Argument (Monadic) Telic Predicates

The first prediction made was that Spanish reflexive *se* would be obligatory with one-argument telic[19] predicates when the main verb was in Spanish, and optional when the verb was in English. In the data collected, four examples were found dealing with Spanish reflexive *se* and an English verb.

(27) Se   había   *washed*   *out.*
     REFL   had   washed   out
     'It had washed out.'
     (Pfaff 1979, 300)

(28) Se   *dressed*   *up*   *a*   *little.*
     REFL-3PS   dressed   up   a   little
     'She/he dressed up a little.'
     (Jacobson 1977, 185)

(29) Hay   dos   cursos   que   se   *interlock.*
     have   two   courses   that   REFL   interlock
     'There are two courses that interlock.'
     (Milian 1996b)

(30) Y   ya   no   se   *wake*   *up*   nunca   más.
     and   already   no   REFL   wake   up   never   more
     'And he doesn't wake up anymore.'
     (Moyer 1992, 488)

As we can see, (30) illustrates a construction involving a reflexive Spanish *se* and a verb in English, *wake up*. The equivalent of this verb in Spanish is the reflexive verb *despertarse*. With two argument predicates, this verb becomes transitive, *despertar* 'to wake something or somebody up'. *Wake up* in English may be used as both a transitive and an intransitive verb. The derivation of (30) is shown in (31).

(31)

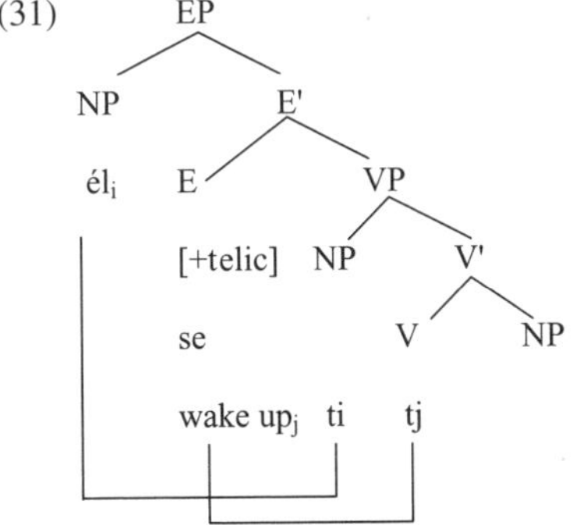

As we can see in (31) the subject is elliptical. The reflexive *se* is filling the head position of the event phrase, because telicity is an uninterpreted feature responsible for the movement of *wake up* to the head of the Event Phrase to have its telicity checked. In the absence of a measuring object, *se* becomes the only way to check telicity. The subject, a third person, originates in the specifier position of the VP and rises to the Spec of the Event Phrase because it is a clitic of this verb and is therefore adjoined.

(32) Y   ya no   *wake*   *up*   a   los   niños.
      and   already   wake   up   to   the   kids

      'And he doesn't wake up the kids anymore.'

Example (32) is also grammatical. Even though *se* is absent, there is an object measuring and delimiting the event, *a los niños*.

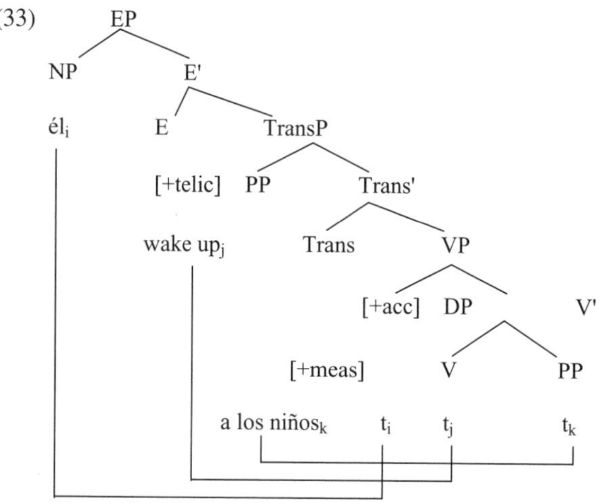

As we can see in (33), *a los niños* rises to the Spec position of the TransP, where it checks the [accusative] and the [measure] features with the head of the Trans Phrase. Even though *se* is absent, it is still a telic event. In the absence of the clitic, the verb must raise and check the telic feature. The subject then rises to the Spec position of the Event Phrase, hence the person and number agreement with the clitic (Sanz 1996). However, (34) is ungrammatical.

(34) *Y   ya   no   *wake*   *up*   nunca   más
       and   already   no   wake   up   never   more

      'And already no wake up never more'

In the absence, first of the object, and then of the clitic *se*, it is impossible to check telicity. Telicity is interpretable in English, but it is contained in a projection that also contains uninterpreted features. Since it cannot be checked, it cannot be erased either, and the derivation crashes as a result.

(35) a. Va   a   *reenlist.*
      go-3PS to   reenlist
      'He/she is going to reenlist.'
      (Reyes 1982 1)
   b. Se va a *reenlist.*
   c. **He/she is going to* realistar.

Example (35a) shows a mixed monadic telic predicate with an English verb *reenlist* and a Spanish auxiliary *(Él/ella) va a* 'He/she is going to'. Since the main verb is in English, reflexive *se* is optional, and it does not need to fill the head of the Event Phrase. Thus, both *Va a reenlist* and *Se va a reenlist* are possible as in (35b). However, when the main verb is in Spanish, the sentence becomes ungrammatical without *se*, as (35c) illustrates.

10.5.2 Codeswitching Involving *ser, estar,* and *be*

Our second prediction was that codeswitching will be allowed between a Spanish copulative verb (*ser, estar*) and its attribute in English, as long as *ser* is used with adjectives in English that signal individual-level properties and *estar* with adjectives signaling stage-level properties. Mixed examples (36)–(41) provide a summary of the findings regarding the use of the Spanish copulas *ser* and *estar*, and English *be*.

(36) Yo no estoy *ready* para este *party.* (estar + *stage-level prop. state*)
    I   not be-1PS ready for   this   party
    'I'm not ready for this party.'
    (Milian 1996b)

(37) Está   *underground.*   (estar + *stage-level adj.*)
    is   underground
    'It's underground.'
    (Moyer 1992, 423)

(38) Tú   no   estás   bien   *informed.*   (estar + *stage-level adj.*)
    you not are   well   informed
    'You're not well informed.'
    (Moyer 1992, 437)

(39) Es *obvious.*   (ser + *individual-level adj.*)
    is   obvious
    'It is obvious.'
    (Milian 1996b)

(40) Es   *refreshing.*   (ser + *individual-level adj.*)
     is   refreshing
     'It's refreshing.'
     (Moyer 1992, 419)

(41) Tú   eres   *teenager.*   (ser + *individual-level adj.*)
     you   are   teenager
     'You are a teenager.'
     (Coltharp 1970, 34)

When speakers engaged in codeswitching choose to start with the copula in Spanish, they have already checked a functional projection with strong features, because the aspectual features of *ser* and *estar* to express states (as opposed to passive processes), [–eventive] and [+/–permanent], are uninterpreted in that particular language. Therefore, the speakers' only choice is to use an appropriate adjective in English—that is, an adjective that indicates individual-level properties with *ser* and stage-level properties with *estar*.

(42) *You   are   insoportable, Dad.*   (*ambiguous: stage-level or*
      you   are   unbearable, Dad   *individual-level*)
      'You are a pain, Dad.'
      (Milian 1996b)

Nevertheless, if speakers choose to begin with the copula 'be' in English as in (42), which is underspecified for the feature [+/–permanent], they may choose either an individual- or a stage-level property adjective in Spanish, depending on what they intend to say. If the adjective is also ambiguous, the sentence might be interpreted as either a [+permanent] or a [–permanent] state. However, if the speaker chooses an unambiguous adjective as in (43), the interpretation of the sentence becomes very clear.

(43) *I'm   not   terca.*   (*individual-level property*)
      I'm   not   stubborn   ([+*permanent*])
      'I'm not stubborn.'
      (Pfaff 1979, 305)

Example (44) shows what happens with a Spanish copula and an underspecified adjective.

(44) No   están   *free.*   (estar + *underspecified adj.*)
     no   are   free   ([+/–*permanent*])
     'They're not free.'
     (Pfaff 1979, 305)

In (44), the adjective *free* is underspecified regarding the properties individual-level versus stage-level. In this case, the presence of *estar* clearly shows that *free* is being interpreted as a stage-level property. With *ser,* however, *free* would have been interpreted as an individual-level property, as (45) shows.

(45) No son *free.*
     no are free
     'They are not free.'

10.5.3 Codeswitching and Passives

Our third prediction, namely that mixed resultative passives would be constructed with *estar* and mixed passives expressing processes with *ser*, cannot be discussed because no examples involving passives were found in the data. This lack of mixed-passive utterances may simply be due to chance, in which case more data is needed, or else it might indicate that proficient bilingual speakers engaged in codeswitching do not tend to produce these kinds of mixed utterances for various reasons. Further research on this topic may provide insight into why mixed passives did not occur at all, and into whether this is related to the fact that the feature [+/–eventive], which distinguishes both types of passives, is uninterpreted in Spanish and interpretable in English.

10.5.4 Other Findings in Relation to the Data

The data collected disputes some of the constraints that have been put forth in recent years regarding codeswitching and verbs. First, it shows that codeswitching is possible between auxiliaries and gerunds or participles, and between a modal and an infinitive (contrary to Di Sciullo, Muysken, and Singh 1986; Belazi, Rubin, and Toribio 1994; Lipski 1985; Poplack 19821; McClure 1981; Mahootian 1993), as illustrated in (46)–(50). Second, it confirms that codeswitching is allowed between external or internal arguments and the verb, irregardless of these arguments surface in subject or object position (as opposed to Poplack 1982; Mahootian 1993; Bentahila and Davies 1983; Belazi, Rubin, and Toribio 1994). This is shown in (51) and (52).

(46) Estoy   *fixing*   *it.*   (CS *auxiliary + gerund*)
     am   fixing   it
     'I'm fixing it.'
     (Milian 1996b)

(47) Nos   va   a   *blackmail.*   (CS *auxiliary + infinitive*)
     us   go-3PS   to   blackmail
     '[She] is going to blackmail us.'
     (Milian 1996b)

(48) Luisa   tiene   que   get   used   to   think.   (*CS modal + infinitive*)
     Luisa   has   that get   used   to   think
     'Luisa has to get used to think.'
     (Milian 1996b)

(49) *But   she's   gonna*   regañarte.   (*CS auxiliary + infinitive*)
     but   she's   gonna   scold to you
     'But she's gonna scold you.'
     (Zentella 1997, 44)

(50) Yo creo   que   apenas   se   había *washed   out*.   (*CS auxiliary + participle*)
     I   think that barely   itself had   washed out
     'I think it had barely washed out.'
     (Pfaff 1979, 300)

(51) ¿Quieres   *carrots*?   (*CS verb +direct object*)
     want-2PS   carrots
     'Do you want carrots?'
     (Milian 1996b)

(52) Porque   yo   ya   *had   it   nailed   down*   (*CS subject + verb*)
     because I   already had   her nailed   down
     'Because I already had her nailed down'

It is also worth mentioning that various examples attested that mixing occurs between the verb and the particle/preposition of a phrasal verb.

(53) Me dijo   que   pusiera todo   el   mugrero *up*.   ([*+telic*], [*+measure*])
     me told   that put   all   the dirt   up
     'He told me to put the dirt up.'
     (Pfaff 1979, 302)

In (53) the main verb is in Spanish and the particle in English. The verb *poner* lacks the feature [+telic], since *el mugrero* is only a measuring object, not a delimiting one. However, by adding *up*, the event is delimited, and the verb *poner* clearly becomes telic. Therefore, the compositional nature of accomplishments is clearly reflected in codeswitching: the measuring direct object is in Spanish, and the delimiting particle in English. Nevertheless, this preliminary conclusion needs further research.

Finally, I would like to draw attention to the following examples, which involve Spanish *hacer* 'do' and an English infinitive.

(54) Su   hija   hace   *teach*   allá   en   San   José.
     her daughter   does   teach   there   in   San   José
     'Her daughter teaches over there in San José.'
     (Pfaff 1979, 300)

(55) Ellas   me   hacen   *telephone*   cada   semana.
      they   me   do   telephone   every   week
      'They telephone me every week.'
      (Moyer 1992, 309)

According to Pfaff (1979, 301), this pattern involving the construction *hacer* + English stem is "reminiscent of the expansion processes of creolization." A total of twelve examples of this type of construction were found, which indicates that the issue deserves some attention. It could be argued that *hacer* is being used as an auxiliary verb that carries the Tense and Agr features, but that lacks any meaning at all, as in other constructions involving auxiliaries.

10.6 Conclusion

In this chapter, a set of naturally occurring Spanish-English CS data from several authors and three different communities has been analyzed from a minimalist perspective. Instances of codeswitching involving a verb and its arguments have been selected from a vast corpus to show that this type of switching is constrained by the aspectual features of the Event Phrase proposed by Sanz and Bever (2001). These features also constrain predicate types in monolingual grammars.

The data presented have demonstrated that constraints on codeswitching cannot be established by setting different switching points in a sentence, by identifying a matrix language and an embedded language, or by identifying system versus content morphemes and the language they come from. Instead, codeswitching research should focus on identifying uninterpretable and interpretable features in each of the participating languages in codeswitching, and how their different interpretability allows for possible and impossible switches. There is no need to propose new constraints because they already exist in the grammars of the participating languages. Nor is it necessary to propose a third grammar to account for codeswitching.

The syntax-semantics interface hypothesis proposed by Tenny (1988, 1994), together with the assumptions of the Minimalist Program (where strong functional categories play a crucial role in determining movement, parameters, and disambiguation), provide a central frame from which several language contact phenomena and language acquisition (first and second) can be analyzed. As Sanz (1996, 14) has pointed out, "The theory of features permits us to understand how facts about the interpretation of sentences can be encoded as functional categories and thus have syntactic consequences."

Extending the idea posited by minimalism that for a derivation to converge *uninterpretable* features must be checked and erased before LF, it has been shown that in intrasentential codeswitching derivations are likely to crash when speakers assign an incorrect interpretability to aspectual features (i.e., uninterpreted when it is interpretable and the other way around), or when there is a mismatch between aspectual features of the verb and the features of the argument. More research is needed on the role of aspectual features constraining monolingual and bilingual utterances.

The question remains whether codeswitching constraints are universal or not. While the aim of universality should be maintained, "issues like particular networks and the creation of particular codeswitching norms" (Boeschoten 1998, 34) should be kept in mind. It is at the heart of linguistics to unveil the universal mechanisms of language acquisition and processing. In this sense, codeswitching can shed some light on the nature of lexical entries, and on how these lexical entries are inserted into a grammatical frame. However, a greater consensus on the type and source of the data, as well as on the criteria used to classify it, is essential to the progress of codeswitching research, and specifically to research on the nature of lexical entries and how they are inserted into a larger syntactic frame.[20]

Notes

This chapter has greatly benefited from the feedback provided by Melissa Moyer and Montserrat Sanz. Their help, support, and advice are greatly appreciated.

1. According to Chomsky's Minimalist Program (1995), checking for agreement takes place between features of functional categories and features of words. There must be a content word in the sentence that has the same feature as the feature of the functional projection that needs checking. The content word must move to the functional projection that hosts the feature. If the feature is strong, movement is overt. If the feature is weak, movement is covert.

2. It is beyond the scope of this chapter to offer a detailed explanation of the Minimalist Program and the main tenets of lexical semantics. Some background knowledge on the part of readers is assumed.

3. According to Sanz (1996, 25), *aktionsart* properties are properties of entire sentences, not of verbs. Objects are crucially related to event type, and the event type determines the function of the external argument.

4. The concept of *aktionsart* or mode of action has been the focus of attention of authors like Tenny (1988; 1994) or Levin and Rappaport Hovav (1995), who have devoted much research to the study of the syntax-semantics interface. The mode of action does not just affect the verb lexical entry, but also the predicate and its internal arguments. As a result, some authors like Davidson have pointed out the need to create an argument called *event*, which would integrate the properties of the mode of action

of the sentence. The concept of event must be distinguished from argument, since event is the result of combining all the elements in the sentence, and it has nothing in common with the arguments that are subcategorized by the verb.

5. As Sanz and Bever (2001, 147) point out, "The functional category Event Phrasethat projects and has features, in the same manner as Tense, ... is a formalization of what semanticists have been arguing since the 1960s: that there is an event argument in sentences."

6. As Sanz and Bever (2001, 157) note, "Most people assume that bilinguals have the same underlying conceptual features, regardless of which language they happen to be speaking. Thus, they offer a unique population, in which conceptual and semantic bases of sentences are constant, but the mapping onto syntactic derivations can differ."

7. Source: Conversations among working-class Mexican-American speakers in El Paso.

8. Source: Mexican-American males and females, thirty-eight to fifty-seven years old, married, Mexican-American spouse, primary school, West San Antonio.

9. Source: Conversations among students from California State University at Fresno and the University of Texas at Austin, and texts for an ongoing survey of San Antonio Spanish.

10. Source: Recordings of conversations between the author and other bilingual Chicanos in Arizona.

11. Source: Samples of data obtained through recordings of conversations between 1983 and 1985. Approximately 150 hours of audio-recorded conversations with 50 Mexican American bilinguals living in East Los Angeles were transcribed. About 20 hours were recorded by student assistants, and the rest were conversations between the author and speakers. The speakers, who include men and women of different ages, were categorized in three groups according to the length of their stay in the United States.

12. Source: Students from New Mexico University.

13. Source: Conversations between Pedro and Zoraida. All the instances of CS were made by Zoraida, a Puerto Rican female residing in The Bronx, who had arrived in New York at the age

14. Source: Conversations among twenty Puerto Rican residents of the stable bilingual community of El Barrio, New York, on 102nd Street. These speakers showed varying degrees of bilingual ability. The conversations were tape-recorded by Pedraza, a member of the community.

15. Source: Conversations among twenty fluent bilingual Puerto Rican families with thirty-seven children, living in El Barrio, New York, and tape-recorded in 1979 and 1980. The samples in the data selected come from boys and girls interacting with each other. These children were found to speak six language variants: Standard Spanish, Puerto Rican Spanish, Puerto Rican English, African American Vernacular English, New York English, and Hispanicized English.

16. This corpus compiles ten hours of naturally occurring conversations among four bilingual Puerto Rican Spanish-English families living in Columbia, SC. They tape-recorded the conversations themselves in their homes over a three-month period.

Speakers were not directed regarding conversational topics; various domestic matters dominate the conversations.

17. As Lipski (1985) has pointed out, when we compare the different Spanish-English communities in the United States, there do not seem to be many qualitative differences among them, but rather differences of ethnic identification and solidarity, language attitude, and social and historical background. Furthermore, there are intragroup differences according to area, length of residence, and socioeconomic factors. Although all these sociolinguistic factors influence the type and frequency of *intrasentential* Spanish-English CS data from different communities, we expect the same universal constraints to apply to data from different communities, as several authors like Poplack (1982) have proposed. The same perspective has been adopted in this study, and the data has been classified according to Event types and not according to author and community.

18. A number of considerations favor the use of naturally occurring data as the basis for testing hypotheses regarding grammatical structure in codeswitching (Milian 1996a). First, codeswitching is often stigmatized as "broken language." Such views lead to negative evaluations of codeswitching by bilingual members of the larger community. The result is that grammaticality judgments, even those of speakers who themselves codeswitch frequently, are contaminated. Second, a related point is that speakers may be embarrassed by utterances containing CS and may therefore be unwilling to identify with codeswitching. Third, because codeswitching often occurs in *ingroup* conversations in which speakers are even unaware that they are engaging in codeswitching, when these same speakers are asked to make grammaticality judgments on isolated sentences, they often perform quite differently from trained linguists. In addition, "trained linguists" are "more aware" of implications of the data for grammatical theory. Fourth, naturally occurring data is sometimes criticized because it is uncontrolled (i.e., situational factors where it is collected often vary); however, situational factors are not absent in grammaticality judgments. In fact, intuitions are a type of performance. Fifth, some examples from naturally occurring data may be dismissed as performance errors; however, studies that report all relevant examples from a substantive corpus, such as the one studied here, cannot be dismissed.

19. Telic features can be checked in the following ways: (1) directly by the verb, when this is inherently telic; (2) through an object delimiting the verb, which as a result acquires the feature [+/−telic]; and (3) through reflexive *se*.

20. The main problem with current research in codeswitching is that authors do not agree on the same terminology to account for codeswitching phenomena. The arguments put forward by Myers-Scotton (1993) and Poplack (1982) on the issue of borrowing versus codeswitching elements are worth mentioning here. According to Poplack, switching differs from borrowing depending on the level of phonological, morphological, and syntactic integration: the more integrated the constituent, the more likely it is to be considered a switch. On the other hand, Myers-Scotton (1993, 1995) believes that both types of lexemes, despite their differences, show the same type of morphosyntactic integration, and their occurrence can be explained by the constraints imposed by the Matrix Language Frame Model. A second criticism is that the degree of proficiency of bilinguals, as well as situational factors, are not always specified by

authors using naturally occurring data. This often leads to confusion and hinders progress in codeswitching and bilingual research in general.

References

Amastae, Jon, and Lucía Olivares, eds. 1980. *Spanish in the United States: Sociolinguistic Aspects*. Cambridge: Cambridge University Press.

Belazi, Heidi, Edward Rubin, and Almeida Toribio. 1994. Codeswitching and X-bar theory: The Functional Head Constraint. *Linguistic Inquiry* 24 (2): 221–237.

Bentahila, Abdelai, and Eirlys Davies. 1983. The syntax of Arabic-French code-switching. *Lingua* 59:301–330.

Boeschoten, H. (1998). Codeswitching, codemixing, and code alternation: What a difference. In Jacobson, R. (ed.) Codeswitching Worldwide, pp.15–24. Berlin/New York: Mouton de Gruyter

Carlson, G. 1977. References to kinds in English. Doctoral dissertation, University of Massachusetts at Amherst.

Chomsky, Noam. 1995. *The Minimalist Program*. Cambridge, MA: MIT Press.

Coltharp, Lurline. 1970. Invitation to the dance: Spanish in the El Paso underworld. In Glenn G. Gilbert (ed.), *Texas Studies in Bilingualism*, 7–17. Berlin: Walter de Gruyter.

Davidson, D. 1967. The logical form of action sentences. In N. Rescher (ed.), *The Logic of Decision and Action*, 81–95. Pittsburgh: University of Pittsburgh Press.

Di Sciullo, Anna Maria, Pieter Muysken, and Rajendra Singh. 1986. Government and code-mixing. *Journal of Linguistics* 22:1–24.

Dowty, D. R. 1979. On the semantic content of the notion of "thematic role." In G. Chierchia, B. Partee, and R. Turner (eds.), *Properties, Types and Meaning*, vol. 2, 69–129. Dordrecht: Kluwer Academic Publishers.

Dowty, D. R. 1991. Thematic proto-roles and argument selection. *Language* 67:547–619.

Durán, Richard P., ed. 1981. *Latino Language and Communicative Behavior*. Norwood, NJ: Ablex.

Higginbotham, J. 1996. On events in linguistic semantics. Ms., MIT and Somerville College, Oxford.

Jacobson, Rodolfo. 1977. The social implications of intra-sentential codeswitching. In Ricardo Romo and Raymund Paredes, eds., *New Directions in Chicano Scholarship*, 183–207. San Diego: University of California.

Jacobson, Rodolfo. 1982. The social implications of intra-sentential code-switching. In Jon Amastae and Lucía Elías-Olivares, eds., *Spanish in the United States*, 230–255. Cambridge: Cambridge University Press.

Jacobson, Rodolfo. 1990. *Code-Switching as a Worldwide Phenomenon*. New York: Peter Lang.

Jacobson, Rodolfo. 1998. *Codeswitching Worldwide*. Berlin: Mouton de Gruyter.

Jake, Janice L., and Carol Myers-Scotton. 1996. Verbs in Arabic/English codeswitching and lexical structure. Paper presented at the Symposium on Codeswitching and the Nature of Lexical Entries, LSA Annual Meeting, San Diego.

Jake, Janice L., and Carol Myers-Scotton. 1997. Codeswitching and compromise strategies: Implications for lexical structure. *International Journal of Bilingualism* 1:25–39.

Joshi, Aravind. 1985. Processing sentences with intrasentential codeswitching. In David R. Dowty, Lauri Karttunen, and Arnold Quickly, eds., *Natural Language Parsing*, 190–205. Cambridge: Cambridge University Press.

Language Policy Task Force. 1984. *Speech and Ways of Speaking in a Bilingual Puerto Rican Community*. New York: Center for Puerto Rican Studies.

Levin, Beth, and M. Rappaport Hovav. 1995. *Unaccusivity: At the Syntax-lexical Semantics Interface*. Cambridge, MA: MIT Press.

Lipski, John M. 1985. *Linguistic Aspects of Spanish-English Language Switching*. Tempe: Arizona State University, Latin American Studies Center.

MacSwan, Jeff. 1997. A minimalist approach to intrasentential code switching: Spanish-Nahuatl bilingualism in Central Mexico. Doctoral dissertation, UCLA.

MacSwan, Jeff. 1999. *A Minimalist Approach to Intrasentential Codeswitching*. New York: Garland.

MacSwan, J. 2000. The architecture of the bilingual language faculty: Evidence from codeswitching. *Bilingualism: Language and Cognition* 3 (1): 37–54.

MacSwan, J. 2013. Code switching and linguistic theory. In T. K. Bhatia and W. Ritchie, eds., *Handbook of Bilingualism and Multilingualism*, 2nd ed., 223–350. Oxford: Blackwell.

Mahootian, Shahrzad. 1993. A null theory of codeswitching. Doctoral dissertation, Department of Linguistics, Northwestern University.

Mahootian, Shahrzad. 1996. Codeswitching and universal constraints: Evidence from Farsi/English. *World Englishes* 15 (3): 377–384.

McClure, E. 1981. Formal and functional aspects of the code-switched discourse of bilingual children. In R. P. Duran (ed.) *Latino Language and Communicative Behaviour,* 69–94. Norwood, N.J.: Ablex

Milian, Silvia. 1996a. Case assignment in Spanish/English codeswitching. Paper presented at the Linguistic Society of America Symposium on Codeswitching, San Diego, CA.

Milian, Silvia. 1996b. Spanish/English codeswitching data. Unpublished corpus.

Moyer, Melissa G. 1992. Analysis of code-switching in Gibraltar. Doctoral dissertation, Departament de Filología Anglesa i Germanística, Universitat Autònoma de Barcelona.

Myers-Scotton, Carol. 1993. *Duelling Languages: Grammatical Structure in Codeswitching*. Oxford: Clarendon Press.

Myers-Scotton, Carol. 1995. A lexically-based model of code-switching. In Lesley Milroy and Pieter Muysken, eds., *One Speaker, Two Languages: Cross-Disciplinary Perspectives on Code-Switching*, 233–257. Cambridge: Cambridge University Press.

Parsons, T. 1990. *Events in the Semantics of English*. Cambridge, MA: MIT Press.

Pfaff, Carol. 1979. Constraints on language mixing: Intrasentential code-switching and borrowing in Spanish/English. *Language* 55:291–318.

Poplack, Shana. 1982. Sometimes I'll start a sentence in English y termino en Español: Toward a typology of codeswitching. In J. Amastae , L. Elías Olivares (eds.), *Spanish in the United States. Sociolinguistic aspects*. 230–263. Cambridge University Press, 230–63.

Radford, Andrew. 1997. *Syntax: A Minimalist Introduction*. Cambridge: Cambridge University Press.

Redlinger, Wendy. 1976. A description of transference and codeswitching in Mexican American English and Spanish. In Gary Keller, Richard Teschner, and Silvia Viera, eds., *Bilingual in the Bicentennial and Beyond*, 41–49. New York: Bilingual Publications.

Reyes, Ricardo 1982. Language mixing in Chicano Spanish. In Jon Amastae and Lucía Elías-Olivares, eds., *Spanish in the United States: Sociolinguistic Perspectives*, 154–165. Cambridge: Cambridge University Press.

Sanz, Montserrat. 1996. Telicity, objects, and mapping onto predicate types: A cross-linguistic study on the role of syntax in processing. Doctoral dissertation, University of Rochester.

Sanz, Montserrat, and Thomas G. Bever. 2001. A theory of syntactic interference in the bilingual. In Janet L. Nicol, ed., *One Mind, Two Languages: Bilingual Language Processing*, 134158 Oxford: Blackwell.

Silva Corvalán, Carmen. 1994. *Language Contact and Language Change: Spanish in Los Angeles*. Oxford: Clarendon.

Tenny, Carol L. 1988. "The aspectual interface hypothesis: The connection between syntax and lexical semantics". In Carol L.Tenny, ed., *Studies in Generative Approaches to Aspect (Lexicon Project Working Papers, 24*. Cambridge, MA: Department of Linguistics and Philosophy, MIT

Tenny, Carol L. 1994. *Aspectual Roles and the Syntax-Semantics Interface*. Dordrecht: Kluwer Academic Publishers.

Toribio, Almeida Jacqueline, and Edward Rubin. 1996. *Codeswitching in Generative Grammar*. In Roca, Ana, and John B. Jensen, eds. *Spanish in Contact*, 203–226. Somerville: Cascadilla Press.

Valdés Fallis, Guadalupe. 1981. Codeswitching as a deliberate verbal strategy: A microanalysis of direct and indirect requests among bilingual Chicano speakers. In Richard P. Durán, ed., *Latino Language and Communicative Behavior*, 95–197. Norwood, NJ: Ablex.

Vendler, Z. 1967. *Linguistics and Philosophy*. Ithaca, NY: Cornell University Press.

Zentella, Ana Celia. 1997. *Growing up Bilingual*. Oxford: Blackwell.

Part IV Codeswitching and Language Processing

11 A Minimalist Parsing Model for Codeswitching

Edward P. Stabler and Jeff MacSwan

A fully lexicalized grammar can represent the knowledge of a bilingual or multilingual speaker simply by putting lexical items from the various languages together. This conception suggests that multilingualism should be a quite natural state, an idea that fits well with a conception according to which every adjustment in register or dialect for context is regarded as a kind of codeswitching (CS), as is the use of various constructions by language learners who are entertaining several hypotheses about the language (Roeper 2000; Yang 2000). Thus, multilingualism is universal. This conception of CS is very appealing, since it does not invoke any special mechanisms to control the interaction among the languages.

However, some restrictions are needed, since codeswitching does not occur at arbitrary positions in an utterance. MacSwan (1999, chapter 1, this volume) proposes that they can be accounted for without special mechanisms. His proposal is, roughly, that the syntactic elements of various languages can mix freely, but the morphophonologies of various languages have different properties and cannot be mixed. Hence, codeswitching is possible only at those points in an utterance that would not disrupt morphophonological dependencies. (See MacSwan and Colina, chapter 8, this volume, for discussion.)

A computational model of language analysis has been proposed by Stabler (2001), which separates morphophonological and syntactic processing and is explicit and general enough to allow proposals like MacSwan's to be realized. Furthermore, the realization should be immediate—that is, no special mechanisms should be needed. Given the grammatical assumptions that MacSwan makes, the computational model should immediately yield the predicted CS abilities. This chapter will show that this is true. The computational realization of the proposal also draws attention to some grammatical assumptions that are rather surprising and that deserve further exploration.

11.1 The Architecture of Multilingual Grammars: Evidence

Much work on intrasentential CS assumes that there must be specific constraints and mechanisms that define the interaction of languages (Poplack 1981; Joshi 1985b; Belazi, Rubin, and Toribio 1994; Myers-Scotton, 2001). In such frameworks, differences in grammaticality, such as those expressed in the English-Spanish codeswitches in (1), are captured in terms of constraints or principles that govern the interaction of the two grammars.

(1) a. The   students   *habían*   *visto*   *la*   *pelicula*   *italiana.*
         the   students   had   seen   the   movie   Italian
     b. *The   student   had   *visto*   *la*   *pelicula*   *italiana*
         the   student   had   seen   the   movie   Italian

However, other work has focused on developing a theory of codeswitching that takes only requirements of the mixed grammars to determine grammaticality in mixed-language constructions (Pfaff 1979; Woolford 1983; Lipski 1985; Mahootian 1993; MacSwan 1999, 2013). This latter approach is preferable for general reasons of parsimony and should only be abandoned if forced by the data.

The interaction of grammars in the derivation of codeswitching is problematic in nonlexicalist models, and especially in the "parametric" theories of language variation that have received much attention (Chomsky 1981; Hyams 1986; Lightfoot 1989; Gibson and Wexler 1994; Fodor 1998). For example, if there is a basic parameter of language variation that determines whether the subject of a sentence can be unpronounced, a "pro-drop parameter," then it seems that Spanish-English bilinguals need to have two, inconsistent settings of this parameter. To determine, then, which parameters are active when sentences are being produced, we need some kind of "control structure" as Joshi (1985a) calls it. Similarly, if there is a basic parameter determining the order of verb and object, then how is the grammar of a Japanese-English bilingual represented, and what set of parameters are active in the production of a CS construction? The simplest ideas do not work. For instance, we could say that in CS constructions, the speaker simultaneously tries to satisfy the parameters of both languages. But this is impossible in most cases, since for example a subject cannot both be dropped and also be pronounced; an object cannot both precede and follow the verb. Another simple idea is that in CS constructions, the speaker switches freely between the parameter settings of the two languages, but in many cases this would allow too much variation. For instance, if separate parameters determine subject-verb and verb-object order, then we would expect that after pronouncing the subject and verb in the order required by one language, a speaker could change parameter settings and produce the object in a position required by the other language. This kind of thing does not happen, as we will see below.

If all syntactic variation is associated with the lexicon, on the other hand, CS may be seen as the simple consequence of using lexical items from two languages in the course of a derivation. The computational system is invariant, and the properties of each lexical item must be satisfied in precisely the same way as in monolingual syntax. MacSwan (1999, 2013) develops a model of intrasentential codeswitching with these characteristics. In his approach, items may be drawn from the lexicon of either language, where each lexical item introduces features that must then be checked in just the same way as monolingual features must be checked. In this lexicalist approach, no "control structure" mediates the contradictory requirements of the mixed systems (MacSwan, chapter 1, this volume). Thus, the grammar of a bilingual simply has lexical items from two different languages. We see how this perspective can be set out very simply and precisely in the following section.

The consequences of this assumption depend on the model of the grammar, though, in ways that might allow an explanation of the restrictions on CS noted above. MacSwan (1999, 2013) makes such a proposal based on a single, simple division in the grammar between syntax and morphophonological processing, a division present in the minimalist grammar that he assumes. The proposal is simply this:

(2)   While syntax can freely compose lexical elements from various
      languages, the units of morphophonology, those elements that are part
      of the head structure, "below X^0" in the syntax, cannot be broken up
      and mixed.

MacSwan argues that this hypothesis is independently motivated by the fact that the morphophonological component of grammar uses ordered rules or ranked constraints, and hence is quite unlike the free generation of structure in syntax, discussed in detail in MacSwan and Colina (chapter 8, this volume). In any reasonable model of grammar, even approaches to grammar that integrate syntax and morphophonology quite tightly, the morphophonology will have the special property of being sensitive to phonological features of stems and affixes, and the rules with that property are language-specific, supporting something similar to (2).

First note that (2) rules out classic problems such as those presented in (3), after Poplack (1981). Since morphophonological operations must apply to the X^0 sequences derived by the syntax, word-level mixtures such as these are not permitted.

(3)   a. *Juan está   *eat*-iendo.
         Juan be/1Ss   eat-DUR
            'Juan is eating.'
      b. *Juan *eat*-ó.
         Juan eat-PAST/3Ss
            'Juan ate.'
      c. *Juan *com*-ed.
         Juan eat-PAST
            'Juan ate.'
      d. *Juan eat-*ará*.
         Juan be/1Ss eat-FUT/3Ss
            'Juan will eat.'

If, however, an English lexical stem is treated with both Spanish phonology and morphology, as in the case of borrowing, no ill-formed constructions result:

(4)   a. Juan   está   parqueando   su   coche.
         Juan   be/1Ss park-DUR   his   car
            'Juan is parking his car.'
      b. Juan   parqueó   su   coche.
         Juan   park-PAST/3Ss his   car
            'Juan parked his car.'
      c. Juan   parqueará   su   coche.
         Juan   park-FUT/3Ss his   car
            'Juan will park his car.'

Following the strong Lexicalist perspective of Chomsky (1970), Chomsky (1995b) assumes that morphologically complex items, such as *walked*, are formed internally within the lexicon, with the properties [walk] and [past] already specified (see Newmeyer 2009, for discussion). Borrowing, then, may be viewed as an operation whereby a new stem is introduced into a specific lexicon where morphologically complex items are formed before entering the lexical array.

Now let us consider some instances of CS involving classic cases of head movement. Rizzi (1982) and many others have treated restructuring verbs (aspectuals, modals, verbs of motion) as involving syntactic reanalysis, or V^0-to-V^0 incorporation, as Roberts (1998) proposed. (Compare Cinque 2004, and Cardinaletti and Shlonsky 2004.) The Italian aspectual *essere* is used with a past participle in passive-impersonal *si* constructions. In constructions such as (5a), *essere* is used as a restructuring verb, allowing promotion of the embedded object to matrix subject position, shown in (5b).

(5) a. Si   è   dato   un   regalo.
       si   essere given   a   gift
       'A gift is given.'
    b. Un   regalo si   è   dato.
       a   gift   *si   essere* given
       'A gift is given.'

On Rizzi's original (1982) analysis, restructuring has applied to (5b) but not to (5a), forcing the promotion of [NP un regalo] in the former example.

However, note that a very different pattern of judgments emerges when codeswitching is involved in constructions like (4). Consider the French-Italian facts in (6) (MacSwan 2000).

(6) a. Si   è   *donné*   *un*   *cadeau.*
       si   essere given   a   gift
    b. *Un   cadeau si   è   donnè.
       a   gift   *si   essere* given

The movement of [NP un cadeau] indicates that V^0-to-V^0 incorporation has occurred in (6b), just as it did in (5b). The verbal complexes are identical in (6a) and (6b): a mixture of the Italian aspectual auxiliary *é* immediately adjacent to the French past participle *donné*. Thus, the unacceptability of (6b) indicates that codeswitching in restructuring configurations is prohibited, just as (2) predicts. Other ungrammatical codeswitched constructions that appear to result from restructuring are given in (7), for English-Spanish, and in (8), for Nahuatl-Spanish.

(7) a. *The students *habían* seen   the   Italian movie.
        the   students had   seen   the   Italian movie
    b. *The students had   *visto* *la*   *pelicula* *italiana.*
        the   students had   seen   the   movie   Italian

(8) a. *Ni-k-neki   *compr-aré*   *ropa.*
        1S-3Os-want   buy-1Ss/FUT   clothing
        'I want to buy some clothes.'
    b. ??Quiero   *nikoas*   *tlakemetl.*
        1S-3Os-want   1S-3Os-buy-FUT   clothing
        'I want to buy some clothes.'

Consider another instance in which codeswitching below X^0 is disallowed. Zagona (1988) establishes with a number of tests that Spanish *no* is a clitic on its verb. Under similar tests for Nahuatl, the negative element *amo* appears to behave much like English negation, syntactically independent of the verb it precedes. Accordingly, barring other factors, codeswitching between Nahuatl *amo* and a Spanish verb should be licit, while codeswitching between Spanish *no* and a Nahuatl verb should be illicit, just as the data indicate:

(9) a. **No*   ni-tekiti-toc.
         not   1S-work-DUR
         'I'm not working.'
     b. *Amo*   estoy   trabaja-ndo.
         not   be/PRES/1Ss   work-DUR
         'I'm not working.'

Other examples of this sort are reviewed in MacSwan (2013, chapter 8, this volume), but for present purposes the relevant insight is this: codeswitching below X^0 is not permitted, as predicted by hypothesis (2).

We may now turn to a consideration of basic word order in CS—first SVO versus VSO, then SVO versus SOV. . We take the universal base structure to be underlyingly SVO with a VP-internal subject for both SV and VS languages. V^0 raises to T^0 (=Agr^0) to value ϕ-features. If the subject checks its EPP feature in the specifier position of T^0, then an SVO order results. If not, then the resulting word order will be VSO. Thus, the typological distinction between SVO and VSO languages is captured in terms of the EPP feature.

Because mixed-language heads are ruled out by (2), if V^0 raises to T^0 to value ϕ-features, then both elements will necessarily have been drawn from the same lexicon, each representing a separate language, otherwise the complex would be ill-formed. As a result, the language of the verb will determine the language of T^0, hence the characteristics of its EPP feature, precisely as the codeswitching facts in (10)-(14) (MacSwan, 2004) require: if the verb is from an SVO language, the subject should occur preverbally, whether it is from an SVO language or not; if the verb is from a VSO language, the subject should occur postverbally, regardless of the requirements of the language of the subject.

(10) *VS verb (Irish), SV subject (English) (Stenson 1990, 180)*
     Beidh   *jet lag* an   tógáil a   phàirt ann.
     be-FUT   jetlag   taking its part in-it
     'Jet lag will be playing its part in it.'

(11) *VS verb (Irish), SV subject (English) (Stenson 1990, 180)*
     Fuair sé *thousand pounds* get-PA he.
     'He got a thousand pounds.'

(12) *VS verb (Brenton), SV subject (French) (Pensel 1979, 68)*
     Oa   ket   *des armes.*
     be-3S   IMP NEG   of-the arms
     'There were no arms.'

(13) *VS verb (Brenton), SV subject (French) (Troadec 1983, 35)*
Setu   oa   *l'état-major*   du-se   barzh ti   Lanserot.
there be-imp the military-staff down-there in   house   Lanserot
'There was the military staff down there in Lanserot's house.'

(14) *VS verb (SLQ Zapotec), SV subject (Spanish)*
2-S-to'oh   *mi*   *esposa*   el   coche.
DEF-sell   my   wife   the   car
'My wife will definitely sell the car.'

Now consider the placement of objects in codeswitching contexts. If an object moves covertly out of the VP-shell to the specifier position of v' (a preverbal position), then the elements remain in the order SVO for purposes of PF. If the object moves overtly, however, an SOV word order is derived at PF. The parameter responsible for this difference is associated with v'. If the Case feature of v' triggers covert movement, SVO is formed; if it triggers ovent movement, SOV results. It is natural to assume that the verb undergoes a checking relation with v' by head movement, guaranteeing that the language of the verb will determine the position of the object at PF, just as in the case of subjects. These facts are attested:

(15) *VO (English) verb, OV object (Farsi) (Mahootian 1993, 152)*
Tell them you'll buy *xune-ye jaedid* when you sell your own house.
tell them you'll buy house   new   when you sell your own house
'Tell them you'll buy a new house when you sell your own house.'

(16) *OV verb (Farsi), VO object (English) (Mahootian 1993, 150)*
Ten   dollars   *dad-e*.
ten   dollars   give-PERF
'She gave ten dollars.'

(17) *VO verb (English), OV object (Japanese) (Nishimura 1985, 76)*
We   never   knew   *anna*   *koto*   *nanka*.
we   never   knew   such   thing   sarcasm
'We never knew such a thing as sarcasm.'

(18) *OV verb (Japanese), VO object (English) (Nishimura 1985, 129)*
In   addition,   his   wife   *ni*   *yattara*
in   addition,   his   wife   DAT   give-COND
'In addition, if we give it to his wife'

(19) *VO verb (English), OV object (Korean) (Lee 1991, 130)*
I ate *ceonyek* quickly.
'I ate dinner quickly.'

(20) *OV verb (Korean), VO object (English) (Lee 1991, 129)*
    Na-nun   *dinner*-lul   pali   meokeotta.
    I-SM   dinner-OM   quickly   ate
    'I ate dinner quickly.'

The data considered in this section appear to justify MacSwan's assumptions about the architecture of the language faculty for bilingual speakers. Assuming that all crosslinguistic variation is lexically encoded, syntactic operations of the computational system can be invariant. Then a bilingual may be assumed to have a unitary system of syntactic operations responsible for mapping lexical sequences to syntactic structures. However, the language faculty also requires operations for forming morphologically complex lexical items (like *walked* and *caminó* 'he walked'), and conceivably these operations cannot combine elements from different languages. MacSwan (1999) points out, for example, that if each language has a distinct set of ordered rules (or even a distinct ranking of universal constraints), it is not easy to see how any merging of the systems would be possible (compare MacSwan and Colina, chapter 8, this volume). So we can suppose that a bilingual speaker has discrete phonological systems for each language, and only the computation of syntactic structure can be common among various linguistic systems.

This picture of the bilingual language faculty also makes sense of evidence of abilities to distinguish distinct languages very early in simultaneous infant bilingualism. Early work on bilingual language acquisition proposed that children initially use both linguistic systems in an undifferentiated manner (Leopold 1970; Swain 1972), and that a gradual process of separation begins with the lexicon, then moves on to morphology, and finally to syntax (Volterra and Taeschner 1978; Grosjean 1982). However, critics of this perspective charge that, on close analysis, there is no compelling evidence for the presence of an undifferentiated language system in early bilinguals (Meisel 1989, 1994; Genesee 1989). Children are able to determine quite early that the input data they are considering constitutes two distinct morphophonological systems.

In the next section, we present the minimalist formalism of Stabler (2001), which will derive monolingual and codeswitched SVO, VSO, and SOV structures, and provides a parsing model with distinct syntactic and morphophonological components. As we will see, this model immediately captures many of the facts reviewed above, but some puzzles come up that are discussed in the final section of the chapter.

11.2   The Architecture of Multilingual Grammars: A Formal Model

Recent attempts to reduce the mechanisms of grammar while maintaining the empirical coverage of earlier theories (Rizzi 1990; Kayne 1994; Chomsky

1995b) inspired the simple formal model of the basic mechanisms of transformational grammar in Stabler (1997, 2001). Realizing MacSwan's proposal in this system will show how easily a lexicalized grammar allows CS, and how the separation of a morphophonological component restricts the positions in which switching can occur. The realization also suggests a notion of "extent of integration" of two grammars, allowing for the role of learning in CS constructions.

11.2.1 Syntax

Adopting the idea that all language variation is lexical, a formal minimalist grammar is just a finite set of lexical items. Each lexical item has some specification of its pronunciation, together with a sequence of features. There are six kinds of features:

Categories	N,D,V,A,P, …
Selectors	=N,=D,=V,=A,=P, …
Select and incorporate	$\Rightarrow$N,$\Rightarrow$D,$\Rightarrow$V,$\Rightarrow$A,$\Rightarrow$P, …
Select and hop	N$\Rightarrow$,D$\Rightarrow$,V$\Rightarrow$,A$\Rightarrow$,P$\Rightarrow$, …
Licensees	-wh,-case, …
Licensors	+wh,+case, …

The lexical item that is the English noun *movie* is represented as the lexical item

movie::N

The $::$ simply indicates that this is a lexical item, and it separates the indication of the phonological features (here given just by the standard spelling of the word) from the sequence of features. If we assume that a name like *Maria* is a lexical determiner phrase that needs Case, the lexical item would be

Maria::D -case

If we assume that the transitive verb *praise* selects two determiner phrases, then we might have a lexical item like this:

praise::=D =D V

A lexicon is a finite set of items like this.

The operations that combine these lexical items into complexes are assumed to be universal and innate. Rather than representing the complexes we build with X-bar structure trees, we will label the internal nodes of a phrase with a mark that just points to its head. So for example, rather than the X-bar structure on the left, we will use the structure on the right:

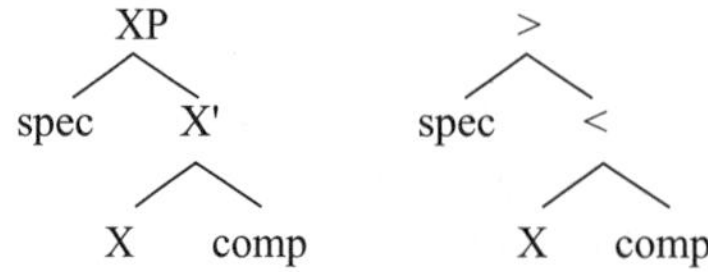

With this notation, it is always possible to tell what the maximal projection of a tree is: the maximal projection of X is the largest subtree that has X as its head. Consider the following tree, for example:

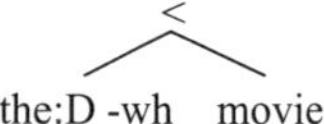

the:D -wh   movie

We can see that this is a determiner phrase, a DP, since following the arrows down from the root, we get to a leaf with the category D. So the whole tree is the maximal projection of that head. The complement of D is also a maximal projection, since there is no higher node that has the leaf node labeled *movie* as its head. So in this notation, as also in Chomsky (1995a) for example, a head can be a maximal projection.

It remains only to define the operations Merge and Move. *Merge* applies to two trees (where lexical items are regarded as the limiting case of one-node trees), when the head of the first tree begins with a selector of a category that is at the head of the second tree. For example, the two lexical items mentioned above could be merged to yield another tree we have already seen, shown again here on the right:

praise::=D =D V   Maria::D   ==>   <
                                                        praise:=D V   Maria

The selection feature =D checks the categorial feature D, and both are deleted: the first argument is attached as a complement. The resulting tree is still a verb phrase that selects another D, but now the complement position is filled and so the second selected element is attached as a specifier:

                <   they::D   ==>   >
           praise:=D V   Maria   they   <
                                                                  praise:V   Maria

A select and incorporate feature can select and incorporate a complement (but not a specifier). The incorporated head is "left adjoined" to the selector, which we indicate with <o as shown here:

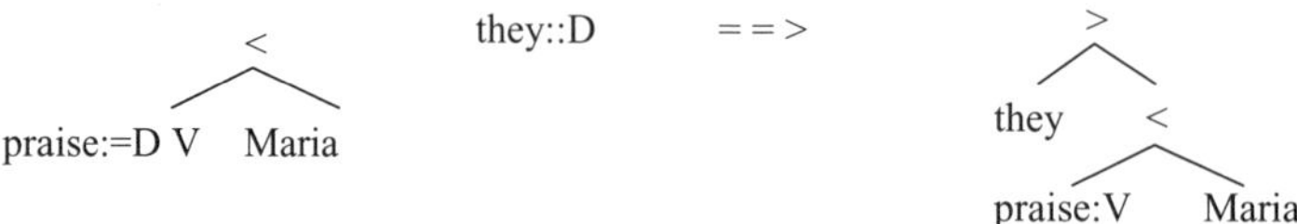

-s::=>V T   <   ==>   <
                       have:V   eaten   o>   <
                                                           have   -s:T   eaten

And finally, a select and hop feature can select and lower to the head of a complement (but not a specifier). The lowered head is "right adjoined" to the selector, which we indicate with <o as shown here:[1]

The particular action of Merge on any given pair of trees is completely determined by the features involved, and if it applies it always checks and deletes exactly two features.

The second operation on structures is *Move*, an operation that applies to a single tree whose head begins with a +f feature for some f, when the tree contains exactly one other head that begins with -f. In such a case, the maximal projection of the -f head is moved to become the specifier of the root, checking and deleting both the +f and -f. For example, writing e for empty phonological structures:

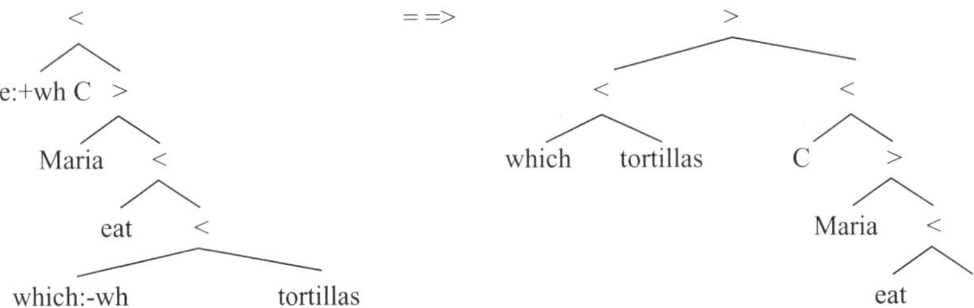

Notice that this movement is "phrasal" in the sense that it always moves a maximal projection. Movement is overt, leftward, and always to a c-commanding position. Notice that the trace position is left simply as an empty node, since the trace will play no role in the rest of the derivation.

These operations Merge and Move have been rigorously defined and studied in a number of papers. Michaelis (1998) proved that the languages definable with these operations are efficiently parsable, and efficient parsers were in fact found and presented in Harkema (2000), and Morawietz (2000), and these were extended to include head movement in Stabler (2001). The simplest parsing methods are the so-called CKY-like methods, which build structure bottom up, exactly as we do when we use Merge and Move in a derivation. Examples will be presented in the following sections.

We can already see, just from the definition of the grammars, that if G1 and G2 are grammars, then the union of G1 and G2 is also a grammar; the class of minimalist grammars is "closed under finite unions" in this sense. Furthermore, as will become clear, letting the language L(G1) be the set of phonological sequences that can be parsed as complete CPs, the language L(G1 union G2) is always a superset of both L(G1) and L(G2), and often it is a strict superset. That is, when two grammars are combined, the resulting language always includes everything that was in both languages, and often includes more. The "more" is exactly the CS expressions.

11.2.1.1 Multilingual Syntax: Some Examples

As explained in the previous section, a lexicon is a finite set of lexical items. The following grammar is presented in Stabler (2001) as a simple, illustrative model of a standard account of the basic clause structure of English. According to this account, the auxiliaries and modals are incorporated into tense, but main verbs stay in situ and the tense affix "hops" down to them. In the following grammar, the order of English auxiliaries and tense affixes is captured by letting the (singular, third-person, present) tense affix -*s* incorporate a Modal, Have, or Be, but hop down onto a selected main verb:

e:: =T C	e:: ⇒T C	e:: ⇒T +wh C
-s:: ⇒Modal +k T	-s:: ⇒Have +k T	
-s:: ⇒Be +k T	-s:: =v +k T	-s:: v⇒ +k T
will:: =Have Modal	will:: =Be Modal	will:: =v Modal
have:: =Been Have	have:: =En Have	
be:: =Ing Be	been:: =Ing Been	
e:: ⇒V =D v	-en:: ⇒V =D En	-ing:: ⇒V =D Ing
eat:: =D +k V	laugh:: V	
the:: =N D -k	which:: =N D -k -wh	
king:: N	pie:: N	

Let's step through a derivation of *the king eat -s*. First we merge the lexical items *the* and *king* to form the tree on the left, which would usually be depicted with an X-bar tree like the one on the right:

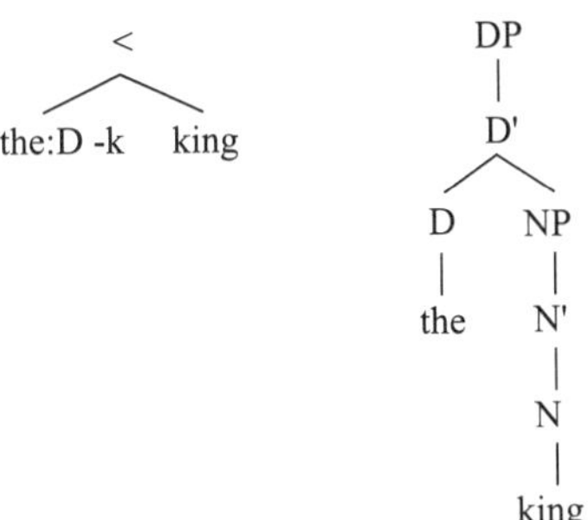

We can also let the lexical item *eat*, which is a V, get selected and incorporated by the "light verb" *v*, which has no phonetic content of its own:

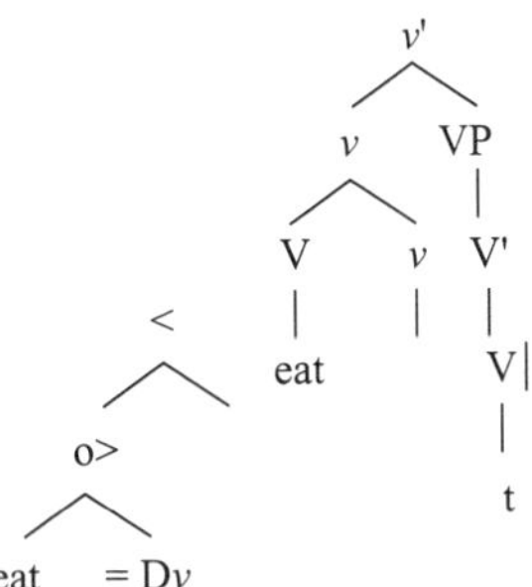

Now the *v*P *eat* selects the DP *the king* as subject. Notice that the DP still has an unchecked "Case" feature -k:

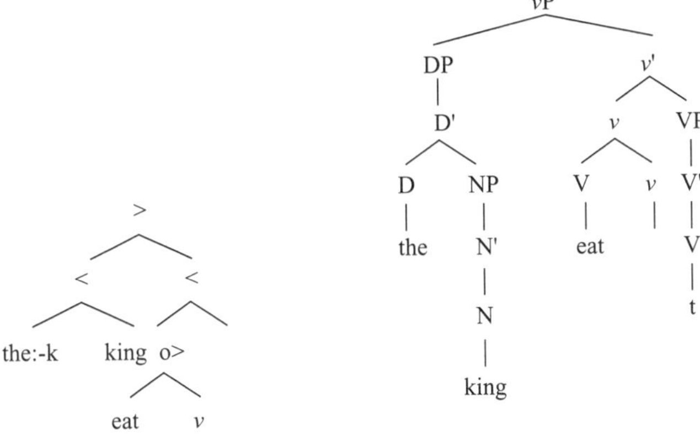

Now the *v*P can be selected by tense, and the tense morpheme -*s* "hops" down
to the head of the *v*P:

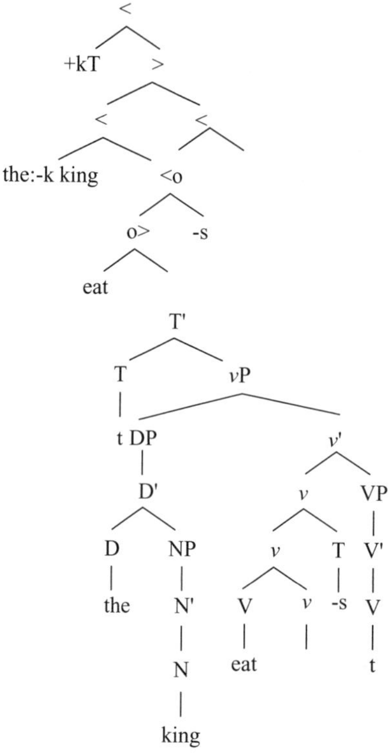

The subject can then move to the specifier of tense to have its Case features
checked:

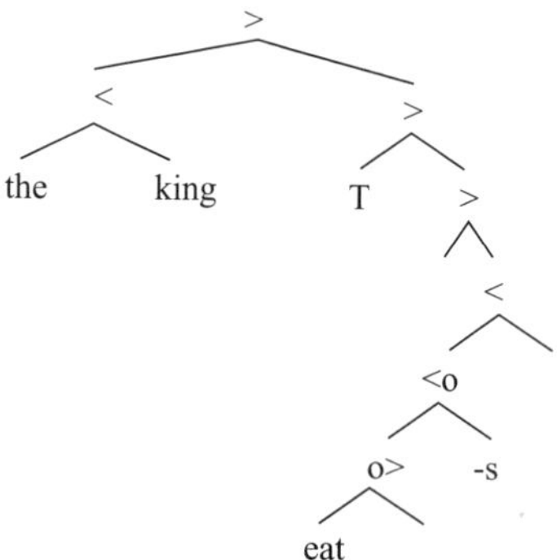

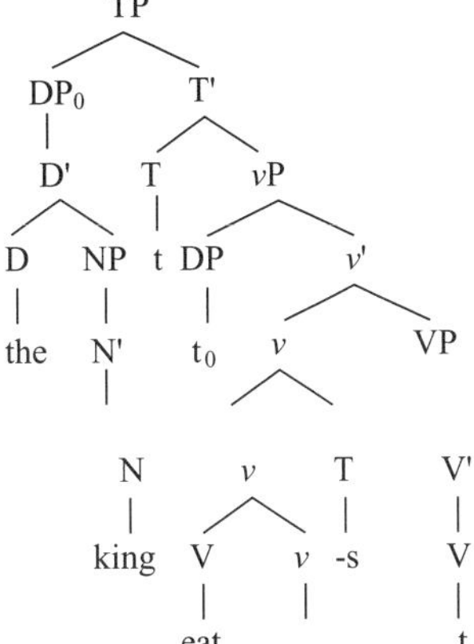

And finally, this structure is selected by the lexical complementizer to form a complete CP:

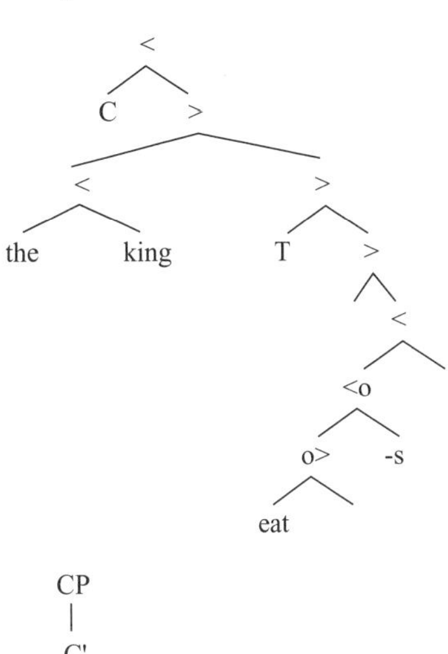

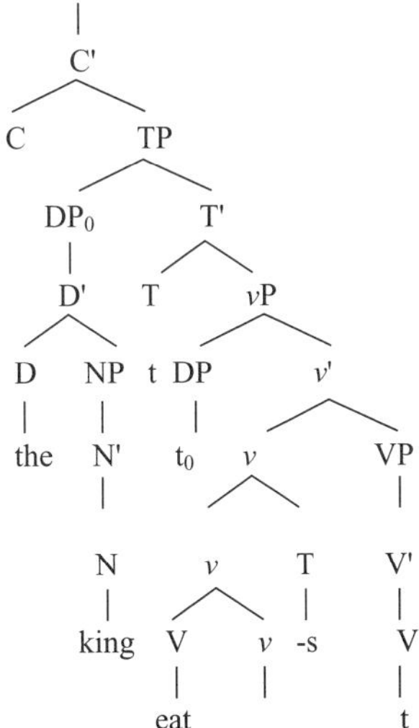

The first structure makes it clear that the derivation is "completed" in the sense that all syntactic features have been checked except for the C that indicates this is a CP, while the second structure is preferred by linguists for the obvious reason: it shows much more about the history of the derivation. Both structures are computed efficiently by various parsing methods, as mentioned above. We can see that in this structure, there is one incorporation step V-to-*v*, one affix-hopping step I-to-*v*, and one movement to check the Case feature of the subject.

With a different selection of lexical items we can derive:

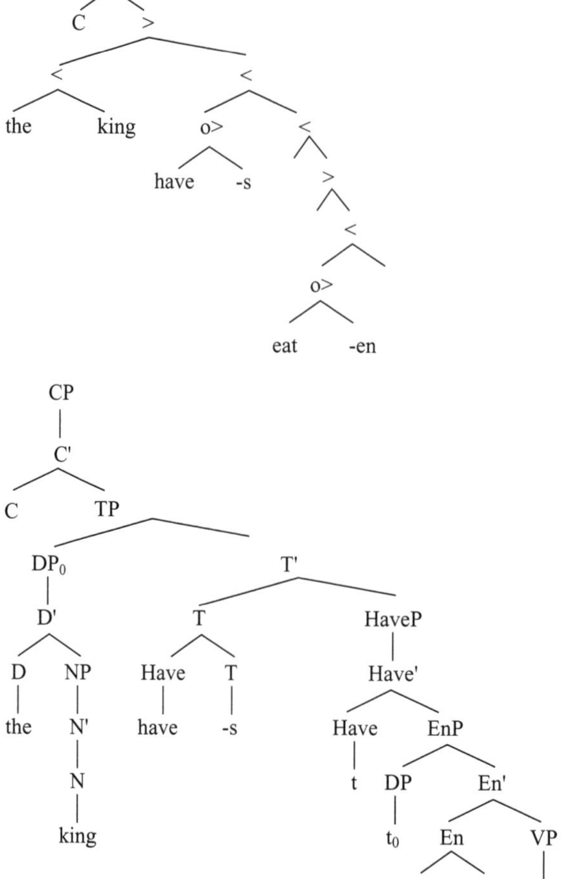

The grammar also allows *wh*-movement:

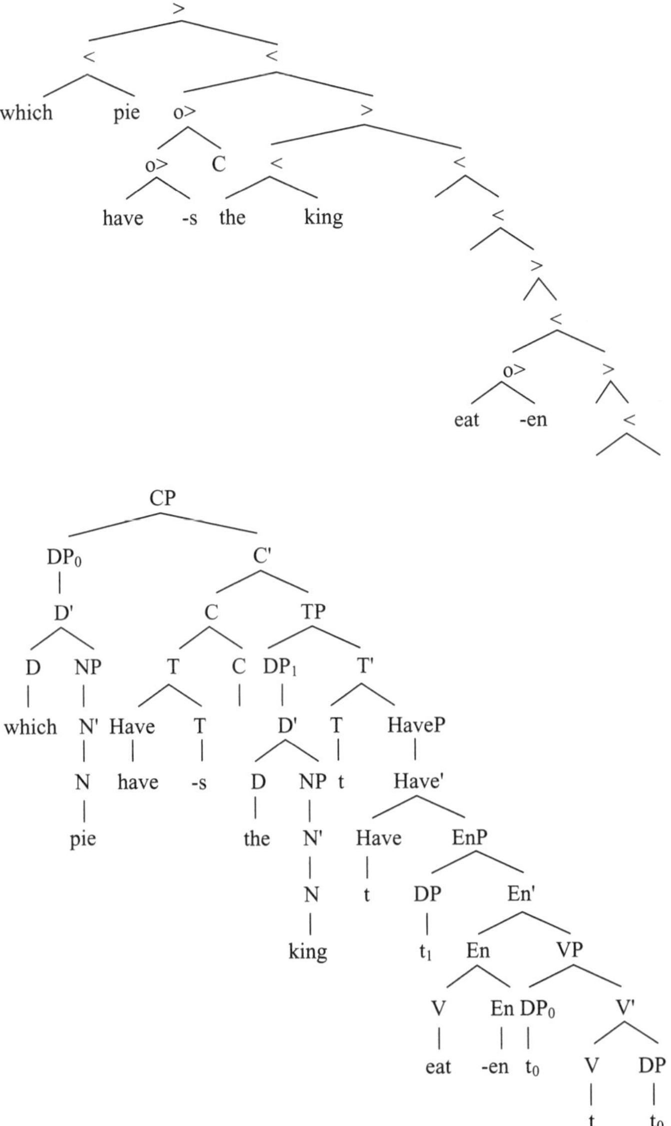

We can see that in this structure, there are three incorporation steps, two movements to check Case, and a movement to check the *wh*-feature of the subject.

Now, suppose that we add some lexical items from another language, such as these Spanish words:

-e:: =v +k T   -a:: ⇒Have +k T
haber:: =En Have   -ido:: ⇒V =D En
comer:: =D +k V   comer:: V   reír:: V
el:: =N D -k   cuál:: =N D -k -wh
rey:: N   pastel:: N

As with the English grammar, this one is obviously very simplified, but it illustrates the main point that we want to make about CS in the syntax. In the first place, simply by adding these seven Spanish words, we can derive structures like this:

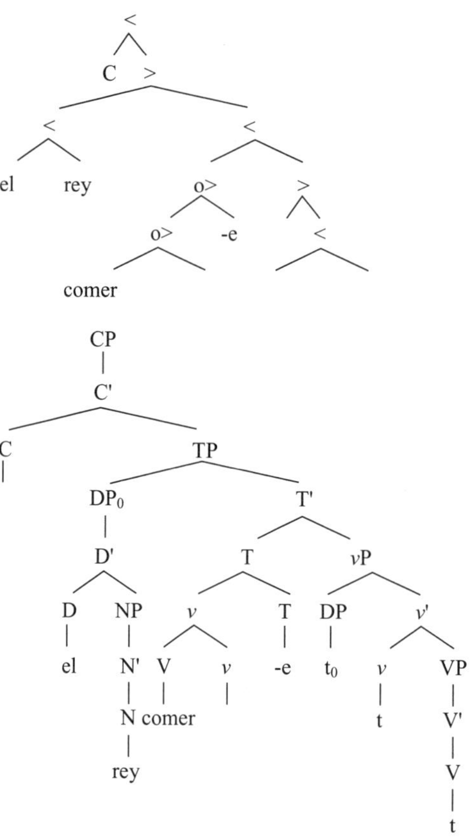

What is more interesting is that we also derive the CS structure:

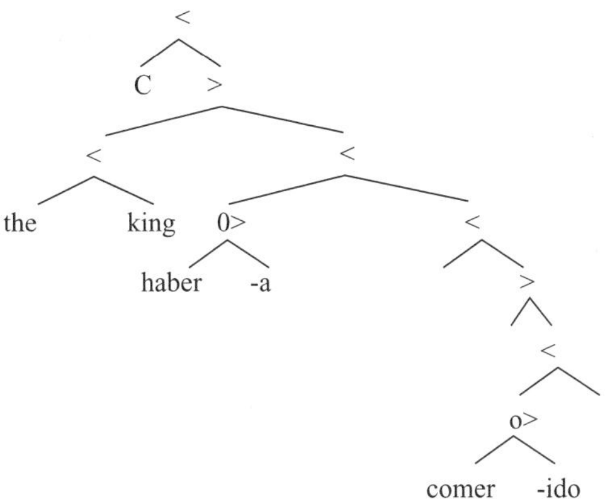

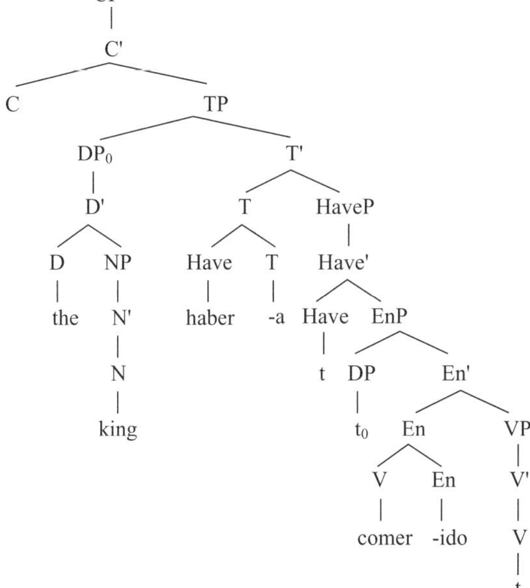

This is similar to good CS structures like (1a), and these structures emerge immediately, using only the mechanisms Merge and Move that are presumed to be universal.

Some puzzles remain, though. In particular, it is easy to see that the lexical items above will also allow us to derive structures like the following:

(21) *The king eat -*e.*

(22) *The king have *a* eat -*ido.*

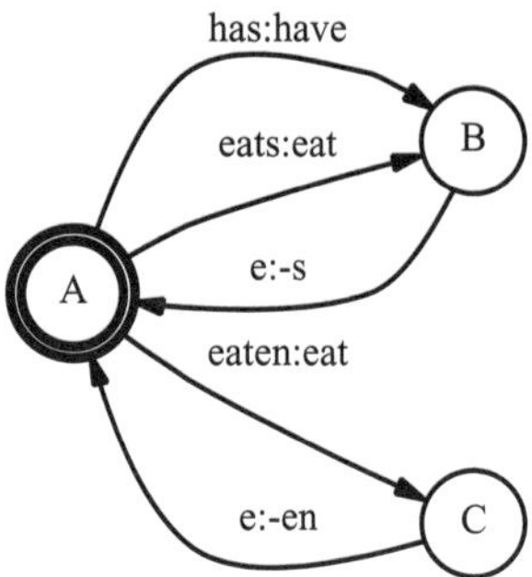

Figure 11.1
A simple finite-state machine

(23) *The   king   have-s   *comer*   *-ido*   *el*   *pastel.*
       the   king   has   eat   -en   the   pie

These are not good CS examples—compare (3) and (1b) above. In the next
section, we will see how to rule out examples like (21) and (22). The problem
with (23) is more interesting and we will consider it more carefully.

11.2.2 Morphophonology

There are various computational models of morphology and phonology. Since
almost all processes are local and surface oriented, finite-state representations
of these components do surprisingly well (Ellison 1994; Eisner 1997; Kaplan
and Kay 1994; Koskenniemi 1983). For the English part of the grammar in
the previous section, we want a morphological analysis of English to recognize
that *has* can be analyzed as *have -s*, *eats* can be analyzed as *eat -s*, and *eaten*
can be analyzed as *eat -en*. A simple finite-state machine like the one depicted
in figure 11.1 can encode these ideas.

To analyze an input, we begin in state A and traverse an arc labeled *x*: *y* and
y to accept *x* and analyze it as including *y*. We continue in this way through
the whole input, to reach a "final state" that is indicated by the double circle.
So in the simple machine in figure 11.1, we begin in state 0, and we can accept
has, outputting *have* and going into state B. Then to complete the analysis we
must be in a final state, so we traverse the arc back to state A, accepting the
empty string *e* and outputting the affix *-s*.

   We can get a simple version of *do*-support by analyzing *does* as the surface
realization of a stranded affix *-s*. Continuing in this way we can cover all of
the English forms allowed by the English syntax given above, yielding the
slightly complex machine shown in figure 11.2. So when we get an input string

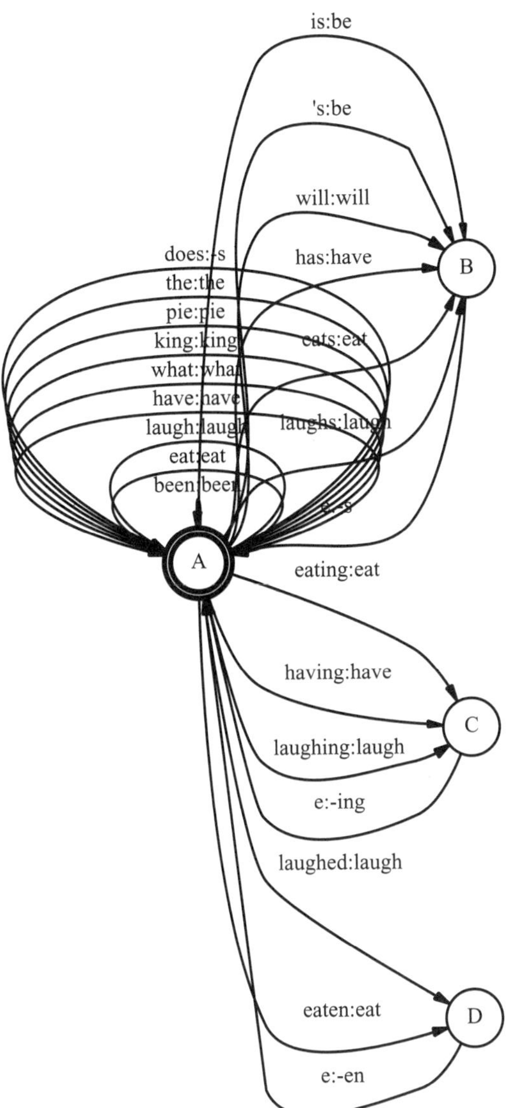

Figure 11.2
A simple finite-state morphology

like *what has the king eaten*, we can first compute all the possible morphological analyses by following all paths from the start state A to a final state to accept this string. In this case, there is only one such path, and it yields the output analysis *what have -s the king eat -en*. This can then be analyzed by the syntactic parser as described above.

11.2.2.1 Multilingual Morphophonology

Now suppose that we add morphophonological rules to the English machine described above. The input *come* can be mapped to *comer -e*, *ha* can be mapped to *haber -a*, and so on. Unlike the addition of lexical items in the syntax, the addition of these mappings does not introduce any word-internal CS at all. Consequently, we immediately have an explanation of why examples (21) and (22) are out, and this will extend to the examples in (3). The morphological analyzer by itself simply will not be able to accept words that mix elements from two languages. Example (23) remains to be explained, and we turn to it now.

Notice that the sequence of morphemes *the king has comida el pastel* will be mapped unproblematically to *The king have -s comer -ido el pastel*, and the grammar given above will, in fact, prove that this sequence of elements can be parsed as a complete CP. Since many Spanish-English speakers find structures like this one unnatural, as mentioned in the discussion of (1), we would like to block this structure. Notice that the Spanish-English codeswitching allowed by the lexicon above is so extensive because the categories of the Spanish elements are exactly the same as we already had in the English grammar. Furthermore, according to the specifics of the English auxiliary system coded by using categories that have unique English phonological realizations, *En* is the category of the affix *-en*, *Ing* is the category of the affix *-ing*, and so on. We needed these specific categories, because *-en* is our representation of the unique affix selected by the auxiliary *have*, and similarly for the other categories. When we added the Spanish lexical items above, we let the Spanish *ido* have the category *En*, which is perhaps not right. Suppose that we adjust the Spanish lexical items given above as follows:

haber:: =Ido Have   -ido:: ⇒V =D Ido

With this change, the problematic (23) cannot be derived, while the unproblematic CS examples are still derived as before.

This suggests that CS is based on exploiting the analogies between the categories of different languages, and it opens a place for learned codeswitching patterns that have been observed by Muysken (1998) and others.

11.3 Conclusions

The formal model presented here is very simple, but it has enough structure to realize the basic hypotheses with which we began. We have seen that the hypotheses from MacSwan 1999 can be expressed as the following independent ideas:

(24) When the syntax is lexicalized, so all crosslinguistic variation is due to the lexicon, CS is immediately predicted for mixed utterances.

(25) The extent of codeswitching in the syntax is based on the extent to which the categories of the different languages are assimilated, which allows for the influence of learned CS patterns.

(26) Morphophonology, based on linear position and ranked constraints, does not allow word-internal CS.

As the other chapters in the book have revealed, there is much more to say about each of these simple ideas, but the first steps taken here have been very straightforward, and so prospects for more sophisticated computational models of codeswitching language users look very good.

Note

1. Features that trigger right-adjoining head movement and left-adjoining affix lowering are provided in Stabler 2001a, but will not be needed here.

References

Belazi, H. M., E. J. Rubin, and J. A. Toribio. 1994. Code-switching and X-bar theory: The functional head constraint. *Linguistic Inquiry* 25:221–237.

Cardinaletti, Anna, and Ur Shlonsky. 2004. Clitic positions and restructuring in Italian. *Linguistic Inquiry* 35:519–557.

Chomsky, N. 1970. Remarks on nominalization. In R. Jacobs and P. Rosenbaum, eds., *Readings in English Transformational Grammar*, 184–221. Waltham, MA: Ginn.

Chomsky, N. 1981. *Lectures on Government and Binding*. Dordrecht: Foris.

Chomsky, N. 1995a. Bare phrase structure. In G. Webelhuth, ed., *Government and Binding Theory and the Minimalist Program*, 383–439. Cambridge, MA: MIT Press.

Chomsky, N. 1995b. *The Minimalist Program*. Cambridge, MA: MIT Press.

Cinque, Guglielmo. 2004. "Restructuring" and functional structure. In Adriana Belletti, ed. *Structures and Beyond: The Cartography of Syntactic Structures*, 132–191. Volume 3. Oxford: Oxford University Press.

Eisner, J. 1997. Efficient generation in primitive optimality theory. In *Proceedings of the 35th Annual Meeting of the Association for Computational Linguistics*.

Ellison, M. T. 1994. Phonological derivation in optimality theory. In *Proceedings of the 15th International Conference on Computational Linguistics*, COLING 1994, Volume 1: 1007–1013. Philadelphia, PA: Association for Computational Linguistics. Also available at the Edinburgh Computational Phonology Archive.

Fodor, J. D. 1998. Unambiguous triggers. *Linguistic Inquiry* 29:1–36.

Genesee, F. 1989. Early bilingual development: One language or two? *Journal of Child Language* 16:161–179.

Gibson, E., and K. Wexler. 1994. Triggers. *Linguistic Inquiry* 25:407–454.

Grosjean, F. 1982. *Life with Two Languages*. Cambridge, MA: Harvard University Press.

Harkema, H. 2000. A recognizer for minimalist grammars. Paper presented at the Sixth International Workshop on Parsing Technologies, IWPT2000, 111-122. Trento, Italy: ITC-IRST

Hyams, N. 1986. Language Acquisition and the Theory of Parameters. Boston: Reidel.

Joshi, A. 1985a. How much context-sensitivity is necessary for characterizing structural descriptions? In D. Dowty, L. Karttunen, and A. Zwicky, eds., *Natural Language Processing: Theoretical, Computational and Psychological Perspectives*, 206–250. New York: Cambridge University Press.

Joshi, A. 1985b. Processing of sentences with intrasentential code-switching. In D. Dowty, L. Karttunen, and A. Zwicky, eds., *Natural Language Processing: Theoretical, Computational and Psychological Perspectives*, 190–205. New York: Cambridge University Press.

Kaplan, R., and M. Kay. 1994. Regular models of phonological rule systems. *Computational Linguistics* 20:331–378.

Kayne, R. 1994. *The Antisymmetry of Syntax*. Cambridge, MA: MIT Press.

Koskenniemi, K. 1983. Two-level morphology. University of Helsinki, ms.

Lee, F. 2000. VP remnant movement and VSO in Quiaviní Zapotec. In A. Carnie and E. Guilfoyle, eds., *The Syntax of Verb Initial Languages*. Oxford: Oxford University Press.

Lee, M. H. 1991. A parametric approach to code-mixing. Doctoral dissertation, State University of New York at Stony Brook.

Leopold, W. F. 1970. *Speech Development of a Bilingual Child*. New York: AMS Press.

Lightfoot, D. 1989. The child's trigger experience: Degree-0 learnability. *Behavioral and Brain Sciences* 12:321–375.

Lipski, J. 1985. *Linguistic Aspects of Spanish-English Language Switching*. Tempe: Center for Latin American Studies, Arizona State University.

MacSwan, J. 1999. A Minimalist Approach to Intrasentential Code Switching. New York: Garland.

MacSwan, J. 2000. The architecture of the bilingual language faculty: Evidence from codeswitching. *Bilingualism: Language and Cognition* 3 (1): 37–54.

MacSwan, J. 2004. Code switching and linguistic theory, pp. 415–462. In T. K. Bhatia & W. Ritchie (eds.), *Handbook of bilingualism*. Oxford: Blackwell.

MacSwan, J. 2013. Code switching and linguistic theory, pp. 223–350. In T. K. Bhatia & W. Ritchie (Eds.), *Handbook of Bilingualism and Multilingualism*, 2nd edition. Oxford: Blackwell.

Mahootian, S. 1993. A null theory of codeswitching. Doctoral dissertation, Northwestern University.

Meisel, J. M. 1989. Early differentiation of languages in bilingual children. In L. K. Obler, ed., *Bilingualism across the Lifespan: Aspects of Acquisition, Maturity, and Loss*. New York: Cambridge University Press.

Meisel, J. M. 1994. Code switching in young bilingual children: The acquisition of grammatical constraints. *Studies in Second Language Acquisition* 16:413–439.

Michaelis, J. 1998. Derivational minimalism is mildly context-sensitive. In *Proceedings, Logical Aspects of Computational Linguistics, LACL'98*. Grenoble. http://www.ling.uni-potsdam.de/~michael/papers.html.

Morawietz, F. 2000. Chart parsing and constraint programming. In *Proceedings of COLING-2000*.

Muysken, P. 1998. Accommodation strategies in language contact. In Utrecht Congress on Storage and Computation in Linguistics.

Myers-Scotton, C. 2001. The matrix language frame model: Developments and responses. In R. Jacobson, ed., *Codeswitching worldwide II*, 23–58. Berlin: Mouton de Gruyter.

Nishimura, M. 1985. Intrasentential code-switching in Japanese and English. Doctoral dissertation, University of Pennsylvania.

Newmeyer, F. 2009. Current challenges to the Lexicalist Hypothesis: An overview and critique, pp. 91–116. In William Lewis, Simin Karimi, Heidi Harley, and Scott Farrar, eds. *Time and Again: Theoretical Perspectives on Formal Linguistics: In Honor of D. Terrence Langendoen*. Amsterdam: John Benjamins Publishing.

Pensel, I. 1979. Testeni. *Hor Yezh* 126:47–73.

Poplack, S. 1981. Syntactic structure and the social functions of code-switching. In R. P. Duran, ed., *Latino Language and Communicative Behavior*. Norwood, NJ: Ablex.

Rizzi, L. 1982. *Issues in Italian Syntax*. Dordrecht: Foris.

Rizzi, L. 1990. *Relativized Minimality*. Cambridge, MA: MIT Press.

Roberts, I. 1998. Have/be raising, move F, and procrastinate. *Linguistic Inquiry* 29:113–125.

Roeper, T. 2000. Universal bilingualism. *Bilingualism: Language and Cognition* 2.

Stabler, E. P. 1997. Derivational minimalism. In C. Retoré, ed., *Logical Aspects of Computational Linguistics*, 68–95. Lecture Notes in Computer Science 1328. New York: Springer-Verlag.

Stabler, E. P. 2001. Minimalist grammars and recognition. In C. Rohrer, A. Rossdeutscher, and H. Kamp, eds., *Linguistic Form and Its Computation*. Stanford, CA: CSLI.

Stenson, N. 1990. Phrase structure congruence, government, and Irish-English code switching. *Syntax and Semantics*, 23:167–197.

Swain, M. K. 1972. Bilingualism as a first language. Doctoral dissertation, University of California, Irvine.

Troadec, B. 1983. Tri fennad-kaoz gant an Itron Bernadette Troadec. *Hor Yezh*, 71–127.

Volterra, V., and T. Taeschner. 1978. The acquisition and development of language by bilingual children. *Journal of Child Language* 5:311–326.

Woolford, E. 1983. Bilingual code-switching and syntactic theory. *Linguistic Inquiry* 14:520–536.

Yang, C. 2000. Knowledge and learning in natural language. Doctoral dissertation, MIT.

Zagona, K. 1988. Verb Phrase Syntax: A Parametric Study of English and Spanish. Kluwer: Boston.

12 Language Dominance and Codeswitching Asymmetries

Ana Teresa Pérez-Leroux, Erin O'Rourke, and
Gretchen Sunderman

12.1 Introduction

Intrasentential codeswitching—that is, the use of more than one language in
the production of a sentence—has been noted to follow regular grammatical
and stylistic patterns (Timm 1975, Lipski 1978, Poplack 1980, Woolford 1983,
MacSwan 2004, 2009, chapter 1 [this volume], and many others). Discussion
surrounding codeswitching concerns its status as evidence for the integrity (as
opposed to the fusion) of the two grammatical systems involved. The basic
observation is that switching has observably restricted distributions. Linguists
have described specific patterns of language alternation in terms of grammatical constraints, and they have accordingly proposed various theoretical models
to account for such constraints.

Syntactic models of codeswitching restrictions can be differentiated by
means of two criteria: first, how they treat questions about the scope of application of the proposed constraints (i.e., are constraints universal or relevant
only to the interaction of specific language pairs?), and second, how they treat
issues of directionality in language switching (i.e., is codeswitching asymmetric?). We understand the notion in the sense defined by Joshi (1985), as
when a category of the matrix or base grammar can switch to another category
in the embedded grammar, but not vice versa). In this chapter we measure
online processing of mixed sentences to explore these issues. Specifically, we
examine the validity of some (presumably universal) constraints on codeswitching (between subjects and predicates, and before embedded clauses), and find
that they seem to apply in an asymmetric fashion, with language dominance
being the variable that determines asymmetric performance.

The chapter is organized as follows. Section 12.2 examines various grammatical models of codeswitching. Section 12.3 discusses processing research
on language mixing, with a focus on the question of the cost of language
mixing. Section 12.4 reports a reaction-time study testing codeswitching

among highly fluent Spanish-English bilinguals. Experimental materials included single-language and mixed-language sentences designed to test switching between pronominal and lexical subjects and their predicates, and at the left edge of embedded clauses, before and after the complementizer. Sections 12.5 and 12.6 present discussion and conclusions, respectively.

12.2 Grammatical Models of Codeswitching

12.2.1 The Null Hypothesis

Much research on codeswitching follows the general path advocated by Woolford (1983), which suggests that restrictions in the distribution of switching points emerge from the free interaction between two grammatical systems. Under this perspective, termed the Null Hypothesis (Mahootian 1993), parsimonious accounts of codeswitching should avoid proposing grammatical mechanisms relevant to codeswitching alone. While generally sharing this goal, models vary substantially on the basic assumptions required to implement the Null Hypothesis, as well as on the content of their specific grammatical predictions. We discuss below the differences between various models, concentrating on the following questions: first, is the application of the proposed constraints universal (in a typological sense), and second, is their application symmetrical (from L1 to L2 and from L2 to L1) or not?

12.2.2 The Linguistic Scope of the Proposed Constraints

Codeswitching models can be broadly classified according to the scope of the restrictions they predict (i.e., are the constraints on switching generally applicable to all language pairs, or only to some?). On one side of the spectrum are models that propose fixed constraints applicable to all possible language pairs. Among the first proposed general constraints was Poplack's (1980) Equivalence Constraint, which predicted the grammaticality of switches that resulted from congruent word-order patterns. Other proposals aiming at universal scope include Di Sciullo, Muysken, and Singh's (1986) Government Constraint (ruling out codeswitching between a governor and the governed category) and Joshi's (1985) Constraint on Closed-Class Items (CCIC) (which ruled out switches between a closed-class item and an open-class item). The role of word order, government relations, and functional (i.e., closed-class) elements was further explored in subsequent universal scope models. Mahootian (1993) and Mahootian and Santorini (1996) integrate issues of government with issues of directionality by suggesting that the language of a head determines the phrase structure of its complement. Incorporating minimalist insights into the study of language switching, Belazi, Rubin, and Toribio (1994) propose a Functional

Head Constraint (FHC) (which rules out switches between functional heads and their complements). The FHC has been criticized on empirical grounds, because of many obvious counterexamples (for instance, it prohibits switches between determiners and nouns). It has also been criticized on theoretical grounds, because it requires the coding of "language" as a special formal feature, and because of introducing feature checking between heads and complements. This is problematic because heads and their complements are not considered checking domains under some theories (Mahootian and Santorini 1996; MacSwan 1999). In fairness, it must be pointed out that the formal difficulties of the FHC disappear if it is understood as stating the formally unproblematic and intuitively appealing notion that all extended projections of a category (in the sense of Grimshaw 1991) are generated within the same language.[1]

Other models, assuming that the mechanisms excluding sentences in single-language utterances are the same as the mechanisms excluding ungrammatical codeswitching sentences, predict language-specific distributional restrictions on codeswitching on the basis, not of a fixed constraint, but on the properties of the specific grammatical components interacting in a given language pair (Lipski 1998; Muysken 2000). For instance, examining various (presumably universal) constraints proposed in the literature, Choi (1991) presents evidence that these simply do not surface in Korean-English codeswitching. Rejecting broad-application universal constraints, Choi argues for a number of viable specific language-pair constraints, which originate from the need to maintain the integrity of a particular language pair. MacSwan (1999, 2004) arrives at a comparable perspective by applying to codeswitching the logic of minimalist syntax, in which ungrammaticality is the result of a conflict between lexical entries and the formal features entering a derivation.

12.2.3 The Issue of Asymmetry

Codeswitching models also diverge in how they deal with issues of directionality in language switching constraints: Do constraints apply identically from L_A to L_B and from L_B to L_A? Although theoretically oriented accounts tend to be inherently symmetric (Di Sciullo, Muysken, and Singh 1986; Belazi, Rubin, and Toribio 1994, etc.), and accounts interested in language processing such as Joshi (1985) and Myers-Scotton (1993) seem to favor an asymmetric view, this correspondence is accidental, as we show below in our discussion of MacSwan.

Joshi (1985) approaches codeswitching from the perspective of language generation. Assuming on the part of the bilingual (i) a balanced and consistent knowledge of language, (ii) fluent, uninterrupted speech production, and (iii) simultaneous activation of both members of the language pair, he proposed systematic interaction between the two grammars in language production/ processing. In this view, both speaker and hearer agree that a given sentence is generated in one of the languages (the matrix language), with the other language (the embedded language) interacting systematically with the matrix language, in particular, obeying a constraint on closed-class items (CCIC). Myers-Scotton's model adopts this matrix/embedded language distinction, but it modifies the form and spirit of the constraints. In her formulation, the matrix language frames the surface positions as well as "system" elements, which include some closed-class items and inflections. The embedded language, in contrast, can only supply content morphemes. A highly problematic aspect of the matrix language model is the vague and unorthodox approach to the notion of "system" (as opposed to "content") morphemes. Closed-class elements are considered system morphemes, but semantic factors such as discourse emphasis may lead to a reclassification as a content morpheme, with criteria that seem grammatically unclear. Also problematic is the treatment of matrix language selection as a dynamic process, open to change within the same interaction. Although sociolinguistic and psycholinguistic criteria are invoked, token frequency is the sole criterion used in the identification of the matrix language. This approach empties all the predictive power of the model, since counterexamples are allowed to reflect ad hoc switches in the base (i.e., matrix) language.

One contribution of Myers-Scotton's work is the reintroduction into the debate of issues of asymmetry in the operation of constraints. The problem of asymmetry is clearly different from the problem of universality, but the two have often been confounded in the linguistic literature. Most often, these matters are not treated separately when researchers reflect on the desirable properties of a given model. Joshi's CCIC aims to achieve general scope, and asymmetry is a fundamental property of his model. Myers-Scotton's original matrix language framework is also an inherently asymmetric model, but by allowing contextually tied changes of matrix language, it fails to generate clearly testable predictions. In subsequent work on the notion of matrix language, Jake, Myers-Scotton, and Gross (2002) restrict its application to the CP domain. These authors suggest that only one language is the source of the morphosyntactic frame structuring the bilingual CP. In formal terms, this means that only one language supplies the formal features used in the derivation of the CP, but that this language can switch across CPs.

MacSwan's minimalist model does not directly address asymmetry, but has the interesting characteristic that the differences in the formal features listed for the functional lexicons of the grammars involved allow switching points to vary (asymmetrically) across language pairs. In other words, his minimalist model allows language-specific scope of restricted distributions, and indeed he finds examples of this: Spanish negation cannot precede a Nahuatl verb, but Nahuatl negation can precede a Spanish verb. The flexibility depends on the features encoded in lexical entries of the two negative particles (the former is a clitic, the latter is not). Importantly, the syntactic difference can be independently established for the lexical entries and formal features available in the monolingual grammar. For this reason, the model favors asymmetry in places where the inventory of formal features of the two languages is divergent.

12.2.4 Methodological Issues

It is important to stress that the different studies discussed so far share similar explanatory and empirical goals, because this fact may be lost in the diversity of approaches pursued. When findings across different researchers are not congruent, methodological issues are used as a last resort to settle a dispute. The problem of verifiability is worsened by sociological factors specific to the study of bilingualism.

Data gathering on monolingual grammars proceeds by a less-than-perfect but most of the time reasonably smooth interaction between positive data (corpus sentences) and negative data (grammaticality judgments that define the boundaries of the possible sentences). In bilingual research, both forms of data gathering involve further methodological limitations, both qualitatively and quantitatively. Corpus data based on spontaneous production, although preferred by some on the basis of ecological validity, are generally not coded with sufficient phonological detail, such as the degree of phonological integration, small pauses, or intonation breaks. The potential problems are easy to illustrate. For instance, a Spanish-English corpus may contain determiner-noun switches such as (1):

(1)   The jefe *was here.*   (*determiner + noun*)
       the boss was here

Some theories predict determiner-noun switches to be ungrammatical (such as the FHC), while others (such as the Equivalence Constraint or the Government Constraint) may predict the same switch to be grammatical. Insufficiently detailed data coding allows the transcription to be ambiguous between (2a) and (2b):

(2)   a. The jefe was here.
       b. The ... "jefe" ... was here.

Sentence (2a) supports the view that deteminer-noun switches are grammatical, whereas sentence (2b) supports the opposite view.

Quantity of data is an additional factor limiting the strength of inferences from corpus studies. Most sentences in a given bilingual corpus are not mixed, so that description of the behavior of specific boundaries typically relies on data that are often statistically insufficient. Missing examples may be the result of possible (but unattested) boundaries, and speech errors could be counted as instances of grammatical switches. Grammaticality judgments, the often preferred source of data for low-frequency constructions in monolingual research, are considered by some researchers to be methodologically vulnerable or even sociolinguistically suspect in bilingual populations. In practice, the usual difficulties in obtaining clear judgment data from speakers are compounded by the stigma attached to codeswitching. This point has been made elsewhere (see, for instance, Azuma 1991).

In sum, methods used yield data that underdetermine the increasingly sophisticated nature of the theoretical claims, a problem many authors have already noted. Both caution and the use of multiple methods for triangulation have been recommended in the literature (Rubin and Toribio 1995; MacSwan 1999). In general, codeswitching research has underutilized the experimental techniques developed for the study of bilingual memory and bilingual processing. Some of these approaches are suitable and are already in use for the study of syntax, both in the cognitive psychology literature and in second language acquisition research. When viable in a given population, these methods may provide fine-grained means of testing the status of particular constraints, as well as a better operationalization of the notion of base language.

12.2.5 Subject Pronouns in Codeswitching

The absence of switching involving subject pronouns was observed early in the literature on Spanish-English switching (Timm 1975; Lipski 1978). Timm (1975) was the first to note that bilinguals who will freely codeswitch at other points in the sentence will object to switches between subject pronouns and verbs:

(3)   *Yo *went.*
      'I went.'

Poplack (1980, 260) questioned this observation: "Why should it be possible to switch codes between a subject and a verb only if that subject is not pronominal?" Later evidence from other languages is mixed. Choi (1991) identifies eighteen tokens of subject pronoun–predicate switches in his Korean-English corpus, but Azuma's (1991) Japanese-English study finds no evidence of switching with pronouns. The evidence is difficult to assess, since reported data often does not allow readers to make the comparison required: How much less frequent are pronoun switches in comparison with other types of subject-predicate switches? Berk-Seligson's (1986) data on Spanish-Hebrew alternations shows a high disproportion between overall switches with pronouns in comparison with other NPs: 0.3% versus 40%. Unfortunately, neither the function of these pronouns and NPs nor a relative baseline of pronoun frequency is discussed. In the token cited in her article, the subject happens to be a demonstrative pronoun and not a subject pronoun, which leaves open the question of subject pronoun switches.

A detailed study of codeswitching with pronouns is that of Jake (1994). She finds clear (but asymmetric and typologically specific) restrictions on the distribution of subject pronoun switches. In her analysis, null subject languages (Spanish, Arabic, Japanese, etc.) and clitic subject languages (French, etc.) have subject pronouns that are "system" morphemes, whereas non-prodrop/ nonclitic subject languages such as English have subject pronouns that are classified as "content" morphemes. Use of embedded language pronouns (of the content type) is excluded for sentences where the matrix language has system subject pronouns. For instance, a Spanish pronoun may not be embedded in an utterance where English is the matrix language. She identifies embedded language pronouns (for languages of the second type) in mixed constituents, but only if they are focused pronouns ("discourse-emphatic," in her terms) or indefinite pronouns in argument (i.e., nonclitic) position. To explain examples like (4), Jake (1994, 284) claims that "an emphatic EL pronoun from English is congruent with an emphatic pronoun in Spanish, the ML."

(4) *You* estás diciéndole la pregunta in the wrong person.
     'You are asking the question to the wrong person.'
     (Sankoff and Poplack 1981)

Interestingly, Jake finds no evidence of switching with expletive pronouns in any of the languages involved. These observations, although fascinating, are difficult to generalize because they are framed in the grammatical terminology of the MLF, where notions such as categorical status (clitics vs. nonclitic) and thematic status (expletive vs. thematic subjects) are lumped together under the system-content contrast.[2]

Further empirical evidence on pronouns is found in MacSwan's (1999) study of Nahuatl-Spanish contact (both null pronoun languages, and hence with subject pronouns classified as system morphemes). He identifies instances of Spanish pronouns functioning as subjects of Nahuatl sentences. Since Nahuatl should be the matrix language by the frequency-based criterion of

Myers-Scotton, these sentences falsify the predictions of the MLF, which would prohibit lexical insertion of embedded language morphemes.

An interesting fact in MacSwan's Spanish-Nahuatl data is the existence of grammatical-person asymmetries. His participants accepted switches between a Spanish subject pronoun and the predicate in the case of third-person subject pronouns, but rejected parallel switches involving first- and second-person subject pronouns. Nahuatl subject pronouns were marginal or ungrammatical with Spanish verbs.

(5)   *Yo ni-k-koa-s   tlake-me-tl.
       I 1Sg-3Osg-buy-Fut garment-Pl-NSF
       'I will buy clothes.'

(6)   *Tú ti-k-koa-s   tlake-me-tl.
       you 2Sg-3Osg-buy-Fut garment-Pl-NSF
       'You will buy clothes.'

(7)   El/Ella 0-ki-koa-s   tlake-me-tl.
       He/she ∅-3Osg-buy-Fut garment-Pl-NSF
       'He/she will buy clothes.'
       (MacSwan 1999)

Codeswitching appeared only when subject agreement was absent—that is, with a third-person Nahuatl verb. In MacSwan's minimalist terms, restrictions on codeswitching arise for the same reasons ungrammaticality arises in single-language utterances: either the derivation crashes (some features remain unchecked) or is canceled (there is a feature mismatch). The Tense head must match in features with the subject pronoun, but the two languages do not fully match with respect to pronoun features, and the restriction described follows from this. Spanish encodes gender on pronouns, but Nahuatl does not. When overt agreement is missing, the verb does not have to raise and there is no feature mismatch. Spanish verbs always raise and the feature mismatches with the Nahuatl pronouns cancel the derivations.

12.2.6   Complementizers and Codeswitching

Another syntactic context under debate is the switching between a matrix clause and its embedded complement, and whether complementizers can be switched. Both switches before and after the complementizer are attested in the literature:

(8)   *Italian-French* (Di Sciullo, Muysken, and Singh 1986)
       Basta che *marche*.
       '(It) suffices that (it) works.'

(9) *English-Irish* (Stenson 1990)
    I am telling you *go raibh faitíos orainn.*
    I am telling you that be-PA fear on-us
    'I am telling you that we were scared.'

Word-order-based constraints such as Poplack's Equivalence Constraint predict the left edge of an embedded clause to be an unproblematic switchpoint in languages with comparable word orders. In contrast, models focusing on functional morphemes or on structural configurations argue about potential restrictions involving the complementizer. In Joshi's approach, switching the complementizer, a closed-class item, would result in ungrammaticality. Di Sciullo, Muysken, and Singh (1986) would derive the same effect from the government relation existing between the verb and the embedded CP. Mahootian (1993) derives it from the complement status of the CP. In contrast, Belazi, Rubin, and Toribio's FHC predicts ungrammaticality for switches between the complementizer and its complement. MacSwan's Nahuatl-Spanish corpus does not suggest evidence of restrictions in this environment, and the issue is left open.

In the Myers-Scotton framework what matters is not the switching point, but the fact that the complementizer itself appears in the matrix language. Reviewing data from a variety of languages, she argues that "COMPs in ML [Matrix Language] + EL [Embedded Language] constituents come only in ML (except in some cases such as the troublesome Lingala one). Also, ML COMPs may head ML sentential complements; but EL sentential complements (as islands) may have only ML or null COMPs" (Myers-Scotton 1993, 132).

The MLF differs from other theories in that the ungrammaticality of complementizer switches is evaluated as relative to the setting of a matrix/embedded language. In a more recent version (Jake, Myers-Scotton, and Gross 2002), the model specifies that the ML does not change within a single bilingual CP. Under that formulation, one may assume that the MLF predicts that switches before Comp are favored over switches after Comp.

At this point it is relevant to distinguish between approaches that use the notion of switching constituents versus that of switching points. Because linear approaches are not valid models of natural language sentences, the only valid expression of the notion of switching point is as referring to a switch between a given node and its c-command domains. Approaches that assume a base language (Joshi 1985, Myers-Scotton 1993, or Jake, Myers-Scotton, and Gross 2002) tend to treat switches as insertional (i.e., the insertion of a node or whole constituent inside a base language structure), whereas most generative-oriented models view even the insertion of a single lexical item within a constituent as two switches, one expressing the relation between the lexical item and the base sentence into which it was inserted, and then the other between the lexical item and its c-command domain. For instance, in a given sequence V Comp N, where the whole sentence is in L_A, but Comp is in L_B, the sequence is considered to contain two switches: one switch in the relationship to the verb in L_A and the CP projection of an L_B Comp, and a second switch in the merging of that L_B Comp to an IP in L_A. So, for the purpose of the present study, we focus on switches involving a whole clause. In this way, we isolate the effect of one switch without involving a second switch. Specifically, we seek to test the effect of switching at the juncture of a verb and its embedded (CP) complement, and between a complementizer and its (IP) sentential complement.

12.3 Language Dominance and the Processing of Language Mixing

Some fundamental questions about codeswitching cannot be addressed using traditional linguistic methodologies. Is there a processing cost to codeswitching? What determines how words in mixed utterances are recognized? We consider these questions in order to examine the potential contribution of online studies in settling some of the empirical disputes in the codeswitching literature. Although writers on bilingualism have marveled at the seemingly effortless ability to go from one language into the other, we have limited understanding of the nature of the process that underlies this skill.

The observation that both languages are activated in parallel in bilinguals' two language systems during comprehension and production is now commonplace in the psycholinguistic literature (See de Groot 2011 for a complete overview of the current literature in pscyholinguistics related to bilinguals and multilinguals.) Much of the research investigating language activation and selection has focused on the lexical level and the question of how the parallel activation is resolved (i.e., how specific words are selected.) Fewer studies have focused on the psycholinguistic processing of mixed language sentences. In the next section, we review some of the earlier studies that focused on mixed language utterances.

Some of the early research on bilingual memory used mixed-language sentences as stimuli, thus generating indirect observations about the effect of sentence-internal language mixing. Altarriba et al. (1996) explored the effect of sentence context in mixed-language utterances, testing whether these effects were operating at a conceptual or at a lexical retrieval level. For high-frequency words, subjects had longer fixation times in high-constraint sentences than in low-constraint sentences. Sentence context appeared to influence conceptual-level expectations about upcoming words in a sentence, as well as specific lexical-level expectations about the word (i.e., language of the target item). In a subsequent study testing the cross-language semantic effect of repetition (i.e., with translation equivalents), Altarriba and Soltano (1996) found important differences between the processing of words in lists as opposed to inside mixed sentences. They obtained a 13% facilitation recall effect when translation equivalents were embedded in lists, in contrast to a 3% inhibitory recall effect when sentences were embedded in a mixed sentence such as (10):

(10) Mike learned to drive y empezó a manejar al trabajo. (drive-manejar)
      'Mike learned to drive and began to drive to work.'
      (Altarriba and Soltano 1996)

The inhibition effect in their results was, however, much smaller than previous findings. In a reply to Altarriba and Soltano, McKay and colleagues argued that the semantic blindness effect could be increased with manipulations of variables such as length, speed of presentation, and predictability of switching point (MacKay et al. 1996).

The relevance of this debate for the codeswitching literature pertains to the question of a processing cost for codeswitching—a large inhibition effect indicates a processing delay introduced by language mixing. Altarriba and Solano pointed out that some of MacKay and Miller's (1992) sentences were linguistically substandard, because at times they inserted a Spanish translation equivalent into an English semantic frame, mixing the languages in a way that was not natural to a bilingual person (i.e., their stimuli contained "ungrammatical switches"). To avoid similar problems, Altarriba and Soltano placed their switched nouns conservatively, at intersentential boundaries in conjoined sentences. MacKay et al. (1996) replied—incorrectly—that such observations were irrelevant to the question of the size of the inhibitory effect. If the mixed-language stimuli consisted of ungrammatical switches, it is very likely that the delay effect would not be a result of inhibition but instead a response delay caused by ungrammaticality.

The findings from research on phonological production and perception in mixed sentences support the view that delay effects do not originate from switching the lexicons alone. Soares and Grosjean (1984) reported on a series of short studies in which codeswitched words were gated (parceled out and presented in segments) showing that guest languages with ambiguous segments are initially recognized as belonging to the base language. This bias diminished with successive exposure to language mixing. Li (1996) also examined spoken word recognition in mixed sentences, using first a self-paced presentation gating procedure, and subsequently a shadowing procedure. His results indicate that Chinese-English bilinguals can recognize codeswitched words with the same amount of information as required by monolingual English listeners. For mixed sentences, words with guest language phonetics were easier to process, so that phonetically distinct codeswitched words were processed faster than comparable, phonologically adapted, "borrowed" words.

Other sources of evidence on bilingual production are congruent with this finding. Grosjean and Miller (1994) discuss prior perception research indicating the presence of a momentary effect of the base language, such that a bilingual subject is slightly delayed in recognizing a guest language word. Testing whether this base language effect existed in production, they came to the conclusion that pronouncing codeswitched words was no different from pronouncing the same words in a monolingual context: no base language phonetic momentum was carried over to the switched segments.

Several early psycholinguistic studies examined mixed language for its own sake. Kolers (1966) and MacNamara and Kushnir (1971) found a cost for intrasentential codeswitches as compared to intersentential codeswitches. Later work by Wakefield (1975) indicated that switching appeared to be faster at major constituent boundaries than in phrase-internal positions. Some of these studies have been critiqued for the uncontrolled selection of the target stimuli, which resulted in unnatural examples of mixed-language sentences. Rakowsky (1989) tried to correct some of the previous methodological problems. Her study compared sentences where switching took place at phrasal boundaries with sentences where switching took place across phrase boundaries. These are illustrated by (11) and (12), respectively. Sentences were also counterbalanced across languages.

(11) In the spring, *los árboles son verdes*.

(12) In the spring, the *árboles son* green.
      'In the spring, the trees are green.'
      (Rakowsky 1989)

In her study, the whole sentence was presented on screen and disappeared when the subjects responded by pressing a key to indicate their judgment of the sentence's felicity. Her subjects (fluent Spanish-English bilinguals) had similar reaction times for switches at phrasal boundaries as for monolingual sentences, but slower reaction times for phrase-internal switches. While corroborating the view that codeswitching is rule governed, these results cannot evaluate online processing of specific switchpoints for two reasons. First, the phrase-internal switches involved at least two points of switching: the onset of the guest language and the return to the base language, thus involving two switchpoints around a variety of functional words. Second, the whole-sentence mode of presentation did not permit an online measuring delay at the specific moment of codeswitching.

Azuma (1991) studied intrasentential codeswitching with the goal of exploring speech-planning models. In an elicited imitation study, subjects had longer reaction times and more errors in sentences where closed-class words were switched than for switches of open-class words. One of her studies contrasted switching of prepositions versus nouns using sentences that mixed English (a prepositional language) and Japanese (a postpositional language).

(13) hoomonkyaku   ni   kuruma   *by*   ko-naiyoo   tanonda
      visitor   to   car   by   come-NEG   asked
      '… asked visitor not to come *by* car'

(14) hoomonkyaku   ni   *car*   de   ko-naiyoo   tanonda
      visitor   to   car   by   come-NEG   asked
      '… asked visitor not to come by *car*'
      (Azuma 1991)

The second study contrasted determiner-versus-noun switches among English-Spanish bilinguals.

(15) … estaba bastante enfadado porque *his* equipo había perdido …
      '… was fairly mad because *his* team had lost …'

(16) … estaba bastante enfadado porque su *team* había perdido …
      '… was fairly mad because his *team* had lost …'
      (Azuma 1991)

As in Rakowsky's study, we are unable to assess the result of one specific switchpoint because there is both a switch into a guest language and a return to the base language.

Finally, Azuma (1993) conducted a production study, which elicited spontaneous switching by instructing subjects to shift languages in the middle of the sentence whenever a tone was heard. Subjects seemed to be packaging phrases in one language, given that most switches were performed at phrasal boundaries. This phrasal integrity effect extended to fairly complex constituents: when subjects heard the tone in the middle of a relative clause, they completed the construction without switching (235). These subjects did not produce unintelligible utterances when forced to switch midsentence and basically respected the integrity of words and phrases. These results, although interesting on their own, do not directly address questions relevant to the evaluation of specific syntactic models of codeswitching.

12.4 Study

12.4.1 Goals of the Study

An online study was designed to explore proposed syntactic constraints as well as issues of asymmetry in codeswitching. In a population of highly fluent Spanish-English bilinguals living in the United States, we tested the effect of switching between predicates and their preceding subjects (both lexical and pronominal), and between main and embedded clauses (before and after the complementizer).

Our goal was to explore the following questions:

a. Is there a processing cost for mixing languages intrasententially?
b. If there is a cost, is it the result of the ungrammaticality of sentences where languages are mixed at noncongruent points, or does it affect both grammatical and ungrammatical switches?
c. Can categorically perceived ungrammaticality of certain switchpoints be quantitatively measured using an online task?
d. If ungrammaticality can be measured, is the sensitivity to the ungrammaticality of switches symmetrical with respect to language (i.e., equally detectable from L_A to L_B as from L_B to L_A)?
e. Does language dominance affect patterns of sensitivity to the grammaticality of given switching points?

12.4.2 Participants

Twenty-seven fluent Spanish-English bilinguals were initially recruited in the study. All participants were university students who had learned Spanish as a first language. They were rated both by the experimenters and by themselves as highly fluent bilinguals. They came from diverse national backgrounds, had a minimum of six years of schooling in each of the languages, and had spent a minimum of four years living in the United States. In a post-task questionnaire, all participants acknowledged being exposed to reading in both languages, being exposed to language switching in their present environment, and having ongoing active exposure to both languages. Some of them acknowledged positive attitudes toward switching, but the majority did not.

One subject failed to complete the study, and four others were excluded on the basis that they had atypically slower reaction times (one subject had an average reaction time of 1022, well over 2.5 standard deviations from the group mean; $M = 657$ ms, $SD = 79$ ms). For discussion of the other three excluded participants see section 12.4.5.1.

Table 12.1
Test sentences classified by syntactic boundary tested and language guise

Boundary	Guise	Example	Predicted status
NP-VP	SE	Los estudiantes *went* to the store.	Grammatical
	ES	The students *fueron* a la tienda.	
	SS	Los estudiantes *fueron* a la tienda.	
	EE	The students *went* to the store.	
pro-VP	SE	Yo *went* to the store.	Under debate
	ES	I *fui* a la tienda.	
	SS	Yo *fui* a la tienda.	
	EE	I *went* to the store.	
V-Comp	SE	Dije *that* they didn't go to the store.	Under debate
	ES	I said *que* ellos no fueron a la tienda.	
	SS	Dije *que* ellos no fueron a la tienda.	
	EE	I said *that* they didn't go to the store.	
Comp-IP	SE	Dije que *they* didn't go to the store.	Under debate
	ES	I said that *ellos* no fueron a la tienda.	
	SS	Dije que *ellos* no fueron a la tienda.	
	EE	I said that *they* didn't go to the store.	

12.4.3 Test Materials

To explore processing sensitivity to the grammaticality status of these various switchpoints, each sentence was presented across different language conditions or "sentence guises": two single-language guises (English-English and Spanish-Spanish), and two mixed-language guises (Spanish-English and English-Spanish). The presentation of each token sentence in these guises was counterbalanced across four blocks of subjects. Table 12.1 reflects the counterbalancing schema for each of the four syntactic conditions: NP-VP, pro-VP, Comp-IP, and V-Comp. The target word to be named is presented in this table between asterisks, and it reflects the first word to be switched at the specific boundary under study.

Test materials contained eighty tokens, with twenty per sentence type. Each subject was presented first with a ten-sentence practice block, and then with two blocks of forty sentences each of varying sentence types, language guises, and language of naming (i.e., the language of the target word named). The computer randomized the order of presentation of sentence tokens. Individual sentences were counterbalanced for guises across groups, so that each of the four different groups saw a given sentence in only one of the four different guises. Subjects were instructed to name any word presented between asterisks. Sentences varied in length. The position of the target word within the sentence also varied in order to prevent an anticipation effect. A *t*-test conducted on the effect of the length of the sentence and position of the target word showed no significant differences ($p > .05$) between early and late presentation of the stimulus word. This factor was then removed from further analysis.

12.4.4 Procedures

Participants were invited to participate in a study of language processing in English and Spanish. No specific mention of codeswitching was made in the recruitment or the pretest materials. Instructions were presented in English by an experimenter known to the participants to be bilingual. The experiment began with the participant pressing a key to start the presentation of the sentences on the screen. Sentences appeared in randomized order, presented word by word in a rapid serial visual presentation mode (RSVP) at 150 ms intervals, using a script programmed in SuperLab for MacIntosh. Participants were instructed to read the sentences silently on the screen, but to name out loud any word presented between asterisks as quickly as possible. The computer measured the reaction time (RT) in milliseconds (ms) from the onset of the presentation of the target word to the onset of naming. A separate audio recording was made to verify the correct reading of the target word.

After completing the online task, participants filled out an extensive language history questionnaire. Questions included the number of years of experience in each language, the language of their basic social networks, and a Likert scale self-assessment of their listening, speaking, reading, and writing proficiency in English and Spanish. After completing this questionnaire, they were debriefed about the goals of the study.

The results of the self-assessment indicated that all participants reported Spanish as their L1 and also reported having extensive experience in English. However, they seldom considered themselves equally fluent in speaking, writing, comprehending, and reading in both languages. Accordingly, and as discussed in section 12.4.5.1, we determined relative language dominance for each individual by comparing the total self-ratings for all categories in the two languages. Those participants with higher overall self-assessment in Spanish were considered Spanish dominant; those participants with higher overall self-assessments in English were considered English dominant. Three participants who produced a balanced self-description were considered Spanish dominant since their reported L1 was Spanish, resulting in an even split of the participants in each dominance grouping.

12.4.5 Results

12.4.5.1 Data Analysis

The few incorrect naming trials produced by participants were excluded from the analysis, resulting in less than 2% of the data being eliminated. We also

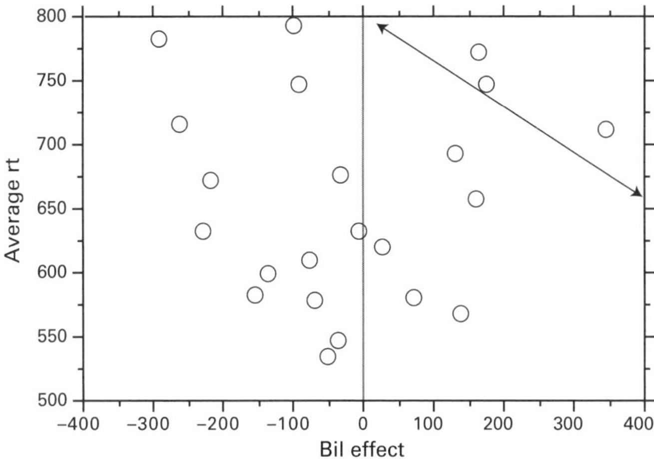

Figure 12.1
Codeswitching effect for individual participants presented according to their average reaction times. The arrow isolates the three individuals with the highest codeswitching effect.

excluded outliers, defined as tokens beyond 2.5 standard deviations from a participant's mean, and any response time less than 300 and more 3000 ms. The mean individual response for each sentence type was calculated for the following factors: Guise (i.e., mixed-language vs. single-language sentences), and Language of naming (according to the language of the target word).

Despite our efforts at homogeneous sampling (all participants were clearly highly fluent in both languages), the initial examination of the language history questionnaire revealed differences in self-ratings of proficiency in the two languages and differences in attitudes toward switching. For these reasons, we explored individual differences in the treatment of mixed-language sentences. By subtracting the average reaction times of mixed-language sentences from those of the single sentences we computed what we called a "bilingual effect"—that is, the overall processing cost of the mixed-language sentences presented. Negative scores in figure 12.1 indicate slower reaction times for mixed sentences, the predicted behavior. Most participants exhibited some codeswitching effect, or were within one standard deviation from zero effect. A group of participants displayed the most unusual behavior of having slower reaction times for single-language sentences than for mixed-language sentences.

Participants with the higher bilingual effect were not evenly distributed across counterbalancing blocks: three belonged to the second block and two

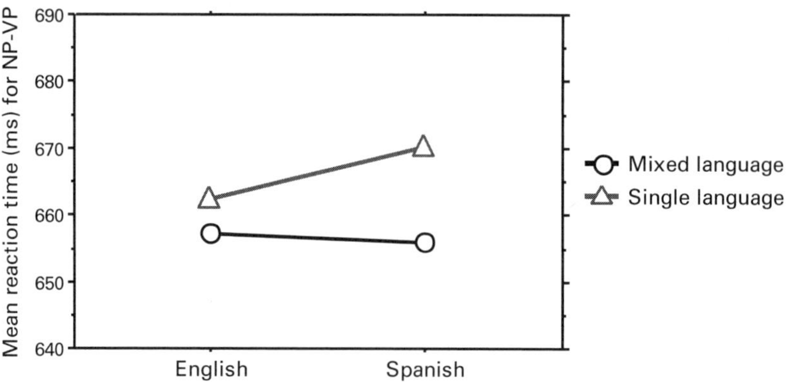

Figure 12.2
Average reaction times per guise per language of naming in the NP-VP
condition

to the third block. This suggests the possibility of an imbalance in the materials. Furthermore, we noted that the three participants with the higher RTs also happened to have had the highest bilingual effect. These participants were then excluded from the statistical analysis.

12.4.5.2   Switching between Subjects and Predicates

The effects of guise and language of naming were analyzed separately within each of the syntactic conditions. For the two conditions between subject and predicate, the NP-VP switchpoint was presumed by all theoretical accounts to be unconstrained, but the pro-VP switchpoint was predicted by some accounts to be a restricted switchpoint. The average of each participant's scores for the NP-VP condition shows few differences between conditions, although presentation of the single-language Spanish sentences elicited slightly slower reaction times. Figures 12.2 and 12.3 display the results for the switches between subject and predicate.

A repeated-measures analysis of variance (ANOVA) on reaction times to the NP-VP condition showed no significant main effects or interactions (Guise, $F_{1,21} = 0.954$, $p = 0.340$; Language of naming, $F_{1,21} = 0.055$, $p = 0.816$; Guise * Language of naming, $F_{1,21} = 0.256$, $p = 0.619$). These results are compatible with the results of an item analysis. A repeated-measures ANOVA on the average response per item also shows the main factors and interaction to be nonsignificant (Guise $F_{1,17} = 0.291$, $p = 0.596$; Language of naming, $F_{1,17} = 0.169$, $p = 0.687$; Guise * Language of naming, $F_{1,17} = 0.581$, $p = 0.456$).

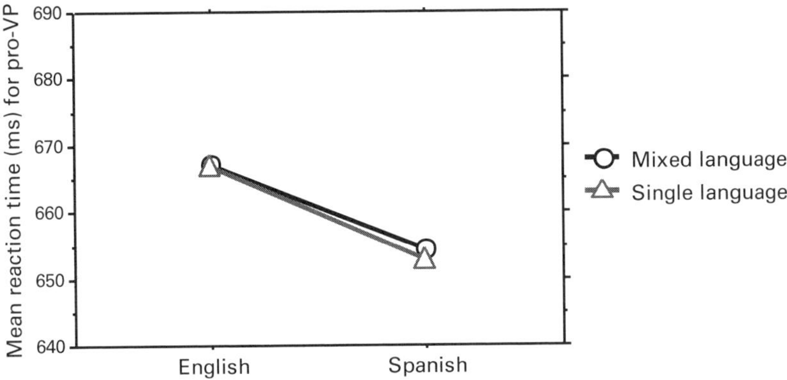

Figure 12.3
Average reaction times per guise per language of naming in the pro-VP
condition

For switches between subject pronouns and predicates, there was a small
but consistent (and almost significant) difference in language of naming. There
was no difference between the mixed-language and the single-language condition, and no significant interaction (Guise, $F_{1,21} = 0.003$, $p = 0.956$; Language
of naming, $F_{1,21} = 3.315$, $p = 0.083$; Guise * Language of naming, $F_{1,21} = 0.002$,
$p = 0.963$). There is a 28 ms delay for the mixed-language condition when
naming in English, but this did not prove significant in a t-test ($p = 0.589$).
The item analysis shows comparable results (Guise, $F_{1,17} = 0.291$, $p = 0.596$;
Language of naming, $F_{1,17} = 0.169$, $p = 0.687$; Guise * Language of naming,
$F_{1,17} = 0.581$, $p = 0.456$). The mixed-language delay in English persisted in
the item analysis (22 ms) but again failed to be significant.

12.4.5.3 Switching between Clauses

Although clausal switches are frequently attested, the precise location of compatible switching is debated, with most analysis favoring the possibility of
switching between the verb and the complementizer of its clausal complement.
Some syntactic accounts specifically rule out switching between the complementizer and its IP complement.

In the case of the V-Comp condition, the data show a small but nonsignificant delay in participants' response to mixed-language sentences. Statistical
analysis shows that the effect of guise misses significance and that there are
nonsignificant differences in the language of naming, nor is there significant
interaction between the factors (Guise, $F_{1,21} = 2.497$, $p = 0.129$; Language of
naming, $F_{1,21} = 0.395$, $p = 0.536$; Guise * Language of naming, $F_{1,21} = 0.077$,

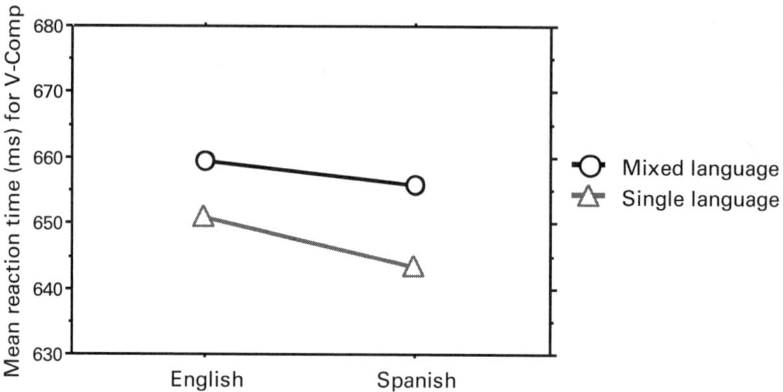

Figure 12.4
Average reaction times per guise per language of naming in the V-Comp
condition

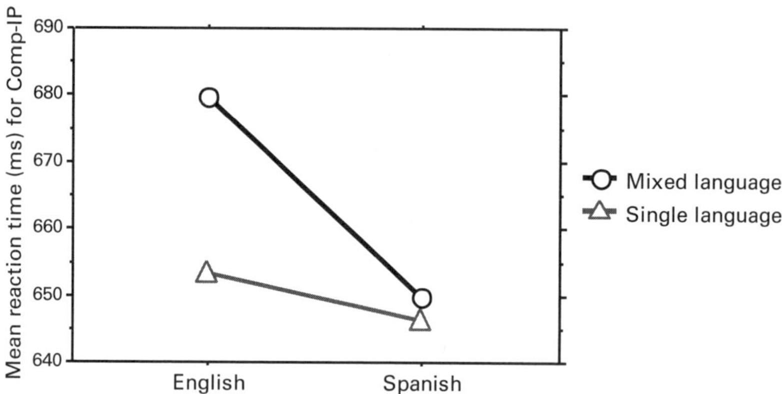

Figure 12.5
Average reaction times per guise per language of naming in the Comp-IP
condition

$p = 0.783$). Item analysis confirms this (Guise, $F_{1,17} = 0.091$, $p = 0.766$; Language of naming, $F_{1,17} = 2.516$, $p = 0.132$; Guise * Language of naming, $F_{1,17} = 0.574$, $p = 0.460$). See Figure 12.4.

The analysis of the Comp-IP condition reveals a more complex picture, because there is a more substantial effect of guise and of language of naming (with the mixed-language condition showing an asymmetric effect of codeswitching when naming in English but little difference in Spanish). See figure 12.5.

The statistical analysis shows that these main effects approach but fail to reach significance. Moreover, the interaction is not significant (Guise, $F_{1,21} = 2.517$, $p = 0.128$; Language of naming, $F_{1,21} = 3.156$, $p = 0.090$; Guise * Language of naming, $F_{1,21} = 1.151$, $p = 0.296$).

12.4.5.4 The Role of Dominance in Codeswitching

In a second round of analysis we exploited participants' self-rating as English dominant or Spanish dominant to examine whether language dominance introduced asymmetry in the patterns of sensitivity to codeswitches in the relevant conditions. By further partitioning our sample size, we decreased the statistical power of the analyses, but this was considered relevant in order to tease out the effect of language dominance. Again we submitted the data to a repeated-measures ANOVA on the mean score per subject, this time with the following factors: Guise * Language of naming * Language dominance.

In the case of the NP-VP condition, the dominance analysis did not add new information. As predicted, there were no significant main effects or interactions (Language dominance, $F_{1,20} = 0.243$, $p = 0.627$; Guise, $F_{1,20} = 1.111$, $p = 0.305$; Guise * Language dominance, $F_{1,20} = 0.861$, $p = 0.364$; Language of naming, $F_{1,20} = 0.035$, $p = 0.854$; Language of naming * Language dominance, $F_{1,20} = 0.225$, $p = 0.640$; Guise * Language of naming, $F_{1,20} = 0.356$, $p = 0.557$; and Guise * Language of naming * Language dominance, $F_{1,20} = 1.044$, $p = 0.319$). As figure 12.6 shows, we find comparable reaction times for all conditions except for the English-dominant participants naming in Spanish, which had slower response times to the single-language conditions. This difference of ~34 ms was not significant ($p = 0.244$).

For the pro-VP condition, English-dominant participants had longer reaction times for single-language conditions, particularly naming in English (estimated difference of ~27 ms, nonsignificant at $p = 0.589$). The Spanish-dominant subjects had a delay in codeswitching when naming in English, also nonsignificant (estimated difference of ~23 ms, nonsignificant at $p = 0.173$). None of these differences was significant. The overall ANOVA again shows patterns of nonsignificance, with the effect of language of naming approaching significance (Language dominance, $F_{1,20} = 0.000$, $p = 0.999$; Guise, $F_{1,20} = 0.006$, $p = 0.941$; Guise * Language dominance, $F_{1,20} = 2.112$, $p = 0.162$; Language of naming, $F_{1,20} = 3.014$, $p = 0.098$; Language of naming * Language dominance, $F_{1,20} = 0.227$, $p = 0.639$; Guise * Language of naming, $F_{1,20} = 0.006$, $p = 0.940$; and Guise * Language of naming * Language dominance, $F_{1,20} = 0.112$, $p = 0.741$). Mean responses to the pro-VP condition by language dominance are presented in figure 12.7.

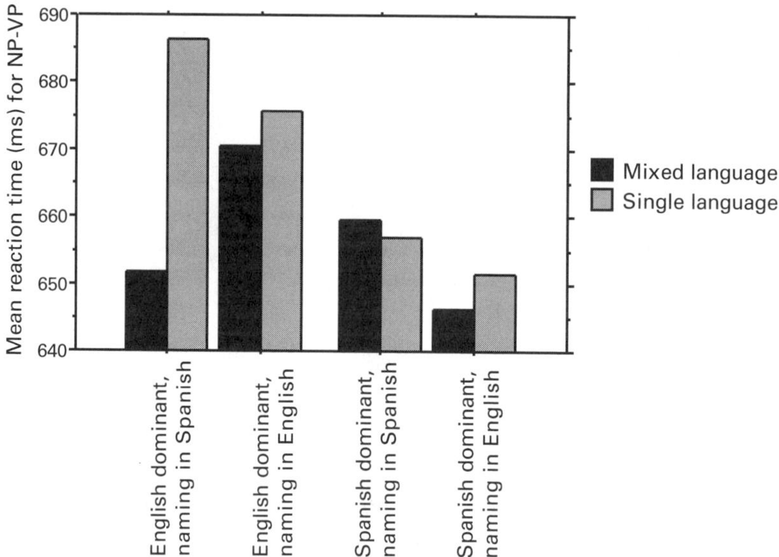

Figure 12.6
Dominance analysis of mean participant performance in the NP-VP condition

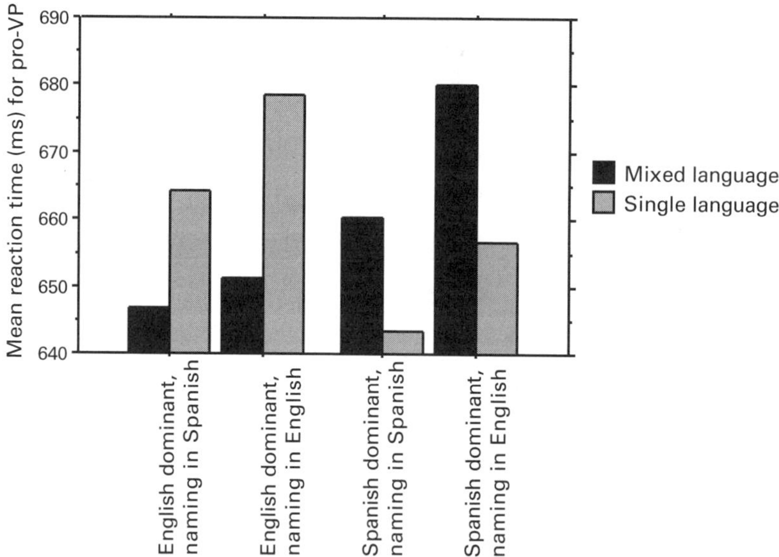

Figure 12.7
Dominance analysis of mean participant performance in the pro-VP condition

The dominance analysis of the V-Comp condition shows for the most part patterns of nonsignificance (Language dominance, $F_{1,20} = 0.007$, $p = 0.932$; Guise, $F_{1,20} = 3.026$, $p = 0.097$; Guise * Language dominance, $F_{1,20} = 2.003$, $p = 0.172$; Language of naming, $F_{1,20} = 0.349$, $p = 0.561$; Language of naming * Language dominance, $F_{1,20} = 0.052$, $p = 0.822$; Guise * Language of naming, $F_{1,20} = 0.059$, $p = 0.811$; and Guise * Language of naming * Language dominance, $F_{1,20} = 0.100$, $p = 0.755$). Note, however, that the effect of guise approaches significance, with the data suggesting no differences for the Spanish-dominant participants, but a small cost of codeswitching for the English-dominant participants. These differences were not significant (for naming in English, estimated difference is ~21 ms, $p = 0.203$; for naming in Spanish, estimated difference is 20 ms, $p = 0.160$). Data for V-Comp by language dominance is presented in figure 12.8.

For the Comp-IP condition, most main factors and main effects are nonsignificant, with the effects of guise and of language of naming approaching significance (Language dominance, $F_{1,20} = 0.139$, $p = 0.712$; Guise, $F_{1,20} = 2.299$, $p = 0.145$; Guise * Language dominance, $F_{1,20} = 0.108$, $p = 0.746$; Language of naming, $F_{1,20} = 2.816$, $p = 0.109$; Language of naming * Language dominance, $F_{1,20} = 1.369$, $p = 0.255$; Guise * Language of naming, $F_{1,20} = 0.923$, $p = 0.348$). Notably, the interaction of Guise * Language of naming *

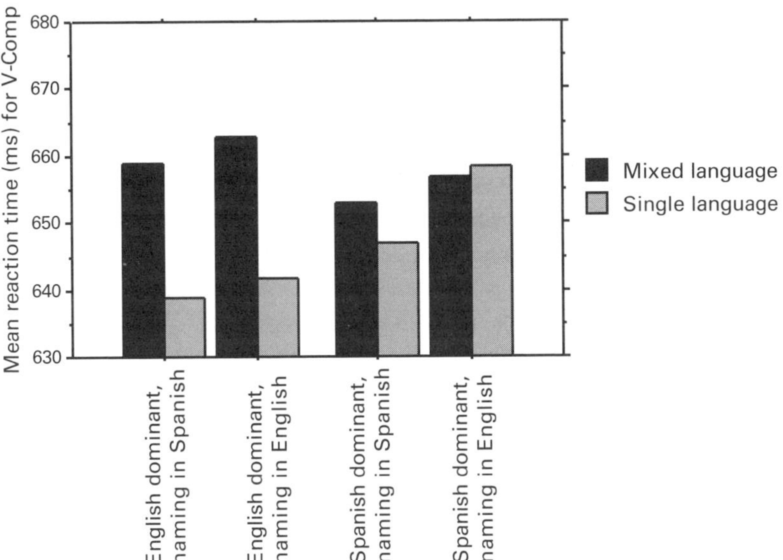

Figure 12.8
Dominance analysis of mean participant performance in the V-Comp condition

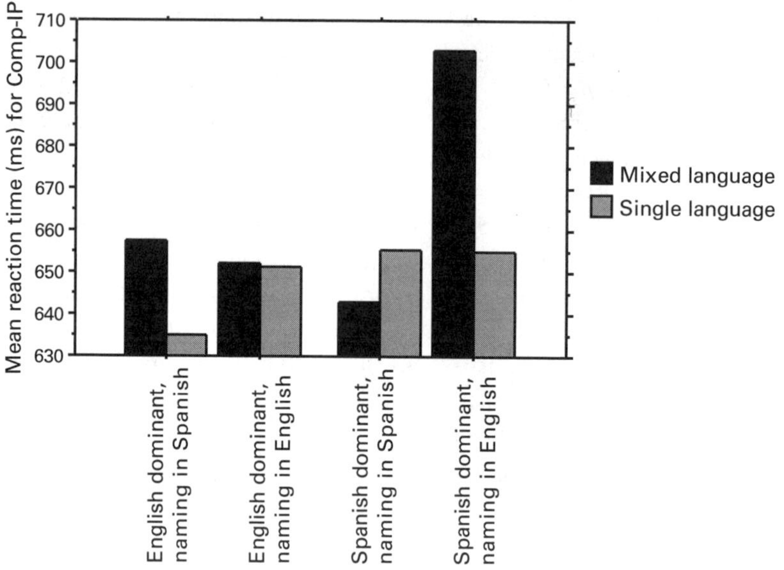

Figure 12.9
Dominance analysis of mean participant performance in the Comp-IP condition

Language dominance barely misses significance at $F_{1,20} = 4.180$, $p = 0.054$. The effect is likely due to the responses given to the English naming condition by participants rated as dominant in Spanish, as can be seen in figure 12.9.

The slight cost of codeswitching that appears for the English-dominant participants naming in Spanish was not significant (estimated difference is ~22 ms, $p = 0.356$), but the codeswitching delay for the Spanish-dominant participants when naming a word in English after a Spanish complementizer was significant (estimated difference is ~48 ms, $p = 0.043$).

12.5   Discussion

For switching between subject NPs and their predicates, the data provide no support for the existence of a codeswitching cost. This result is desirable and expected, because it confirms the standard description of such switches as grammatical in the various qualitative and quantitative studies of Spanish-English codeswitching. In contrast, the lack of clear results for pro-VP runs counter to prior descriptions of Spanish-English codeswitching. Our own bilingual intuitions as well as work on the elicitation of grammaticality judgments (Brown 1994) indicate that switching predicates after pronominal subjects is odd. The possibilities outlined by Jake, that such sentences can be made felicitous by pragmatic factors (i.e., ungrammaticality effects can be neutralized by the effect of focus), remain open. The decontextualized sentences employed in the study allow participants a certain degree of interpretive freedom, with the possibility of "rescuing" the sentence by giving the pronoun a focused interpretation. However, this type of speculation is beyond the methodology employed in this study.

Switches involving embedded clauses resulted in interesting patterns. Both conditions gave rise to faster reaction times in the codeswitched presentations. Partitioning the data by dominance shows that the effects are not evenly distributed. For the V-Comp condition, the English-dominant participants were responsible for the effect, which was more apparent when naming a Spanish *que* after an English matrix clause. The only effect of codeswitching that resulted in statistical significance appeared in the Comp-IP condition, when Spanish-dominant participants had to name an English word after a Spanish *que*. That the interaction in the Comp-IP condition is significant suggests that dominance is an explanatory factor for grammatical sensitivity to codeswitching patterns. In fact, that the result is significant at all is remarkable since in the dominance analysis the data were further partitioned and the sample size for each condition reduced. Therefore, this result suggests the need for asymmetric models that take dominance into consideration. The observed asymmetry seemed determined rigidly by language dominance: Spanish-dominant participants reacted to Comp-IP but English-dominant participants did not. The findings elicited show support for the complementizer predictions of the FHC, but mainly for Spanish-dominant subjects, suggesting that it is this particular layer of functional projection (the CP extension of IP) whose integrity needs to be preserved for these subjects. English-dominant participants may also have been affected by switches between verb and complementizer, particularly when this complementizer was to be named in Spanish. This suggests the possibility of lexically linked accounts (i.e., that restrictions are specific to functional heads such as Spanish *que*), a suggestion that resonates readily with MacSwan's minimalist model.

While we will not speculate at this point on a specific syntactic analysis for these results, we can use them to evaluate in general terms the type of model required. These data can be interpreted in favor of asymmetric models that are linguistically based, such as Choi or MacSwan. The findings also suggest that dominance determines which functional layer bilinguals are interested in matching to the preceding language environment. However, these findings do not rigidly dictate the ungrammaticality of certain switchpoints. The dynamic effect of dominance, if validated in future research, may help explain the amount of disagreement about the basic facts of codeswitching.

12.6 Conclusion

Like Azuma (1991) and Rakowsky (1989), we observed no effect of grammatical codeswitching. These findings can be understood as stating that participants in a bilingual processing mode (which our participants could certainly be believed to be in—see Grosjean 1997 for a discussion) do not have a cost of codeswitching, confirming the linguistic description of codeswitching as an effortless, natural language phenomenon, not driven by language limitations. The mixed-language effect appeared in specific syntactic environments in specific groups of bilinguals, supporting the now-commonsense view that codeswitching is grammatically constrained.

The methodological challenges inherent in the online study of codeswitching are substantial: experimenters must carefully control the sentences while at the same time striving to produce potentially good tokens for codeswitching. A variety of factors such as dialect-specific lexical preferences or the kind of prosodic factors that may emerge in the visual presentation of words (such as word length, specific prosodic patterns of actual tokens, etc.) may also introduce additional noise in the design. Indeed, item analyses revealed the presence of some highly unbalanced items, and additional control of these factors is imperative in future research. Our experimental design, by counterbalancing across language of naming and mixing, already controls for a good deal of the variability. However, the intricate pattern of results elicited often fell short of achieving significance. It is possible that a simple increase in sample size can strengthen the statistical power of these results (a sample of twenty-two is modest for this type of study). It is also possible that those unaccounted factors such as lexical choice may prove to play a fundamental role in determining the viability of switching, as suggested in the qualitative literature (Valdés-Fallis 1976), or of prosody (Grosjean, personal communication). These factors alone could explain Azuma's (1991) results, because his switches are of prosodically minimal constituents, which as closed-class items could not be stylistically or lexically motivated. Since our switches started with lexical items (except in the case of the V-Comp condition) and continued afterward, the first switched words were not prosodically small and contained lexical items that seemed (at least to us) plausibly switchable.

The findings in this study clearly favor linguistic theories of codeswitching, while acknowledging the need to integrate these with psycholinguistic models. To illustrate, under sentence planning approaches, whole-embedded clauses should present no problem for the parser and result in no codeswitching effect (for a related proposal see Jake, Myers-Scotton, and Gross 2002). From a syntactic perspective, one wishes to raise the question of how a phrase is sliced: like any functional projection? as a maximal extended projection? For instance, the latter perspective is assumed for prepositional phrases in Azuma (1991), but it is not entirely clear how we should apply it to the intricate functional structure of clauses. We found effects at the edge of the CP as well as the IP, and this finding is not explainable under a sentence planning approach. It also suggests that both Belazi, Rubin, and Toribio (1994) and Mahootian and Santorini's (1996) views of switching with embedded sentential complements were partially correct and not incompatible with each other.

We conclude by acknowledging that tighter lexical control of sentence stimuli is required to strengthen this type of experimental approach, and that the issue of individual differences with respect to language dominance among bilinguals also deserves further attention. We believe that the psycholinguistic study of codeswitching can help shape linguistic models of codeswitching and can contribute data fundamental to the evaluation of competing theoretical alternatives.

Notes

1. Grimshaw (1991) had suggested that functional projections are extended projections of a head, a proposal now seen as a natural assumption. Under this view the sentential and clausal layers are extended projections of the verbal predicate, and the DP layers are extended projections of the nominal head, which may raise as high as a PP (but note that this is not exactly what their model predicts). This perspective predicts uniformity within a given CP, while not requiring it to extend into the extended nominal projections.

2. It is not clear either why indefinite pronouns (which have lexical content and the same surface distribution as lexical NPs) should not simply be included with other lexical NPs and are instead examined in contrast to subject pronouns. Myers-Scotton's (1993) afterword to her book *Duelling Languages* notwithstanding, the grouping of these variables into a single distinction (system-content) is problematic, because it introduces new primitives (the system-content distinction) involving a fusion of formal and semantic criteria. A more productive approach is to keep criteria separate and to investigate the effects of specific grammatical components independently. Rather than redefining the status of pronouns, one may wish to treat this phenomenon not within the primitives of the grammar but with other aspects of the syntax/semantics of focus, given unrelated but obviously relevant evidence that focused pronouns elicit binding theory anomalies in pronominals (Authier 1998).

References

Altarriba, Jeanette, Judith F. Kroll, Alexandra Sholl, and Keith Rayner. 1996. The influence of lexical and conceptual constraints on reading mixed-language sentences: Evidence from eye fixations and naming times. *Memory and Cognition* 24:477–492.

Altarriba, Jeanette, and Emily Soltano. 1996. Repetition blindness and bilingual memory: Token individuation for translation equivalents. *Memory and Cognition* 24:700–711.

Authier, Jean-Marc. 1998. When syntax overrules semantics. In Pius N. Tamanji and Kiyomi Kusumoto, eds., *Proceedings of NELS* 28:33–42. Amherst: GLSA, University of Massachusetts.

Azuma, Shoji. 1991. Processing and intrasentential codeswitching. Doctoral dissertation, University of Texas at Austin.

Azuma, Shoji. 1993. The frame-content hypothesis in speech production: Evidence from intrasentential codeswitching. *Linguistics* 31:1071–1093.

Belazi, Hedi M., Edward J. Rubin, and Almeida J. Toribio. 1994. Code switching and X-bar theory: The Functional Head Constraint. *Linguistic Inquiry* 25:221–237.

Berk-Seligson, Susan. 1986. Linguistic constraints on intrasentential code-switching: A study of Spanish/Hebrew bilingualism. *Language in Society* 15:313–348.

Brown, Esther. 1994. The prodrop parameter and restriction on code-switching. Ms., The Pennsylvania State University.

Choi, Jae Oh. 1991. Korean-English code switching: Switch-alpha and linguistics constraints. *Linguistics* 29:877–902.

De Groot, Annette M. B. 2011. *Language and Cognition in Bilinguals and Multilinguals: An Introduction.* New York-Hove: Psychology Press.

Di Sciullo, Anna Maria, Pieter Muysken, and Rajendra Singh. 1986. Government and code-mixing. *Journal of Linguistics* 22:1–24.

Grimshaw, Jane. 1991. Extended projections. Ms., Brandeis University.

Grosjean, François. 1997. Processing mixed language: Issues, findings, and models. In Annette de Groot and Judith Kroll, eds., *Tutorials in Bilingualism*, 225–254. Hillsdale, NJ: Erlbaum.

Grosjean, François, and Joanne L. Miller. 1994. Going in and out of languages: An example of bilingual flexibility. *Psychological Science* 5:201–206.

Jake, Janice. 1994. Intrasentential code-switching and pronouns: On the categorical status of functional elements. *Linguistics* 32:271–298.

Jake, Janice, Carol Myers-Scotton, and Steven Gross. 2002. Making a minimalist approach to codeswitching work: Adding the matrix language. *Bilingualism: Language and Cognition* 5:69–91.

Joshi, Aravind. 1985. Processing of sentences with intrasentential code-switching. In David R. Dowty, Lauri Karttunen, and Arnold Zwicky, eds., *Natural Language Parsing*, 190–205. Cambridge: Cambridge University Press.

Kolers, Paul A. 1966. Reading and talking bilingually. *American Journal of Psychology* 3:357–376.

Li, Ping. 1996. Spoken word recognition of code-switched words by Chinese-English bilinguals. *Journal of Memory and Language* 35:757–774.

Lipski, John. 1978. Code-switching and problems of bilingual competence. In Michel Paradis, ed., *Aspects of Bilingualism*, 250–264. Columbia, SC: Hornbeam.

Lipski, John. 1998. Review of *Government and Codeswitching: Explaining American Finnish*, by Helena Halmary. *Language* 74:874–875.

MacKay, Donald G., Lise Abrams, Manissa Pedroza, and Michelle D. Miller. 1996. Cross-language facilitation, semantic blindness, and the relation between language and memory: A reply to Altarriba and Soltano. *Memory and Cognition* 24:712–718.

MacKay, Donald G., and Michelle Miller. 1992. Semantic blindness: Repetition suppression at the semantic level. Ms., UCLA.

MacNamara, John, and Seymour Kushnir. 1971. Linguistic independence of bilinguals: The input switch. *Journal of Verbal Learning and Verbal Behavior* 10:480–487.

MacSwan, Jeff. 1999. *A Minimalist Approach to Intrasentential Code-Switching*. New York: Garland Press.

MacSwan, Jeff. 2004. Code switching and grammatical theory. In Tej K. Bhatia and William C. Ritchie, eds., *The Handbook of Bilingualism*, 283–311. Malden MA: Blackwell.

MacSwan, Jeff. 2009. Generative approaches to code-switching. In Barbara Bullock, Almeida Jacqueline Toribio, eds., *The Cambridge Handbook of Linguistic Code-Switching*, 309–335. New York: Cambridge University Press.

Mahootian, Shahrzad. 1993. A null theory of codeswitching. Doctoral dissertation, Northwestern University.

Mahootian, Shahrzad, and Beatrice Santorini. 1996. Code switching and the complement/adjunct distinction: A reply to Belazi, Rubin, and Toribio. *Linguistic Inquiry* 27:464–479.

Muysken, Pieter. 2000. *Bilingual Speech: A Typology of Code-Mixing*. Cambridge: Cambridge University Press.

Myers-Scotton, Carol. 1993. *Duelling Languages: Grammatical Structures in Code-Switching*. Oxford: Oxford University Press.

Poplack, Shana. 1980. Sometimes I'll start a sentence in Spanish y termino en español: Toward a typology of code-switching. *Linguistics* 18:581–618.

Rakowsky, Amy. 1989. A study of intrasentential code-switching in Spanish-English bilinguals and second language learners. Doctoral dissertation, Brown University.

Rubin, Edwin J., and Almeida Jacqueline Toribio. 1995. Feature checking and the syntax of language contact. In Jon Amastae, Grant Goodall, Mario Montalbetti, and Marianne Phinney, eds., *Contemporary Research in Romance Lingusitics*, 177–185. Amsterdam: John Benjamins.

Sankoff, David, and Shana Poplack. 1981. A formal grammar of code-switching. *Papers in Linguistics: International Journal of Human Communication* 14:3–43.

Soares, Carlos, and François Grosjean. 1984. Bilinguals in a monolingual and a bilingual speech mode: The effect on lexical access. *Memory and Cognition* 12:380–386.

Stenson, Nancy. 1990. Phrase structure congruence, government, and Irish-English code-switching. *Syntax and Semantics* 23:167–198.

Timm, Lenora A. 1975. Spanish-English code-switching: El porqué y how-not-to. *Romance Philology* 28:33–45.

Valdés-Fallis, Guadalupe. 1976. Social interaction and code switching patterns: A case study of Spanish/English alternation. In Gary Keller, Richard Teschner, and Soledad Viera, eds., *Bilingualism in the Bicentennial and Beyond*, 54–80. New York: Bilingual Press.

Wakefield, James. 1975. Language switching and constituent structures. *Language and Speech* 18:14–19.

Woolford, Ellen. 1983. Bilingual code-switching and syntactic theory. *Linguistic Inquiry* 14:520–536.

Contributors

Shoba Bandi-Rao — Borough of Manhattan Community College, CUNY
Rakesh M. Bhatt — University of Illinois at Urbana-Champaign
Sonia Colina — University of Arizona
Marcel den Dikken — CUNY Graduate Center
Anna Maria Di Sciullo — University of Québec at Montréal
Daniel L. Finer — Stony Brook University
Kay E. Gonzalez-Vilbazo — University of Illinois at Chicago
Jeff MacSwan — University of Maryland
Sílvia Milian Hita — Escola Oficial d'Idiomes del Prat
Monica Moro Quintanilla — University of Oviedo
Pieter Muysken — Radboud University Nijmegen
Erin O'Rourke — University of Alabama
Ana Teresa Pérez-Leroux — University of Toronto
Edward P. Stabler — University of California, Los Angeles
Gretchen Sunderman — Florida State University
Almeida Jacqueline Toribio — University of Texas-Austin

Index

X' Theory, 19, 63, 96, 155n5

Yang, C., 257
Yiddish, 111n8
Yoon, J.-M., 59n20

Zagona, K., 96, 203–204, 261
Zanuttini, R., 103
Zapotec, SLQ, 22, 263
Zentella, A. C., 237, 240, 246
Zubizarreta, M. L., 107
Zwart, C. J.-W., 170